A history of International Relations theory

'This wide-ranging and popular work has already established itself as a standard treatment of the subject'

European Journal of International Relations

'Many a graduate student could pass his or her international relations theory comprehensives if she committed the book to memory. The undergraduate lives in constant need of historical and theoretical perspective'

Choice

Torbjørn Knutsen introduces ideas on international relations expressed by thinkers from the High Middle Ages to the present day and traces the development of four ever-present themes: war, wealth, peace and power. The book counters the view that international relations has no theoretical tradition and shows that scholars, soldiers and statesmen have been speculating about the subject for the last 700 years.

Beginning with the roots of the state and the concept of sovereignty in the Middle Ages, the author draws upon the insights of outstanding political thinkers, from Machiavelli and Hobbes to Hegel, Rousseau and Marx; and contemporary thinkers such as Woodrow Wilson, Lenin, Morgenthau and Waltz who profoundly influenced the emergence of a discrete discipline of International Relations in the twentieth century. Fully revised and updated, the final section embraces more recent approaches to the study of international relations.

Torbjørn Knutsen is Associate Professor of International Relations, University of Trondheim.

A history of International Relations theory

Second edition

Torbjørn L. Knutsen

Manchester University Press

Manchester and New York

Distributed exclusively in the USA by Palgrave

First edition 1992
Second revised, expanded edition 1997

Published by Manchester University Press
Oxford Road, Manchester M13 9NR, UK
and Room 400, 175 Fifth Avenue, New York, NY 10010, USA
www.manchesteruniversitypress.co.uk

Distributed exclusively in the USA by
Palgrave, 175 Fifth Avenue, New York, NY 10010, USA

Distributed exclusively in Canada by
UBC Press, University of British Columbia, 2029 West Mall,
Vancouver, BC, Canada V6T 1Z2

British Library Cataloguing-in-Publication Data
A catalogue record for this book is available from the British Library

Library of Congress Cataloging-in-Publication Data
Knutsen, Torbjørn L.
    A history of International Relations theory / Torbjørn Knutsen. — 2nd ed.
    p.   cm.
    Includes bibliographical references and index.
    ISBN 0–7190–4929–6 — ISBN 0–7190–4930–X
    1. International relations—History.   2. International relations—Philosophy.
I. Title.
JX1391.K58   1997
327.101—dc20   96–33348
                                                                           CIP

ISBN 0–7190–4929–6 *hardback*
     0–7190–4930–X *paperback*

First published 1997

10 09 08 07   10 9 8 7

Typeset in Great Britain
by Northern Phototypesetting Co Ltd, Bolton
Printed in Great Britain
by CPI Bath

Contents

Contents

Maps, figures and tables

Preface

The first edition of this book was completed during the summer of 1991 and mailed off in mid-August. But by the time it reached the publisher, world events had transformed the face of international politics. On 19 August a failed communist coup shook the Gorbachev regime, catapulted Boris Yeltsin to fame and power and cracked the foundations of the Soviet Communist Party. The subsequent dismantlement of the old Stalinist Party apparatus caused the international communist movement to unravel and forced radical movements all over the world into defensive retreat.

These events closed the books on the Cold War. They also closed several introductory texts to International Relations, many of which were so encased in Cold War issues and concepts that the unravelling of the global communist movement made them obsolescent by the Fall term. So when the publisher invited me to prepare a second edition of this book, I was grateful for the opportunity to replace the former concluding chapter. The original intention was to provide a new chapter that would trace the post-Cold War fade-out of the three traditional paradigms – Realism, Rationalism and Revolutionism – and account for the fade-in of newer and more varied approaches. But page-limits have a way of defeating even the best of intentions. The first drafts of the new concluding chapter quickly burst at the seams. Early pruning efforts tended to produce dull catalogues of names and arguments. In the end, in the interest of readability, I found it necessary to exclude several contemporary contributions to International Relations theory from this chapter – among the regrettable casualties of pruning are feminist theories (Grant and Newland 1991; Sylvester 1994), Third-World perspectives in general (Ngugi 1986; Gordon 1989) and the Orientalism debate in particular (Said 1987; Howard 1995); the Democratic-Peace thesis (Russett 1993; Gates et al. 1996), normative theories (Frost 1986; Nardin and Mapel 1993), ecological approaches (Sprout and Sprout 1965; Vogler and Imber 1996) and other contributions to *fin-de-siècle* International Relations scholarship.

The new conclusion demanded a new beginning. As if to illustrate Croce's famous maxim that all history is 'contemporary history', the new closing discussion of post-Cold War affairs led to substantial revisions in the opening presentation of medieval politics. The new first chapter is longer than the old one, but it has a clearer focus and a better organizing claim, and these two things together ensure a less long-winded account. Compared to the substantial revisions of Chapters 1 and 10, the intervening Chapters 2–9 have merely benefited from some nipping here and some tucking there.

My reading of older sources has been made possible with the kind co-operation of countless librarians – among whom I owe the staffs of the university libraries in Trondheim, the Library of Congress, the British Library and the Bibliothèque nationale a particularly deep debt. My writing has benefited from the patient help of colleagues who have commented on the revised manuscript. I owe special thanks to Jennifer Bailey, Erling Berge, James Der Derian, Yale Ferguson, Scott Gates, Naeem Inayatullah, Mark Katz, Jonathon Moses, Iver Neumann, David Phelps, Georg Sørensen and Silke Vogel. Also, this book would not be what it is without the incredulity and enthusiasm of the fine students at the University of Trondheim. I have not always agreed with the criticisms offered. And as I have privileged some comments over others, it stands to reason that the published result is no one's responsibility but my own. But I can carry that responsibility more confidently for having received criticism early and thus having been forced to express my points with greater clarity.

Torbjørn L. Knutsen,
Trondheim, August 1996

To HAK who explained to me the love of power;

and to JLB who showed to me the power of love.

Introduction

Why a history of International Relations theory?

This book counters the common assumption that the study of International Relations has no theoretical tradition. This assumption is evident in the misconception of students who enter introductory courses of International Relations expecting to be informed about current events. It is also reflected in the many textbooks in which most of the theories discussed have been formulated within the life-span of the teacher.[1]

International Relations theory distinguishes itself in this respect from Political Theory. Whereas the beginning student of Political Theory is introduced to a tradition which begins with ancient Greek authors and evolves continually up to our own times, the beginning student of International Relations is introduced to no comparable chain of classics. The tradition of Political Theory is reconstructed from great works by Plato, Aristotle, Augustine, Hobbes, Locke and Rousseau to mention only a few. International Relations is considered too recent a discipline to contain any comparable chain of 'classic texts' (Wight 1968, p. 1).

Definitions, limitations and foci

Theories enlighten. A theory is a set of related propositions that help explain why events occur the way they do. A theory is an abstract, conjectural or speculative representation of reality. Thus, one does not ask of a theory whether it is true or false; rather, one asks whether it is enlightening. To theorize is to speculate with an intention to understand or explain.

It has been observed that speculation about the state goes back to antiquity, whereas speculation about the relations between states goes back little further than to World War I. This book disputes this observation. It argues that scholars, soldiers and statesmen have, in fact, speculated about the relations between states since the modern state emerged four or five centuries ago. It identifies the major concepts and themes of these speculations and it indicates the tradition of

1

International Relations theory through modern history – i.e. that part of Western history which is bracketed by the Renaissance and the Reformation on the one hand, and by the Second Industrial Revolution and World War I on the other. It notes that this tradition has often been shaken and altered by large-scale war. World War I is a case in point: this war did not so much give birth to International Relations theory as give the tradition a major jolt, a new emphasis, a higher popular profile, a new self-consciousness, a mission and a new direction of development. This book discusses International Relations theory on both sides of this major jolt.

Where can we find the most salient speculations about relations between states? Most immediately, we find them in the tradition of Political Theory. For while speculating about the state, many political theorists have also speculated about the relations between states. Sometimes these speculations have been brief 'asides', but at other times they have been spelled out at great length. Machiavelli's book on war, Rousseau's discussion of 'Perpetual Peace' and Hume's treatise on 'the Balance of Power', are cases in point. Observation of and speculation about international politics are found in other places, as well: diplomatic missives, advice to heads of state, texts of International Law, autobiographies and correspondence of statesmen and soldiers. These are texts which contain much material for a historical reconstruction of International Relations theory.

The chief problem of this study is not that there are too few sources, but that there are too many and that they are diverse and uneven. To simplify the selection and the analysis of the sources, and to facilitate the presentation of the argument, this book reduces the sources to manageable proportions in several ways. First, it defines the topic under investigation – the tradition of International Relations Theory – rather narrowly: its primary focus is the interactions between sovereign states (Holsti 1987, p. 9). Consequently, past speculations which seek to account for such interactions are given priority. Concerns about war and about military and economic capabilities of states are important elements of this discussion.

Second, this definition limits the study in time and space. It makes it natural to begin the study with an account of the evolution of its major constituent unit and its characteristic properties and to follow their evolution over time. This makes the 'state' the primary object of the discussion and makes 'sovereignty' the primary concept. The histories of the two are intimately intertwined through modern history. By the *state* is meant the territorial state: an independent political community 'which possesses a government and asserts sovereignty in relation to a particular portion of the earth's surface and a particular segment of the human population' (Bull 1977, p. 8). This concept of the 'state' emerged out of the tumultuous politics of the late–medieval period in Western Europe. And this historical fact furnishes the present study with its primary spatial site: it is inordinately preoccupied with Western events and with European theorists.

By *sovereignty* must be understood the ultimate source of legitimate authority over the state. This concept of sovereignty has constituted the core concern in the long tradition of Political Science. Whereas Economics has been organized around the problematic of 'wealth', Philology around 'language' and Medicine around the 'health' of the human body, Political Science has been organized around the problematic of 'sovereignty'.

Third, the book uses the tradition of Political Theory as its primary source for information about speculations on relations among states. Other sources are also consulted. However, to use them in other than a supportive mode, as purveyors of historical context and ambience, would have produced a very different (and much larger) work.

The nature of International Relations

International Relations deal with human behaviour in the largest of all social groups: the international society. This society has two characteristic features which distinguish it from other human groups. First – most obviously but also most overlooked – membership in the international society is obligatory. Most other human societies offer, in principle at least, voluntary membership: an individual member can leave if he wants to, and the ultimate sanction which can be applied to individuals who refuse to obey the rules of sociability is expulsion. It is the peculiar nature of international society that membership in it is compulsory (Carr 1964, p. 95). States cannot alter their geographic location; territories cannot be made to go away.

Also, international society lacks an ultimate authority. Many efforts have been made to organize a world government, yet no true world legislature exists which makes rules and laws that emphasize the cohesive and sociable side of human interaction. Although there exists an elaborate body of international law, there exists no global executive power authorized to enforce these laws. In domestic society, laws and sanctions are devised and applied by controlling political institutions that act in the name of society – domestic society has legislative and executive institutions, represented by a prime minister, a president or a king. International society has no such supreme institution. Theories about international society distinguish themselves from other political theories by being preoccupied with human behaviour in an *anarchical society*.

The absence of a supreme authority does not mean that human sociability is removed from international society altogether, as some authors maintain. Rather, it means that the sociable nature of humanity is de-emphasized in international actions, and that allowances are made for a larger share of egotistical, unilateral behaviour. The traditional way to justify this greater allowance of egotism is to emphasize the concept of sovereignty. Modern International Relations has been dominated by the twin notions of the presence and the absence of sovereignty. Applied to relations *within* states, this involves the belief that there is a final and

3

absolute authority in society. Applied to relations *among* states, it expresses the antithesis of this belief – i.e. the principle that internationally, over and above a collection of societies, no supreme authority exists. With the concept of sovereignty as its fulcrum, the study of International Relations has traditionally been preoccupied with the dichotomies of 'war' and 'peace', 'anarchy' and 'order'.

The nature of International Relations theory

When did scholars and statesmen begin to study sovereign states and speculate about the nature of their interaction? It is useful to distinguish between two phases in the development of International Relations theory. The first phase involves the emergence of the basic concepts of its discourse. This phase, which is covered in Part One of this book, largely coincides with the 'long sixteenth century.' This was an age in which Renaissance discoveries in space (the Americas) and time (Greek and Roman cultures) altered the traditional conceptions of world geography and history. It was also an age in which the Reformation challenged the Medieval outlook upon which these old conceptions rested. It was during this crowded and tumultuous era that the key concepts of International-Relations theorizing, such as 'state' and 'sovereignty', found their first secular definitions. Major contributors to this formative first phase were Iberian lawyers like Vitoria and Italian historians and civil servants like Machiavelli and Guicciardini.

The second main phase involves the continued discussion of these concepts and their inclusion in larger, explanatory frameworks. This phase is discussed in Part Two of the book. It began during the violent, final stage of the Religious Wars; it lasted through the modern ages, until the very end of the nineteenth century; and it can be sub-divided into several shorter periods of about a century each. A chapter is devoted to each such period. During the first of these periods, roughly covering the seventeenth century, the basic legal and historical concepts of the first phase were synthesized into larger, secular systems of thought. Jean Bodin is among the first of these synthesizers. Not only did he provide a decisive clarification of the key concept of 'sovereignty', he also initiated a discussion of the interaction between sovereign actors. The characteristic feature of such interaction, Bodin recognized, is that no supreme authority exists above the participating princes. Thus, no legal agent can intervene to arbitrate in contests between them. In such an environment, it is essential that princes keep their promises. A few years later, Gentili, Hobbes and others would refer to Bodin's observation as the principle of *pacta sunt servanda*.

Thomas Hobbes is another great synthesizer. He was not the first theorist to apply the concept of a social contract to describe relations between princes; however, he was the first to use the related concept of a pre-contractual state of nature as an analogy to interstate relations. This analogy was a decisive conceptual innovation, and it has since dominated discussions of International Relations. Some social theorists, like Spinoza and Pufendorf, agreed with Hobbes' depiction of interstate interaction; they elaborated on the pessimistic image of international politics as red in tooth and claw.

Other authors developed alternative visions in which international interaction was seen not in terms of relations between sovereign princes, but as interaction between rational individuals – usually between self-interested merchants. Émeric Crucé, for example, optimistically depicted a harmonious condition marked by co-operation and harmony among men. His vision was later pursued by William Penn, the Duc de Sully, Abbé St. Pierre, Jeremy Bentham and several others.

Still other seveneenth-century theorists struck a middle position between the pessimism of Hobbes and the optimism of Crucé. Hugo Grotius, for example, another of the great early synthesizers, depicted international interaction as an anarchic activity; however, he held that it could be much improved by the acceptance of a codex of international law built on human reason, common interest and past habits of peaceful interaction.

These basic visions of interstate interaction were largely maintained in subsequent centuries. However, they were restated in various contexts and coloured by the intellectual outlook of different epochs. Seventeenth–century speculations were built around a basic, mechanical view of human society – reflected most typically in the traditional balance-of-power arguments of the age. Eighteenth-century theories were marked by a pervasive vision of the self-equilibrating properties of human interaction. Nineteenth-century speculations were dominated by images of 'progress' or 'evolution'.

A third major phase of International Relations theory emerged around 1900. This contemporary phase is discussed in Part Three of the book. The transition from the modern to the contemporary phase was not marked by a clear rupture. When the study of International Relations emerged as an academic discipline after World War I, it was dominated by the mental furniture of nineteenth-century theorizing. However, the orderly arrangements which the old macro-theoretical propensities had imparted to the study of society and politics were waning. In the words of Charles Tilly (1984, p. 17): 'The nineteenth century's legacy to the twentieth century's social scientists resembles an old house inherited from a rich aunt: worn, overdecorated, cluttered, but probably salvageable.'

After World War I, the studies of International Relations were furnished by the Enlightenment *meublement* from the epochs of optimism and idealism. After World War II, this was replaced by furniture in stern First Empire style. The 1950s and 1960s were dominated by a pseudo-realist perspective tempered by nineteenth-century notions of 'modernization' and 'development'. But increasingly, post-war speculations have been conducted in an atmosphere which resembles that of the sixteenth century – a fragmented field, split among various basic principles. Since 1970, the study of International Relations has been torn among an increasing variety of competing approaches. During the 1980s, and especially after the Cold War was brought to a close, the discipline has grown more fractured and fragmented than ever.

The purpose of the study

International Relations theory seeks to explain why international events occur the way they do. Most theorists speculate about the relations between sovereign states; their intention is to understand patterns of political interaction between and among states. Some of them want to go further; they seek to tease from these patterns of interaction general principles – laws or law–like statements – by means of which they can explain past events and predict events in the future.

Aristotle laid the foundation for the study of politics with the proposition that man is by nature a political animal – a *zoon politikon*. He argued that attempts to derive knowledge about politics from the endowments and behaviour of man-in-isolation are misguided. Man, Aristotle emphasized, cannot exist outside a social context: 'He who is unable to live in society, or who has no need because he is sufficient for himself, must be either a beast or a god.'

Political theorists ever since have accepted Aristotle's argument that political actors are influenced by the social context they inhabit. Increasingly, they have also accepted that the same maxim applies to political theorists: they, too, are shaped and coloured by the culture, the imagery and the mythology which form their perceptions, their experience and their knowledge. As this social context changes – from one geographical area to another, or from one historical epoch to the next – men are moulded in different forms and their speculations are given different modes and flavours.

Perceptions of international politics are no exception. International Relations theory, too, varies across space and time. To trace the history of a subject matter which constantly undergoes mutations and transformations, as this book tries to do, is much like hunting chameleons. When Robert Heilbroner set out to write a brief history of capitalism, he faced this problem of the constant transformation of his subject matter with the following attitude. 'It is helpful,' he observed,

to approach this daunting task by reminding ourselves that understanding, explanation and prediction are universal attributes of human experience, not achievements of social science – never complete, but rarely completely inadequate. They are attained in varying degrees in different social circumstances. Thus the problem for our consideration is not whether we can understand, explain or predict, at all ... but the limits of our capacity to do so (Heilbroner 1986, p. 180).

This brief survey of the history of International Relations theory takes Heilbroner's advise *ad notam*. International Relations theory (like other social-scientific disciplines) does not 'evolve' in the sense that it steadily accumulates a body of knowledge about a constantly confined subject-matter. Consequently, the purpose of a survey is not to depict the evolution of International Relations theory from its palaeological past and arrive at a mature, complete set of explanatory principles. Rather, the task is a more modest one. It is to sketch some of the ways in which past observers have struggled to understand the nature and logic of international politics, arrange these diverse sketches in rough chronology and place them into the political and intellectual climate of their age.

If this mosaic is well done – and if the readers are willing, at times, to step back and view the work from a little distance – they may glimpse the outline of an analytic tradition.

Part 1
Preludes

1

Gods, sinners and the origins of International Relations theory[1]

Where should we look for the origins of an International Relations theory tradition? Some authors (Dougherty and Pfaltzgraff 1981) claim that we should begin with World War I. But this is too late. Long before World War I, a large body of literature existed which discussed issues of war, wealth, peace and power in international relations – as this book seeks to show. Others (Kauppi and Viotti 1992) argue that we should begin with the dawn of recorded history. But this is too early. No sustained connection exists between the famous discussions of Xenophon, Thucydides and other classical authors and the arguments of modern theorists.

There are many reasons why discussions about the origins of International Relations theory are littered with disagreements. One reason is that discussions often are clouded by an unclear idea of what 'tradition' means. It is therefore useful to distinguish at the outset between a 'historic tradition' and an 'analytic tradition' (Gunnell 1978). A 'historic tradition' is commonly defined as a self-constituted pattern of conventional practice. A historic tradition of International Relations may be traced back to antiquity – to Xenophon, Thucydides, Herodotus, Livy, Plutarch and other ancient authors who discussed causes of war and described practices of containment and counterbalance, and who claimed that kings and princes will always try to divide in order to conquer and form alliances better to defend. However, one cannot safely infer from political practices the existence of political theories. It has been argued that balance-of-power practices are integral to politics; that they are not necessarily deduced from theory; that they follow as naturally from political interaction as one fencer's parry follows another's thrust. David Hume (1985, p. 337), for example, maintained that ancient accounts convey little more than the existence of 'common sense and obvious reasoning'.

An 'analytic tradition' refers to an inherited pattern of thought or a sustained intellectual connection through time along which scholars stipulate certain concepts, themes and texts as functionally similar. As an analytic tradition the study of International Relations can hardly be traced back more than a few centuries. Many authors testify to the existence of balance-of-power practices in ancient Greece. Some of them also testify to the existence of balance-of-power theory. Thucydides (1972, p. 48), for example, explains quite clearly that he intends to draw lessons for posterity, for the sake of 'those who want to understand clearly the events which happened in the past and which (human nature being what it is) will, at some time or other and in much the same ways, be repeated in the future'. However, neither Thucydides nor any other classical author can alone demonstrate the existence of a 3000-year-long tradition in International Relations; their accounts do not add up to a *sustained* intellectual connection across the ages. Their arguments faded from Western scholarship when Greece fell to Macedon and Rome. And when Rome collapsed, they slipped out of view altogether.

Yet it is precisely the collapse of Rome which marks the beginning of the present study. On the face of it, it seems unlikely that the beginnings of a sustained intellectual connection among International-Relations themes and concepts could emerge from the primitive, rough and turbulent era which followed the collapse of Rome. But several authors of the 'Dark Ages' touched on some of the broader issues of international affairs. Cassiodorus (490–583) briefly discussed issues of war and peace in his *History of the Goths*; Gregory of Tours (538–94) touched on issues of diplomacy in his *History of the Franks*; and Paul the Deacon (720–99) noted both themes in his *History of the Lombards*. Pope Gregory the Great (590–604) wrote about the experiences of his youth when he was Rome's ambassador to Byzantium and negotiator with the Lombards. It seems worthwhile briefly to investigate some of these authors before this era is dismissed as theoretically barren.

The fall and rise of the Far West

It is true that interstate relations did not exist in the early Middle Ages. Not really. At least not in the modern sense of the term. Yet international practices existed. Comments on such practices existed too during the Dark Ages of Cassiodorus no less than in the antiquity of Thucydides. The preconditions therefore also existed for international theorizing.

The Dark Ages
The Roman Empire had imposed unity and order upon Europe, Asia Minor, the Middle East and the northern coast of Africa from about 500 BC. By the fourth century AD, the politics of the Empire were riddled by corruption and paralysis. The armies gained influence. The generals fought each other and recruited bands of barbarians to serve under them. They seated and unseated emperors. Roman cities faltered under the impact of such military rivalries. Industry and commerce decayed. Since the eastern regions of the Empire remained stronger,

wealthier and more unified, emperor Constantine moved the imperial capital to Byzantium (Constantinople) in AD 330. Soon the great Roman Empire split into a Western and an Eastern half.

In this weakened state, the Empire faced a sudden wave of great migrations (380–450). It was assaulted by the Goths who came from south Russia, threatened Constantinople about AD 380, tore through Greece in 396 and sacked Rome in 410. The entire Empire shook. Its western half collapsed. The old, gigantic empire split into local, self-sufficient, impoverished fragments. Or more precisely put, it split in two: into a consolidated eastern half and a fragmented western half.

The eastern part of the Roman Empire survived the great migrations. It clung to its Roman traditions under the onslaught of the barbarians. From its splendid capital in Byzantium, the East Roman Empire managed to ensure the traditional unity of Orthodox religion and authoritarian politics. The Byzantines secured the survival of the empire partly by repelling the barbarian onslaught by armed force, and partly by deflecting it by diplomacy – in 489, for example, the emperor Zeno gave Theodoric, the leader of the Ostrogoths, permission to conquer Italy² and rule in the emperor's name. Throughout the Middle Ages, Byzantium remained the principal European city. But the Byzantine empire closed itself defensively off from the rest of the world, and took no leadership in European events.

The western half of the Roman Empire unravelled under the impact of the great migrations. Communications ground to a halt. Production and trade choked. Two centuries afterwards, Europe had no coherent existence. The area had unravelled into a great jumble of tribes, military raiders, villages, manors, monasteries and trading towns. Kingdoms rose under exceptionally strong rulers, but fell apart again under weaker ones.

The early Church; the early Empire
Various institutions emerged during these centuries to provide some measure of unity and order in the Far West. The most important of these was the Church. It maintained, against all odds, the rudiments of a common Western identity through the Dark Ages. It kept the Christian religion alive. It conserved the remnants of Roman civilization. It spread the light of religion, learning and literacy to the north-western periphery.

The Church became an important force partly because it offered the only ordering structure of central administration in those chaotic times, and partly because conversions of barbarians contributed to its growing might. Such conversions were actively promoted by missionaries and were often sponsored by the pope. They extended Catholic Christendom northwards, and steeped the Far West in a common culture. The conversions of the Anglo-Saxons in the seventh century and the Germans in the eighth were important milestones in medieval history. The Catholic religion and the Latin language provided, together with the memories of Roman law and various remnants of imperial institutions, some measure of cultural unity to the fragmented continent.

A second important force for unity was the German and Frankish kingdoms which rose – often with support from the pope – and fell during the early Middle Ages. One such kingdom was built by a Germanic king, Clovis (466–511), who conquered much of Western Europe and briefly unified it into a vast kingdom.[3] Another important kingdom was built by the Frankish king *Carolus Magnus* or Charlemagne (768–814). He obtained the support of the Church, and was even crowned Emperor of the West by the pope himself in AD 800. Charlemagne came close to imposing some of the prestige and governmental machinery of the Roman emperors upon Europe. In the process he became a powerful competitor to the pope and prepared the grounds for a new, secular conflict between pope and emperor concerning power and authority over vast Western territories. But the Carolingian empire (like the Merovingian empire before it) did not long survive its founder. It disintegrated in all but name soon after Charlemagne's death.

The demise of the Carolingian Empire was quickened by new waves of destructive migrations. Magyar, Viking and Arab assaults threatened to bring chaos to the Far West in the eighth and ninth centuries. Charlemagne had developed a formidable cavalry force, but it was slow, cumbersome and ineffective when faced by warriors who emphasized swiftness – like the Magyars on their light steppe ponies or the Vikings, who harassed the Carolingian coasts in the their rapid vessels. Magyar tribes emerged from the Hungarians plains and attacked northern Italy and Germany. Vikings descended upon the coasts and rivers of the British Isles and the Continent's Atlantic rim. Saracens attacked the Mediterranean coasts of Italy and France. Arab armies, flying the flag of the new religion of Islam, conquered all Iberia during the first half of the eighth century and launched incursions into the heart of the Rhône valley.

The recovery of the West

The second wave of foreign invasions destroyed the order which Charlemagne had imposed upon the Far West. But in some places the foreign onslaught also spurred constructive actions which stimulated the growth of military tactics and organization. The most consequential of these developments concerned the evolution of knightly cavalry tactics. These had evolved in the Carolingian empire. But since it was immensely expensive to equip armoured knights, they were for a long time considered too costly to maintain. However, frequent Viking and Magyar attacks in the ninth century made some Frankish regions realize that it was better to make heavy, regular payments to local knights who remained in residence and on call, than periodically to be exposed to devastating barbarian raids. Counts and other administrators enfeoffed knights who promised military service in return for rights to collect income from one or more villages. In one sense, then, these barbarian invasions triggered a reaction which in some places produced stable order on the local level. The origins of feudal society, in short, lie with the heavy cavalry which evolved within the Carolingian empire.

The evolution of cavalry – which amounted to a military revolution in its day – produced the trunk of the feudal order: a supreme class of specialized warriors ('vassals') who received large land grants ('fiefs') in exchange for armed service. When the Carolingian empire collapsed, the warrior class remained a distinguishing feature of the post-imperial order. But without the empire to contain it, it was not harnessed to any clear political purpose. Legally, its members were liegemen or vassals of kings (of whom Charlemagne had been the greatest). But in practice they could ignore royal orders; the new monarchs had neither the fiscal base nor the military power to enforce their claims. Europe thus fell under the rule of armoured lords who assumed authority to govern all those who lived on their fiefdom. They administered justice, collected taxes and agricultural produce and claimed labour service and military service from the residents. And in the process they evolved from a military élite to a social élite. Its members called themselves *nobiles* in the Roman fashion and appropriated various late imperial titles such as *comes* (count) and *dux* (duke).

It may be argued, crudely, that early feudal society was an elaborate supply system which ensured that mounted knights were equipped and maintained. Mounted warfare was specialized, costly and exclusive, and gave feudal society its military bearing and its knightly code of chivalry. However, even at the height of their power, military aristocrats could never do precisely as they liked. They inhabited a 'heteronomous' political framework. Their own authority was circumscribed by that of others. Their freedom of action was limited by a web of allegiances and obligations.

The word 'feudal' is derived from *feudum* ('fief'), which in essence was land which a lord bestowed upon his vassal by investiture in return for services. This etymology suggests a crucial point: that the entire feudal structure rested on entitlement to land. When this is said, another crucial point must be added: that a fief was not simply defined by drawing clear 'boundaries' around it and giving it as 'property' to an individual owner. No, a fief was an amalgam of conditional property and private authority – property was conditional in that it carried with it explicit social obligations which limited a lord's freedom of action; authority was private in that the rights of jurisdiction over the inhabitants of a fiefdom resided personally in its ruler. The system was rendered more complicated still by the prevailing concept of usufructure, which meant that different lords could have different titles to the same landed property. As a result, the medieval system of rule reflected a patchwork of overlapping and incomplete rights of government (Ruggie 1986, 1993; Strayer 1970); a lattice-like web in which 'different juridical instances were geographically interwoven and stratified, and plural allegiances, asymmetrical suzerainties and anomalous enclaves abounded' (Anderson 1979, pp. 37f). Medieval politics was a heteronomous system in which even the highest lord found himself circumscribed. His actions were restricted by other high lords – by popes (who were able to modify, if not control, the behaviour of clerics and noblemen) or by monarchs (like those that developed in England, France, Germany and in the Iberian Peninsula before AD 1000[4]). He was limited by towns and structures of trade, which gradually revived at the turn of the millennium and stimulated the rise of walled cities and powerful city-states in Italy, the Rhineland and the Low Countries.

States existed, but they did not reign supreme (Meinecke 1957, p. 27). Medieval Europe was not really a state system; it was a shifting kaleidoscope of political arrangements among monarchs, nobles, clerics and towns.

Three medieval civilizations

By AD 950 three distinct civilizations existed in the Western World, confronting each other around the Mediterranean: the Byzantine, the Arabic and the 'barbarian' civilizations.

Byzantium

The first civilization of the High Middle Ages was the Byzantine Empire. It was contained within the Eastern Roman Empire, which had survived the onslaught of the Great Migrations. It included Asia Minor, the Balkan Peninsula and scattered parts of Italy. Byzantium was Christian in religion and Greek in language and culture. Geographically, it guarded the Straits of Bosporus. Spiritually, it guarded the Graeco-Roman tradition in its Orthodox, Christian version. Commerce and navigation were continued on much the same level as in ancient times. For most Christians, the Byzantine Emperor represented the world's supreme ruler; and Constantinople, which had about 1,000,000 inhabitants by the tenth century and the largest urban population in the known world at the time, was the world's pre-eminent city.

The rulers of Byzantium constantly faced the threat of invasion. In dealing with it, they developed the arts of war and diplomacy. The better to combat the barbarians, the early Empire built an efficient field army, small but with great mobility and personally attached to the emperor. In response to changes in barbarian tactics, the armoured cavalry gained steadily in importance after the sixth century. These developments are treated in the *Peri Polemon* (or 'On the wars') – eight books on the long struggle of emperors Justin I (518–27) and Justinian I (527–65) against the Persians, the Vandals and the Goths. The books were written by Procopius of Caesarea (*c*.500–70?), and reflect his ambition to emulate Thucydides.

Procopius was not unique in having studied ancient texts on history and warfare. Such texts were collected and copied in schools, universities and libraries. Byzantine libraries were richly stocked with classical literature – including many important works which have since disappeared. The inhabitants were highly aware of the long heritage of civilization they represented. Byzantine scholars

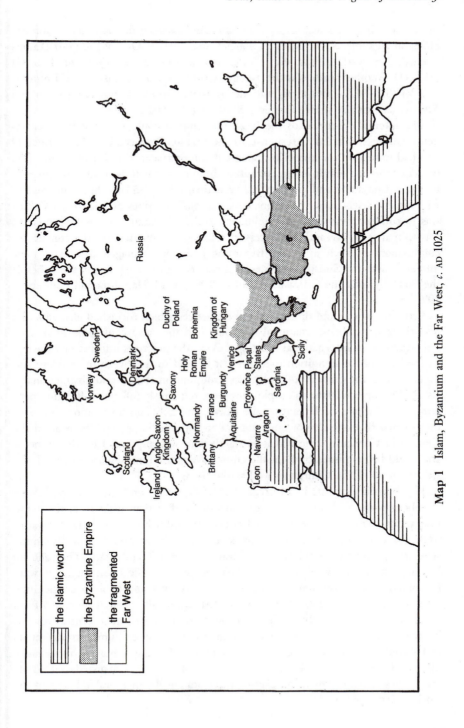

Map 1 Islam, Byzantium and the Far West, *c.* AD 1025

drew upon these classical texts to compile handbooks, anthologies and commentaries on all subjects, including diplomacy and warfare. One of the most famous manuals on warfare was the *Strategicon*, written under Emperor Leo III (717–41). Another study was the *Tactica*, written under the auspices of Emperor Leo VI (886–912) – but apparently derived from an older manual (also entitled *Strategicon*) written under Emperor Maurice (582–602).

The internal resources of the Byzantine empire could not sustain a permanently successful military response to the threatening invaders. The emperors also had to rely on the arts of containment, counterbalance and negotiation. One principal method employed in Byzantine diplomacy was to weaken their enemies by fomenting strife and rivalries between them. A second method consisted in winning the friendship of neighbouring nations by bribes and flattery. A third was to convert their heathen neighbours to the Christian faith. A final method was to marry off Byzantine princesses to foreign potentates. By the concurrent employment of such methods, Byzantine emperors managed to extend their influence over the Sudan, Arabia and Abyssinia, and to keep at bay the tribes of the Black Sea and the Caucasus (Nicolson 1988, p. 10; Hamilton and Langhorne 1995, pp. 17f).

Activities of war and diplomacy were practices which furnished elements to a historic tradition of international relations. Did they also contribute to an analytic tradition of International Relations? Were the practices informed by theory? In the light of the definition used here, it is hard to see Byzantine warfare and diplomacy in the early Middle Ages as grounded in theory and abstract analysis. Rather, both warfare and diplomacy were religiously informed. Religion penetrated the whole of Byzantine life. Civil and religious institutions were so intertwined that one cannot understand one without the other. The head of the Church in Constantinople was a patriarch who was appointed by the emperor and could be dismissed by him; the emperor was the representative of God and was the head of the Church as well as the State.

The Emperor's court had a large staff of diplomats and interpreters, but its members performed foreign-service functions rather than tasks of analysis and theorizing.[5] Universities entertained educators and scholars, and their libraries were stocked with a wealth of Greek and Roman literature. But Byzantine scholarship occurred within the joint frame of Church and State. The scholars had a thorough knowledge of the whole range of classical learning, but were hampered by an authoritarian Church/State structure and by an overwhelming reverence for the ancients. They commented ceaselessly on texts inherited from the past, but rarely doubted them and never subjected them to critical review. They composed endless streams of commentaries, compendiums, abridgements and anthologies, but produced few contributions of lasting scholarly importance. 'Age after age, innumerable pens moved, lakes of ink were exhausted, but no literary work remains which can claim a place among the memorable books of the world' (Artz 1967, p. 112).

The Islamic world

The second medieval civilization was characterized by the political-religious institutions of the Caliphate. It stretched from the Iberian peninsula across North Africa, through the Middle East and Persia and far into India; it was geographically the most extensive of these civilizations, and intellectually the most advanced. Islam was its religion. Arabic was its language.

The Arab civilization was built by tough and ruthless means. The Muslims were at the outset cavalry warriors – indeed, Muhammad was a strategist and military leader; and the remarkable expansion of Islam after his death shows that his successors, too, were shrewd strategists. They possessed the ability to observe their enemies, emulate the strong, and learn and adapt militarily to changing circumstances. In their encounters with Byzantine cavalry, they organized a heavy cavalry. And, most astonishingly, these former desert-dwellers built warships in great numbers and launched two great land-and-sea invasions on Constantinople in the late seventh century.

The early caliphal empire, governed by the Umayyad dynasty (661–750), retained old Arab manners. But when the Umayyad dynasty was toppled (AD 750), the new Abbasid dynasty reformed government procedures and moved the seat of empire to Baghdad. This implied a turning away from the empire's Arab roots and its Bedouin sentiment, and an embrace of a sedentary, urban culture. Baghdad lay on the intersection of Middle Eastern trade routes. As the capital of a growing empire, the city grew rapidly in wealth, power and size – counting some 800,000 inhabitants by the tenth century (and was then, after Constantinople, the second largest city in the known world). Its political culture was marked by merchants and professional classes. A complex network of communications intersected in Baghdad. The city lay on the central routes of the *caravans*. These were encouraged by trade and by pilgrimage, and helped reinforce the unity of the Islamic world. Merchandise moved along these routes. So did ideas and arguments – in the tangible form of documents, books and letters, or in the human form of teachers, students, preachers and pilgrims. No city could compare with ar-Rashid's Baghdad. Not even the court of Charlemagne could rival that of the Caliph in splendour, sophistication and scholarship.

The Abbasids valued education and learning. Schools were systematically built, usually in connection with mosques. By AD 900 nearly every mosque had an elementary school (Artz 1967, p. 150).[6] Abbasid scholars studied the translated works of the Graeco-Roman tradition. Many of them were influenced by Aristotle. Others were informed by non-Western impulses – especially by a distinctly Persian genre of political commentaries known as the 'mirror of Princes'.[7]

Did Islamic writings on foreign affairs introduce an analytic tradition of International Relations? It may be argued that the existence of an analytic tradition is not supported by a scrutiny of Abbasid texts. Warfare and diplomacy were, in Baghdad as in Constantinople, religiously informed. Civil and religious institutions were intimately intertwined. The Abbasid state was, in essence, a theocracy – not in the Western sense of a state ruled by the Church and the clergy, since neither existed in the Muslim world, but in the more literal sense of a polity ruled by God. Its political discussions were anchored in theology rather than secular analysis and theory. The Abbasids publically professed to base their rule on the religion of Islam, and acknowledged the embryonic Islamic law as the legal basis of their society. Abbasid foreign policy was based on the notion that history was moving inexorably towards global peace and order conferred by the only true Faith. Until Islam emerged victorious, however, the world was divided between one area, which was Islamic (*dar al-Islam* or the 'Abode of Islam') and one area which was not (*dar al-Harb* or the 'Abode of War'). Between the two there was a state of war of some kind – either in full flood in the form of Holy War (*jihad*), or else in a temporary armistice.

But it may also be claimed that religious maxims played a smaller role in Arab speculations on politics than is commonly assumed. The Islamic perspective of world politics was mitigated by pragmatism. The permanent tension between *dar al-Islam* and *dar al-Harb* did not prevent peaceful relations and cultural and commercial exchanges. It was not uncommon for Caliph and Emperor to exchange poets or scholars as gifts or on loan; and it was possible for non-Muslims to take up residence in Muslim territory and engage in commerce. Muslim scholars embraced the ancient Graeco-Roman heritage, including Thucydides and Aristotle. By keeping alive arguments which were lost in the West, they maintained a tradition. And that this was a living, analytic tradition is demonstrated by the fact that the Arabs did more than simply translate the old texts and comment on them. To a greater degree than their colleagues in Constantinople, Muslim scholars went beyond the texts (Grunebaum 1946). They extracted the organizing ideas and arguments, which they turned, twisted and placed in new contexts. Thus it is quite conceivable that the Arabs sustained an analytic tradition of International Relations. This tradition would then draw partly on the Graeco-Roman world and partly on the Persian. This is a possibility that few Western scholars have seriously explored.

The Far West

In the company of the Caliphate and the Byzantine Empire, the remainder of Europe hardly deserves the denotation 'civilization'. The far western parts of Europe, which the Caliphate had been unable to conquer and Byzantium unwilling to hold, were filled with busy, barbarian kings who did their best to maintain a semblance of order on their savage turfs. Political unity had long been dissolved by migration and reversion to heathen tribalism. Most languages were Germanic, but were not written down. Most religions were an intricate folklore of myths and stories reverberating with echoes of a Christian past. There was no sense of loyalty to embracing and supreme institutions like a state (Wallace-Hadrill 1956). The old Roman roads had fallen into neglect; their flat stones were often removed and used as convenient building-blocks. Travel was rendered dangerous by brigandage and highway bandits.

The Church was a lingering centre of power and a source of order. Trade had died down. Communications were rudimentary. But the pope had a chancery which collected diplomatic records in specialized archives under the direction of and authority of the 'masters of the rolls'. Also, Charlemagne's court at Aix-la-Chapelle (or Aachen), near the mouth of the Rhine, included a chancery – an office which was elaborately organized with a large clerical staff under the charge of a 'chancellor'. Such archives reveal that envoys of Rome and Aachen did not merely represent the interests of their respective masters; they also furnished reports on the internal situation in foreign courts and on the relations of those courts towards each other. These early medieval envoys, then, were sent to foreign courts for other reasons than their gifts of eloquent oration. They were also sent for their trained powers of observation and the soundness of their judgement. In the education of envoys, then – in the routines used by the medieval chanceries to train their powers of observation and develop the soundness of their judgement – lie important precursors to the systematic study of International Relations.

When Charlemagne created an empire, and thus erected a powerful political competitor to the pope and prepared the grounds for a secular conflict between pope and emperor, it was a political watershed in Western history. When he created a scholarly as well as a political and administrative centre for his growing empire, it was an intellectual watershed as well. Charlemagne created a splendid court at Aachen to which he summoned prominent scholars from all parts of Europe. He exchanged cultural gifts with Caliph Harun ar-Rashid and Empress Irene. He established a court library which included a collection of ancient authors. He initiated a campaign to establish schools and teach literacy near the cathedrals and in the monasteries of his realm. Such initiatives greatly improved conditions of scholarship, and represent a turning-point in the history of Western political thought. The conflict between pope and emperor was systematically discussed at the Carolingian court. Lasting questions were formulated about the nature of power and the division of political authority between religious and secular actors all over the Christian world. If the pope's authority came from God, where did the emperor's authority come from? From the pope (as the pope maintained)? From God (as the emperor argued)? Or from men (as the seven princes and prelates who were later to elect the emperor would subsequently claim)? These questions reflected a high-pitched struggle which dominated European politics for centuries. The debates which ensued broke out of the realm of theology and, unlike similar debates in Constantinople and Baghdad, entered the province of International Relations theorizing (Fichterman 1964).

When Charlemagne died, the Carolingian empire unravelled. The Church remained as a virtual monopoly of medieval scholarship, and tended to collapse all knowledge into theology. Western debates on warfare and diplomacy occurred within a religiously founded discourse. But the surrounding society was more unsettled and diverse in the Far West than in Byzantium and the Caliphate. The West was never reconstituted as a single, unified empire sanctioned by a central religious authority. Rather, the West remained a politically heterogeneous area which, during the ninth and tenth centuries, evolved a peculiar plurality of power centres in the form of independent territorial states. These states were justified by doctrines drawn from Christian theology. Although the Church retained a virtual monopoly on Western scholarship, no standardized theology entirely overwhelmed European values and norms. Ancient, local legal codes were, for example, never entirely extinguished. They continued to make an imprint on local political institutions and processes. Also, the peculiar system of states which emerged in the Far West presented an opportunity for independent intellectuals to manoeuvre between Church and State, to move from one state to the next, to attach themselves to one court or another.

But we are getting ahead of the story.

Sources of Western political theorizing

While the lights of Byzantine and Islamic culture burned most brightly, the Far West was, by comparison, illuminated by a dim twilight. 'Culturally Latin Christendom, like a ruined family that could no longer maintain its old dwelling, came to live in a few rooms of the cellar' (Artz 1967, pp. 179f). Some achievements in political theory were accomplished around the time of the collapse of Rome – as evinced in the works of Ambrose, Bede, Capella and others. However, early medieval scholarship was not marked by creative independence and original thought. Virtually all of these scholars built on the same ultimate explanatory authority: the Bible, *the* source of wisdom that provided answers to all questions. The Bible was the central repository of knowledge in Western medieval civilization.

Religion
The Bible explained that the world had been created in six days by God for an ultimate if inscrutable purpose. Although created perfect, man had fallen from grace into sin and error, thereby incurring the penalty of eternal damnation. But God had, in his infinite benevolence, provided a way of atonement and salvation through a propitiatory sacrifice of His only son. Helpless in himself, man could still be permitted, through God's mercy and by humility and obedience to His will, to obtain pardon for sin and error. Life on earth was just a temporary probation, a means to a greater end. In God's appointed time, this world would come to an end. The Earthly City would be swallowed up in flames, and good and evil men would be separated. The good and faithful would be gathered with God, and dwell in his Heavenly City in perfection and felicity for ever. But the evil and recalcitrant were reserved a place of everlasting punishment. This biblical argument provided the bedrock basis for medieval political theorizing. The key assumption of the vision was that good men go to heaven and bad men go

to hell. But an important additional factor was added with the concept of original sin. This concept provided the most important explanation for the occurrence of conflicts and war – and, besides, it provided a key precondition for the immense power of the medieval Church.

The assumption of original sin was most importantly developed by Augustine of Hippo (354–430). Augustine lived in North Africa in the early fourth century and witnessed the fall of Rome from afar. He lived in the rich, isolated backwater of Carthage around AD 400. In 410, when Alaric the Goth sacked Rome, Augustine understood that the whole gigantic bureaucracy of the Roman Empire was destined to unravel. Under the pressure of these apocalyptic events he worked intensely to offer some way of escape. With Christian dualism as his vantage point, Augustine wrote *The City of God*. The argument flows from the notion that man inhabits two parallel realities: this world of violence, war, hunger and misery on the one hand, and the Kingdom of God on the other. Augustine argued that social life is divinely ordained. However, because of Adam's original sin which man inherits, the human race has been condemned in its first origin. 'Life itself, if life it is to be called, bears witness by the host of cruel ills with which it is filled', he writes (Augustine 1954, p. 474). Because of his sinful and corrupt nature, man requires government and coercive laws. And as an act of mercy, God has created laws to impose some order upon the sinful and corrupt human society. He has also created monarchs and princes and given them authority to enforce the laws and maintain civil order. God has, according to Augustine, given kings and princes a just reason to use violent means to preserve the safety of the State! A good citizen should therefore obey his government. This secures the order and peace which man so obviously cannot keep on his own. Man is always at risk, unless aided by the Church. This medieval world view was not challenged for several hundred years. It infused all social theorizing until the High Middle Ages.

Augustine delivered the premises for medieval political studies. Its students never really considered the possibility that human behaviour could be studied in and of itself, or that political authority could be granted by anyone else but God. Furthermore, political studies were the province of a tiny, Church-educated élite. Theories were deduced from theological axioms, and tended to reflect Augustine's pessimistic assumptions about the corrupt and sinful nature of man. Scholars of the Church may have condemned war, and may have denounced the excesses of cruel tyrants and the conquests of strong rulers. But they argued that such behaviour was a natural consequence of man's wicked and sinful nature. Also, they did not condemn war on principle. For they maintained, with Augustine, that certain wars were just. Defensive wars, for example, waged to maintain traditional order against the onslaught of barbarian marauders, were considered just. So were wars waged on God's behalf against the infidels.

Rome's struggle against the invading barbarians was, according to Augustine, an example of a just war. It was a case where Christian defenders of order sought to combat an enemy of both Faith and order.[8] The example showed that the moral qualities of men like Cicero had made the empire great. They had been devoted to the common good and their devotion had been enforced by imperial authority and power. Yet, these men had been misguided in glorifying Rome rather than God, argued Augustine. They had insisted on allegiance to temporal affairs rather than the natural and eternal values of the Christian faith. They had glorified the City of Man (*civitas terrena*) rather than the City of God (*civitas dei*) (Momigliano 1963). This duality between the two realms of human existence was also discussed by Pope Gelasius I (492–96). He, too, drew a sharp distinction between State and Church, but unlike Augustine, he argued that *both* institutions reflect the will of God: thus both are equally 'natural' and equally just. However, the State and the Church have different tasks to perform, Gelasius claimed. The State, represented by the emperor, should concern itself with temporal issues, whereas the Church, represented by the pope, should deal with mankind's spiritual needs.

Augustine and Gelasius introduced to medieval Europe a political doctrine which benefited the Christian Church and, ultimately, the pope. It explained that all monarchs and princes of Europe had their authorities from God. And since the pope was God's representative on earth, the kings and emperors owed obedience and submission to Rome. This doctrine sanctioned the notion that there exists a universal community of man, under God, represented by the Christian Church. No temporal body, neither civilian nor military, could assume absolute authority over it. When the Roman Empire caved in, the political structure it had imposed upon Europe unravelled, but the visions of Augustine remained. They were guarded and managed by a network of bishops and priests and overseen from Rome by the authority of the pope, who imposed some measure of mental unity on the Far West.

In the centuries after the demise of Rome, all scholarly activities in the Far West were dominated by the Christian clergy. This meant the eclipse of the pre-Christian speculations of classical political philosophy – including the Greek concept of the *polis* and the Roman concept of *imperium*. It also meant the hegemony of an Augustinian notion according to which all the inhabitants of the world were unified in a human community (*humanitas*). This community consisted of all peoples and all races. It was unified under God, and transcended the smaller communities of the village, the town or the State. This notion of 'humanity' unified the human species under a supreme principle, 'so that there is no room for distinction between Greek and Jew, between circumcised and uncircumcised, or between barbarian and Scythian, slave and free man. There is only Christ: he is everything and he is in everything' (Colossians 3:11).

Throughout the Middle Ages, the intellectuals of the Far West thought of themselves as belonging to this large human community. There were wars and quarrels, uprisings, doctrinal disputes, the great struggle for paramount influence over Church and State between pope and emperor. But through it all, there continued to be 'a belief in the actual unity of Christendom, however variously felt and expressed. This belief was a fundamental condition of all medieval political thought and activity. This universal notion reverberates through late medieval visions of a peaceful world' (Lange 1919, p. 98). In his *De monarchia* [*c*.1313], Dante Alighieri (*c*.1265–1321) called for the establishment of a world-state. It should be governed by one all-powerful ruler who was as unselfish as he was omnipotent, and could end all conflicts, suppress all tyrannies and bring about universal peace.

Religion and law

The scholarship of the medieval Church allowed no essential difference between the various branches of knowledge. It derived its concepts from theology, and drew no clear distinction between knowledge about nature and knowledge about man. The one conspicuous issue of international politics of the age, the political debate between pope and emperor, was maintained within a theological discourse.

The Church exercised a solid dominance over medieval scholarship. But it was not the exclusive font of Western wisdom. Other sources of knowledge and authority existed. One of the most important of these was 'custom' or 'customary law'. Although the Middle Ages was rife with conflict and violence, medieval society attached a great respect to customary law. And although disputes were regularly settled by force (especially when kings were disputants), medieval Europeans were as busily engaged in litigation as they were in battle. Every great estate was hung about with lawsuits. Rights, titles and privileges were constantly granted, revoked and reaffirmed. By the High Middle Ages, legally demonstrable privileges had become the universal cement of European society.

In contrast to Byzantium, whose jurisprudence drew directly upon the legal heritage from Rome, Western scholars drew upon two legal traditions: canon law and customary law. Canon law was developed by Church leaders and informed by Christian theology, but was anchored in Roman law. Customary law, by contrast, represented a codification of customary behaviour. It had its origins centuries back among barbarian chieftains and kings (Keen 1963).

The stubborn persistence of customary law is an important factor in the development of political theory in the Far West. First, it included a unique, perhaps even a proto-democratic, element of popular involvement (Szücs 1990, pp. 27ff). It was derived ultimately from the people who, at least tacitly, had given it their consent; and it applied to vassals and lords alike. It had 'percolated up from below' (Ferguson and Mansbach 1988, p. 53), and applied to individuals by virtue of their membership in a tribe or local group. Chieftains, princes and kings were subject to customary law, which therefore limited the power and authority of central rulers and protected the interests of their subjects.

Second, customary law was a centripetal force in early European politics. It was local in conception. It perpetuated local privileges and immunities deter-

mined by inherited status. It cemented the forms of localism which characterized the feudal order and was an obstacle to all attempts to reassemble the Far
West into a unified empire.

Customary law regulated a wide variety of feudal, manorial, urban and royal
affairs. Two aspects of customary law are of particular interest for the student
of politics. The first of these pertains to economic activities (Berman 1983, p.
333). During the eleventh century, customary rules which regulated transport
and commerce were formalized and basic concepts and institutions of orderly
mercantile relations emerged. By the middle of the twelfth century, the so-called
lex mercatoria ('the law merchant') governed a special class of people (merchants)
in special places (fairs, seaports, cities and towns).

The second relevant aspect of customary law pertains to war. Warfare was not
really subject to any control during the Middle Ages; Germanic tribesmen entertained no clear idea that war was wrong – let alone illegal. Yet they entertained
some rudimentary notions of fair conduct – including the chivalrous treatment
of imprisoned soldiers and heralds. These notions, as reflected in customary law
on war and diplomacy, may be considered an early source for International Relations theory.

Religion, law and foreign policy
Canon law and customary law can be considered separate sources of International Relations scholarship. In practice, the two cannot easily be separated.
Christian scholars would, for example, provide good justifications for extant
principles of customary law which governed the treatment of soldiers and heralds. Influenced by the codes of Christian morality, Western scribes and scholars lamented the destruction wrought by war and pitied the innocent victims.
And from this lamentation rise important medieval efforts to regulate war
through ecclesiastical and royal legislation. A concept of The Peace of God (*pax
ecclesiae*) arose in the 990s from the Church synods as an effort to forbid, under
threat of excommunication, acts of warfare and violence against ecclesiastical
property and against innocent persons (clerics, pilgrims, women, merchants and
peasants). A concept of The Truce of God (*treuga dei*) emerged in the eleventh
century from the Church as an attempt to forbid fighting on certain days of the
week and during certain seasons and Church festivals. It was expressed by many
bishops in the second quarter of the century. It was repeated by Pope Urban II
at the Council of Clermont (1095), and this served as a reminder which renewed
and generalized the concept. Subsequent condemnations of wars and warfare
met with considerable popular support and evolved into veritable anti-war movements. Several European localities proclaimed a Peace of God or a Truce of
God.

These concepts of peace were steeped in Christian morality and in the universal vision of a human community (*humanitas*). And, like all universal visions,
it had a downside. In some interpretations the idea of humanity implied a duty

to defend Christianity. In others it implied a Christian duty to convert heathen peoples – an interpretation that was bolstered by Christ's command to go out and 'make disciples of all nations' (Matt. 28:19). Both interpretations fuelled the Western expansionism which began on the eve of the twelfth century and which was first manifest in the crusades.

It is a testimony to the two-sided nature of the Christian concept of peace that Pope Urban II, who spoke in favour of regulations within Christendom at the Council of Clermont, proposed on the same occasion (1095) the First Crusade against Islam. The pope recalled that the land of the Holy Sepulchre was under Muslim domination, and he promised full remission of sins to everyone who joined an expedition to liberate Jerusalem. People from all over the Far West answered his call. Driven by religious ardour, adventurism, greed or other motives, they joined the crusaders who followed the old Byzantine main road across Asia Minor. Their captures of the Seljuk capital of Nicaea (1096) and the Syrian city of Antioch (1097) opened the way to the Holy Land. They conquered Jerusalem in 1099 and founded a number of Christian principalities in its immediate vicinity (Runciman 1992). These small settlements, outposts of Christendom, were constantly threatened by adjacent Muslim societies. Several Western expeditions were equipped to assist them and to consolidate the Christian presence in Palestine. None of them were infused with the zeal of the First Crusade, and none were as successful.

Crusades, states and interstate relations
The crusades were armed expeditions. They involved issues of logistics and strategy which were discussed and decided by military commanders. But the crusades were also religious ventures. They were pilgrimages in need of theological justifications, and these were provided by the Church. Ultimately, it was the pope who sanctioned each crusading initiative and, formally at least, financed them. Also, it was the pope who provided the justification. This he found in the just-war theory of Augustine. Urban II justified the crusades as assistance to the Orthodox Christians in the East who were besieged by the Muslims. Later popes portrayed the crusades as defences of Western Christians who had settled in the Holy Land. During the twelfth century, the theme of the Holy Land was increasingly stressed, suggesting that the holy places (the Holy Sepulchre and Jerusalem) were indispensable to Christians who had been expelled by the Muslims. Ultimately, when the pope argued that the final purpose of the crusade was to defend Christianity, this meant in practice an effort to liberate the Holy Land. This became the main, justifying goal of the crusades.

The crusades involved the clash of two very different political worlds, the Christian West and the Islamic East, and they had important effects on both of them. In the East, the crusades helped unify and militarize the Muslim world. They caused the Muslims to co-ordinate their armies and to invest more of their resources in military forces, and left them both stronger and more hostile.

Towards the end of the twelfth century the Muslim world found an outstanding leader in Saladin, fielded bigger armies, and recaptured Jerusalem (1187): the crusader states in Palestine and Syria were doomed and Byzantium was threatened.

In the West, the crusades helped developed more co-ordinated, powerful and confident states. First, the crusades were vast ventures. Earlier warfare had been amateurish and small-scale. The crusades involved a sudden increase in army size. They reflected a veritable revolution in organizational ability, and show that, at the threshold of the twelfth century, the Far West was wealthy, powerful, confident and co-ordinated enough to stage vast assaults on the world outside (Ganshof 1995, pp. 82f).

Second, the crusades were intercontinental operations. Early medieval warfare had consisted of small-scale, local affairs. But the crusades created, for the first time since the Roman Empire, armies which operated according to intercontinental strategies. They reflected a broadening of the strategic visions of the Westerners, a kind of world strategy which had the papacy in the centre. The pope was, ultimately, the paymaster of the ventures, and he was able to direct funds to whatever theatre of war he felt needed it most at the time. Compared with the situation in the tenth and eleventh centuries, when warfare in Europe was almost local, the twelfth century witnessed the eruption of intercontinental operations.

Third, the crusades were sustained expeditions. Early medieval warfare had involved short, explosive campaigns. So the crusades imposed new, heavy demands on traditional systems of mobilization. In fact, the old feudal system of raising armies could no longer cope with the demands imposed by lengthy periods of campaigning abroad. It became clear, around 1300, that the old system would no longer do. New ways of raising and maintaining armed forces were needed. Ways which could evolve only when powerful kings emerged as independent actors on the political scene. Monarchs had emerged at the centre of a new form of web or organization, and the nobility was increasingly given the role of recruiters (Strayer 1955, pp. 163ff). The monarch drove the nobility out to recruit soldiers. And he promised those who were willing to serve that, in return for their services, they would be paid a certain sum of money per day or per week.

Two intertwined developments blaze through these changes in military and political organization. The first is the transition from an old-type feudal army, essentially based upon obligation, to a new-type army which was based upon payment for service. This required available cash and the rapid growth of modern, centralized fiscal institutions.

The second development concerns the nascent centralization of economic and political power in the hands of the monarch. It altered the royal relationship with important domestic groups – it eroded the position of landed aristocrats and enhanced the influence of urban traders and financiers. The position and authority of the aristocracy began to erode in the thirteenth century. This erosion continued through the fourteenth century, and it was expressed in a steady decline in the role of the noble horseman in war. Heavy cavalry was repeatedly defeated by lighter adversaries as the fourteenth century progressed – the battles of Lake Copaïs (1311), Crécy (1346), Poitiers (1356), Nájera (1367) and Aljubarrota being cases in point. By the time of Tannenberg (1411) and Agincourt (1415) the functions of noble Knights had largely been reduced to ceremonial displays of style, splendour and opulence. Their traditional role in warfare had been undermined by well-trained, well-organized infantry armies. The king no longer depended exclusively on the military services of the nobility.

The king downgraded his relations with the nobility as the infantry element of his armies mushroomed. This downgrading was hastened as soldiers and officers increasingly demanded to be paid in money, and presented the king with a desperate need for ready cash. As a result he began to cultivate good relationships with new social groups which were wealthy and taxable. Most particularly, he upgraded his relationship with urban commercial classes, merchants and bankers. And in order to tax these wealthy groups more easily, the king brought them in as participants in the new institutions of royal decision-making. During the thirteenth century, the new and wealthy classes were included in royal deliberations over matters of national expenditures. By the fourteenth, this practice was common enough to be formalized. And the formalization foreshadowed the growth of parliamentary politics in England, Spain, France and other emerging territorial states of the Far West. It stimulated the growth and the consolidation of territorial states along the Atlantic Rim of Western Europe.[9] And the simultaneous evolution of these states meant the emergence of a European interstate system.

The (r)evolution of medieval knowledge

During the Dark Ages, faith had been the major source and support of scholarly speculation. 'Let us believe in order that we may know', insisted Augustine, who had applied reason in order to fortify faith. In the High Middle Ages, however, reason began to supplant faith as the chief support of Christian thought. This upgrading of reason was sustained by a variety of cultural, economic and political factors. It may have its preconditions in peculiar features of Judaeo-Christian thought – such as the linear notion of time and of salvation as the outcome of an effort in and through history (Niebuhr 1949, pp. 15ff). It was conditioned by the growth of cities and by a 'higher artisanate' which found access to the company of educated scholars in the late Middle Ages – a development which stimulated the rise of a group of free entrepreneurs, craftsmen-inventors and quasi-intellectuals who belonged to neither the Church nor the State. In effect, this development gave rise to a group of independent intellectuals, who were constantly in search of princely patronage and who were therefore cosmopolitan, who had a nose for novelties and who tended to exploit the opportunities such novelties afforded (Needham 1969, p. 193).

Most famously, the upgrading of reason and the development of political theorizing was stimulated by the rediscovery and dissemination of pre-Christian texts on economics, politics and logic. Manuscripts were discovered in the Far West. Some were found in the old, great Western cities like Athens or Rome. For example, a digest of the *Corpus Juris Civilis* – the voluminous collection of laws compiled by Emperor Justinian I (527–65) – was discovered in Ravenna in 1071, and triggered a revolution in legal and political thought. Others were found in monasteries. For although the Dark Ages descended upon the Far West for seven or eight centuries, classical, non-Christian scholarship was not entirely lost. Much of it was preserved by a type of religious institution which emerged rapidly during the fifth and sixth centuries and grafted itself on to the ancient infrastructure of the Church: the monasteries. Serious and sensitive persons all over the Far West could reject the barbarian world around them and retire into the calmer communities enclosed by the monastery wall. These religious communities were self-sufficient, and were usually left unmolested by rough neighbours who held them in religious awe. As the monastic communities spread northwards during the seventh century, they also disseminated ancient manuscripts. In a world of violence, these were islands of calm which copied and kept the knowledge of Graeco-Roman scholarship.

Most of the manuscripts, however, were discovered outside the West. Some were found in the universities and libraries of Byzantium, where large collections of ancient texts had been compiled and preserved through the Dark Ages (James 1968a, b). But the largest discoveries were made in the Arab world. When Christian soldiers broke through the Arab defences of Al-Andalus in the eleventh century, they did more than reconquer Iberian territory; they also captured the products of the sophisticated Arab civilization – the houses, the mosques, the public baths, the bookshops and the libraries. Such discoveries sparked an intellectual revolution in Europe. Northern scholars came across the Pyrenees and around the Provençal coast to study and steal the greatest book collections the West had ever seen. They immediately encountered a major problem: most of the books were written in Arabic, which the Western scholars could not read. So they got the Arab texts translated – often by Toledan Jews – into Spanish. Then Christian scholars would convert the Spanish translations into Latin for the rest of Europe. And during the process they soon realized that the Arab texts were themselves translations – many of them from ancient Greek and Roman manuscripts that had long been given up for lost after the fall of Rome. From the late eleventh century onwards, all kinds of texts flooded back across the Spanish mountain passes with their old/new knowledge: architecture, astronomy, biology, botany, chemistry, engineering, pharmacology, geometry, mathematics, medicine, optics, philosophy, physics, zoology. The job took 150 years, and it profoundly altered Western civilization.

There were two major problems with all this new knowledge. It arrived in a confusing mass, and it competed with pre-existing religious orthodoxy. But, soon, a solution was discovered to both problems: Aristotle. First, in hitherto unknown Aristotelian texts, Western scholars found a systematic arrangement of all human knowledge. In the *Organon*, for example, Aristotle had first divided all knowledge into three kinds (practical, productive and theoretical); then he had subdivided these into a vast array of specializations. Aristotle had put everything into place.

Secondly, Aristotle was known and trusted. The Church had long known of him. Indeed, they had already incorporated some of his arguments into their theology. Church scholars could therefore neither ignore nor reject Aristotle's newly discovered writings which were now being made available. Some of the Christian scholastics even suggested that Aristotle might assist them in deducing an exhaustive, solid and consistently rational defence of Christianity. Thomas Aquinas (1225–74) was one of the scholars over whom the new Aristotelian translations cast their spell. He undertook to provide a firm, logical basis for Christian theology; to combine Catholic doctrine and Aristotelian philosophy into one perfectly rational system. The fruit of his labours was the *Summa Theologica*.

Thomas Aquinas was Italian by birth. He studied and taught in Paris, Cologne, Naples and Rome. On his many travels, he noted the political and economic changes which occurred all over Europe – he observed the rise of 'new monarchies' in France, Spain and England; he witnessed the re-emergence of city-states in Catalonia and Northern Italy; he noted the growth of manufacture, trade and communication and the advent of new merchant classes; and he read the recently-discovered philosophy of Plato, Aristotle and other early advocates of reason. Building partly on Church orthodoxy and partly on Aristotle, Aquinas claimed that the world was created by God in seven days as an organized whole in which each constituent item had a proscribed place and obeyed rules specific to its position. Each rock, plant, animal, human and angel had its specific position in the great order of things. When a rock fell to earth, it obeyed the rule which said that lifeless objects seek to lie still on the surface of the earth. And when a man acted, he obeyed the rule of reason. God was the embodiment of perfect reason, and the more rational a man was, the nearer he was to God.

Aquinas' argument had important consequences for political theory. First, it modified Augustine's claim that man was corrupted by original sin. In Aquinas' view, man's physical and mental abilities were vitiated but not destroyed. This attitude, together with the claim that the crucifixion of Christ involved a restoration of man's original status, provided a more optimistic analysis of the human condition. Since man was rational, he had the capacity to follow the law of God consciously. He could, through his own will and devotion, improve his faculties of reason and thus approach God.

Second, Aquinas' argument revived Aristotle's claim that man is by nature a political being. His argument that politics is the interaction of rational men acting out their God-given nature sharply contradicted Augustine's view that political authority is merely a compensation for the corrupt and sinful nature of man.

Third, Aquinas' argument made politics part of the God-given, rule-bound order of the universe. Politics became 'participation in the eternal law by a rational creature'. This 'eternal law' was partly revealed in the Bible – Aquinas identified the Ten Commandments and the Sermon on the Mount as its most authoritative expression. Also, the eternal law could be partly grasped by human reason. The part of God's law which could be uncovered by human reason Aquinas called 'natural law'. The discovery of natural law was not a prerogative of Christian men (Aquinas 1947, p. 1011). It helps all humanity to separate right from wrong and to direct their actions towards the good and just. Since just actions lead to happiness, natural law tells humanity to act justly, and it promises happiness in return for individuals as well as society – including international society.

Aquinas discussed medieval states, the supreme purpose of which was to maintain peace.[10] These states were heteronomous societies. They were not clearly delineated territorial states in the modern sense of the term, but porous polities whose 'public territories formed a continuum with private estates' (Anderson 1979, p. 32). The State existed, but it did not reign supreme. 'Law was set above it; it was a means of enforcing the law' (Meinecke 1957, p. 27). So when Aquinas discussed war and peace, he did not have relations among states in mind. Consequently, Aquinas' discussions can seem unclear when read with modern eyes (and informed by modern territorial distinctions between domestic and international affairs). On the one hand, Aquinas deplores war and recommends its avoidance as far as possible, for 'it produces little good and it wastes much more than it produces'. On the other, he defends the right of war and claims that war is justified if it is waged on the authority of the sovereign, for a just cause and with the right intention of preventing injustice. In Aquinas' famous words:

In order for a war to be just, three things are necessary. First, the authority of the sovereign by whose command the war is to be waged. For it is not the business of a private person to declare war, because he can seek for redress of his rights from the tribunal of his superior ...

Secondly, a just cause is required, namely that those who are attacked should be attacked because they deserve it on account of some fault. Therefore Augustine says [...]: 'A just war is usually described as one that avenges wrongs, when a nation or state has to be punished, for refusing to make amends for the wrongs inflicted by its subjects, or to restore what it has seized unjustly.'

Thirdly, it is necessary that the belligerents should have a right intention, so that they intend the advancement of good, or the avoidance of evil. Hence, Augustine says [...]: 'True religion does not look upon as sinful those wars that are waged not for motives of aggrandizement, or cruelty, but with the object of securing peace, of punishing evildoers, and of uplifting the good.' For it may happen that the war is declared by the legitimate authority, and for a just cause, and yet be rendered unlawful through a wicked intention (Aquinas 1947, pp. 1359–60).

The peculiar Western context

An account of the origins of International Relations theory must begin with the intellectual and political development of the medieval Far West. It must include a discussion of medieval law – both canon law (as expressed in the early attempts to limit warfare such as the 'Peace of God' and the 'Truce of God') and those elements of customary law which dovetailed with Church doctrines (most notably the *lex mercatoria* and the emerging codes of conduct among chieftains and kings).

The account must also include the emergence of the territorial state and the European states system. For it was in the unique context of the simultaneous evolution of several territorial states along the North-Atlantic rim that the medieval codes of conduct and rules of law were applied to issues of war and peace and diplomatic interaction. In the Byzantine and Islamic civilizations, such issues were studied in an imperial context. Political scholars were bound by the values of Church and Mosque and by the concerns of empire. Here, scholarship was an integral part of the imperial state, whose primary objective was to maintain law and order. Here, speculations on world affairs tended to be universalist extensions of the order of empire. But in the Far West emerged a multi-state alternative to empire. And this emergence is a first unique factor of the development of the Far West, and helps to illuminate the region's early discussions on international relations.

Some medieval scholars struggled to grasp the precise nature of these emergent states and their interaction. In their struggles lies a decisive contribution to the growth of International Relations theory. One of these contributors was Thomas Aquinas. His political thought leans heavily on Augustine and on Aristotle. By relying on Augustine's discussions of war and peace, Aquinas elaborated on the ancient idea of a God-given natural law. By combining Augustine's idea of natural law with an Aristotelian notion of man as 'by nature a social and political being', Aquinas established a connection across time that has proved to be one of the most solid lines in the intellectual tradition of the West. By relying on Aristotle, Aquinas drew connections backwards, thus forging theoretical links between Christian theology and the political thought of Europe's classical past. By elaborating upon the classical connection between the State and man's moral life, he drew connections forwards: he reintroduced a natural-law theory of the State which would blaze through the political though of the West until far into the eighteenth century.

Another important contributor to the early development of International Relations theory was Pierre Dubois (1233–1322), who had attended Aquinas' last lectures at the University of Paris. Dubois wrote *De recuperatione Terre Sancte* ('The Recovery of the Holy Land') around 1306. The title indicates that Dubois was arguing for the necessity of launching a new crusade to wrest Palestine out of Muslim hands. But it was also a discussion of how to obtain peace and stability in Europe. Dubois opposed the establishment of a world-state. He criticized the idea – which most of his contemporaries entertained – of a universal empire. Instead he advocated a federation of Christian states. He recognized the rise of several territorial states in Europe. And he feared that any effort to unify them through some revival of the Roman Empire would lead to wars and disaster. Thus, he proposed instead the establishment of a council of states designed to decide all interstate quarrels by arbitration – and in the act produced the first rough draft for the organization of Europe's separate states (Bozeman 1960, p. 247).[11]

A more careful discussion of Dubois would pinpoint three important properties of early International Relations theorizing. First, that the first fumbling arguments were intensely informed by Christian themes and precepts. Second, that a multi-state system was emerging along the Atlantic rim and that it was reshaping European politics and Western political theorizing in fundamental ways. And third, that this development did not merely give early International Relations scholars something to theorize about; it also provided a social environment within which they were permitted to theorize with imagination and independence. The evolution of several independent states involved the evolution of several courts and of local interpretations of Church doctrines. The growth of the multi-state system in the Far West was, in fact, attended by a multi-centred environment of scholarship within which independent and diverse political theorizing was allowed to occur.

The rise of a multi-state system in Europe was attended by the growth of a body of intellectuals who were independent of Church authority. Pierre Dubois is a case in point. He was employed not by the Church, but by Philippe le Bel – an ambitious French monarch who treated the papacy with suspicion and disrespect. Another example is Marsiglio of Padua (*c.*1275–1343). Marsiglio was first employed by the university of Paris and later by several secular rulers. He, too, understood that important political changes were wrought by the rise of the modern state and a European state system. He struggled to identify the qualities which express the essence of the modern state. In his *Defensor pacis* ('Defender of the Peace', 1324), he 'manipulates phrases and struggles to express the idea of state sovereignty' comments Artz (1967, p. 299). But 'sovereignty' was beyond the range of his Latin vocabulary, and Marsiglio never really arrived at a satisfactory concept.[12] But his effort was breathtaking. The first part of Marsiglio's treatise is a theory of the State which foreshadows later theorists – such as Bodin. He draws on Aristotle (but not on Augustine or Aquinas). But he differs from contemporary Aristotelians by arguing that the State is designed solely to serve man in society. Marsiglio portrays the State as independent of God. He sees law as independent of any higher law; for him, the essence of law lies in its enforceability, and its ultimate source in the people. The right to make law backed by coercive force lies with the more substantial citizens, argues Marsiglio. They should meet in an assembly and delegate the direction of government to the ruler, he continues. Having established that absolute authority (or 'sovereignty' as Bodin would have called it) belongs to the State, and that no superior power exists above the State, Marsiglio begins the second part of his treatise, which quickly develops into an intense criticism of the pretensions and usurpations of the papacy. He rejects any claim of papal supremacy over temporal affairs. Later, in his *Defensor Minor*, Marsiglio goes as far as to encourage the seizure of Church property by the secular powers of the State.

Aquinas, Dubois, Marsiglio and others sensed how the evolution of the modern State wrought momentous changes in European politics. Their efforts to grasp these changes constitute a key source of early International Relations theory. It is important to appreciate that these efforts occurred within the discursive tradition of the Church, and that the first, fumbling theories were intensely informed by Christian themes and precepts. But it is also important to realize that a multi-state system was emerging along the Atlantic rim of Europe at this time, and that it was attended by the growth of intellectuals who were independent of Church authorities. The steady increase in their number and the growth of their social importance is a unique feature in the development of the Far West (Needham 1969). This uniqueness helps explain why International Relations theorizing orginated in the ascendant multi-state system of Western Europe (rather than in the imperial systems of the Near or the Middle East). Nowhere did this multi-state ascendancy create a more intense political environment than in renaissance Italy – to which it is natural to turn for the next growth phase of International Relations theory.'

2

The roots of the Modern Ages:
Renaissance interstate politics

The seeds of International Relations theorizing were sown in the fragmented and rural High Middle Ages, and they took centuries to grow. Their growth was attended by the evolution of the modern state. By the fifteenth century, the evolution is not as far developed as is often believed. Renaissance authors like Machiavelli are often presented as modern political theorists. Yet, their speculations clearly reverberate with antique and medieval echoes.

When Machiavelli wrote about states and politics, he had the city-state in mind, not the modern nation-state. Also, he focused primarily on domestic politics; he drew his lessons about the behaviour of princes from politics within states, not politics among states. And when he discussed issues of war and peace, his perspective was tactical and practical rather than strategic and theoretical. He was an important pioneer in the field of political theory, but his direct contributions to International Relations theory are surprisingly modest. Here, his younger contemporary Francesco Guicciardini may have played a more important role.

Renaissance politics

'In the history of the world, no civilization has appeared to be more completely rural than that of the Middle Ages', writes Georges Duby (1968, p. xi) about the sparsely populated, heavily forested Far West of the tenth and eleventh centuries. In spite of powerful, centralized institutions like the Holy Roman Empire and the papacy, medieval Europe was fragmented; it was plagued by invasions and shifting personalized rule. Under these conditions, life and property were precarious. Social and economic relationships were organized in highly localized networks of production and protection. These conditions changed dramatically after AD 1000 .

The medieval sentiment

Renaissance theorizing emerged from an environment which was steeped in Christian theology. Medieval education and discussion took place within Church institutions. These acknowledged no essential difference between the various branches of knowledge. They drew no distinction between knowledge about nature and knowledge about man. In the final instance, they subordinated all existence to participation in a dramatic morality play, dominated by the four themes of God, Nature, Prescription and Obedience.

God was the dominant theme. He was conceived as an omnipotent and omniscient intelligence; a master dramatist who has planned an infinitely complex, cosmic drama in the smallest detail. Finished in idea before it was enacted in fact, God had, even before the world began, already written the last syllable of recorded time. And his drama was unalterable (Becker 1932, p. 7). Man must accept God's drama, because he could not alter it. His fate was to play the role he was assigned. In order for him to play his role according to the divine text, the authorities of Church and State – deriving their just powers from the will of God – were instituted among men to dispose them to submission and to instruct them in their proper lines.

Nature was a second theme of medieval speculation. Nature was seen as perfect, good and eternal, simply because it was created by God, who *is* Perfection, Goodness and Eternity. All things made by man, by contrast, were clumsy and temporal infringements upon God's perfect work. There was therefore no distinction between 'natural' and 'good' in medieval thought. And the two core questions of political theory – 'Why should man obey the state?' and 'What is the good state?' – had no meaning. The state was part of God's great plan; created by God for the benefit of man, it was natural and therefore good by definition.

Prescription and *obedience* were two final themes of the medieval, Christian drama. The two were intimately intertwined. Man could use his intelligence and identify the laws which God had invested in the universe. These laws were natural and good, and imperfect man would be wise to emulate them. If man could live according to God's laws, he would live a good and natural life, and he might receive forgiveness from God on the day of final judgement. He might save his soul and attain an afterlife of eternal bliss. In the medieval mind, human reason was subordinate to a larger theological purpose. The function of intelligence was therefore to demonstrate the truth of revealed knowledge, to reconcile diverse and pragmatic experience with the rational pattern of the world as given in faith.

In the High Middle Ages, the function of science was to scrutinize God's two primary creations: the World and the Bible. God had left clues in both creations, and He had equipped man with intelligence and reason to find these clues and read in them God's intentions. The primary duty of scientists was to compare the clues found in nature with the clues found in the Bible, identify God's intentions as clearly as possible, and then create rules and prescriptions for all human activities. Only by obeying these prescriptions could man hope to attain salvation (Foucault 1973, pp. 25ff).

Emergence of modern notions
The evolution of the feudal order had brought a marked improvement of social stability in the core areas of Europe. During the eleventh century the development evinced an accelerating tendency to concentrate political power and centralize command in the hands of royal courts. This development was remarkably quick along Europe's Atlantic rim. Here a rudimentary system of monarchic states evolved rapidly – before AD 990 it did not exist; by AD 1100 a complex macropolitical structure consisting of territorial states was being consolidated (Tilly 1994).

The rise of territorial states altered the social processes in Europe. From a long-term, large-scale perspective, this development improved the social stability in core areas of Europe. Travel became safer. People ventured further away from their village or local fortress-town to cultivate new land or to exchange their products. Horses were effectively harnessed and shod for heavier work. Iron ploughs made possible new techniques of agriculture, such as crop rotation, which produced higher yields. Watermills and windmills were more frequently built and used to grind corn, press oil, saw lumber and, by the fourteenth century, make paper. Such innovations encouraged the evolution of new, more productive systems of social organization (White 1972).

Gradually, life was transformed. Commercial networks branched across Europe, stimulated by the crusades, which offered great opportunities to entrepreneurial individuals – principally the merchants of northern Italy, who were so conveniently located both across the crusaders' path and on the thriving trade routes to the Eastern Mediterranean and Asia. This transit trade was a great stimulus for the city-states in Northern Italy. Many Italian rulers saw the need for interstate agreements to encourage the smooth flow of trade. Slowly, treaties between these city-states produced the basis for diplomatic interaction and swept away traditional webs of cumbersome feudal laws. Merchants met regularly at the fairs and markets which spread across the map of Europe like shoots of climbing ivy: St Denis, Foggia, Champagne, Lyons and others. By one estimate, trade increased as much as twenty times during the eleventh and twelfth centuries (Southern 1953, p. 44).

The most astounding developments occurred in the northern regions of the Italian peninsula. By the year 1400, Italy was a kaleidoscope of social formations. In the south, where the High Middle Ages witnessed several changes of dynasty – Muslim, Viking, Angevin and Aragonese chieftains had succeeded one another as rulers – lay Naples and Sicily. In the centre, the papal states stretched across the Apennines from Rome to Ravenna. In the north were the wealthy merchant cities of Milan, Venice, Genoa and Florence. Here, strong city governments controlled not only their own immediate vicinity but hundreds of square miles of rural territory as well. The city-states had developed vast territorial domains around themselves.

In the late fifteenth century, five major city-states dominated peninsular politics: the republics of Venice and Florence, the papal states and the principalities of Milan and Naples. Some of these states were controlled by a prince or despot, like Milan. Others governed themselves as republics – like Florence, a city which allowed its inhabitants great freedom to pursue their own interests, undisturbed by popes and monarchs. Although each of the city-states differed greatly from the others in their histories as well as by the nature of the institutions, the regular interaction between these five major city-states increasingly assumed the character of a state system (Franke 1968; Baron 1952).

The emergence of this state system, which is generally considered to be the first modern example of a family or a system of states, was intimately related to the decline of the two dominant medieval institutions of the papacy and the Holy Roman Empire. Both institutions embodied the medieval conception of a universal community. The decline of this conception and its replacement with alternative views of political organization opened up the floodgates of power politics within the Italian city-states and produced a political environment in which the idea of a *'raison d'état'* – a reason or justification for the security of the state – became a predominant principle. This evolution included the establishment of a diplomatic system; a network of permanent embassies with accredited diplomats, foreign policy analysts and advisers in addition to an elaborate structure for the rapid transport and the safe storage of diplomatic dispatches (Nicolson 1954, pp. 27–31; Elton 1981).

Perceptions and politics in the Renaissance world

Most of the city-states of Northern Italy had grown wealthy from ventures of trade and finance. Already in the High Middle Ages, merchants and bankers from Italy had played central roles at the fairs of Champagne and Lyons and at the permanent markets which succeeded them in Paris, Bruges and London. By the year 1300, the network of Italian banking spanned all the major market centres of Europe – the Peruzzi of Florence, for example, were represented by partners and salaried employees in 15 locations all across Western and Northern Europe (Roover 1965, pp. 80, 85).

This growth of commerce wrought changes in the social conditions of Europe. It created new patterns of social relations, caused new problems and triggered new attitudes to old ones. The rise of a financial and entrepreneurial élite in core areas of Europe not only altered the social structures, it also changed social attitudes. It fuelled the growth of a new transnational class of people who 'saw business facts in a different light and from a different angle; a class, in short, that was *in* business, and therefore could never look at its problems with the aloofness of the schoolman' (Schumpeter 1954, p. 78). This new class accumulated

Map 2 Italy at the end of the fifteenth century

and controlled wealth. It attained an increased social presence as well as power
to assert its own interests.

As the business man's social weight increased, he imparted to society an
increasing dose of his mind. 'The particular mental habits generated by the work
in the business office, the schema of values that emanates from it, and the attitude to public and private life that is characteristic of it, slowly spread in *all*
classes and over all fields of human thought and action' (Schumpeter 1954,
p. 78). Starting from their professional needs and problems, craftsmen, bankers,
merchants, rulers and artists began to develop funds of tools and knowledge –
mechanics, credit, navigation, chains of economic command and a social division
of labour. This initially practical reservoir of knowledge evolved outside the university scholarship dominated by the Church. It gave rise to a body of secular
or 'lay' concerns.

Lay scholars had long existed in the West (Needham 1969). In late fifteenth-century Italy they began to outnumber the scholars of the Church. The new urban élite in the wealthy city-states like Venice and Florence grew obsessed with the secular aspects of human history and philosophy. Their concerns with moral and civic questions are reflected in the style, decorum, character and education of the age. The rediscovery of Greek and Roman artefacts mushroomed towards obsessive proportions among the *nouveau riche* élite.

The lay, classical scholars were professionally concerned with ancient affairs, and became known as *humanists*. They were in high demand at Italian universities and with the better families. They had studied Greek and could teach it to others. They read and interpreted the classical texts – as did Marsilio Ficino, who translated all Plato's works into Latin. They edited and wrote commentaries on the classical texts. They devised new methods of historical investigation that enabled them to position old manuscripts in time and distinguish originals from copies and forgeries. The humanists were something new in European society: lay scholars who made a living from their knowledge in secular affairs. They rediscovered what Graeco-Roman writers had meant by the 'liberal arts': the liberating effect on mind and imagination of the study of great literature and philosophy.

By breaking the Church monopoly of learning, the fourteenth- and fifteenth-century humanists initiated a revolution in education and scholarship. Their independence challenged the Church. Their analyses of original texts identified errors in authoritative Church documents. Even the Bible was shown to contain errors of translation – and Lorenzo Valla ignited a major controversy when he applied a new method of criticism to a document on which the papacy based its temporal claims, and showed that it was a clever forgery. The activities of the humanists, then, contributed to the erosion of traditional Church authority, at least in matters of science and scholarship.

Any description of the Renaissance spirit must include accounts of the new individualism of the age, the fascination with classical culture and the emergence of a unique historical self-consciousness. The new individualism is reflected in the Renaissance preoccupation with heroes and hero-worship, and with the central concept of *virtù*. The fifteenth-century hero possessed elements of both traditional feudal-chivalric values and new urban-cultural attributes. The Renaissance gentleman was the great individual who shaped his own destiny by skill and insight. The ideal of the virtuous gentleman is portrayed in Castiglione's best-selling *Book of the Courtier* (1528), a handbook of etiquette which portrays the ideal courtier in terms of the old chivalric virtues (physical dexterity, courage, skill in combat, courtesy) as well as the new urban ones (knowledge of classical philosophy, appreciation of art, eloquence and good taste). This ideal of the virtuous gentlemen reflects a new emphasis on individualism as a value in its own right.[1]

Another feature of the Renaissance was the enthusiasm for classical culture.

Renaissance scholars discovered in ancient texts a society which they found appealing. Much of the action in the ancient texts took place in urban environments comparable to their own city-states. It appeared from this classic literature that ancient Greece and Rome had been places where a man of means was looked up to – which was just what the *nouveaux riches* of Florence and Milan wanted to hear! In authors like Thucydides and Tacitus they found descriptions of individuals who reasoned, took calculated risks, gambled, and conquered difficulties or were vanquished by their obstacles.

Business men were quick to respond to the Italian mania for ancient culture. They scurried all over southern Europe for artefacts and manuscripts, and discovered an astonishing quantity of texts and fragments covering a variety of topics – agriculture, astronomy, etiquette, ethics, geometry, good living, history, philosophy, poetry, politics, post-prandial speaking, rhetoric ... – all of which were studied with care. Some enterprising merchants hired ships and organized regular package-tours to Athens and Rome. The more expensive tours even included a humanist scholar who would guide the *nouveau-riche* citizens of Florence and Venice in their search for ancient, valuable items that could teach them to behave like their high-cultured ancestors. And like all adventurous and wealthy tourists, they bought everything in sight, carried their souvenirs home, showed them off to their friends and told them about the trip.

Increasingly, copyists like Francesco Poggio[2] were recruited by princes, merchants or bankers. Agents of Palla Strozzi, one of the richest men in Florence, procured from Greece Plutarch's *Lives*, Aristotle's *Politics* and Ptolemy's *Cosmography*. In 1423, Giovanni Aurispa arrived in Italy with 238 manuscripts from Greece. Among these were Thucydides' *Peloponnesian War*. It was translated from Greek by Lorenzo Valla in 1485, and had an immediate impact on Renaissance humanism.

The intensely sought-after Greek and Roman manuscripts provided fledgling scholars with sustained and systematic discussions of political theory. Some complete works of the classical period had been known and studied before the fifteenth century. Euclid and selections from Aristotle and Plato and others had been accessible since the High Middle Ages, but through often inexact Arab translations. Immense horizons were opened by the sudden influx of classic masterpieces in the 1420s and 1430s:

The *Iliad* and *Odyssey*, the tragedies of Aeschylus, Sophocles and Euripides, the comedies of Aristophanes, the odes of Pindar, the eclogues of Theocritus, the histories of Herodotus, Thucydides and Xenophon, the character studies of Theophrastus, the speeches of Demosthenes, the dialogues of Plato, the writings of Cynics, Stoics and Neo-Platonists, the speculations of the Ionian philosophers, the medical writings of Hippocrates and Galen, the geography of Ptolemy and Strabo – it was as if these masterpieces had been written all at once and suddenly given to Florence (Cronin 1967, p. 51).

The knowledge discovered in these classical texts was pre-Christian. They had none of the wealth- and fun-denying properties of the Church doctrines. The educated Renaissance man identified more easily with the classical accounts of complex human beings who faced complex human problems than with the Church's predictable, one-dimensional stories of saints who were saved and sinners who were punished.

A new generation of authors began to emulate the classic texts. The spirit of civic humanism pervaded the writings of Leonardo Bruni (1369–1444), who traced the historical evolution of Florence. His *History of the Florentine People* (1610) attributed the power and wealth of Florence to her republican government, from which flowed beauty of style, courage, industriousness, strength and other instances of Renaissance *virtù*. It is the conception of *virtù* which guides Renaissance discussions of politics. And the primary Renaissance theorist of *virtù* is Niccolò de Bernardo Machiavelli (1469–1527). The concept is evident in his *Discourses*, but explicitly invoked in *The Prince* – Machiavelli's famous, short, extreme, epigrammatic articulation of the concerns of the age.

Machiavelli: between *virtù* and self-interest

Machiavelli contributed greatly to political theory. His contribution to International Relations theory was less. He really focused on politics within states, not among states. And when he alluded to interstate relations, he does not use the modern balance-of-power concept.[3] He explains political action either in terms of the old, conceptual pair of *fortuna* and *virtù*, or else invokes the more modern concept of self-interest.

Machiavelli's understanding of *fortuna* and *virtù* draws on old, pre-humanist ideas, and is most evident in the first part[4] of *The Prince*. Translators agree about the first term, *fortuna*, and translates it as 'fortune'. The term is derived from the goddess Fortuna, who has been worshipped in Italy from the earliest times, always portrayed as a controller of destinies. Originally, Fortuna was the goddess of prosperity; later she became the goddess of chance (and thus identified with the Greek Tyche, a capricious dispenser of good and ill luck). Machiavelli largely uses the term 'fortune' in a secularized and descriptive sense: rather as a synonym for 'event' or 'chance occurrence', but with a dramatic edge to it – in one context Machiavelli compares fortune to a violent river; in another to a sudden storm.

Translators disagree about the second term, *virtù*. Some translate it as 'virtue' (which is misleadingly wide), others as 'prowess' (which may be too narrow, but is closer to the mark). *Virtù* is derived from the word *vir* which means 'man'; and it is obvious from Machiavelli's usage that the term reverberates with the masculine ideal of the Renaissance gentleman. Castiglione (1959, p. 295) saw this ideal as involving both genius and determination; properties that made for greatness in literature and artistic creativity, as well as in statesmanship and war. The 'strength of a lion' and the 'cunning of a fox' are political virtues for Machiavelli, because possession would increase the chances of a prince to master the twists and turns of fortune. He 'must be a fox in order to recognize traps, and a lion to frighten off wolves. Those who simply act like lions are stupid. So it follows that a prudent ruler cannot, and must not honour his word when it places him at a disadvantage' (Machiavelli 1961, pp. 99f). He must *appear* to be trustworthy, truthful, honest and good, but be careful not to go too far. For 'if he has these qualities and always behaves accordingly, he will find them harmful'. However, if he only pretends to have them, then they will be of great political service. The prince 'should appear to be compassionate, faithful to his word, kind, guileless, and devout. And indeed, he should be so. But his disposition should be such that, if he needs to be the opposite, he knows how' (p. 100). Machiavelli, then, loaded his understanding of *virtù* with qualities of cunning, leadership, command and other abilities which would enable a ruler to master the twists of 'fortune' and to ride off the frequent storms of Italian politics. His explanations are rife with sexual overtones. *Virtù* can harness *fortuna* 'because fortune is a woman and if she is to be submissive it is necessary to beat and coerce her' (p. 133; Pitkin 1984). And because *fortuna* is capricious and malicious, *virtù* must be malicious, too. If there is no other way open.

In addition to the conceptual pair of *fortuna* and *virtù*, Machiavelli also develops a more typically modern concept to explain political action: self-interest. This principle is evident in the second part of *The Prince*, which discusses military power as the foundation of the state. It is most notable in Machiavelli's discussion of the several types of armed force. Indeed, the principle first appears when Machiavelli explains the behaviour of soldiers: armies can be composed of mercenary, auxiliary or national troops, or of a mixture of the three. Mercenary troops are always dangerous, for there is 'no loyalty or inducement to keep them on the field apart from the little they are paid, and this is not enough to make them want to die for you' (p. 77). Auxiliary troops (i.e. troops which are supplied by another state to assist your own) are even more dangerous, for they obey the orders of another ruler, and 'you are left in a lurch if they are defeated, and in their power if they are victorious' (p. 83). National troops are the best. These are the only troops a prince can depend on, for they live with their families on the very territory they are set to defend and they depend upon victory for continued survival. Machiavelli's explanation is distinctly modern. It makes good sense for mercenaries and auxiliary troops to desert when wars break out: bravery in war entails a risk which is higher than the salary can compensate for. The national soldier, by contrast, fights neither for a salary nor for his prince, but for himself. Thus, it makes good sense for the national solder, who is a subject and a citizen with a family and a property to defend, to fight for the survival of the state in which he has concrete stakes. The explanatory principle to which Machiavelli appeals in this second part of *The Prince* is, in short, the self-interest of the modern, rational individual.

In the third part of the book, Machiavelli uses this concept of rational self-interest to explain the behaviour of successful princes. Also, he draws no distinction between the interests of the prince and those of the state. The two converge. The prince fully represents the state and embodies its interests. It is therefore in the interest of the state that a prince should feel free to break his word whenever he deems it necessary. By the same token, the prince should not feel obliged to keep his promises if he thinks this would be counter to state interests; the prince must learn 'to be a great liar and deceiver', but he must also learn to conceal this important skill. Princes must always act according to the best interests of the state; they do not answer to ordinary moral rules. In politics, and most particularly in interstate politics, there exists a different morality; it is governed by the self-interest and the security of the prince/state (Meinecke 1957; Ferrari 1860). Many despots have found in Machiavelli's book good excuses for doing anything they felt necessary to keep themselves in power. Through this principle, Machiavelli has greatly influenced rulers – such as Henry IV of France, who is said to have had a copy of *The Prince* in his pocket when he was assassinated.

The fourth and final part of *The Prince* deals with the political situation in Italy in Machiavelli's own time. Its analysis is guided by the old conceptual pair of *fortuna* and *virtù*. Here he argues that fortune is the arbiter of only half of man's actions. The remaining half is governed by man's own will and his *virtù*. This claim, which implies than man is largely the maker of his own fate, reverberates with Renaissance individualism and represents a resounding break with the medieval belief that man's fate is authored by God. Distinctly modern is Machiavelli's final chapter – which many readers consider the key to the entire book. Here Machiavelli expresses the hope that Italy can unify, grow strong, and cast off the curse of foreign intervention which is threatening to grind the country to pieces. This chapter is significant because it amounts to a plea, not to a benevolent God, but to a prince who possesses the secular virtues – the will, the cunning, the strength and the rational self-interest – Machiavelli has set out above. However, the chapter is significant for another reason as well: it introduces patriotic intent as a motivating force in political action. It is Machiavelli's hope that a virtuous prince will raise a national army, unify Italy, chase the foreign invaders off Italian soil and restore the country to independence and glory. This plea embodies nothing less than modern Europe's first doctrine of national liberation.

Guicciardini: chronicler of power

Machiavelli shows some influence from Thucydides – he was for example affected by the ancient historian's psychological portrayal of political leaders. However, Machiavelli adopted neither Thucydides' method nor his balance-of-power theory. But others did. One of the most significant of these – at least from an International Relations perspective – is Francesco Guicciardini (1483–1540).

Whereas Machiavelli seems to have treated *The Peloponnesian War* 'as only a reservoir of stories from which he selected a few' (Bondanella 1973, p. 17), Guicciardini found in Thucydides' account instructive elements towards a deeper understanding of interstate relations.

Although Guicciardini drew theoretical insights from antique authors, most of his discussions concern political issues of his own day. And in order to appreciate his arguments, it is necessary to note the political uncertainties which were unleashed upon Florence in his lifetime. When Guicciardini was born, Lorenzo de' Medici ('the Magnificent') was the ruler of Florence. Strong and cunning, he maintained order not only in Florence; his imaginative diplomacy helped preserve order among the five central Italian states (Florence itself, Venice, Milan, Naples and the Papacy). When Lorenzo died in 1492 (aged 44), his diplomacy unravelled. His son Piero took over, but had none of his father's qualities. Regional uncertainties erupted into crisis in 1494, when Charles VIII of France invaded Italy. Piero surrendered Florence. The citizens considered this a cowardly act. They revolted, expelled Piero and, under the influence of the religious leader Savonarola, declared Florence a republic with Christ as its only ruler.

The Florentine rebellion was supported by Spain. Spanish rulers had long been wary of French expansionism. And when the French invaded Italy in 1494, Spain reacted swiftly with an invasion of its own. The resulting Franco–Spanish war constituted the international context of Italy's early sixteenth-century politics. Machiavelli's and Guicciardini's works must read as texts written in the shadow of 'The Italian Wars' – a protracted foreign rivalry during which French and Spanish armies fought over Italy. The Italian city-states were rendered helpless. Italian rulers were often reduced to agents of French or Spanish interests, and Italian city-states lost their former independence (Machiavelli 1961, pp. 133ff).

In 1498, the pope took sides in the war. He turned against Spain and Florence, and ordered the trial of Savonarola for heresy and for fomenting public strife. Savonarola was tried and burnt at the stake. However, the Florentine Republic survived under the leadership of Piero Soderini – who in turn employed Machiavelli (as a secretary of the Council of Ten) and Guicciardini (as ambassador to Spain).

Guicciardini's life

Guicciardini was born in 1483 into one of the oldest and most important families of the Florentine aristocracy. In 1498 he enrolled as a student of law at the University of Florence. After three years he transferred to the University of Ferrara – largely because his father wished to have a member of the family (and a share of the family fortune) in a more secure city in the event of political upheavals. He received the doctorate in civil law in 1505, and began to write. He wrote a history of his family. And he began a more ambitious study of the history of Florence.

Guicciardini's writing was interrupted in 1509, because he became entangled in high-stakes political games. He was elected to minor posts in the Florentine Republic. Then he was appointed as Soderini's ambassador to the court of King Ferdinand of Aragon. Finally, he married Maria Salviati – an act which had dire consequences, because the marriage represented an open declaration of political sympathies: the Salvatis strongly opposed the powerful Medici family. So in 1512, when the Medici family overthrew Soderini's government and took power, Guicciardini's goose was cooked. He was forced to give up his ambassadorship in Spain, return to Florence and open up a law practice there. He also resumed his writing.

In 1516, Guicciardini entered the service of the pope. He served the papacy for the next 20 years, showed himself as an efficient administrator, and was rapidly promoted.[5] Italy was at this time caught up in the complex struggle between the kings of France (Francis I) and Spain (Charles V, who was also Holy Roman Emperor). This struggle is commonly referred to as the 'Italian Wars', although it really was a contest for the dominance of Europe. It injected immeasurable suffering and destruction into Italian politics. Guicciardini became, in this critical period for Italy, Pope Clement VII's trusted foreign-policy adviser. He counselled the pope to manoeuvre delicately between the rival rulers of France and Spain, while maintaining control over Italy. On Guicciardini's advice, the pope first supported Charles V of Spain in the fighting which ended in the battle of Pavia (February 1525), during which Francis I was defeated. In a clear balance-of-power move, the pope then joined France's Francis I and helped establish the League of Cognac, whose aim was to contain the ambitions of Charles V.

Guicciardini retired from politics in 1538. During the final years of his life he worked on his most ambitious work, *The History of Italy*. It covers Italian politics between 1494 and 1534, the most chaotic and formative period of the Italian Wars. He was working on the final revision of this book when he died in May 1540.

Guicciardini's works

In spite of his busy and successful career as a diplomat and papal adviser, Guicciardini was a prolific author – while ambassador in Spain, he wrote a book on Spanish politics and a collection of essays; after the death of Pope Leo X he began a work on Florentine politics; and during a difficult few years after 1527 he composed several biographical works.[6] In addition, through a period of 18 active years, he wrote a series of observations and thoughts on a variety of subjects. He incessantly revised and rewrote this collection, which is known as his *Ricordi*. This collection of maxims or aphorisms represents the harvest of an active and turbulent life.

Some of Guicciardini's *Ricordi* were rules that instructed his family on how to maintain their status and reputation. Others were comments on political events. But all of them reflect the author's experiences in Renaissance Italy. They leave an impression of cruel and corrupt rulers, driven by ambition and vice. The *Ricordi* are infused with a bleak and cynical view of the human condition. They attribute the sufferings of man to human failings. They warn against trusting individual rulers, because they follow their desires rather than their reason (Gilbert 1965, p. 288; Ferrari 1860, pp. 277ff). And he puts little faith in the wisdom of the popular masses – which he likens to a 'mad animal, full of a thousand errors, of a thousand confusions, lacking in taste, in discernment, in stability'. He refers to the clergy as 'bands of ruffians' among whom he had seen nothing but ambition, avarice and sensuality (C-28).[7]

Guicciardini's masterpiece is his *History of Italy*. It has had a lasting influence because of its description of the relations among the Italian city-states. Tracing the welter of alliances, wars and diplomatic moves that shaped Italian politics in the late fifteenth century, Guicciardini draws an image of a city-state system which is self-regulating owing to some balance-of-power mechanism. This image, which posterity has inherited of Renaissance Italy, depends to a great degree on Guicciardini's account. There is no question that his account embodies balance-of-power arguments. He writes about Lorenzo (the Magnificent) de' Medici (1448–92): 'Realizing that it would be most perilous to the Florentine Republic and to himself if any of the major powers should extend their area of domination, he carefully saw to it that the Italian situation should be maintained in a state of balance, not leaning more toward one side than the other' (Guicciardini 1969, pp. 4f).

Several questions are begged by this description. One question concerns the representative nature of Lorenzo's policies: was Lorenzo a politician of exceptional skill or was his approach to politics a common one among Italian rulers? The most probable answer is that Lorenzo was unique. Lorenzo was humanist, a poet and a sponsor of the arts; also he was, by all accounts, a master of affairs of state – including foreign affairs. And it is evident from Guicciardini's own account that Lorenzo approached the ideal of a Renaissance gentleman to an uncommon degree; a soldier and a scholar who possessed 'all the signs and indications of virtues that are apparent and of value in civic life'. Lorenzo was such an important force in Italian politics, Guicciardini explains, that when he died in 1492 the stability of Florence ended – indeed, the entire Italian city-state system unravelled. Clearly, Lorenzo was no ordinary politician, and his political skills ought not be considered representative of all Renaissance rulers.

Another question concerns Guicciardini's description of Lorenzo's policies: did this unique ruler entertain a balance-of-power theory? The most probable answer is that he did not. For, in the letters that Lorenzo wrote, no clear and consistent balance-of-power logic guides his foreign-policy arguments. Lorenzo might, indeed, have been more skilful than most; however, like other tyrants of his day, he conducted his foreign policies on an *ad hoc* basis and not according to any master model. The balance-of-power arguments which are found in Guicciardini's *History*, then, are likely to be creations of its author rather than convictions common also to its protagonist.

It is unlikely that Lorenzo acted on any balance-of-power theory. But it is likely that Guicciardini portrayed him as if he did. Like other Renaissance rulers, Lorenzo strove to obtain short-term gains and not to establish lasting, interstate relationships. His decisions were quick, his moves were sudden. Gradual creation of confidence and goodwill were unknown values in Renaissance politics, which was guided by opportunism rather than planning. For the Renaissance rulers, interstate affairs was a game of hazard for high and immediate stakes: 'it was conducted in an atmosphere of excitement and with that combination of cunning, recklessness and ruthlessness which they lauded as *virtù*' (Nicolson 1954, p. 31). But Guicciardini used balance-of-power arguments to explain the actions of Lorenzo. Thus it is *he*, rather than Lorenzo, who deserves a place among the earliest modern International-Relations theoreticians.

Rediscovering Thucydides

Since Guicciardini was an experienced diplomat, scholars have often assumed that his descriptions of Italian statecraft reflect common diplomatic practices. This is hardly the case. It is likely that Guicciardini extracted the balance-of-power principle not from the diplomatic practices of his day but from the historic accounts of classical authors, which he then applied to contemporary practices. Most probably, he found it in Thucydides, whose *Peloponnesian War* is the first recorded political and moral analysis of a nation's war policies.

Thucydides discusses the causes and the nature of the war between the ever-active, innovating sea-power of Athens and the slower-moving, more cautious land-power of Sparta. Throughout his long narrative, Thucydides kept rigidly to his theme: a chronicle of battles and sieges, of alliances made and broken and, most important, of the effect of war on peoples – of the inevitable 'corrosion of the human spirit'. He discusses the character and influence of the most outstanding political leaders of the age. And these studies of character had a pervasive influence on the Renaissance humanists who sought to emulate his style.

According to Thucydides the Athenians argued that 'the strong do what they have the power to do and the weak accept what they have to accept' (Thucydides 1972, p. 402). The implication that a strong ambitious state can be contained by an alliance of smaller states was to influence International Relations theory in subsequent centuries (Lebow and Strauss 1991).

Thucydides' discussion of alliance politics and warfare among ancient Greek city-states made Italian humanists see parallels in the competition among the Italian city-states of their own day. Humanist historians like Guicciardini adopted Thucydides' balance-of-power vision. After a millennium of neglect, Thucydides was reconnected to Western political theory. His impact on subsequent International Relations theory cannot be fully appreciated unless he is considered a citizen of two distinct ages: Renaissance Italy as well as ancient Greece.

Conclusion

It was Machiavelli's formulations which attracted the critics' attention – during the seventeenth century it was commonly held that *The Prince* was inspired by the Devil; and in Elizabethan England, Niccolò Machiavelli was identified with Old Nick, and Satan was at times unflatteringly referred to as 'machiavellian'. Guicciardini largely escaped the attention of angry moralists – although his writings sometimes make Machiavelli appear reasonable and compassionate by comparison.

It was Machiavelli's stark deviation from the God-centred medieval system of thought that provoked this harsh reaction. If he has been vilified for centuries, it is chiefly because he broke so resoundingly with the medieval world-view. Machiavelli was born .t the end of the Middle Ages, and realized that the medieval dream of a politically united Christendom was a meaningless vision. This realization was shocking to men whose whole intellectual background was based on Christian theology. Machiavelli was a humanist, and like Guicciardini and other humanists he believed that scholarship based on analysis of historical events could shape policy. Such analysis ought not be confused with ethical and moral concerns, he claimed. He saw his task as describing things as they really happen and not speculating on things as they might be. What really happens, Machiavelli insists, is that effective rulers act exclusively in their own political interest. Guicciardini agrees – indeed, he extends this principle to all political actors; even 'those who preach liberty so convincingly have as their objective their own personal interest' (C–66).

With such claims Machiavelli and Guicciardini express the rupture between medieval Christendom and the modern age. And it is this rupture which makes them so important. They deviated from orthodoxy. They were also in sharp revolt against many of the propositions of traditional political theory. Where the medieval outlook was dominated by concerns about God, Machiavelli and Guicciardini were concerned with the State. Where the medieval philosophers saw nature as a divine creation which encompassed human society, they saw nature as a given and considered it separate from society (which they saw as fashioned by man). Where medieval thinkers sought to prescribe divine rules by which man could live a virtuous life and save his soul, they sought to describe human behaviour in order to infer lessons about the conditions for individual freedoms.

From God to The Prince

Machiavelli and Guicciardini removed God from scholarly attention. They did not do this explicitly by denying God's existence. They did it implicitly by quietly directing attention elsewhere; away from the salvation of the soul towards the security of the State. Disregarding theological concerns, they argue that there exists two moral realms, each with its specific interests and its specific code of ethics. On the one hand is the code which emphasizes justice, honesty, compassion and other virtues of traditional Christianity. On the other is the code which applies to the interest of the State. Machiavelli is most explicit in this regard. In the relations among states, God is no longer the legitimizing, moral authority; *The Prince* is. And Princes obey a moral code entirely their own.

Guicciardini agreed. He, too, describes Renaissance politics as a turbulent and dangerous game played by men who are 'false, insidious, deceitful and cunning' (C–157). And the prince for whom Guicciardini writes must remain constantly alert to challenges which threaten to unravel his state and to opportunities which may serve to strengthen it. To assert himself, the prince must always be guided by self-interest (C–218); he must simulate and hide his intentions (C–49, 104), exaggerate his power (C–86) and cover up his weaknesses (C–196). To safeguard his state, the prince must disregard the individual virtues of civil society and instead consider the collective interests of the state – thus, although it is humanly desirable to discuss things openly, it is politically prudent never to reveal one's own affairs (C–184); although lying is morally reprehensible, it is politically expedient, and the prince must learn to practise it well (C–37). Guicciardini's prince inhabit a ruthless world in which revenge is not only sweet, but necessary (C–72,74), and security means that your enemies are unable to harm you, although they should intensely wish to do so!

From nature to society
Unlike the medieval philosophers, who were concerned with the relationship between the State and God, Machiavelli and Guicciardini focused on the State as a self-sufficient entity – as ancient theorists had done. However, they pushed the classical perspective one logical step further: they conceived of the State as a self-sufficient actor which continually interacted with other states, and they vested in it a legitimizing authority for political acts. Because every State was part of an interstate context, it needed to concern itself with its own security, with armies and with leadership. For Machiavelli, the prince was the personification of the State. Thus, he portrays the prince as a self-sufficient, self-reliant actor who must seek to make himself as independent as possible of other actors. Including God.

Where medieval philosophers saw society as part of a great, God-given, natural order of things, Machiavelli and Guicciardini saw society as man-made. They saw the State as an artificial, temporal creation which must be ceaselessly monitored and tended to by men. Thus, by replacing God with the State, they also replaced nature with society. And again, they pushed the argument as far as it would go: nothing, they reiterated, is superior to the State. No consideration of justice or cruelty, praise or shame is to interfere with the necessary task of maintaining the State and of preserving the prince's freedom of action. Guicciardini took the last, extreme, step explicitly. He self-consciously removed God

51

from political considerations altogether. In God's place he put 'the reason and practice of states' (Guicciardini 1994, p. 159).

From prescription to description

Machiavelli and Guicciardini replaced the prescriptive concerns of medieval thought with descriptive analysis. Machiavelli was a practical man, and his *Prince* a practical book. And 'since my intention is to say something that will prove of practical use to the enquirer,' he notes, 'I have thought it proper to represent things as they are in real truth, rather than as they are imagined' (Machiavelli 1961, p. 90). Guicciardini agreed.

This attitude 'was a sword which was plunged into the flank of the body politic of Western humanity, causing it to shriek and rear up' (Meinecke 1957, p. 49). Machiavelli and Guicciardini do not concern themselves with how princes ought to behave; they seek to explain how successful princes in the past have, in fact, behaved. Machiavelli's exposition of the ethical code of princes enraged many humanists. To them, Machiavelli explained that he had not invented this code, he had simply described something which already existed. Successful princes have always distinguished between private morality and the interests of the State; they all know that they 'cannot observe all those things which give men a reputation for virtue, because in order to maintain his state he is often forced to act in defiance of good faith, of charity, of kindness, or religion' (Machiavelli 1961, p. 101).

This attitude also enraged the Christians. They believed that he not only accepted man's sinful nature but that he considered it a positive virtue. This position was worse than wicked: it disregarded the Day of Judgement, on which all injustice would be punished. In response to the Christians, Machiavelli said nothing. His silence is eloquent, indeed epoch-making; 'it echoed around Christian Europe, at first eliciting a stunned silence in return, and then, a howl of execration that has never finally died away' (Skinner 1981, p. 38). Machiavelli's silence represents a resounding rupture with medieval preoccupations.

Although Guicciardini had the same clinical and descriptive approach to politics as Machiavelli, he escaped the criticism which humanists and Christians levied against it. Machiavelli became the favourite *prügelknabe* of the moralists. Guicciardini merely became 'the first of the Machiavellians' (Rubinstein 1970, p. 19).

Reason, Free Will and Determinism

By making men masters of their own destiny, Renaissance humanists ushered in a distinctively modern political outlook. By portraying man as his own master, and denying that God or nature impose limits on human action, they made a resounding rupture with the medieval world view. Whereas medieval scholars found man's distinctive characteristic in 'reason' tempered by 'faith', Renaissance authors found it in the power of man's 'free will'.

This does not mean that the Renaissance men denied human rationality; they simply changed it. Machiavelli, for example, reduced it to a matter of calculation. For the medieval scholars 'reason' meant the ability to distinguish just from unjust acts; for Machiavelli 'reason' becomes the ability to compute ways to realize one's will. As the Aristotelians (like Aquinas) celebrated man's wisdom, Machiavellians celebrated man's freedom. This is obvious in the final part of *The Prince* where Machiavelli, wondering whether *fortuna* or *virtù* is the most determining principle in the life of a man, stresses the importance of the latter to an unprecedented degree: 'So as not to rule out our free will, I believe that it is probably true that fortune is the arbiter of half the things we do, leaving the other half or so to be controlled by ourselves', writes Machiavelli (1961, p. 130).

On this point Machiavelli and Guicciardini diverge. In the great debate on the respective role of *virtù* and *fortuna*, Machiavelli stresses the former and Guicciardini the latter. '[Y]ou cannot deny that Fortune has great power over human affairs', Guicciardini writes in maxim C–30. 'We see that these affairs constantly are being affected by fortuitous circumstances that men could neither foresee nor avoid. Although cleverness and care may accomplish many things, they are nevertheless not enough.' Guicciardini, then, seems more pessimistic about the human condition than Machiavelli. He is more conscious of the limits of human reason. He is more sceptical about man's ability to learn from History and from observing political events (C–114). This leads him to counter Machiavelli's faith in reason and free will. He writes in maxim C–128:

In affairs of state, you should guide yourself not so much by what reason demonstrates a prince ought to do, as by what he will most likely do, according to his nature and his habits. Princes will often do what they please or what they know, and not what they should. If you guide yourself by any rule other than this, you will get into very great trouble (Guicciardini 1970, p. 73).

This observation strikes at the very foundations of Machiavelli's *Prince* as a guide to political action. At the same time, it consolidates a key principle in modern International Relations analysis: in order to understand the actions of a statesman, it is not enough to understand his rational calculations; it is necessary to understand the history and the interests of the state which he represents.

Final remarks

Political theory was revolutionized during the Renaissance. During a few busy decades of the early 1500s, the Western world-view was irreversibly altered as the old theological discussions yielded to a new expansive modern discourse. It focused on states, not on God; it presented the State as a man-made thing and saw politics as a ceaseless activity necessary to sustain the State. International Relations theory made small progress by comparison. Renaissance manuals on war and on diplomacy, the two types of commonly-written texts in which one would expect to find theoretical approaches to international politics, are remarkably a-theoretical. The military manuals of the age demonstrated one thing clearly: that the nature of warfare changed dramatically after Charles VIII invaded Italy with French troops in 1494 and ignited the Italian Wars. Robert de Balsac noted the changes almost instantly; his *Nef des Princes et des Batailles* of 1502 describes the deployment in the field of new French and Spanish weapons systems, such as light artillery and handguns. Machiavelli, too, notes the introduction of new, destructive weapons systems in his *Art of War* of 1521. Battista della Valle goes one step further in his *Libro continente appertenentie ad Capitanii* of 1528; he includes field guns in his diagrams of efficient battle formations. But all these books concentrate on describing technical aspects of war – provisioning armies, setting up and guarding camp, marching formations and battle tactics (Hale 1981, pp. 276f). They contain little International Relations theory. During the final quarter of the century, however, International-Relations theorizing would also begin to gain momentum.

These remarks on Renaissance military manuals also apply to writings on diplomacy. They, too, reflected the sudden changes of the age – for example by suddenly embracing the notion of a 'reason of state' in a big way. Guicciardini was apparently the first author to use the term in its modern sense; by the final quarter of the century it had become a fashionable catchword. It proliferated in diplomatic manuals, and even found its way into the title of several late-sixteenth-century books. This suggests a more self-conscious attitude to the ends and means of diplomacy and interstate politics. However, it does not notably advance the understanding of international relations. It took time before the implications of the notion of a 'reason of state' made their mark on International Relations theorizing. This, however, is part of a story which is more appropriately told in the next chapter.

Part 2
The Modern Ages

3

Guns, ships and printing presses: the sixteenth century and the birth of the modern world

International Relations theory appeared in the sixteenth century. It emerged alongside the painful twin-birth of the modern state system and the modern world economy. Its growth was part of a process which eroded old institutions and overthrew traditional truths, but which did not replace the old conceptions with new certainties. It was a central part of the intellectual anxiety of that sprawling, tumultuous epoch which marked the transition from the medieval to the modern world. It was an age torn between the beliefs of the medieval mind and the concerns of the modern age.

The sixteenth century began as an age of vicious warfare between competing universal truths. It ended as an age of anxious relativism. The interminable warfare of the age failed to provide solutions to any of the fundamental questions over which the wars were fought. The failure to produce a healing peace forced forth new investigations of the causes and justifications for war, and the construction of new sets of rules to regulate relations among the powerful monarchs.

The emergence of the modern world can be captured through analysis of three key inventions which appeared in Western Europe in the long sixteenth century: firearms, the compass and the printing press. These inventions had political implications. They changed society and altered the relative ability of social groups to punish and reward. They altered European society and profoundly affected international interaction.

Social innovations, economic changes and political power

No one knows who invented gunpowder. The ancient Chinese certainly possessed it. It came via the Islamic empire to Europe. The Europeans put it to purposeful military use in the late 1400s, and thereby altered the distribution of political power among the emerging states. Monarchs who acquired guns vastly enhanced their military power. This made their neighbours insecure and compelled them to acquire similar weapons. The arrival of gunpowder, then, caught the monarchs of Europe on the horns of a security dilemma (Hertz 1950). Guns made battles more destructive and warfare more costly. And the rising costs of warfare in early sixteenth-century Europe had immediate political consequences. They made political power increasingly dependent upon national wealth, and pressured kings and princes to invent new ways of raising revenues. This, in turn, stimulated the growth of the modern state and the state system.

Taxation was one way of raising revenues. Long-distance trade was another. But such trade was a fairly recent option: it was made possible by new ship models and improved means of navigation. Such maritime innovations also made possible expeditions of discovery and adventure. Later, when cannons were fitted to the new ships, the Europeans were enabled to pillage and colonize America, Africa and Asia. Colonization, then, attended trade as a way in which the states of Western Europe could raise much-needed revenues. And with these new sources of revenues the new European monarchs could build larger armies and equip them with more guns. Trade and colonialism stimulated the growth of trade routes between Europe and other regions; they fuelled an international network of communications and transport which would provide the scaffolding of the modern world economy.

The printing press spread the culture of the Renaissance, with its enthusiasm for ancient texts, it knowledge and its entrepreneurial spirit, to the rest of Europe. It also fuelled the dissent within the Church and hastened the religious fragmentation which we call 'the Reformation.'

The gunpowder revolution and political change
The feudal organization of society sustained a class of noble landowners and trained them as warriors. The advent of gunpowder destroyed this class. The mounted warriors became easy targets for the new handguns and cannons. And when it became obvious that an untrained footsoldier equipped with an arquebus could kill a nobleman from a safe distance, the *cavalry* lost its leading role in warfare; the warrior-noblemen were rendered obsolete in war, and the cavaliers saw their position in civil society eroded as well. The *infantry* became the important branch of the armed forces of the Renaissance. The cost of a footsoldier with a gun was a fraction of the cost of a nobleman with horse and entourage, and encouraged the kings of Europe to invest in infantry. Army sizes expanded rapidly as a result. Also, the introduction of field-guns during the Italian Wars gave rise to a third, distinctly modern, branch of the armed forces: the *artillery*.

As armies grew in size and complexity during the Italian Wars, the costs of equipping an army skyrocketed. Even the wealthiest aristocrat could no longer afford to raise large armies of professional soldiers. Only the king could afford the expenses of modern warfare – 'the man who had at his disposal the taxes of an entire country was in position to hire more warriors than any other' (Braudel 1972, p. 657).

In this way, the military revolution of the fifteenth and sixteenth centuries furthered the rise of 'the new monarchies' in Europe (Tilly 1994). Larger armies meant soaring military expenditures. This stimulated rulers to find more efficient ways to collect and manage taxes. And these efforts, in turn, stimulated the creation of the modern state. They consolidated the power of the monarch, thus contributing to the early absolutist form of European states; they made the king less dependent on the landed aristocracy, but upgraded his relations with the commercial classes in the expanding towns, thus encouraging the rise of the *Ständestaat* (Poggi 1978, pp. 36ff) and preparing the grounds for the systems of popular representation of West-European politics. The fiscal apparatus was, in short, 'the institution which pulled the other institutions in its wake' (Schumpeter 1976, p. 141).

Evolution in transport, revolution in commerce
Politics within states were altered by the intense royal efforts to extort funds from their populations. Politics among states also changed, as monarchs searched for ways to extort revenues from the extra-European regions. Long-distance travel was made possible by new Iberian ship models which improved the speed and comfort of sea travel. It was also stimulated by new developments in mathematics, astronomy and mapmaking which enhanced the accuracy of navigation. With the improvement of the compass and the innovation of the astrolabe, seafarers no longer found it necessary to scurry along the crowded coasts of Europe, navigating from one island to the next. They boldly struck out into the open oceans of the globe.

Throughout the fifteenth century, ocean traders grew more prominent in coastal towns of Southern Europe. The evolution was notably brisk in Iberian cities such as Lisbon and Oporto, where trade mushroomed both in luxuries and in bulk goods. This growth of trade stimulated an emancipation of the mercantile strata of society from traditional controls.

It is easy to exaggerate the rise of the mercantile classes, for the greatest merchant of all was the Crown. The most famous of all the royal merchants was Henrique Infante de Portugal, better known as Prince Henry the Navigator. Henrique's historical fame rests on his founding of a naval academy, a veritable 'think tank', to which he brought some of the best mapmakers and astronomers of Europe. He was among the first monarchs systematically to finance his activities with income from colonial exploits – from the import of dyes and sugar into Portugal from West Africa and the Atlantic islands, and from the capture and sale of African slaves.

Henrique inaugurated an age of expansion (sometimes referred to as an 'Age of Discovery'). His success demonstrated to other monarchs the wealth and power which awaited them in overseas expansion. Thus, 'discovery' was attended by a fever of competitive colonization and war. The improved military capabilities which characterized the competition among monarchs at home, also provided superior forces to conquer new lands abroad. Guns mounted on ships enabled the seafaring nations of Europe to rapidly expand along the Mediterranean, African, Asian and American coasts.

The Infante Henrique also exemplifies a more subtle and psychological effect of overseas expansion: it stimulated a new entrepreneurial spirit among people who understood that overseas expansion opened up substantial opportunities for gain and fame. The discovery of the New World created an awareness of new opportunities, and this awareness in itself provided a stimulus to further change.

Movable type, revolution in thought
The advent of print altered the way in which human thought was expressed, disseminated and preserved (Eisenstein 1993). Once introduced, the new technology of the movable typeface was quickly propagated throughout Europe. Around 1450 Johann Gutenberg completed his first set of printed Bibles; by 1470, printing shops had appeared in Cologne, Basle, Rome and Venice. After 50 years, an estimated 8,000,000 books had been printed (Mandrou 1978, pp. 27ff).

The first printed texts were Bibles, prayer books, sermons and breviaries. Then followed all kinds of entertaining texts – stories, fables of varying quality, and the spectacularly successful chivalric romances (Leonard 1949). Among the sixteenth-century best sellers were also a wide variety of handbooks and manuals. How-to books of all kinds – agriculture, building, design, fashion, pottery, tool-handling, surveying – together with maps, calendars and tables for weights and measures were among the most popular printed products. Last but not least, Greek and Latin classics were printed – a practice which undoubtedly saved several ancient texts written on animal skins that had grown mouldy or brittle with advancing age.

Printing spread texts and theories beyond the narrow scholarly élite. The immediate result was to bring dissent and confusion to established bodies of knowledge. This was, for example, quite apparent in the emerging disciplines of geography and cartography. Geographers described the various countries in the world – their inhabitants, their climate, their resources – and provided important information for traders and buccaneers. Cartographers drew maps. They identified places where trade and pillage were most promising, and determined the quickest and safest routes to those places. It did not take long for descriptions and maps to provoke conflicts between lay scholars and traders on the one hand and orthodox Church authorities on the other. The scholars noted that new knowledge about the world flatly contradicted traditional, Bible-based contentions about the division of land and water and about the inhabitants of the earth. The new cartographic representation of a round earth, turning both upon itself and around a fixed sun, contradicted the official vision of the Church: a flat earth in the centre of a universe arranged around Palestine.

Furthermore, printing exacerbated dissensions within the Church. As religious texts were printed and spread, it became obvious that the Church was not unified, but that its members entertained a diverse array of ideas and interpretations. Sermons and tracts spread to every corner of Europe with the advent of print, and revealed that churchmen in different regions had widely different interpretations of even the most basic doctrines of the Faith. The theologians of Spain had quite different views from their colleagues in Rome – not to mention how different they were from the theologians of France, Poland, Denmark and the many German principalities.

The heterogeneity of the Church, revealed by the art of printing, triggered a flood of demands for Church reform. The last straw was added to centuries of accumulated dissatisfaction when Church authorities allowed entrepreneurial clerics to raise revenues by mass-printing letters of indulgence – documents given to the faithful in return for prayer, penitence, pilgrimage or, most shockingly, hard cash. Demands for Church reform had been voiced since the Middle Ages. However, these demands did not constitute any unified reform movement, for they, too, assumed different forms in different social and geographical locations. Printed matter changed the nature of the protest. It spread the consciousness of diversity within Christian Europe; but it also spread certain unifying key ideas and the names of key authors who symbolized different schools of interpretations.

One of these key ideas was the claim that religious faith was a private matter. This notion was formulated by several authors; the most famous were Martin Luther and Jean Calvin. Luther formulated the first, more obedient and passive challenge to the established doctrine that religious faith was demonstrated in acts – generally by participation in public ceremonies and sacraments. Since sacraments could not be properly administered without the clergy, salvation could not be achieved without the Church hierarchy. Luther denied the clergy their indispensable role. He (and Calvin) claimed that individual intentions were a better indicator of faith than collective rituals; that faith was 'nothing else but the truth of the heart'.

This theory was revolutionary. It captured a sentiment of individuality and privacy which appealed to the merchants and the rising middle-class artisans of the age. The way in which the theory was disseminated was also revolutionary: in 1517, Luther formulated his argument in the form of ninety-five points of trenchant criticism of corrupt Church practices and nailed them up on a church door. His expectations of a scholarly discussion of his grievances were rudely shattered when his friends printed up the *Ninety-five Theses* and distributed them. Within a fortnight, they were discussed all over Germany; within a month, all over Europe (Eisenstein 1993, pp. 151ff).

Events quickly spiralled out of control. The explosive political potential of the new teachings was most immediately realized where the merchant and middle classes were most numerous and found a ready ally in the ruler. In Holland, in

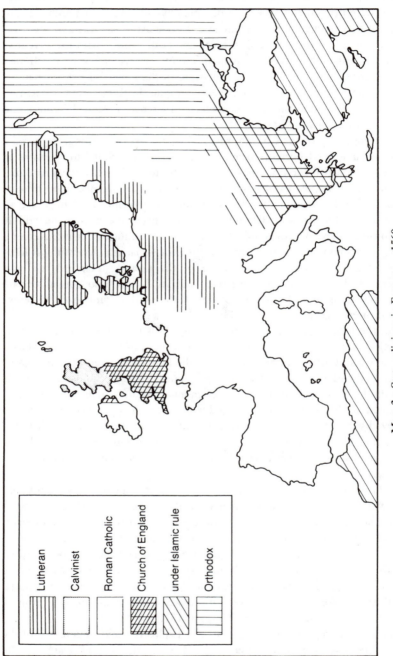

Map 3 State religions in Europe, *c.* 1560

Lutheran

Calvinist

Roman Catholic

Church of England

under Islamic rule

Orthodox

states and free cities in the Holy Roman Empire and in England, revolutions were fomented by demands for religious freedoms. The clamour for religious reform was often embraced by statesmen and monarchs to further their own political interests. In the predominantly rural, relatively poor areas of north-western Europe – in Northern Germany, England and Scandinavia – Protestant Reform was particularly successful, because it was championed by monarchs who sought to strengthen royal power at the expense of the established Church.

A time out of joint

A key question of political theory emerged from this turbulence: What is the relationship between religion and war? On the one hand, many spokesmen of the established Church maintained the right to wage war against infidels and heretics. Spanish jurists in particular argued that heretics should be punished by war; that heretics and infidels set themselves outside the law of God and nature, and therefore have no true jurisdiction. On the other hand, several jurists, historians and philosophers recognized that soldiers and statesmen found in religion effective justifications for political aims.

Towards the end of the sixteenth century, the penchant of kings to justify their adventurism with religious arguments was increasingly noted by the jurists of the age. Vitoria was among the first Spanish jurists to warn against the dangers of making religion a cause for war. He observed that, if religious doctrine could legitimize war, then every prince would always declare his own war a holy one. Gentili agreed, arguing that religious claims are often 'said to be inventions of the most greedy of men and to be cloaks for their dishonesty'. Religion is a relationship between man and God, he maintained. It is divine in origin, and 'since the laws of religion do not properly exist between man and man, therefore no man's right is violated by a difference in religion, nor is it lawful to make war because of religion', he argued. 'A man cannot complain of being wronged because others differ from him in religion' (Gentili 1964).

The argument that religion is not a sufficient justification for war supports a distinctly modern understanding of religious faith as a personal concern and an individual right. The case for religious tolerance was fuelled by political stalemate. It increased as the religious wars dragged on with no clear victor in sight. In 1555 the concept of tolerance was advanced in the Treaty of Augsburg, which proposed a compromize solution to the religious strife between various German principalities. The treaty proclaimed that it ought to be up to the individual prince to determine the religion of his realm. Although this position was diplomatically expedient, it remained intellectually unsatisfying. The time was not yet ripe for the tolerance of the religious authority of princes; this position would have to wait for another century to be generally accepted as the principle of *cuius regio, eius religio*. The Treaty of Augsburg, did however, inaugurate a period of intense debate about princely authority in war and religion. The debate did not end until the Treaty of Westphalia in 1648 more clearly expressed the terms on which the new international order was to be based. The long interval between the two treaties of Augsburg and Westphalia marked a steady increase in the pitch of the religious war in a divided Europe. It also marked one of the most formative periods in the history of international relations theory.

Contradictions of the age
The mounting pace of social change divided social philosophers. Several political thinkers struggled to re-establish the old intellectual certainties in the face of turbulent times and uncertain futures (Ferrari 1860, pp. 298ff). But all were torn between the comfortable certainties of traditional knowledge and the intellectually engaging emerging spirit of tolerance; between the ethical and the pragmatic; between Aquinas and Machiavelli. Innocent Gentillet defended traditional doctrines in his *Anti-Machiavel*. Francis Bacon put in a good word for Machiavelli in his *Essays*.

The struggle with the changing times is evident in the writings of Justus Lipsius (1517–1606). He repudiated Machiavelli and sought to resurrect the traditional concept of *virtù* as a quality marked by rigorous morality, wisdom, justice, courage and temperance – virtues which accord with the Greek and Roman classics as well as with established Christian values. In the first chapters of his *Politics* of 1589 Lipsius elaborates a classical definition of *virtù* and laboriously establishes it as the moral basis for princely rule. But then he abruptly raises the question of whether the prince can, in fact, be expected to measure up to such high ethical standards. After all, he remarks, we do not live in Plato's *Republic*, but in a world where men are known to be duplicitous, if not downright evil. Accordingly, we would be exceedingly naive if we did not realize that princes often use both deception and fraud to further their political objectives.

A similar struggle is apparent in the works of Tommaso Campanella (1568–1639), a Dominican monk, a passionate philosopher poet and a political revolutionary. A prominent transition figure, Campanella sought to reconcile Catholic theology with Renaissance science. His books contain both some of the most retrograde astrological superstitions and religious fanaticisms and some of the most progressive notions of his day.[1] Campanella taught that the world had two centres: one associated with the earth and marked by darkness, cold and hatred; another associated with the sun, and marked by brightness, warmth and love. He identified Machiavelli as the primary theorist of the earth, and castigated him for having reduced religion to a political tool and destroyed the spiritual community of man with a nefarious doctrine of egotistic reasoning and individual interest. He saw his own political thoughts as an antidote to the Renaissance humanists, and spelled them out in *La città del sole* ('The City of the Sun') of 1602. It is a political dialogue in the tradition of Plato's *Republic* and More's *Utopia*, proposing an ideal state governed by reason, love and social solidarity. But it also contains shrewd comments on contemporary politics. The duality is even more apparent in his *Discorsi politici ai principi d'Italia* ('Political Discourses to the Princes of Italy') (159?). Here Campanella portrays European affairs as formed by a double tension: a contest between Turk and Habsburg on the one hand, and between Habsburg and Valois on the other. In effect, Campanella opposes Renaissance humanism one moment, and borrows from it the next. In one place he angrily opposes the notion of a 'reason of state'; in another he uses it. He even employs the balance-of-power principle: he notes that Italian rulers assist France in order to contain Spain, and adds that this policy would be reversed if Spain were to decline and France become the greater Power. Such contradictions express the paradox of the age: even the fiercest opponents to Machiavelli borrow from him and finish by emulating him. What in fact happened to Campanella 'was that the evil enemy of Machiavellism, against which he was bitterly struggling, gained and held possession over him himself from the very first' (Meinecke 1957, p. 102).

Comparable contradictions are evident in the works of Giovanni Botero (1540–1617). On the first pages of his *Reason of State* (1956 [1589]) Botero declares himself an opponent of Machiavelli; he insists, like Lipsius and Campanella, that justice and integrity are qualities requisite in a ruler. Yet, by the time he draws his conclusions, Botero has adopted many of Machiavelli's arguments. For example, he recommends that a ruler appear virtuous not because such conduct is good in itself, but because it earns him goodwill and prestige (Botero 1956, p. 96). He agrees that self-interest lies at the core of all political action – 'that in the decisions made by princes interest will always override every other argument' (p. 41). He even repeats Machiavelli's claim that the self-interest of the prince is identical to the interest of the State – that 'in the last resort *ragione di stato* is little else but *ragione d'interesse*' (quoted in Meinecke 1957, p. 69).

The first five books of Botero's *Reason of State* address the same themes as Machiavelli's *Prince* – the nature of the State, the necessary skills of the ruler, the different classes of people and how to best treat them, etc. The sixth book marks a transition from internal to external concerns; from domestic affairs to foreign policies and international relations. Like most sixteenth-century authors, Botero lists the accepted facts of practical affairs – the raising of armies, the building of fortresses and the maintenance of garrisons. But he also displays a much wider scope and a more fertile imagination than his contemporaries. Some of his observations are brilliant – as when he explains how Italy and Germany have been kept at peace because their powers have been 'equally balanced' (Botero 1956, p. 125). Others are odd – as when he argues that some rivers of the world are well suited for trade and navigation because their waters are particularly thick and slimy.

One of the most original aspects of Botero's international analysis is his emphasis on economic factors. Whereas Machiavelli and Guicciardini argued that armed force is the ultimate basis of the State, Botero adds (in Book 7) that production and international trade are also crucial, for such activities create wealth by the means of which a prince can purchase means of force. Botero also explains (in Book 8) that to be powerful, a country must possess a numerous population, because many citizens provide many soldiers, more taxes and a greater economic efficiency. However, it is crucial that the population does not grow to exceed the country's resource base. For if this should happen, it would cause scarcity, misery, disease and jealousies, and would erode the unity and strength of the state.[2] Unless the prince conducts an active policy of colonialism and exports the surplus population to foreign lands – 'like swarms of bees leaving the hive when they would die from disease or overcrowding if they remained' (p. 156).

Two sixteenth-century traditions: Spain and Italy

In 1492, Columbus first sighted the New World. His discovery was followed by 15 years of coastal expeditions which established the existence of an enormous American land-mass. After 1508, the pattern of discovery changed. Spain began to establish permanent bases on the Greater Antilles to serve as bases for future expeditions. The first probings were completed in 1518. Over the following two decades, Spanish soldiers undertook a full-scale conquest of the entire American interior. Hernán Cortés conquered the Aztec empire of Mexico in 1519; Francisco Pizarro destroyed the great Inca empire of the Andes in 1533. From the hearts of the two fallen native empires, the conquistadors fanned out over South America in the pursuit of El Dorado. By 1540, after only about 25 years of intense effort, the great age of the *conquista* was over. The new age that opened up offered boundless opportunities for persons seeking adventure and profit; it also offered conceptual turbulence and legal and ethical dilemmas.

Politics and empire: the Iberian tradition
Cortés and Pizarro conquered the Americas with a brilliance and daring which fired the imagination of future generations. In their wake came colonists, whose cupidity drove them to commit unspeakable cruelties against the natives. Their actions were condoned by a substantial body of legal and religious sophisms. The influential Juan Ginés de Sepulveda (1490–1573), Charles V's priest and Philip II's educator, for example, defended this policy of pillage and extermination. Bartoloméo de Las Casas (1474–1566), on the other hand, gained fame as an indefatigable champion of the rights of the Indians (Alker 1992). In an age in which travel to the New World was physically demanding and dangerous, he crossed the Atlantic 14 times to plead with the King of Spain for just and humane treatment of the natives. The debate reached its apex when, in 1550, Sepulveda and Las Casas held their famous dispute before a committee of theologians and jurists at Valladolid (Hanke 1974). Las Casas won this duel of minds. But it was a victory in a debate on legal theory and moral

philosophy; in the real world the cruel treatment of Indians continued unabated. The population of Spanish America declined from an estimated 50 million in the early sixteenth century to only 4 million in the seventeenth (Stavrianos 1981, p. 80).

The moral and legal aspects of the wars against the Indians remained under discussion in Spain, and the continuing debate had the effect of enlarging the conception of international relations. Authors such as Francisco de Vitoria (1480–1549) and Domingo Soto (1494–1560) extended the scope of international law, giving maritime matters a more systematic treatment. The debate was particularly intense at the famous university in Salamanca, home of the illustrious 'primo professor', Vitoria. In 1532, he issued *De Indis noviter inventis* ('On the Indians Recently Discovered'), which discusses whether Spain was entitled to rule the new peoples that the conquistadors had discovered in the new world. This treatise was followed by *De jure belli Hispaniorum in barbaros* ('On the Right of the Spanish to Wage War against the Barbarians') (153?), which discusses the circumstances under which Spain's war against the Indians may be justified. These two brief treatises complement each other. The first discusses the preconditions for peace; the second, the reasons or justifications for war. Together they constitute one of the first sustained expositions in Western thought on the law of peace and war.

In his first treatise, *De Indis*, Vitoria does not make any big issue of the conquistadors' presence in the New World. All people have a natural right to travel, he argues. Thus, 'the Spaniards have a right to travel into the lands in question and to sojourn there, provided they do no harm to the natives, and the natives may not prevent them' (Vitoria 1934a, p. xxxvi). He does, however, make an issue of the fact that, when the Spaniards arrived, the Indians were clearly in peaceful possession of property, both publicly and privately. But since the Indians were infidels, could their possession amount to true ownership? The conquistadors had answered this question in the negative, arguing that Christian people for that reason were entitled to seize the goods and the land of heretical indians. Vitoria emphatically rejects this position. For him, the Indians 'had true dominion in both public and private matters, just like Christians, and that neither their princes nor private persons could be despoiled of their property on the ground of their not being true owners' (p. xiii).

In his second treatise, *De jure belli*, Vitoria discusses the legality of the war which the Spanish conquistadors fought against the Indians of the New World. This treatise focuses more on Spanish politics than on the Americas, for it involves the complex question of who has the right to declare war. Vitoria's argument begins with St Augustine's proposition that any private person has a right to defend himself and his property with armed force if necessary. But Vitoria soon transcends Augustine's analogy between private persons and states. He claims that whereas persons can lawfully resort to violent defence only in the moment of danger, states can use armed force for certain offensive purposes as well. States, for example, have the right to avenge themselves and to exact reparations for wrongs suffered in the recent past. In a war between states, then, 'everything is lawful which the defence of the common weal requires. This is notorious, for the end and aim of war is the defence and preservation of the State' (Vitoria 1934b, p. lv). A state's authority to wage war rests with the prince, Vitoria continues, for 'he is its representative and wields its authority; and where there are already lawful princes in a State, all authority is in their hands and without them nothing of a public nature can be done either in war or in peace' (p. lii).

Vitoria acknowledges that although the prince is the pre-eminent representative of the authority of the state, limits must be imposed upon princely action in matters of war. To define those limits, he again relies on Augustine's claim that war is lawful only if it has a just cause. Thus, he is forced to address the question 'What may be a reason and cause of just war?' To answer this question, Vitoria immediately rejects differences in religion, extension of empire and the prince's personal gain as causes of just war. There is only one just cause of an offensive war, he argues, 'namely a wrong received'. An offensive war is just, then, when it is a punishment for the violation of right. However, he warns, war is a most extreme punishment, and not every violation of a right justifies war, any more than every crime in civil society justifies the most extreme punishment of the wrongdoer. When contemplating an offensive war, the prince must seek to balance the defence of the state against the public welfare; he must always be concerned with making the punishment correspond to the measure of the offence and with furthering the cause of justice (p. liv).

Vitoria recognizes that state security, public welfare and justice do not always coincide. Consequently, the prince is often torn between contradictory concerns. The final pages of the *De jure belli* address these various concerns and relate them to the conquistadors' war against the Indians. Vitoria recognizes that religion is used by Christian rulers to extend their empires and amass personal gain and glory. He proposes that the prince consult his advisers before he commits troops in an offensive action. This, he says, will restrain zealous rulers – i.e. princes who are concerned not with private gain as much as with God. He explains that actions of crusading rulers should be limited in order to prevent hasty and frivolous wars.

Vitoria concludes that although there are conditions under which Christian soldiers can lawfully engage in offensive war, religion alone is not among them. Did conditions exist in the New World around 1500 that could justify the wars against the American Indians? In defending themselves, could the Spanish lawfully execute and enslave the Indians? Vitoria's answers are ambiguous. On the one hand, he denies that it is lawful in itself to kill innocent men, women and children. On the other, he acknowledges that innocent bystanders are often casualties of military action and that this cannot be helped – he even admits that civilians may be deliberately killed if sparing them would imperil the success of military operations. Vitoria's argument is complicated by his acknowledgement that, if an enemy refuses to restore things wrongfully seized, the injured party may recoup his losses from innocent as well as from guilty persons. This recognition opens up the way for endless reprisals, as one party and then another each seeks to recoup its losses from civilian populations.

Only one clear point emerges from this final discussion: a sharp distinction drawn between two types of war: war between Christians and pagans on the one hand and war among Christian nations on the other. The enslavement of non-combatants is lawful only in the first type of war, but not in the second. It is a received rule of Christendom that Christians do not become slaves according to the law of war; this enslaving is not lawful in a war between Christians, Vitoria explains (pp. lxiv–lxv).

Politics and counterpoise: the Italian tradition

Vitoria's defence of the Indians is, in some ways, quite modern. For example, his discussion includes assertions of the rights to private property, to travel and trade. In other aspects, the treatise is rife with medieval concerns; the discussions of war and peace, for example, rely on Aristotle, Augustine and Aquinas and their assumptions on divine, natural law. Vitoria's view of politics was dominated by individual decision-makers – by princes and soldiers and, the choices they faced, and by the nature and the moral and legal implications of their acts.

Vitoria's non-Iberian contemporaries tended to pay less attention to individuals and to ethics. Italian theorists in particular emphasized relations between institutions. The Italians tended to view international relations not in terms of ethical choices but in terms of interaction between *states*.

Vitoria wrote in Spain, one of the most religiously orthodox regions of Atlantic Europe and the leading force behind the Counter-Reformation. Botero, Gentili and several others wrote in late-Renaissance Italy, the most pragmatic and vibrant region of Europe. Furthermore, whereas Vitoria was a citizen of an expanding empire, and was concerned with the moral problems of imperial expansion, his Italian counterparts were inhabitants of threatened city-states, and preoccupied with issues of order and security. Such differences in cultural and political context help explain why sixteenth-century Iberian authors formulated the foundations for modern international law, whereas their Italian counterparts developed theories of balance of power. The Italian awareness of interstate relations and state power are obvious in authors like Belli, Paruta, Boccalini and others.[3]

Alberico Gentili (1552–1608) reflected the principles and perspectives of the Italians particularly well. He identifies states, not men, as the basic units of international politics, but he also recognizes that there is a need for a legal codex to regulate the interaction between states. Gentili's most famous work, *De jure belli libri tres* ('The Three Books on the Law of War', 1598), is remarkably free of many of his contemporaries' myopic preoccupations with the shape of fortresses, soldiers' discipline and municipal defence. The first of the books deals with war in general; what it is, who may make it, and what motives or causes justify it. The second book establishes a legal framework for conducting belligerent operations. The third book discusses the conclusions of war. By Gentili's definition, war is a violent conflict between public authorities. In contrast, operations against piracy, for example, cannot be regarded as war. The contending parties in wars must be independent sovereigns or peoples subject to no higher jurisdiction; and pirates obey no sovereign authority.

Princes represent the highest authority of the state, Gentili writes. Because states are subject to no higher jurisdiction, disputes between them will routinely arise. Because the primary duty of the prince is to maintain the security and the well-being of his citizens, such disputes will often erupt in war. This vision of interstate relations echoes Guicciardini's idea of a reason of state. Gentili has little to add to Vitoria or Botero on the nature of war. He does, however, formulate several important insights about negotiated settlement between states. Part lawyer, part politician and part practising diplomat, Gentili drew on his varied experience to define rules which could regulate the conduct between states and minimize war.

For Gentili, disputes between states are unavoidable. When such disputes arise, they can be settled either by negotiation or by force. He accentuates the desirability of negotiated settlements, and proposes that princes submit their differences to third parties for arbitration. Negotiation, however, will only be an option when both (or all) disputing princes voluntarily agree to negotiate. Because there is no higher authority to compel independent princes to negotiate, it follows that if one of them refuses to do so, then only war will settle the dispute.

Although Gentili sees war as part and parcel of interstate interaction, he does not argue that war is the natural condition of mankind. He sees the human species as essentially sociable and gregarious (1964, pp. 53ff). All men are unified by relations of kin and by reciprocal needs, and they owe one another mutual aid. Gentili then extends this reasoning to states by drawing an analogy from his vision of a society of men and applying it to that of a society of states (pp. 67f). On the basis of this parallel, Gentili argues that, subject to the exercise of sovereignty, both the earth and the oceans belong to all. All states have the right to undisturbed maritime navigation, to carry on commercial intercourse and to secure shelter in foreign ports. No state can legitimately deny anyone innocent passage over its territory. These are natural rights of all men, or what Gentili calls 'privileges of nature', and they constitute the fundamental principles of the society of states. For the purpose of defending these fundamental principles, war may be justly declared. In Gentili's words, 'a war will be called natural, if it is undertaken because of some privilege of nature is denied to us by man. For example, if a right of way is refused to us, or if we are excluded from harbours or kept from provisions, commerce and trade' (p. 86).

Denial of the privileges of nature is not only an unlawful injury to the party directly hurt by it; it is also an offence against human society at large. In order to protect and defend these privileges of nature upon which this society depends, other states should rally to the defence of the injured party. It is commonly accepted in civil society, he argues, than an honest man is bound by his honour and his conscience to come to the aid of a fellow man who is injured or endangered. 'We are bound by a natural law ... to aid one another', he writes, and continues:

And if these things are true in the case of private individuals, how much truer they will be of sovereigns, who call one another kindred, cousins, brothers. They will be so much the more true of princes because, if one private citizen does not defend another, there is a magistrate who can avenge the wrongs of private individuals and make good their losses; but there is no one to mend the wrongs and losses of princes, unless it be that same prince, who would prefer to apply a remedy to an evil afterwards, rather than prevent the evil from being done in the beginning (pp. 70f).

Similar attitudes mark Gentili's *De legationibus* ('On Legations') of 1584, which examines the principle of the inviolability of envoys.

Gentili's argument reverberates with the now familiar distinction between domestic and interstate affairs. Domestic politics occur under the watchful eye of a civil magistrate, whereas international politics mean interaction between sovereign states subject to no higher earthly authority. In Gentili's view, the principal reality of international politics is that it concerns states rather than individual human beings. To this distinction Gentili adds that the interaction between states expresses neither complete conflict of interest nor complete identity of interest; it is a complex balance of conflict and co-operation. In their dealings with one another, all states are bound by the rudimentary rules and institutions of the society they form. This argument informes Gentili's less known, posthumously published book *Hispanica advocatio* of 1613. This book contains notes on the cases that Gentili prepared as counsel for Spain against the Netherlands. Even in this partisan setting, Gentili argues a succinct case for a doctrine of territorial sovereignty as the basic principle underlying the rights and obligations of belligerent as well as neutral states.

Conceptualizing sovereignty

In Gentili's society of states, war is not a natural condition. It is, however, a common enough occurrence. It should be fought only for a just cause, by just means and only by those with the proper authority. But Gentili is unclear on the question of who should be considered a 'proper authority'. He approaches the modern notion that only public authorities are entitled to wage war and that only states can be considered such authorities. Through a discussion of the rights and the duties of the prince, Gentili sketches a distinctly modern outline of interstate relations as an anarchical society. However, the seminal clarification of these issues is found not in Alberico Gentili but in Jean Bodin (1530–95), whose clarification rests on two contributions to International Relations theory: on his lasting definition of 'sovereignty' and on his formulation of the principle of *pacta sunt servanda* – the insistence that sovereign rulers must keep their commitments.

The life of Jean Bodin is, like the century he lived in, only imperfectly known. But we know that he was, like Europe itself, torn between the religious theories which proliferated in the wake of the Reformation. He was brought up Catholic, but he studied the Lutheran arguments – indeed, he read them so seriously that he apparently spent some time in prison on charges of expressing Protestant views.

Like many other thinkers of this turbulent age, Bodin was influenced by the methods and theories of Renaissance scholarship. He attended school first in Paris before he transferred to the university in Toulouse. It was a centre of international and humanist learning, visited by scholars from Germany, Italy and Switzerland. About 1550, Bodin embarked upon the study of law. He was a humanist. He did not approach law through the study of cases and arguments; he thought that an understanding of legal principles was best ascertained through the study of history.

Around 1560 Bodin left Toulouse. Disappointed in his ambitions and worried that religious wars would soon engulf the city, Bodin left for Paris. Here he abandoned the teaching of law for its practice. But he found time to integrate his many notes from Toulouse into a pedagogical system, *Method for the Easy Comprehension of History* (1945 [1566]).[4] He interpreted the term 'history' broadly to include the diverse issues of 'the customs of peoples and the beginnings, growth, conditions, changes and decline of all states'. These issues have their analytic origins in Bodin's pedagogical system. However, they also have a historic genesis in a deep religious crisis which confounded sixteenth-century European politics – a crisis which very nearly tore France asunder before Bodin's eyes. Attempts to stem the rapid progress of Calvinism by force sparked sustained resistance. Riots erupted in 1562, and ignited a veritable civil war which lasted for over a generation.

Keenly aware of the political potential of religious doctrines, Bodin echoed a key claim of Vitoria, Gentili and others: that religion is not a sufficient cause for war. His position was based neither on religious doctrine nor on philosophical argument, but on a pragmatic concern for civil order founded in law. Bodin's *Six Books on the Commonwealth* (1967 [1576]) discuss the salient properties of 'the best and most enduring forms of law'. Readers often find the first book dry and confusing, because it contains a wealth of legal definitions and has a tendency to raise theoretical questions only to discuss them in legal and in practical terms. Despite the fact that Bodin never actually identifies the 'best and most enduring forms of law', Bodin's first book is quite readable once two things are understood: first, that its primary purpose is actually not to provide a description of the ideal constitution, but to define the key terms applied throughout the rest of the books; and second, that Bodin's primary concern is a practical one: to identify the best workable regime type for his age.

'Book Two' approaches a description of the good state. It contains a lengthy comparison of three different types of commonwealths: monarchic, aristocratic and democratic. Superficially read, it may appear that Bodin has derived his argument from the similar scheme found in Aristotle's *Politics*. More closely perused, it is evident that Bodin's *Six Books* is intended as a rebuttal to Aristotle; Bodin merely uses Aristotle as a convenient vantage point for his own purposes. Indeed, Bodin appears positively annoyed with Aristotle's accounts, and repeatedly points out the philosopher's shortcomings – a bold, iconoclastic streak for a Catholic educator, but one which was not untypical of the day.

'Book Three' complements Bodin's discussion of various forms of state with a lengthy examination of the essential structures of a just and effective government. His meticulous treatment of actual states reveals his ultimate, practical purpose: he wants to find the most orderly and stable commonwealth in a world whose traditional order is rapidly waning.

This purpose is also evident in the next two books. 'Book Four' is devoted to historical change: it is largely a comparison of the rise and fall of good and powerful states. Bodin singles out civil war and revolutions as special issues of concern. 'Book Five' discusses continuity and order. Again, Bodin raises the issue of revolution, but this time in the context of raising and maintaining armies. In the sixth and final book, Bodin returns to the question of the best form of government. True to his habit of providing pragmatic answers to normative questions, he extols the powerful monarch; and it is unclear whether he held that monarchic rule was conducive to virtue or whether he felt that it could best guarantee social order and political stability.

Bodin's *Six Books on the Commonwealth* are largely devoted to politics within states. Bodin is nevertheless counted among the most important contributors to International Relations theory, primarily because of the conceptual discussions of the dry and elusive 'Book One', notably his discussions of the concept of 'sovereignty'. Bodin realized that although this concept is central to the study of all politics, 'no jurist or political philosopher has in fact attempted to define it' (Bodin 1967, p. 25). He decided to be the first man to do so.

Bodin defines sovereignty as 'that absolute and perpetual power vested in a commonwealth' (1967, p. 25). This brief definition hinges on three decisive postulates. First of all, it implies that sovereignty does not really pertain to individuals, but to states; sovereignty is not a property owned by any one man, it is a quality ultimately vested in a commonwealth. Its precise locus depends upon the type of commonwealth. Bodin explains: 'A state is called a monarchy when sovereignty is vested in one person, and the rest have only to obey. Democracy, or the popular state, is one in which all the people, or a majority among them, exercise sovereign power collectively. A state is an aristocracy when a minority collectively enjoy sovereign power and impose law on the rest' (pp. 51ff).

Bodin's second message is that sovereignty is perpetual; it remains vested in the commonwealth, and is in principle unaffected by the comings and goings of individual men. Individual rulers represent the commonwealth as a communal and historical organism, and are only given sovereignty in temporary trust (alone or in a group, according to rules specified by the type of commonwealth). These rulers 'cannot properly be regarded as sovereign rulers, but only as the lieutenants and agents of the sovereign ruler, till the moment comes when it pleases the prince or the people to revoke the gift' (p. 25).

Thirdly, sovereignty is absolute. It is unconditional and irrevocable; and it is the source of all power and authority inside the commonwealth. 'It is the distinguishing mark of the sovereign that he cannot in any way be subject to the commands of another, for it is he who makes law for the subject, abrogates law already made, and amends obsolete law' (p. 28). This does not mean that a sovereign ruler is entirely exempt from law.

Bodin identifies three limits to sovereign power: divine or natural law, regime type and covenants. First of all, princes are bound by divine or natural law. Although his authority is absolute in relation to other elements of the state, the source of his authority lies in a higher law and his power is limited by the requirements of justice as specified by this higher law. 'There is no prince in the world who can be regarded as sovereign, since all the princes on earth are subject to the laws of God and of nature', Bodin admonishes. 'All the princes of the earth are subject to them, and cannot contravene them without treason and rebellion against God. His yoke is upon them, and they must bow their heads in fear and reverence before His divine majesty. The absolute power of princes and sovereign lords does not extend to the laws of God and nature' (pp. 28f).

Several corollaries follow from this conception that sovereignty is not the personal property of the prince, but rather the incarnation of a principle which could not have a will at variance with the interests of the state. One corollary of great importance is that sovereignty is indivisible. This interpretation challenges the medieval theory of the *Ständestaat*, i.e. a state in which supreme authority was shared among the prince, an aristocracy and representatives of the people. There can be monarchies, aristocracies and democracies, argued Bodin, but never a stable mixed state. In this sense Bodin marks a rupture with medieval political theory.

A second limit is imposed upon sovereign power by what Bodin calls 'the constitutional laws of the realm'. Any lawful ruler is constrained by the type of commonwealth he rules – or, as Bodin phrases it at one point, 'the true sovereign is always seised of his power'. To clarify this point, Bodin defines several attributes of sovereignty, the principal of which is to make the laws of the realm. However, there are certain laws that even the most sovereign of princes can neither make nor unmake. Those are the laws that define the basic rules of operation of the regime type – 'the constitutional laws of the realm'. These laws are given by nature and 'cannot be infringed by the prince. Should he do so, his successor can always annul any act prejudicial to the traditional form of the monarchy, since on it is founded and sustained his very claim to sovereign majesty' (p. 31). An absolute prince, then, cannot transform his monarchy into an aristocracy or a democracy; such a transformation would be tantamount to revolution.

This argument captures a position which was emerging in north-western Europe at the time – most notably around the trade centres on both sides of the British Channel. In the 1560s it was advanced in the Spanish Netherlands, where the northernmost Dutch Provinces rebelled against Philip II of Spain. This argument foreshadows a position which would emerge fully-fledged in the English Civil War nearly a century later: that the monarch is bound by certain basic laws of the constitution of the land. Bodin's discussions on the limits of sovereign princes strongly foreshadow the principle of the constitutional monarchy.

Finally, princely powers are limited by covenants. 'A law and a covenant must not be confused;, Bodin writes. A law is a command made freely by a ruler in the exercise of his sovereign powers – which means that he can make or unmake them at will. A covenant is a mutual undertaking and is equally binding on all parties involved. Even the most absolute king is 'bound by the just covenants and the promises he has made'.

Bodin distinguishes between two types of covenants: on the one hand are those which a prince makes with his subjects. Such agreements are not laws, and a prince does not draw on his sovereign powers in entering into them; thus his covenants are no different from those of other private individuals. He is therefore obligated, like any other private individual, to honour the contracts, oaths and promises he has made. Also, like any other private person, a prince can be released from such covenants only under specific conditions – a commitment can be invalidated if, for example, it is deemed 'unjust or unreasonable, or beyond his competence to fulfil, or extracted from him by misrepresentations or fraud ...'. Bodin, then, sees no difference between the covenants entered into by the prince and his citizens and those which his citizens enter into among themselves. In either case, a covenant is a contract between rational, responsible, private individuals (p. 29).

On the other hand are covenants which a prince makes with other princes. These covenants Bodin calls 'treaties'. He argues that treaties are not 'of the same order as contracts and agreements between private citizens'. For when princes engage in covenants, they make them on behalf of their commonwealths, thus making them in the exercise of their sovereign powers. Since treaties are covenants made between sovereign actors, and no supreme authority exists above these actors, no legal agent can intervene to arbitrate in contests between them. The absence of any supreme authority above the commonwealth emerges from Bodin's discussion as the key characteristic of interstate relations.

The law which regulates the interactions of citizens within commonwealths does not apply to interaction between sovereign princes – on this broad principle Bodin agrees with Machiavelli: in relations between states the power of the sovereign prince is limited only by the power of other sovereign princes. However, Bodin's recognition that princely interaction is not limited by civil law does not mean that interstate relations are conducted in an environment of lawlessness. Rather, it drives Bodin into an argument of how imperative it is that the interaction of sovereign princes be guided by principles of rational and moral conduct. By merit of his acknowledgement of this restriction on state behaviour and in the effort to identify rational principles of interstate conduct, scholars have identified Bodin as a founder of modern international law.

Since interaction between sovereign states is not sanctioned by any supreme authority, there exists only two principles of order in interstate relations: force and faith. Bodin devotes the entire Chapter 5 of Book Five to the ordering effects of force, but his discussion covers little new ground. He draws on Machiavelli's *Art of War* and focuses on issues of order and revolution within states. On one occasion, however, Bodin saddles 'the most powerful of princes' with particular responsibilities for maintaining international order, for 'to him falls the honour of being judge and arbiter' (p. 177). Bodin's comments on international order fall short, however, of the modern notion of collective security. He writes that the sovereign has 'no promise more binding than the undertaking to defend the goals, the life, and the honour of the weak against the strong, the poor against the rich, or the innocent threatened by violence of wicked men' (p. 22). However, he nowhere suggests that peaceful sovereigns owe it to themselves to ally and contain warlike princes. Rather, if a powerful sovereign intervenes to stop quarrels between lesser princes, he does it for reasons of honour. According to Bodin, the primary moral obligation of princes lies not with interstate order but with the laws of nature and the divine principles of decency and justice.

It is the second principle of international order which Bodin makes his major focus: faith in justice. Non-violent, social interaction – among states as well as among individuals – can take place only on the basis of agreements. These will only be made if it is generally believed that they will be upheld once they are entered into. In civil society, systems of justice, sanctioned by the supreme authority of a sovereign power, exist to ensure that the sanctity of agreements is respected. In the interstate arena, however, sovereign princes interact with no supreme authority to arbitrate their conflicts; here agreements are made on the basis of faith alone: 'Since faith is the sole foundation and prop of that justice on which all commonwealths, alliances, and associations of men whatsoever is founded, it should be preserved sacred and inviolable in all cases where no injustice is contemplated' (p. 177).

Agreements between princes are the ultimate basis for interstate interaction, and it is essential that princes can rightly assume that such agreements will be kept once they are entered into. It is only short-sighted princes who make promises they have no intention of keeping, Bodin argues quite pragmatically. For by breaking his word, a ruler will undermine the faith others will have in him. If a sovereign prince is not sure that he can keep his promise, he should not give it (p. 178). Indeed, even when dealing with scoundrels and the enemies of faith, a wise prince should consider himself bound by his word (p. 180). Bodin's insistence that princes must keep all covenants they make is in international law referred to as the principle of *pacta sunt servanda*. It is Bodin's second major contribution to International Relations theory.

The argument which leads up to this principle deserves two brief comments. First, for Bodin a covenant is a an agreement entered into by rational, responsible, private individuals – he repeatedly uses the term 'contract' interchangeably with it. In his *Six Books on the Commonwealth*, Bodin formulates several arguments which would later be elaborated by the contract theorists of the

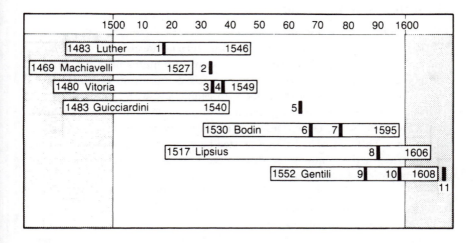

1. *95 Theses* [1517]
2. *The Prince* [1532]
3. *De Indis noviter inventis* [1532]
4. *De jure belli hispaniorum in barbaros* [153?]
5. *History of Italy* [1561]
6. *Method for the Easy Comprehension of History* [1566]
7. *Six Books on the Commonwealth* [1576]
8. *Politics* [1589]
9. *De legationibus* [1584]
10. *De jure belli libri tres* [1598]
11. *Hispanica advocatio* [1613]

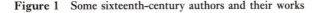

Figure 1 Some sixteenth-century authors and their works

seventeenth and eighteenth centuries – by Thomas Hobbes, John Locke and Adam Smith most famously. These elaborations still constitute the key building-blocks of the liberal political tradition. Bodin was not the only social philosopher to reason in terms of contract, so this was hardly an original contribution on his part.

Second, Bodin's account contains an early distinction between two levels of human interaction. On one level is the society among men; this is the level of the commonwealth. On another is the society of commonwealths. This vision contrasts sharply with the medieval notion that the international society, too, was a society among men. For Bodin, international interaction constitutes a society among sovereign states. His major insight is that, in spite of the constant threat of anomy, this interstate society, too, is governed by identifiable principles of order. The corollary of this insight is that if humanity can identify, strengthen and obey these principles, it can regulate interstate interaction and reduce, and perhaps abolish, war.

The sentiment of the century

The sixteenth century was an era of transition between the Middle Ages and Modern History. It saw the advent of more efficient means of production and new modes of exchange; it witnessed the rise of new means of destruction and new modes of political power. In this era a few countries on the Atlantic rim began to conquer the rest of the globe with capital and with arms.

On the one hand, the century began to tie large sections of the world together on a truly global scale. On the other, it began to divide the world in unprecedented ways. Differences had always existed between the militarily powerful and the powerless nations; now these differences were accentuated by new, European, gunpowder-based weapons systems. Similarly, differences had always existed between rich and poor regions; now these differences were exacerbated by the advent in Europe of new forms of agriculture, of manufactories, long-distance trade and systems of finance.

Also, in the sixteenth century the Catholic Church lost its exclusive domination over the mind of European peoples. The old division between Christians and pagans was replaced by a new division within Europe itself between Catholics and Protestants. Partly because of this new division, Europe turned away from its enduring preoccupation with the Muslim threat. Instead of unifying against the challenge of the infidel Turk, European princes turned against each other. From 1530 on, Europe plunged into a protracted era of internecine destruction intensified by colonial rivalries, religious doctrine, new weapons and new-found wealth. By 1600, the fever of wars had escaped the rational political control of kings and emperors. It degenerated into anarchy and self-perpetuating violence, which reached a climax of brutality and pointlessness in the Thirty Years War (1618–48).

Variations in sixteenth-century theorizing

The sixteenth century was marked by socio-economic change and violent conflict. It was also an age of political theorizing – an activity which both generated conflict and drew momentum from the warfare between competing universal truths. It was an age in which traditional truths were challenged and overthrown before new certainties could be established.

The essence of the century's mentality is hard to pin down. The sixteenth century does not have the clear themes that the fifteenth century had before it and that the seventeenth century would display after it. It was torn between medieval and modern concerns. By the middle of the century, two dimensions had appeared in political thought. One dimension was the conflict between the Catholic and the Protestant interpretation of the Christian heritage; the other was a conflict between a religious and a secular conception of social authority.

The religious dimension spanned the mental distance between the Catholic tradition of Augustine on the one hand and the new, Protestant opposition of Luther and Calvin on the other. The Protestant message appealed to the mercantile and manufacturing middle classes which were slowly emerging along the Atlantic rim. It flourished in countries where monarchs broke with Catholic doctrines. Between 1530 and 1560, kings in Scandinavia, England and Germany broke with the Catholic Church – many of them tempted by the possibility offered by conversion to seize the lands of the Church and include them in the royal household. The pope, fearing an unravelling of his authority, reacted to these defections by summoning a group of eminent churchmen to a Council in Trento to give the old Church a thorough facelift. As a result, the churches in Europe were filled with better music, brighter paintings, more opulent spectacles – in a word, with Baroque art. Also, the defections made the fanatic King Philip II of Spain (1556–98) take it upon himself to head a far-flung Catholic counteroffensive. But the religious reactions of the pope and Philip II produced little new theorizing about International Relations.

The secular dimension of sixteenth-century thought was fuelled by a greater belief in human rationality and by more insistent demands for privacy and individual freedom. The ever-increasing trend of secularization of thought is evident in the many major innovations which appeared in the age: gunpowder, compass, printing press. The printing press, most particularly, was an decisive disseminator of intellectual innovations: of new religious interpretations (Luther, Calvin), new versions of old classics (Plato, Aristotle, Ptolemy ...), new theories about the universe (Copernicus) and, not least, of the innumerable charts, calendars and handbooks which spread among European scholars and statesmen like wildfire.

The sixteenth century was the age of scientific awakening, and the growth of scientific thought was a strong secularizing force. In International Relations theory, the secularizing trend was reflected in the sudden embrace of the concept of a 'reason of state'. In Italy most particularly, a spate of texts on politics and diplomacy emerge. Girolamo Frachetta advertises by his very titles – *Il Principe*, *Discorsi di stato e di guerra*, and *Ragione di stato* – that he pursues the secular, humanist themes of Machiavelli and Guicciardini into the seventeenth century. And he is not alone. Scipione Ammirato, Ciro Spontone, Antonio Palazzo, Pietro Canonhiero, Ludovico Zuccoli, Federico Bonaventura, Gabriel Zinano, Lodovico Settala, Scipione Chiaramonti and others were all informed by the secular concepts of state power and state interests.[5] Even in doctrinaire Spain, the notion strikes root – when Don Quixote was convalescent, he passed the time discussing with the priest and barber 'that which is called the reason of state'.

The emergence of secular theorizing
The emphasis on rationality, individualism and freedom had long been prepared by the Renaissance humanists. Their emphasis on history and classic learning flowered in the fifteenth-century societies of the Italian city-states. However, by the early sixteenth century the Italian Renaissance was near collapse, shattered by the ruinous Italian Wars. At this time, the Italian Renaissance had made little impact on the rest of Europe. North and west of the alps, the vast majority of scholars still accepted medieval authorities as a matter of course. The conceptual context of the new monarchs and their primary advisers was still provided by the traditional teachings of the Church. But, with the advent of printing, the concerns of the Italian humanists spread to other regions of Europe, notably to the dynamic trading centres on the Atlantic coast which experienced an awakening of individualism and concern for privacy. The resulting preoccupation with individuality and the greater interest in the concepts of liberty and private property became evident in both religious and juridical treatises. Bodin, Luther and others argued that faith is essentially a private concern. Bodin insisted that the task of political philosophy is to strike the right balance between the realms of the public and the private (Chartier 1987). Luther argued that salvation could not be achieved through public rituals, but that each individual had to consult his own heart to determine if his acts were motivated by a pure faith in God.

The sixteenth century was not yet a secular age (Fébvre 1942; Bloch 1961). In Spain most particularly, religion still played a decisive role in intellectual life; here the Counter-reformation imposed a uniformity of thought which was fortified with the persuasive power of the Inquisition. In the German principalities and in the Northern Dutch Provinces the Reformation produced its own firebrand Protestant doctrines. All across Europe, in fact, social thinkers were still steeped in religious concerns. Yet during the course of the century religious debates were complicated by secular issues. Protestant demands for religious freedom, for example, were always attended by political considerations. In the Dutch Provinces, a campaign for freedom of religion soon broadened to include demands for individual rights more generally, and then to protests against Spanish taxation. In 1576, broad anti-Spanish sentiments prevailed over narrow religious demands when representatives from all 17 Dutch provinces formed a political union to liberate their territory from Spanish occupation. Religious demands had become political struggle.

At the same time, new elements of pragmatism and tolerance intruded upon the religious debates. After warfare had failed to restore the religious unity of the Christian world, scholars argued that religion alone could not be a just cause of war. Increasingly, princes agreed to disagree on the religious issue. As a result, a consensus of religious tolerance slowly emerged – as evinced in Bodin's propensity to prefer pragmatic solutions to political problems. Indeed, the new tolerance went so far that if excessive religious intensity constituted a major source of political problems at the beginning of the century, then excessive relativism was a cause of trouble towards its end. New knowledge about peoples and customs of the non-European world was collected by soldiers, traders and adventurers and disseminated through the new medium of print. Some information was of a high standard. Much of it was nonsense. Fantastic travellers' tales, mystical forecasts, religious scares and witchcraft panics swept across the West.

The late sixteenth century was an age of great diversity. The optimism and life-affirming attitudes of the Renaissance continued; but the age also witnessed the growth of pessimism and introvert reactions. Proud, conspicuous castles were built in this age; but so were sombre, hidden monasteries. *Carpe diem* ('seize the day') was a popular motto of the age; but so was *memento mori* ('remember you are mortal'). It was an age of intellectual uncertainty. And when new knowledge about the extra-European world arrived, it contributed to the chaotic relativism which rapidly emerged – a view that beliefs and customs vary with time and place and that there are no absolute standards for evaluating human values and conduct. This point of view is illustrated by the French essayist Montaigne, who wrote that one should not judge too harshly a tropical people's habit of eating human flesh. 'I find that there is nothing barbarous and savage in this nation, as far as I have been informed, except that everyone calls barbarian that which is not his own usage', writes Montaigne (1935, p. 18), with tongue only half in cheek.

By the seventeenth century, Europe stood at the brink of political and cultural exhaustion. It was by no means clear which way Europe was going to develop – it might conceivably have fallen into the same kind of chaos as India did at about this time. People were ready to grasp at any certain belief, and this readiness provided a fertile environment for visionaries and charlatans like Nostradamus, Paracelsus and innumerable others. However, this sorry state also provided the womb for modern science. With superstition went doubt. And when doubt was systematized – by thinkers like Bacon and Descartes – new critical methods of thought and knowledge offered promises of a new certitude which, in time, provided Europe with a new epistemological foundation and a new faith in itself. The roots of modern science lie in the confusion of the late sixteenth century. 'The rise of science in the seventeenth century possibly saved European civilization from petering out in a long post-medieval afterglow, or from wandering off into the diverse paths of a genial scepticism, intellectual philosophizing, desultory magic, or mad fear of the unknown' (Palmer 1951, p. 233).

4

Absolutist politics: the seventeenth century and the growth of the interstate system

The long sixteenth century saw the creation of the basic elements of modern international politics – territorial states, sovereign rulers, military structures and overseas ventures. It also witnessed the first stirrings of theoretical considerations about the nature, the operation and the implications of these new phenomena. The seventeenth century integrated these elements into a recognizable state system; it forged it on the anvil of the Thirty Years War (1618–48).

The Thirty Years War was the climax of an escalating religious conflict that had begun with the Reformation a century earlier. It erupted in Europe's middle regions, where it was at first fought by princes who hired military entrepreneurs to provide the Crown with soldiers and weapons. But the war rapidly evolved into a struggle between the entrepreneurs themselves. Soon they lost control. The armies they had created developed into vast, predatory formations which roamed the central parts of Europe in pursuit of the basic necessities of life. They swarmed into villages. They devoured the resources there and moved on like an enormous pack of starving wolves. The villages were left destitute behind. Many of the inhabitants chose to join the predatory pack, living parasitically off its wake. An army of 30,000 men could be followed by twice as many starving men, women and children who supplied a thievish tail to the soldiers' rougher plundering. Armies and camp-followers constituted gigantic, ambulatory slums 100,000 strong, their itineraries directed less by goals of war than by concerns for immediate survival.

The central regions of Europe were economically devastated and politically fragmented by this warfare. Here emerged a class of military adventurers, landless, homeless, pitiless, without religion or scruple, without knowledge of any trade but war and incapable of anything but destruction. Here emerged no centralizing state structures. By 1648, when the Peace of Westphalia was signed, these adventurers had worked up a vested interest in war. Many of the armies mutinied when they heard that a peace treaty was signed. Demobilization drew out for years, as leaderless armies roamed aimlessly across the central regions of Europe in search of food and loot. Many mercenaries were never integrated into civil society; they retained, as bandits, pimps or professional assassins, the parasitic character they had acquired during the long years of warfare.

North-western Europe, by contrast, consolidated its state structures. Historians have often asked why these state structures evolved so rapidly during the seventeenth century. Some find the answer in the Reformation. Distinctly modern state structures evolved in England and Sweden, where monarchs had rejected Catholicism, confiscated Church lands, seized large landed properties, and gained unprecedented economic influence. This argument hardly provides the whole answer. For the evolution of a strong state was particularly marked in France, which remained a staunchly Catholic country and where no confiscation of Church lands occurred.

Other authors propose that the evolution of strong states was a function of the increased power of monarchs, Protestant as well as Catholic. In the late sixteenth and early seventeenth centuries, the kings of Europe became commanders-in-chief of their countries' armed forces. This put them in a position to expand their power over their civil societies. Although this explanation may be closer to the mark, it cannot account for the evolution of state structures in the United Provinces, which were not a monarchy at all, but a rather loose confederation of states.

There is one feature which the United Provinces, France, England and Sweden had in common, and which helps explain the seventeenth-century evolution of their state institutions: they all participated in the Thirty Years War, but only intermittently. They all unified their territories and enhanced the political power of their central institutions in the shadow of war, but without bearing its terrible cost in full.

Troops, tolerance, taxes and the Thirty Years War

During the religious wars, an old division grew increasingly visible in Europe between a western and an eastern half – between a 'Latin' and an 'Orthodox' civilization (Szücs 1990; Geiss 1993). A rough dividing line can be drawn from the Baltic in the north, down along the Elbe river and the Bohemian mountains to the head of the Adriatic Sea. This line divided Europe's trade-oriented western seaboard from its agricultural eastern regions.

A second line can be added: a wavy east-west line drawn from Brussels via Stuttgart and Prague to Warsaw. This second line roughly divides the Protestant northern half from the Catholic southern half of Europe. It crosses the first line in the heart of the Holy Roman Empire, and the intersection coincides closely with the major battlefields of the Thirty Years War. When the war ended in 1648 with the Treaty of Westphalia, territorial states had emerged both in the east and the west. The unruly central regions of the Continent, by contrast, emerged hopelessly fragmented.

Territorial states in a dividing Europe
The Treaty of Westphalia gave sovereignty to the small states in the heart of Europe. Thus it rendered the Holy Roman Emperor politically impotent. According to the Treaty, the Emperor could no longer recruit soldiers, make laws, levy taxes, declare war or ratify peace terms without the consent of representatives from all the states. Since such consent was a practical impossibility, the central region of Europe remained fragmented – for over 200 years it remained a vast, unruly territory which separated the large, trade-oriented, progressive states of western Europe from the agricultural, reactionary states of the eastern interior.

The countries situated to the east of the fragmented middle were largely landlocked. Only a few countries possessed merchant fleets and navies. They participated marginally in long-distance trade, and no significant mercantile class emerged to match the wealth, to challenge the power and to threaten the entrenched social position of the landed aristocracy.

The countries to the west developed differently. Along the Atlantic coast of Europe, political and religious authority also gathered in the hands of the monarch and his court of ministers and advisers. But this development occurred within a unique political setting. Its characteristic features, the most important of which were the representative assemblies, provided the predispositions for participatory institutions – market institutions as well as democratic structures.

The monarchs of western Europe drew two lessons from the Thirty Years War. First, they agreed that the religious conflicts which had fomented a century of rivalries and destruction had to be stopped. So when the war was brought to an end (1648), the monarchs agreed to disagree on the issue of whether Catholicism or Protestantism was the one true Doctrine. They agreed to give the individual king the authority to choose a version of Christianity and impose it upon his country. This agreement (referred to in the peace treaty as *cuius regio eius religio*) meant that the monarchs of Europe should respect each other's choice of religion. It also meant that the king was the supreme religious authority in his own country; that the king (and not the Church) was granted spiritual authority over the inhabitants of his kingdom, and no outside actor had the right to challenge this authority within his realm. This agreement confirmed that *territory* was the key requirement for participation in modern international politics. It consolidated the concept of the territorial state, which thus gained common acceptance in Europe. But it also undermined the influence of rulers who had wielded great political power in the past by virtue of a transcendent principle of authority – a religious or a philosophical belief. The powers of the pope and the emperor, then, were drastically reduced by the agreement which was expressed in the Treaty of Westphalia.

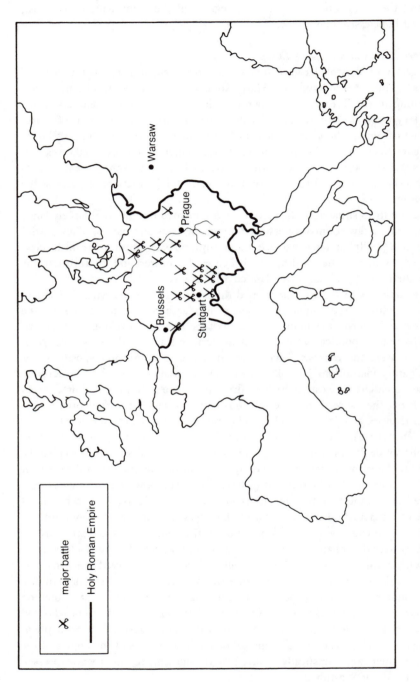

Map 4 The Holy Roman Empire and the major battles of the Thirty Years War (1618–48)

major battle

Holy Roman Empire

Warsaw

Prague

Brussels

Stuttgart

A second lesson which the European kings drew from the Thirty Years War was that hired troops were dangerous. After Westphalia, the kings strove to establish their own, *national* armies. They reserved for themselves the role of commanders-in-chief. Emulating the New Model Armies of Sweden and the United Provinces, officers and men were paid, clothed and equipped by the Crown and commanded by the king or his trusted lieutenants. New military institutions and ancillary services emerged all across the Continent as part of the evolution of modern state structures. Military treasuries, camps, hospitals, and judicial and secretarial institutions proliferated, as did quartermaster and victualling arrangements (Parker 1978). The soldiers' days were increasingly organized by physical training – by ceaseless drill, by marching and by exercises in siegecraft.

This introduction of permanent forces required new military infrastructures to accommodate the men and to produce, store and maintain their military *matériel*. Barracks, depots, payment plans and administrators were developed by all states of Europe. The pioneer was France, where le Tellier and de Louvois created a civil bureaucracy to administer the new forces. This system was, in turn, copied by other European states.

This build-up of such new institutions solved the problems which the military entrepreneurs represented. But it was an extraordinarily expensive process (Finer 1975), and raised urgent new questions of state finances. How should the new forces and institutions be paid for? Kings and royal councillors provided two answers: revenues should be raised by two separate methods: taxation and colonialism.

Different monarchs handled their financial problems in different ways. Their choices of financial strategies depended on the physical size of the nation, its resource base, and the historical experiences of its people. Also, it depended on geographic position: countries along the Atlantic seaboard had the opportunity to increase their national wealth through colonial exploits; land-locked countries in eastern Europe were forced to raise money through other means – through taxation, but also through the conquest of neighbouring territories. The different ways in which the countries of Europe raised new revenues reflected and reinforced a growing division of Europe between an Atlantic and a Continental region.

The necessity for the European kings to cover military costs stimulated the development of more efficient structures and routines of national finance. Finance involves payment services. Financial systems mobilize money, allocate credit and limit, price, pool and trade the risks. In the seventeenth century, the large-scale handling of money and credit was complicated by soaring military costs which weighed down national budgets. Taxes constituted the basic financial resource of the seventeenth-century state (Ardant 1975, p. 165). All over Europe, the fiscal screws were tightened. The monarchs increased old taxes and invented new ones. They also intervened heavily in civil society to stimulate economic development in order to tax it.

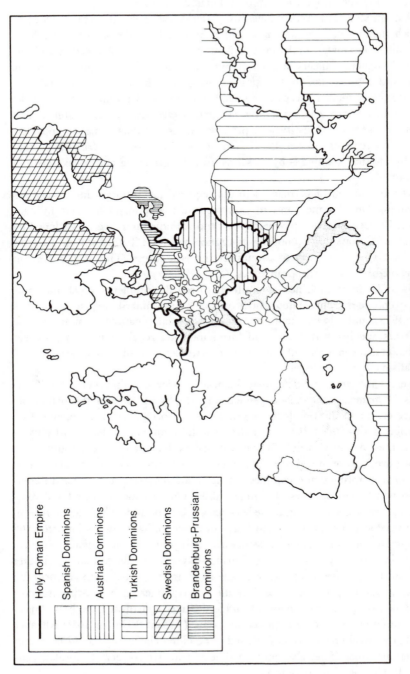

Map 5   Europe in 1648

Holy Roman Empire

Spanish Dominions

Austrian Dominions

Turkish Dominions

Swedish Dominions

Brandenburg-Prussian
Dominions

After the Thirty Years War, Europe was dominated by six nations: Austria, Russia, Prussia, England, France and the United Provinces. The eastern region was dominated by Austria, Russia and Prussia. All three states grew rapidly after 1648, conquering the territories of their immediate neighbours – overrunning the decaying Holy Roman Empire, the Ottoman Empire and the Kingdom of Poland – until their borders met. These areas east of the fragmented Germanies saw little of the commercial revolution and the market expansion which occurred along Europe's Atlantic seaboard. In contrast to the west, where the seventeenth century saw the emergence of a wealthy bourgeoisie and a free mobile labour force, eastern Europe experienced a 'manorial reaction' and a 'refeudalization' of society. After the Thirty Years War the entire region slid back into conditions reminiscent of medieval Europe. The chief socio-economic unit in the east remained the agricultural estate, run by an omnipotent landlord with uncompensated compulsory labour furnished by tenants and serfs. The landlords constituted the only significant political class. They concentrated their military energies on the armies, dominated by noble officers. They developed no significant navies; they took no part in the race for overseas possessions, and developed few mercantile interests (Anderson 1988, pp. 46ff).

The western regions of Europe were dominated by England, France and the United Provinces. Here private enterprise was encouraged by new commercial laws, subsidies and tax exemptions. In England and France, privileges were introduced to expand manufacture. Massive state projects were implemented to improve the roads and canals of the nations. Both countries encouraged the export of domestic manufactures to maximize import earning; both levied heavy taxes on imported goods to discourage money from leaving the country. They established chartered companies, stressed the need for new colonies and built up their navies.

The rise of the Western world
The western nations' new emphasis on naval forces markedly affected their socio-economic structures. The building of ships took time – several years for a good man-of-war. It also required an infrastructure of dockyards, shipwrights, pilots and cartographers. The building of naval forces accentuated the financial problems of the age. However, the creation of a permanent navy also promised a solution: the king could enhance his revenues by supporting ventures of colonialism and long-distance trade. The most important example of state encouragement of private enterprise in order to increase its own revenues was the chartered company. The Crown would issue a charter which included a private company in the realm of royal sovereignty. This would ensure the company a monopoly on a specific trade in a specific area; furthermore, it would enable it to negotiate with foreign rulers, purchase arms, raise armies and fleets, establish garrisons abroad and even declare war and peace.

The first chartered companies had been formed by the Dutch in the second half of the sixteenth century. In the early decades of the seventeenth, England and France followed suit. The English East India Company was created in 1600, the Virginia Company in 1606, the English Amazon Company in 1619–23, and the Massachusetts Bay Company in 1629. Still later, in 1660, came the Royal Adventurers, who pioneered trade in Africa and were replaced a dozen years later by the more tightly organized Royal African Company. The French were not far behind. The powerful ministers Richelieu (1585–1642) and Colbert (1619–83), both of whom effected an unprecedented centralization and concentration of the political and economic power in the person of the king, applied mercantilist measures to increase the wealth of France and make the country a self-sufficing economic unit (Cole 1939).

The mercantilist measures were economic means designed to serve military ends. They added economic power to the religious and the military authorities of the monarchs, strengthened the state structures of western Europe, and blurred the distinctions between trade and war, economics and politics. In eastern Europe, by contrast, societies increasingly exported raw materials and imported west-European consumer goods – foreshadowing the imperialist dependencies (and the anti-imperialist theorizing) of the nineteenth and twentieth centuries.

To put it boldly: along the Atlantic rim, the absolutist state marked a *break* with the feudal order. It emerged in the wake of a disintegrating feudal order; it was 'a compensation for the disappearance of serfdom in the context of an increasingly urban economy' which the political apparatus did not completely control and to which it had to adapt. In the eastern regions of the continent, by contrast, the absolutist state was the repressive *continuation* of the feudal order. It was 'a device for the consolidation of serfdom, in a landscape scoured by autonomous urban life or resistance' (Anderson 1979, p. 195).[1]

The territorial state

The changes which occurred during the religious struggles of the early seventeenth century were expressed in the recognizably modern features of the territorial state. First, the state became defined in territorial terms, occupying a specific area of the earth's surface and surrounding itself with an inviolate boundary.

Second, this territory was governed by a set of institutions loyal to the monarch and staffed with professional bureaucrats, divided into subservient and increasingly specialized departments. These departments, at first devoted to the maintenance of military and fiscal functions, increasingly assisted the monarch in making rational policy decisions, and in implementing and enforcing the decisions made.

Third, the territory contained a population whose identity was partly a product of its monarchs' century-long efforts to inculcate a shared set of myths and symbols of nationhood.

Finally, the state was infused with a new notion of sovereignty. A clarification of the nature of this new notion was made by the mathematician, hobby-states-man and versatile genius Gottfried Wilhelm Leibniz (1646–1716). In his *Caesarinus fürstenerius* of 1677 Leibniz tries to prove that his employer (the Duke of Hanover) has a right of legation, and in the process he develops a new notion of sovereignty. At the outset he defines the Duke's primary problem: the Treaty of Westphalia conferred sovereignty upon all those German rulers who had formerly been included in the Holy Roman Empire; however, it had not abolished the traditional, essentially feudal, structure of the Empire itself. Local German rulers were therefore still enmeshed in old webs of traditional duties, allegiances and jurisdictions. In which sense, Leibniz asked, could the many German princes be said to be sovereign?

Instead of answering the question in legal terms, Leibniz first defines the concept of 'sovereignty' in terms of 'what actually happens in the world today' (1963, p. 340). In his mind, the first condition for sovereignty is a minimum size of territory (pp. 304ff). The smallest principalities – quite abundant at the time as Germany was divided into well over 300 states – could not claim to be treated as equals of the largest in respect of war, alliances and the general affairs of Europe. Smaller territories, not possessing sufficient territory, could 'at best, with their garrisons, only maintain *internal* order'.

A second condition for sovereignty, Leibniz continues, is 'majesty' (pp. 307ff). By this he means the authority that enables a ruler to demand obedience from his people. Majesty is not the same as sovereignty. Majesty involves normative and moral authority, whereas sovereignty means the 'actual and present power to constrain' subjects on their own territories.

In this lies Leibniz' third criterion for sovereignty: the actual control of one's territory by virtue of one's military power (pp. 304ff). Bodin addressed the internal aspects of sovereignty; Leibniz placed these internal aspects into a larger, practical, interstate context. He argues that among the many nominally sovereign princes of the former Empire, only those princes are sovereign who *actually* possess the ability to constrain their subjects without in turn being constrained by a superior power. The decisive criterion thus is actual control of one's 'estates' by one's military power, which excludes any other power within and without. Among the over 300 princes who claimed sovereignty in Germany, Leibniz counted as truly sovereign only those who had the ability to render their territories impermeable to foreign influence. As for the Holy Roman Emperor, whose sovereignty had been vastly reduced by the Treaty of Westphalia, he could enforce his authority or rights only by applying military force (p. 313). The Treaty of Westphalia had made him no different from any other sovereign.

From the notion of impermeability emerges a concept of external sovereignty. With its implicit recognition of this concept, the Treaty of Westphalia laid the legal basis for the modern territorial state. Upon its foundation was erected a new system of international interaction and a new system of concepts and theories by which this interaction could be understood. The Treaty's recognition of the principle of external sovereignty represents the formal recognition and the legal consolidation of the modern interstate system: i.e., a system of political interaction between legally equal territorial states, whose monarchs exercise their authority (their 'internal sovereignty') within well-defined, geographical frontiers, their inhabitants subject to no higher authority. The Treaty of Westphalia marks a decisive shift from a view of international law *above* the states to a law *among* states; the vision of international law as divine in inspiration was replaced by the argument that international law is a codified set of customs or conventions – rules of conduct created and prescribed by the states themselves for the purpose of facilitating interstate interaction.

Absolutism

The two key concerns of seventeenth-century international politics were 'order' and 'wealth'. They were embodied in the twin terms 'absolutism' and 'mercantilism'. The two must be seen as political and economic aspects of the rapid development of the state and of the interstate relations of the age.

The term 'absolutism' entered the language of politics (in French) during the decade after the revolution in 1789. The phenomenon to which the term refers was, of course, much older. During the fourteenth and fifteenth centuries, monarchic power was developing toward monopoly. During the long sixteenth century, kings indulged themselves in international politics. They used marriages and military manoeuvres as their primary diplomatic tools – and kept the Continent in a fever of wars and their courts permanently short of monies. The central idea of absolutism is that the justice and power of a state should be monopolized by the monarch – the reason most typically given is theological: the king is said to possess a divine right to make political dispositions. Jean Bodin foreshadowed this argument. But the first explicit doctrine of the divine right of kings may have been formulated by Pierre de Belloy (1540–1612) who argued, in his *De l'autorité du roi* of 1588, that the monarch was instituted by God and responsible to God alone.

The most famous argument for absolutism may have been formulated by Robert Filmer (1588–1653). In *Patriarcha* (1991 [1637?])[2] Filmer begins his argument by insisting that human society originated with Adam. Kings rule by divine right because God granted all social power to Adam, his direct ancestor. Adam then passed it on to his many decendants through the history of mankind, Filmer continues. This argument has several implications. It implies, first, that mankind constitutes one large family which descends from one single male individual. Since God had fashioned Eve out of Adam's rib and explicitly subjected her to Adam, woman is always inferior to man. And since God created Adam first, and gave him authority over all men who came after him, all men were born subjects to their fathers and inferior to their elders – men were, in a word, born unfree and unequal, and first-born sons were superior to younger brothers.

Filmer's argument also implies that no society ever began with free and equal individuals! Because God had given Adam possession of the whole world and because Adam's oldest son was subject to his father's will, Adam's son enjoyed only as much property as Adam had voluntarily given him. And after Adam's death, his son inherited all his father's property and all his authority and power. After the death of Adam's son, Adam's property and authority was in turn inherited by a line of first-born sons down to Noah. With Noah, the process of patriarchal inheritance changed. Noah, whose family was all that was left of the human race after the flood, made a momentous political decision: instead of keeping to himself the governance of the whole world, he divided it up into four parts. His three sons, Shem, Ham and Japheth, each received a part; and for himself, Noah retained that territory which was to belong to the Chosen People. In Filmer's opinion, then, Noah founded the states of the world.[3] And after Noah the authority of father and political patriarch was inherited by a direct line of succeeding first-born sons. With this argument, Filmer provided a theoretical basis for the principle of primogeniture. According to this principle, the heads of the seventeenth-century states of Europe all derived their kingdom, their power and their political authority from their succession to one or other 'of the sons or nephews of Noah' (Filmer 1991, p. 7).

Filmer's argument was not unique. The idea that the justice and power of a state should be monopolized by the monarch was also justified by the English monarchs James I (1603–25) and Charles I (1625–49) – like Filmer, both of them anchored their claims in the Bible and argued that they were personally chosen by God to govern their people. A most influential expositor of absolutist theory was the French bishop Jacques-Bénigne Bossuet (1627–1704). Like Filmer in England, Bossuet in France formulated an argument for the Divine Right of Kings, hinging it on the proposition that the monarch is chosen by God and responsible to Him alone; kings were God's viceregents in political affairs on earth. But Bossuet was more explicit on one important point: Divine Right may give the king absolute authority in political affairs, but it does not give him the right to arbitrary rule. Bossuet was careful to explain that as citizens are bound by the rules defined by their king, so the king is bound by the rules defined by God. Royal rule must be reasonable and just, like the will of God which it reflects. Thus, a king is sovereign so long as he conforms to the will of God. With this argument – which carries strong echoes of Jean Bodin – Bossuet distinguished sharply between absolutism and arbitrariness (1824, pp. 103–267).

Mercantilism

The central idea of mercantilism is that economic activities should be subordinate to the goal of state-building and the interests of the state. It is largely a theory of statecraft, and must be understood against the background of rivalry of the great powers of seventeenth-century Europe: the United Provinces, England and France. The decisive developments of the age were England's success-ful challenge of the strongest commercial power of the age in Europe, the United Provinces. The rise of mercantilist thought parallels the rise of England as a global power and a world empire.

The 'balance of trade' is a key notion of mercantilism. This idea reverberates through the writings of Walter Raleigh (1554–1618) and John Selden (1584–1641). It is no coincidence that one of the earliest expositors of this notion was Francis Bacon (1561–1626), an early formulator of England's balance-of-power policy. For Bacon, wealth and military capabilities were mutually rein-forcing dimensions of national power – there is, as he put it an unbroken chain 'from shipping to Indies, from Indies to treasure, and from treasure to great-ness' (Bacon, 1852, p. 201). According to Bacon, a favourable balance of trade should be an important foreign-policy goal. This goal can be achieved by estab-lishing colonies that will export raw materials (particularly precious metals) to the mother country and buy products from her.

One of the most popular mercantile arguments was presented by Thomas Mun (1571–1641). His main work, *England's Treasure by Forraign Trade, or the Ballance of our Forraign Trade is the Rule of our Treasure*, was published posthu-mously in 1664. It was very influential and went into several editions. Mun asso-ciated the balance of trade with the 'balance of greatness'. The association between the balance and power and the balance of wealth became obvious during the Protectorate: the military republic of Oliver Cromwell devised the Naviga-tion Act (1651) with the explicit purpose of protecting English shipping from foreign competition.

Underlying the mercantilist thought of Bacon, Selden, Mun and others was the notion that wealth could be translated into naval power, and naval power would protect trade, which would engender more wealth, which, in turn, would strengthen the nation's naval power ... and so on in a beneficial cycle (Heckscher 1935).

Anarchy, reason, contract and order

Absolutism and mercantilism both addressed the issues of human co-operation, wealth and order. The theme of 'order' was a key concern for the trading nations which had experienced first-hand the destructive effects of the Thirty Years War. International Relations theory in the mid-seventeenth century was domi-nated by a quest for a set of regulatory principles which could impose order upon a chaos of competing and self-contained states.

The problem of order was first discussed at the level of individual men rather than the level of states. The discussions began with the Reformation and with the interest it created in the relationship between God, human reason and relig-ious freedom. Several sixteenth-century thinkers agreed that religion is a private concern; that in matters of faith, individuals should be granted freedom of conscience. During the religious wars, social thinkers began to investigate conflicts and war in the light of human reason and individual freedom. During the Thirty Years War, many of them argued that individual freedom was gained at the cost of social order. They speculated that if all were perfectly free, then interaction would produce the most chaotic and violent condition imaginable.

In a 'state of nature' where man is endowed with total freedom, man will have a right to everything – 'men live without a common power to keep them all in awe, they are in that condition which is called warre; and such a warre, as is of every man, against every man', wrote Thomas Hobbes in 1651. In the state of nature, he continued, 'the life of man [is] solitary, poore, nasty, brutish and short' (1951, pp. 185f). Benedict de Spinoza agreed. In a sketch which he wrote in 1670, Spinoza explains that in the state of nature neither reason nor morality can exist; thus, each man 'looks to his own interest, according to his own view and acts at his own advantage, and endeavors to preserve that which he loves and to destroy that which he hates' (Spinoza 1951b, p. 211).

This image of the lawless state of nature became a central concept in seventeenth-century political thought. It drove many thinkers to conclude that the state is necessary to maintain social order. In the state of nature, most authors agreed, man is driven by passion and by egotism. However, since man possesses the faculty of *reason*, he will sooner or later realize that his individual interests are better served by order than by chaos. Therefore he will band together with his fellow men and form institutions which can impose order upon human interaction. This logic developed into two different arguments. On the one extreme were authors like Hobbes and Spinoza, who, intrigued by the apparent paradox of the logic, concluded that man can exercise true reason and true freedom only within the confines of the state. Spinoza, for example, maintained that 'man, who is guided by reason, is more free in a State, where he lives under a general system of law, than in solitude, where he is independent' (1951b, p. 235). This argument rapidly evolved into a secular justification for absolutism.

On the other extreme were authors like John Amos Comenius and Émeric Crucé. Comenius (1592–1670) stressed the importance of education. In a brief proposal entitled *The Angel of Peace* [1628?], he claimed that, in order to make a peaceful Europe, it was essential to introduce children to rational thought and expose them to a common European culture steeped in Christian values. Crucé entertained similar ideas. If man is only granted fuller freedom by his rulers, Crucé writes, he will, guided by reason and by Christian values of 'devotion, sweetness and charity', create a new Europe. Here men could go here and there freely, and mix together without any hindrance of country, ceremonies, or other such like differences as if the earth were, as it really is, a city common to all (Crucé 1972, p. 36).

Émeric Crucé (1590–1648)
Crucé recognizes that Christianity had been used by princes for political pur-

poses. In *The New Cyneas* (1972 [1623]),[4] he writes that the many wars in his age 'are undertaken either for honour or profit, or for the reparation of some wrong, or else from exercise. One could add religion if experience had not made known that this serves most often as a pretext' (Crucé 1972, p. 8). This idea expresses a key lesson of the Thirty Years War.

Crucé also articulates another lesson: that soldiers are necessary in times of war, but that they constitute a dangerous problem in times of peace. He sees soldiers, thieves and savages as the three primary obstacles to the establishment of a new, unified Europe. It is, however, quite possible that, if they were shunned by society, 'even they would think of their own conscience'. Crucé's reasoning foreshadows an important point in social-contract theory:

If they should prefer to continue to live in their own savage fashion, they would not be sufficiently strong to resist so many people who are bound closely by common consent. These good people would descend upon them, hem them in, attack, and kill them like miserable beasts in their lair. War will always be a just measure against them if they cannot be brought to reason (p. 29).

In the interest of social order, wise princes should assist these poor people, and help them find new employment. Soldiers are dangerous because they possess ambition and means of violence, and therefore represent a threat both to the power of their prince and to the general order of society. In order both to secure his own position and to maintain social order, a wise ruler would give his soldiers something to do 'with honour without murder'. Some soldiers could be employed by a police force, or a constabulary, he suggests; others should be encouraged to go into trades which contribute to the wealth and well-being of society, such as agriculture or business (pp. 25f).

About one-third of the way into *The New Cyneas*, the argument changes pace as the author changes topic from conflict and order within states to war and peace among states. Crucé argues that men are rational and equal, and that they understand very well how their interests are better served by trade and co-operation than by war and conflict. He dreams of a new Europe in which men travel freely from one country to the next, for there are, he insists, no major differences between men of different countries. 'Why should I, a Frenchman, wish to harm an Englishman, a Spaniard, or an Indian?' he asks. 'I cannot when I consider that they are men like I am, and that, just as they, I am subject to error and sin, and that all nations are joined by a natural and therefore insoluble bond' (p. 36).

Crucé acknowledges that Europe is divided between a number of sovereign states. He is pragmatic enough to avoid any proposal to dismantle them. However, he does suggest that these sovereign states join together as members of a world organization. He proposes that some neutral, centrally located city be selected as the headquarters of a 'general assembly' to which all the states of Europe should send ambassadors. When differences arise between the states, the ambassadors would assemble and pass judgement after hearing the arguments of the representatives of the contending nations. Crucé's fame rests upon this proposal, for in it subsequent scholars have seen no less than a blueprint for a League of Nations.[5]

Crucé's argument deserves attention for another reason as well: his is the first elaborate peace proposal which assumes that merchants have a vested interest in peace. For Crucé, the basic unit of analysis is the individual man rather than the state; it is the citizen rather than the prince. He claims that interaction between enlightened economic actors leads to interdependent interaction and to peace. Crucé foreshadows nineteenth- and twentieth-century idealism when he awards the merchants and the manufacturers important roles in preserving interstate order. No occupations can compare with these in social utility, Crucé argues. The merchant 'nourishes a state' and the manufacturer 'enriches it'. And if princes saw to it that their subjects were employed in trade and production, they would never again seek amusement in war.

Benedict (Baruch) de Spinoza (1632–77)

Spinoza's argument relies on some of the same axioms as Crucé, but arrives at different conclusions about war and peace in seventeenth-century Europe. Spinoza's discussions are abstract. Unlike Crucé, he selects the territorial state as his unit of international analysis. His discussion is complex, yet stunningly streamlined; it is a vast deductive edifice in which the state has its distinct place in a larger metaphysical system.

It may be unfair to select another entry into Spinoza's system than his own theological axioms. But, in the interest of brevity, Spinoza's discussion of human nature provides a convenient short cut to his political observations. Human beings, Spinoza asserts, are always torn between reason and passion; and the greater their freedom, the more passion dominates. In the state of nature, passion is near-indomitable. Spinoza uses the Latin term *conatus* to describe human passion as a vital, self-protective, self-aggrandizing *élan*. Through *conatus* people seek to avoid injury, resist threats of injury and, if injured, restore themselves out of an inherent principle of self-recovery – unless the injury is so serious as to destroy this *élan* altogether (Scruton 1986, pp. 59f). In the state of nature, people's actions are dominated by *conatus*; by their constant efforts to protect their lives and their belongings.

Reason exists in the state of nature, but in the service of *conatus*. It does not engender any collective agreement as to criteria for right or wrong, good or bad. In the state of nature there is no moral consensus, no politics and no law for people to obey. In the state of nature, every human individual is sovereign. They can do precisely as they please, for 'by sovereign natural right every man judges what is good and what is bad' (Spinoza 1951b, p. 211). In this state of total freedom, the only thing that can stop people in a state of nature from taking from another what they want to satisfy their pleasures is the knowledge that the other is stronger. Only the certainty that their actions will be rewarded by injury and pain will persuade them to refrain from fulfilling their desires.

At some point, Spinoza argues, humans will discover that their existence is better preserved and their pleasures best pursued by co-operation with other people. At that point, people will enter into social agreements. They will pass from the contending disorder of the state of nature to civil society. They will create a 'commonwealth' which is built on mutual assistance and designed to enhance humanity's self-preservation and improve its wealth and pleasures (pp. 201f). In the act of creating the commonwealth, they also make themselves citizens and subjects – 'Citizens, as far as they enjoy by the civil law all the advantages of the Commonwealth, and Subjects, as far as they are bound to obey its ordinances or laws' (Spinoza 1951c, p. 301).

Spinoza's political philosophy is guided by two major insights. First, that the creation of the commonwealth does not alter human nature. In civil society, the end of every human act is the self-preservation of the actor. 'The natural right of every man does not cease in the civil state. For man, alike in the natural and in the civil state, acts according to the laws of his own nature and consults his own interest' (p. 302). The commonwealth does, however, alter people's behaviour, because it constrains by law the means through which they are allowed to pursue their pleasures. It forces people to seek their interest within the law. The law represents reason: it is an elaboration made by enlightened, self-interested humans who seek to preserve social order. It forces the multitudes, whose reason is assumed to remain comparatively undeveloped, to behave according to reason. Thus, the law made by the few becomes a substitute for the imperfect reason of the many.

Second, Spinoza recognizes that the commonwealth does not solve the problem of order. It solves the problem on the level of sovereign individuals; however, it recreates a state of nature in the lawless interaction among sovereign states. Two commonwealths, Spinoza writes, 'stand towards each other in the same relation as do two men in the state of nature'. All commonwealths are sovereign, and have the right to act precisely as they will. This state of nature among commonwealths is exacerbated by the internal order and the division of tasks of the commonwealths. People in the state of nature must divide their attentions between many tasks to keep themselves alive; at times they will be overcome 'by sleep, by disease or mental instability, and in the end by old age'. A commonwealth, by contrast, is a timeless organism where a social division of tasks makes some people soldiers and others providers of food and arms. People who are tired and hungry are relieved by those who are rested and fed; those who are old and tired are replaced by those who are young and eager.

Unlike the individual person, the state is constantly alert. Whereas individuals compete intermittently in the state of nature, states struggle ceaselessly. Whereas war erupts as soon as one state wills it, peace occurs only when several states agree that it is to their mutual advantage – and then, is it unlikely to last:

This 'contract' remains so long unmoved as the motive for entering into it, that is fear of hurt or hope of gain, subsists. But take away from either commonwealth this hope or fear, and it is left independent, and the link, whereby the commonwealths were mutually bound, breaks itself. And therefore every commonwealth has the right to break its contract, whenever it chooses, and cannot be said to act treacherously or perfidiously in breaking its word, as soon as the motive of hope or fear is removed (Spinoza 1951c, p. 307).

Hugo Grotius (1583–1645)

Between the extreme positions of Spinoza and Crucé existed more moderate arguments. The most influential of these was formulated by Hugo Grotius. According to Spinoza, the states of Europe have guarded their sovereign rights jealously, and history has shown no progress towards a civil society of states. Politics among states has always been, and given the limits of human reason is likely to remain, power politics. Grotius shared Spinoza's bleak view of contemporary affairs. In his major work *De jure belli ac pacis* ('On the Law of War and Peace', 1853 [1625]), Grotius observes that the glamour which had attended interstate relations a hundred years earlier had disappeared with the fragmentation of Christendom. In his own time, Grotius observed 'a licence in making war of which even barbarous nations would have been ashamed; recourse was had to arms for slight reasons, or for no reason; and when arms were once taken up, all reverence for divine and human law was thrown away' (Grotius 1853, I, p. lix).

Grotius shared some of Crucé's optimism about the rational and pragmatic nature of international interaction. On the very first pages of the 'Prolegomena' to his *De jure belli ac pacis*, Grotius criticizes the power-focused, state-centred view of politics. He acknowledges that the human is a creature that, like other animals, is impelled by nature to seek its own gratification. But he immediately notes that man is an animal of a quite peculiar kind: man has a unique desire for society – 'that is, a desire for a life spent in common with fellow men, and not merely spent somehow, but spent tranquilly and in a manner corresponding to the character of his intellect'. Then Grotius adds that humans are equipped with language and reason, and that this gives them 'a faculty of knowing and acting according to general principles; and such tendencies as agree with this faculty do not belong to all animals, but are peculiar attributes of human nature'. These peculiar attributes, in turn, drive humans to devise general principles which will guarantee peaceful interaction among sovereign states and thus serve people's desire for a human society. Such general principles will benefit all the actors involved. And as soon as the rulers of Europe realize this, they will begin to devise rules and legal institutions to arbitrate in their conflicts.

De jure belli ac pacis was Grotius' own effort to construct a set of principles and rules designed to regulate international interaction. It helped establish International Law as an independent branch of learning. Although Grotius had several precursors, none of them had considered the subject of international law in its entirety. Some of them, such as Vitoria, had studied the law of war. Others, like Bodin and Leibniz, had investigated the concept of state sovereignty. Still others, like Gentili, pursued the rules of diplomatic interaction. Grotius' main accomplishment was to bring together already existing *disjecta membra* into one masterful synthesis, and to breathe life into it. This constituted a gigantic contribution to the study of International Relations.

Grotius expressed the interests of the United Provinces, the pre-eminent trading nation of his day. His first work, *De jure praedae* ('The Law of Prize and Booty' of 1609),[6] set out his famous doctrine of *mare liberum*: the claim that the open seas are free to all. Grotius' argument is clad in the quasi-religious discourse of the age. It begins with theological claims that God had created all nations different, and that He had provided no nation with all the necessities of life, but distributed the world's bounty unevenly, so that humanity would be forced to trade and exchange. However, the continuation of the argument is pragmatic. It hinges on an appeal to natural law, which Grotius considered to be a product not of divine creation but of human reason and of customary practices.

Grotius' conception of natural law hinges on two theoretical constructs. First, it is sustained by the assumption that each state is founded on a social contract which had, at one point, been established by its citizens. A comparable contract – vaguer, less authoritative, but equally informed by self-interest – could be created among sovereign states. As soon as the rulers of Europe realized that they would all benefit from such a contract, they would devise rules and legal institutions to arbitrate in conflicts between states, Grotius argued. The second basis for a natural law Grotius found in the principle of *pacta sunt servanda* – the respect for promises given and treaties signed. Grotius uses the same pragmatic argument as Bodin to explain that rational actors in an anarchic world soon learn that their best long-term interest is served by keeping the promises they make and by making promises only when they intend to keep them.

Grotius witnessed the destructive effects of the Thirty Years War and the evolution of the various new kingdoms, dukedoms, principalities and cities that emerged from the debris. He acknowledged that there was no prospect of re-establishing the traditional authority which had been exercised in the past by popes and emperors. Neither was there any hope of abolishing or banning war. But Grotius also realized that there was an urgent need to furnish international relations with some new code of behaviour. And he understood that there was a need to humanize the conduct of war, even within modest limits.

Following Bodin, Grotius created a conception of International Relations as political interaction in a *society of states*. He called for the establishment of a set of laws to regulate interstate conduct, and argued that states must accept these laws as binding. These arguments together with his proposal for an exhaustive set of laws, are spelled out his *De jure belli ac pacis*. Since he was a practical and pragmatic man, he did not conceive of this law as created by God. More explicitly than Bodin, Grotius anchored this natural law firmly in human reason and in customary practices. For Grotius, too, then, human reason promised a solution to the problem of international conflict and war (Grotius 1853; Bull 1977, p. 28–36).

Thomas Hobbes: 'twin of fear'

The major themes of seventeenth-century social thought that reverberate through the international speculations of Crucé, Grotius and Spinoza attain a famous expression in the works of Thomas Hobbes (1588–1679). He was born in the same year that the Spanish Armada launched its ill-fated attack on England. News of the approaching Armada seized the country; and when it reached Hobbes' mother, she was so gripped with fear that she gave premature birth: so Thomas Hobbes writes about his own entrance into this miserable world. With reference to this anecdote, he saw himself as 'the twin of fear'. He suggests by this that his fear, insecurity and introspection were major sources of inspiration for his bleak vision of society.

The Spanish Armada was not the only source of Hobbes' fear and insecurity. His uncertain childhood may also have contributed to his depressed visions. His father, a vicar with taste for card games and drink, abandoned wife and children after a violent brawl outside his own church door. Thomas was raised by an uncle and sent away to school in 1592 – the uncle assumed that, at the age of four, Thomas could take reasonably good care of himself.

A third source of Hobbes' pessimistic outlook may be traced to an intellectual crisis which brought his entire body of knowledge and understanding to collapse when he was still young and impressionable. Upon his graduation from Oxford (1608), Hobbes became the tutor of a young nobleman, whom he escorted on visits to France and Italy. Here, a veritable scientific revolution was challenging the established truths of the Church and the Aristotelian tradition of Western philosophy. Hobbes found that the Aristotelian philosophy that he had been taught at Oxford was crumbling before the discoveries of Johannes Kepler, Galileo Galilei and other members of the new scientific movement.

On returning home, Hobbes felt spiritually bewildered. Bereft of his old intellectual moorings, he began to search for new sources of knowledge and insight. He voraciously studied the writings of classical thinkers other than the authoritative Aristotle. Euclid's Elements was for Hobbes what the revelation on the road to Damascus had been for Paul. In Euclid, Hobbes learned to perceive the world through a cool geometric logic, and to trace proofs back through proposition after proposition until he was demonstratively convinced of their true and axiomatic nature.

In Thucydides' *Peloponnesian War* Hobbes, like Guicciardini, found an ambitious attempt to identify regularities in human society, to establish laws which regulated human behaviour. Hobbes saw in Thucydides' discussion of the fate of ancient Athens a salutary warning against democratic rule. But more importantly, he found in Thucydides' accounts of the war between Athens and Sparta a historian's struggle to engender, from observations of social events, conclusions about general forces which shape human behaviour. 'My work is not a piece of writing designed to meet the taste of an immediate public, but was done to last for ever', Thucydides explains. His aim was not to entertain, but to be 'judged useful by those who want to understand clearly the events which happened in the past and which (human nature being what it is) will, at some time or other and in much the same ways, be repeated in the future' (Thucydides, 1972, p. 48). Hobbes read Thucydides' ambitious purpose in the light of the scientific revolution of the seventeenth century, and saw in it an effort to establish the very axioms of human interaction. By 1629 Hobbes had, as a fruit of his intense studies of Thucydides, produced the first English translation of the *Peloponnesian War*.

The final, and undoubtedly the most important source of Hobbes' preoccupation with fear and insecurity, was political. During the 1620s, he had occasion to observe a conflict as bitter and momentous as the one Thucydides had observed 2,000 years before. At home, he experienced the English Civil Wars; on the Continent, he witnessed the ravages of the Thirty Years War. Like Crucé, Grotius and Spinoza, Hobbes was marked by its atmosphere of violence, insecurity and fear. Like Thucydides and Guicciardini, both of whom also wrote in the shadow of destructive warfare, Hobbes entertained a pessimistic view of human nature. He held war to be a natural state of affairs in human society, and argued that the only way to put an end to war is to trust human's reason to form a commonwealth – either by common agreement or by force of arms. This commonwealth must be led by a sovereign monarch who demands absolute obedience from his citizens. He wrote in his masterpiece, *Leviathan* (1951 [1651]): 'There must be some coercive power to compel men equally to the performance of their covenants, by the terror of some punishment, greater than the benefit they expect by the breach of their covenant.'

Hobbes' state of nature

Hobbes sketched a state of nature with the intent of showing what a society would be like without a supreme authority. He describes a condition of violent anarchy or war – 'a Warre, as is of every man, against every man'. International Relations theorists who define interstate relations in terms of an absence of supreme authority and therefore see interstate politics as interaction in an anarchical society, often refer to Hobbes' state of nature as the key analogy of the interstate system (Bull 1977, pp. 46–51).

The logic of proof which underlies this analogy, articulates the geometric logic of the century. Its axioms are clearly expressed in Hobbes' theory of perception and communication. Like prisoners locked up in solitary confinement, who can only communicate by tapping signals on their walls, human beings are shut off from each other by the very medium they depend upon to send their signals.

Alone, separated from the world and isolated from one another, men can only be aware of their own feelings.

From this solipsistic perspective, Hobbes explains that 'good' is simply the name which each individual gives to a 'fancy' which attracts him; 'evil' is the name he gives to unpleasant things. 'Fear' is the 'opinion of Hurt' engendered by the appearance of things which repel him. 'Courage' is the same, with the hope of avoiding that fear by resistance (Hobbes 1951, pp. 118ff). Such notions make a common guiding moral for humanity impossible. They sustain the view that the world is composed of self-absorbed egotists who are constantly in search of felicity and present enjoyment. Since they are all endowed with reason, they all seek to store up means to secure their future content. Hobbes uses the term 'power' to signify these means. He assumes as a 'generall inclination of all mankind, a perpetuall and restlesse desire for Power after Power that ceaseth only in Death'. Thus, wealth is power, friends are power, knowledge is power; and through knowledge, science is power, because science is 'the knowledge of consequence and dependence of one fact upon another' (pp. 150–60).

In the state of nature, in which no government exists and where individual men exercise unlimited liberty, everyone's perpetual search for power results in a constant struggle. If Hobbes' thought does not include any supreme good (any *Summum Bonum*), it does include a supreme evil (a *Summum Malum*): viz the constant fear of a violent death at the hands of others. This supreme evil constitutes a cornerstone in Hobbes' political thought, and its description as a 'time of Warre, where every man is Enemy to every other man' has, by theorists ever since, been considered a forceful analogy to international society. In such a state of nature, 'the notions of Right and Wrong, Justice and Injustice have there no place', for 'where there is no common Power, there is no Law: where there is no Law, no Injustice. Force and Fraud, are in warre the two Cardinall virtues.' In the state of nature, there can be no notion of property, 'no *Mine* and *Thine* distinct; but onely that to be every mans that he can get; and for so long as he can keep it' (p. 188). In the state of nature, then, all men have the same right to all things. Hobbes maintains in a most celebrated passage:

... men live without other security, than what their own strength, and their own invention shall furnish them withall. In such condition there is no place for Industry; because the fruit thereof is uncertain: and consequently no Culture of the Earth; no Navigation or use of the commodities that may be imported by Sea; no commodious Building; no Instruments of moving, and removing such things as require much force; no Knowledge of the face of the Earth; no account of Time; no Arts; no Letters; no Society; and which is worst of all, the life of man, solitary, poore, nasty, brutish, and short (p. 186).

The notion of a supreme evil is important for Hobbes, because natural man will perceive it with his reason, This perception motivates him to enlighten himself and to discover the one basic dictate of reason: 'to look to the preservation and safeguard to ourselves'. Self-preservation, then, becomes the primary axiom in

Hobbes' political system. In the state of nature, there exists no other moral code than the law of self-preservation. This Hobbes refers to as the 'Right of Nature'. No rule is valid in the state of nature, except the rule of self-preservation; no right exists except the right of the strongest. From this one rule and this one right, Hobbes effects a revolution in Western thought. He makes the 'Right of Nature' his political law of gravity, a scientific axiom upon which he builds his entire political system – aided by the method of geometry, the bricks of Natural Law and the clay of fear and reason.

A second axiom of Hobbes' is that all men are equal in the faculties of mind and body. This equality perpetuates the struggle and war which, in turn, leads to the fear of a violent death:

For as to the strength of body, the weakest has strength enough to kill the strongest, either by secret machination, or by confederacy with others, that are in the same danger with himselfe.

And as to the faculties of the mind [...] I find yet a greater equality amongst men ... From this equality of ability, ariseth equality of hope in the attaining of our Ends. And therefore if any two men desire the same thing, which neverthelesse they cannot both enjoy, they become enemies; and in the way to their End [...] endeavour to destroy, or subdue one an other. .... Hereby it is manifest, that during the time men live without a common Power to keep them all in awe, they are in that condition which is called Warre; and such a warre, as is of every man, against every man (pp. 183–5).

In the state of nature, where everyone enjoys full freedom, everyone also lives in perpetual fear of a sudden death at the jealous hands of others. Acting in accordance with the principle of self-preservation, people deduce that, in order to remove that paralysing fear, they must remove its cause: i.e. that must remove everyone's natural right to everything. This can be achieved only if everyone agrees to give up their natural right to everything: each and every one must, on a solemn promise of good behaviour, give up their right to everything. In order to guarantee that this promise is kept, people must create a strong central power. This is done by everyone's promising everyone else that they will obey whatever command some central power shall consider necessary for the peace and defence of all. By giving this unreserved vow of obedience, people create a power strong enough to deter everyone else from breaking their promises.

Hobbes defined 'freedom' as the absence of restraint. He held that absolute freedom is an intolerable condition, and that people must sacrifice some freedom if they are to enjoy any freedom at all. Therefore they build a state designed to provide some restraint and to ensure them the security collectively that they cannot find individually. They create a *Leviathan*, an omnipotent power which can exercise absolute power *within* the state. However, by putting an end to the state of nature between individuals, they have re-established another state of nature *among* individual states. In Hobbes' words:

in all times, Kings and Persons of Soveraigne authority, of their Independency, are in continuall jealousies, and in the state and posture of Gladiators; having their weapons pointing and their eyes fixed upon one another; that is, their Forts, Garrisons, and Guns upon the Frontiers of their Kingdomes; and continual Spyes upon their neighbours; which is a posture of War (pp. 187f).

Sovereignty and power

Like Bodin and Grotius, Hobbes made the concept of sovereignty the fulcrum of his vision of interstate relations. However, whereas Bodin and Grotius associated sovereignty with law, Hobbes associated it with a ruler's absolute and unrestricted force. In his *Leviathan* Hobbes argues that, within the state, rulers can demand unreserved obedience from their citizens. The rulers *are* the state; their interests the state interests; their will the state's will. The ruler is sovereign, and therefore represents the state in relations with other states.

These rulers are sovereign individuals. Because they are *sovereign* individuals, their freedom is restricted by no one. They have not surrendered their Right of Nature. They are hindered by no one in their ceaseless search for felicity and present enjoyment and in their constant quest to store up means to secure their future content, i.e., to accumulate 'power'.

Because rulers of states are sovereign *individuals*, they are essentially equal in body and mind. In their perpetual pursuit of 'Power after Power', some states will inevitably become physically stronger or more wealthy than others. But in the intelligence of their rulers, states are unlikely to differ substantially; and when all factors of power are taken into account, the difference between states is not considerable. Although strength and wealth are primary manifestations of power, they are by no means the decisive sources of power. For Hobbes, knowledge is also power; 'worth, dignity, honour and worthiness ... eloquence, liberality, nobility' are power; indeed, 'reputation of power, is Power, because it draweth with it the adhærence of those that need protection' (p. 150). And most importantly, friends are power, and through confederacy with friends – 'with others who are in the same danger' – even the weakest sovereign can harm the strongest, either by the overt use of force or by covert machination. Hobbes' discussion of self-interested rulers' pursuit of 'Power after Power' provides an elaborate justification for the balance-of-power policy which England conducted at the end of the seventeenth century. It also provides support for the term 'balance of power' – the general use of the term emerged in Europe during the 1660s, just as Hobbes' *Leviathan* attracted the attention of European scholars.

Hobbes and seventeenth-century politics

Hobbes' discussions of the many facets of power and of the calculated use of alliances to contain expansionist monarchs was entirely in tune with the foreign policies of Elizabeth I, who repeatedly intervened to support weaker Continental powers against the might of Spain or France. It also supports the observations of Hobbes' elder contemporary, Francis Bacon, man of letters and Lord Chancellor of England. In a pamphlet 'Considerations Touching a War with Spain' (1852 [1623]), Bacon estimates whether it is possible for England and its allies to contain the forces of Spain. 'The balancing of the forces of these kingdoms and their allies with Spain and their allies', he writes, is a 'great and weighty consideration' for England (Bacon 1852, p. 200).

Towards the end of Hobbes' life, it was no longer Spain but France which represented a threat to England. Under the leadership of Louis XIV (1661–1715), France sought to establish a universal monarchy over Europe and subordinate all other countries in Europe to its will. The response levelled against this expansionist policy was a balance-of-power policy. The efforts to contain French ambitions were chiefly the work of Holland – the small country in which both Spinoza and Hobbes sought refuge from civil war and persecution in their own countries. When France made aggressive moves on the Spanish Netherlands in 1667, William III of Orange immediately dropped all quarrels with England – with whom he had just fought two large mercantile wars (1652–54 and 1665–67) – and signed an Anglo-Dutch alliance designed to contain French expansion. When Sweden became the third member of this anti-French alliance (1668), King Louis XIV found himself overpowered, and withdrew from the Spanish Netherlands. The French withdrawal was immediately followed by the collapse of the Triple Alliance; indeed, Louis XIV had no sooner sued for peace than a secret treaty was signed between England and France (1670) according to which the two great powers divided Holland between them two years later.

These events, in which rulers sign secret treaties one moment and violate them the next, is quite in tune with Hobbes' understanding of the behaviour of sovereign actors. Hobbes maintained that rulers, like other men, are driven by self-interest; he held that, because they are sovereign, rulers are not constrained in their actions by any law. In effect, sovereign rulers enjoy the full Right of Nature, according to which might is the only right. Spinoza agreed (1951b, p. 213; 1951c, p. 309). Both Hobbes and Spinoza accepted the implication that, if any ruler is free to act according to his own will and inclination, then he is also free to break treaties or violate alliances whenever he decides this to be in his interest. Consequently, any treaty of peace or alliance can be trusted to remain in force only as long as the motives for concluding it continues to hold good – thus, when France withdrew from the Spanish Netherlands, the Triple Alliance lost its purpose and immediately collapsed; however, every time the expansionist Louis XIV launched an ambitious military offensive, anti-French alliances were organized by William III to resist his aggression – first in the War of Devolution (1667–68), then in the Dutch War (1672–78) and finally in the War of the Grand Alliance (1689–97).

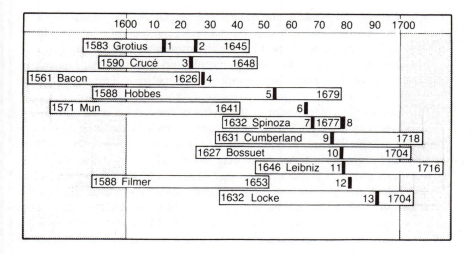

1. *De jure praedae* [1609]
2. *De jure belli ac pacis* [1625]
3. *The New Cyneas* [1623]
4. *Considerations Touching a War with Spain* [1624]
5. *Leviathan* [1651]
6. *England's Treasure by Forraign Trade* [1664]
7. *Theologico-Political Treatise* [1670]
8. *Ethics* [1677]
9. *Enquiry into the Laws of Nature* [1672]
10. *Politique* [167?]
11. *Caesarinus fürstenerius* [1677]
12. *Patriarcha* [1680]
13. *Two Treatises on Government* [1689]

Figure 2   Some seventeenth–century authors and their works

The sentiment of the century

The seventeenth century opened in the name of God. It evolved through conflicts and wars which were fuelled by incompatible religious interpretations. It closed in the name of the absolute monarch and with the secular argument that war could be kept at bay through a policy of counterpoise. During the course of this process, International Relations theory came of age.

This coming of age was indicated by a proliferation of books and treatises which discussed interstate relations. It was attended by a trend towards a more secularized view of political affairs. Social theorists increasingly saw the causes of war less as God's intention to punish man for his sins, and more in terms of properties of human nature and of the interplay of human interests. Hobbes,

Crucé, Spinoza and Grotius, for example, all explained the causes of war in terms of human emotions such as greed and pride; and they all found new hopes for a peaceful social order in people's ability to calculate that human existence would be much improved if human reason could impose limits upon human passions. Also, all of them based their argument on a secular redefinition of the concept of 'natural law'.[7]

This development is apparent in the works of Samuel Pufendorf (1632–94). He was keenly aware of the international changes which had occurred in his lifetime. He saw the Treaty of Westphalia (1648) as a watershed in international history, and distinguished sharply between the chaotic world of war and devastation which preceded Westphalia and the orderly world of self-governing equilibrium which emerged after it. He noted that, before Westphalia, authors like Grotius and Hobbes had been naturally predisposed by chaotic circumstances to ask how man could establish an orderly society. And he realized that, once the Westphalian system of sovereign states was established, it was more natural to ask how one could ensure that sovereign actors would become useful contributors to an orderly Europe. To achieve this end, he argued, it was necessary to devise a new morality which could gain the consent of all Europeans. The essential constituents of this new morality, 'which would teach one how to conduct oneself to become a useful member of human society, are called natural laws' (Pufendorf 1991, p. 35).

Greater secularization: natural law and national interest
The tradition of natural law reaches back to the philosophies of ancient Greece and can be traced through Western social and religious thought. As a preliminary definition, it can be said that 'natural law' denotes a set of principles that transcend the laws of individual societies and of different epochs. Whereas the laws of a given society or a given epoch are transitory and changing phenomena, natural law is a supreme phenomenon which outlives the times and sanctions a supreme, unchanging moral order.

Hobbes, Crucé, Grotius and Pufendorf all anchored their political theories in a secular understanding of natural law. Pufendorf, for example, argued explicitly that if natural law were to furnish Europe with precepts for useful political conduct, then this could not be grounded in religion – for, as the treaty of Westphalia recognized with its principle of *cujus regio eius religio*, Europe was still racked with religious quarrels. Thus, it became important for him to cleanse natural law of its grounding in Aristotelian and Thomistic theology. From the 1660s onwards, his project was to construct a comprehensive secular moral philosophy grounded in natural law and adapted to the conditions of post-Westphalian Europe – a set of universal principles of right deduced from two premises no person could reasonably doubt: a scientifically reconstructed condition common to all persons, the 'state of nature', and the empirically verifiable self-love or concern each person has with their own preservation. Pufendorf helped free International Relations theory from the fetters of theological thought. He sought in his analysis to trace political events back to the rational motives of the agent (Meinecke 1957, pp. 224f).

In this respect, Pufendorf was a representative voice of the times. Several authors of the third quarter of the seventeenth century developed theories of social interaction from speculations about human nature and from notions like 'reason', 'motives' and 'interests'. Most of them were driven by an attempt to replace the pessimistic argument of Thomas Hobbes with a more optimistic alternative (Hintz 1962) – as in the case of John Bramhall's *Catching of Leviathan* (1658). Like Bramhall, many of them were churchmen who were incensed by Hobbes' emphasizing necessity rather than liberty. They saw self-interest as a constant feature of human life. And they reasoned that, since self-interest was universal, it was also universally predictable, and would therefore provide a firm basis on which to build social theory. Some of them devised a theory around the claim that when individuals are allowed to pursue their own interest, great benefits will accrue for society at large. Joseph Lee, for example, opened his argument with a defence of the 'undeniable maxime that everyone by the light of nature and reason will do what makes for his greatest advantage', and he closed it with the claim that 'the advancement of private persons will be the advantage of the publick' (quoted in Appleby, 1978, p. 62). Bishop Richard Cumberland agreed.

Cumberland's *De legibus naturae* ('A Treatise of the Laws of Nature', 1727 [1672]) was explicitly written as an attack on Hobbes. Cumberland argues that man is not only endowed with needs, wants and self-serving reason (which Hobbes had recognized); human beings also have a natural liking for each other and a capacity for benevolence. Cumberland sought to demonstrate that this benevolence did not depend on religious texts, legal authority or the threat of force. Rather, benevolent acts would occur naturally. In a world of rational humans, Cumberland claimed, there are sufficient 'contingent' sanctions in the form of natural rewards for virtue and of punishments for vice to make possible a peaceable and tolerable society even in the absence of civil force. 'I suppose every one seeks *his own* Good, and that *to act in pursuit thereof*, adds to the *perfection* of his Nature,' he writes (1727, p. 215). In pursuit of his own good, each man enters into 'Compacts' with other men 'by which their mutual Happiness may be both secur'd and increas'd ... By *these Methods* the Powers of some will of necessity be counter poiz'd by others' (p. 297). Thus 'governed by the universal Benevolence of all rational Beings towards all, are the principal Causes of the publick Happiness of all' (p. 114).

When Bramhall's, Lee's and Cumberland's notion of self-interest was allowed to inform theories of individual interactions, they foreshadowed the doctrines of liberal moral philosophers like Adam Smith and Jeremy Bentham. When the concept of self-interest was applied to the interaction of princes and statesmen, it greatly enriched the old concepts of *raison d'état* and balance of power. This is notably obvious in the case of the French duke of Rohan (1579–1638). He introduces his book *On the Interest of Princes and States of Christendom* (1673 [1638]) with the observation that 'Princes command their peoples, as they are themselves commanded by Interest ... The Prince may err. His councels may be corrupted. But the Interest alone can never fail; and in proportion to whether it is well or ill understood, it causes States to live or die' (Rohan 1673, p. 7).

Rohan's maxim that 'interest can never fail', was immediately embraced by British analysts. It informed Marchament Nedham's book *Interest will Not Lie, or a View of England's True Interest* (1659) and his newspaper *Mercurius Politicus* (Gunn 1969). By this maxim, any analysis of international relations must begin by defining the interests of states. But how are such interests best determined? Rohan proposed that the most appropriate vantage point is to assess each state's military strength and geographic situation. In addition, it is helpful to gauge each state's cohesive force of religion, its ability to negotiate and enter into alliances and, last but not least, its reputation and ambitions.

The new context of inquiry: the scientific revolution
The growing secularization of the century was attended by greater methodological self-awareness. Theorists increasingly speculated about state interaction in descriptive rather than in prescriptive terms. They still referred copiously to classical authorities; however, they did this with a greater independence than before. They displayed a greater propensity to question ancient wisdom.[8]

These attitudes reflect a larger tendency to question authorities – all authorities, secular (Aristotle, Plato) as well as religious ones (the Church, the Pope and the Holy Roman Emperor). Such attitudes may be related to the incessant wars of the age, and to the powerlessness of priests, philosophers and politicians to deal with them, to the breakdown of traditional law and beliefs and to the emergence in Europe of a state of normative chaos. It made the matter worse that travellers and traders brought new information about peoples, manners and customs of distant new worlds into a violent Europe. In the prevalent state of normative vacuum, such new knowledge only contributed to the relativism of the age.

The way out of relativism was pioneered by scholars who sought to regain man's certainty of mind. Three contributors stand out in this respect as facilitators of the scientific revolution: Bacon, Galileo and Descartes. All three wrote their most influential works around the time of the Thirty Years War. They shared the doubts of the age. They asked how it is possible for man to gain reliable, truthful and usable knowledge. They rejected the methods advocated by the academic tradition of the universities founded in the Middle Ages, and provided alternative methods of knowledge acquisition.

Traditional science had been deductive. But Bacon, Galileo and Descartes argued that deduction alone could produce no new knowledge. For them, truth is not something one could postulate at the beginning of an exploration. It is something one discovers after a process of investigation. Appropriate methods of investigation had long been used by practical cartographers and astronomers. Map-makers did not draw their information from learned authorities and holy texts; rather, they took notes on what sailors and traders could tell about distant lands, systematized the tales, cross-checked the information, and compared notes and extant maps. Star-gazers charted the heavens by observing the skies at night and keeping meticulous logs of their nocturnal observations. Copernicus relied on pre-Christian observations of the paths of planets and stars, and found that their movements did not fit official, geocentric accounts. Brahe observed the skies regularly throughout a long lifetime. He left stacks of meticulous nocturnal notes to his assistant, Kepler, whose calculations replaced the complex orthodox vision with a simple heliocentric model. He summarized the planetary orbits in a few mathematical statements and presented them in this form as 'laws of nature'. Galileo drove the point home by depicting the planetary orbits and drawing individual planets as he had observed them with his own eyes through the lens of a telescope.

The fact that Galileo made his observations through a telescope has a symbolic significance: seventeenth-century science was profoundly optical in its orientation. It emphasized the single sense of human sight. Scientific observation meant selecting a few things from the confusing wealth of the universe, and being content with seeing these things systematically, measuring their apparent size and weight, describing their colour, shape and character, explaining their position in relation to each other and, if applicable, calculating their movement in space. The understanding which accompanied such optical observations was phrased in mechanical terms. The unchallenged exemplar of this scientific vision is Isaac Newton's *Mathematical Principles of Natural Philosophy* of 1687. It demonstrates that all bodies – whether they are located on earth or in the heavens – can be measured, that their motion can be timed and their movement captured in terms of laws described in mathematical formulae. All matter in the universe moves as if every particle attracted every other particle with a force proportional to the product of the two masses and inversely proportional to the square of the distance between them.

New modes of theorizing: interests, states and balance
Seventeenth-century scientific knowledge came to mean knowledge about visible differences between static objects. Botany and biology relied on taxonomic tables. The study of language was presented as a logical system in which each component part performed a specific function. The analysis of wealth examined the circulation of objects (like coins) that could be represented in a system of exchange (Foucault 1973). The study of history was purged of its propensity simply to retell past events – historians increasingly relied on a meticulous examination of things themselves, and then transcribed the information they had gathered in neutralized and faithful words. The study of International Relations

came to mean the study of interrelations between impermeable territorial-states. This obsession with matter in geometric motion informs one of the most mechanical visions in the social sciences: the theory of the balance of power.

Balance-of-power theories were not new in the seventeenth century – they were expressed earlier by Italian theorists like Guicciardini, Gentili and Botero. However, in the seventeenth century the imagery of equilibrium presented itself with unprecedented clarity – as is apparent in the theories of thinkers like Bacon, Mun, Spinoza, Pufendorf, Hobbes and Cumberland (and evident in the practices of William III of Orange, Frederick the Great and Charles II). Also, the phrase 'balance of power' came into general use. It denoted a policy in which one state allied with other states (preferably weaker than itself) against any state which threatened to dominate Europe. Through the balance-of-power principle a state could preserve or maximize its independence of action: by manipulating alliances states could create a counterpoise against any state whose ascendancy they feared. According to this notion, a balance-of-power policy allows a state to throw its weight where it is most needed in order to safeguard its own independence.

One important reason for this improved clarity in balance-of-power theories lies in the new scientific epistemology of the age. With the deductive approach of the orthodox schoolmen ridiculed, Bacon, Descartes and Galileo hastened the evolution of the scientific approach. The natural world was 'de-spiritualized' and 'de-animated'. Whereas the orthodox schoolmen had tended to impute purposes to natural phenomena, the seventeenth-century scientists imposed a mechanical model. The branch of science which had the greatest success was geometry, and its method and mechanical vision are evident in the writings of Descartes, Hobbes, Galileo, Leibniz, Newton and Spinoza. These authors described natural phenomena by identifying the presumably simple motions from which their behaviour could be derived. There was no longer any essential difference between bodies called stones and bodies called animals. Descartes and Hobbes agreed that the world can be reduced to matter in motion. Both conceived of animal bodies as complex machines. Even the spiritually-oriented Leibniz recognized that every organic body of a living being is a sort of God-made machine, or natural robot, which infinitely excels all man-made robots. Indeed, few theorists reflected this *Zeitgeist* better in their conception of international interaction than Leibniz. His vision is very much informed by his overall, teutonically complex image of states as discrete, impermeable, indestructible, animated organisms; all interacting with others, each distinguished from others by its self-consciousness.[9]

A second reason for the improved clarity is that the old notion of balance benefited from the new concept of 'interest'. Pufendorf (1991, p. 35) sensed this when he deemed the Treaty of Westphalia a watershed in international history. Gatien Courtilz de Sandras noted quite explicitly that a new preoccupation with 'interest' suddenly took precedence over dynastic squabbles and religious affinity in European diplomacy (Courtilz 1686, p. 3). The same notion is apparent in Rohan's discussion of European politics. In his words, the interest of a state

always aims at the augmentation, or at least the conservation, of the State. To fulfill its aim, it adapts to the times. So in order to consider well the interest of contemporary Princes, it is not necessary to go very far; it is sufficient to analyse current affairs. Thus we can take as our vantage point the claim that there are at present in Christendom two Powers which represent the two poles from whence descend the influences of peace and war upon the other states: viz. the Houses of France and Spain. That of Spain finds itself suddenly augmented, and has not been able to conceal the ambition of making herself mistress and cause the Sun of a new Monarchy to rise in the West. That of France is forthwith carried to make a counterpoise. The other princes join the one or the other, according to their interest. But for as much as this interest, as it has been well or ill followed, has caused the ruin of some and the greatness of others, I have proposed to publish in this present Treatise: First, what was the true interest of these two mighty powers, and then of the others which seem in some manner to depend on their protection. Next of all I shall show how much has been the digression from this true interest, either because it was not well understood by the Prince or else because it was concealed from him by the corruption of his Ministers (Rohan 1673, pp. 7f).

Rohan was much influenced by Renaissance scholars (notably by Machiavelli, Guicciardini, Boccalini and Bonaventura). But – as should be apparent from his portrayal above of mid-seventeenth-century European politics – Rohan identified the balance-of-power mechanism more keenly than any of his predecessors. The reason is that he has linked the old notion of counterpoise to the new concept of 'interest'. Indeed, he may be the first European theorist to make this link. The Duke of Rohan, Huguenot general and statesman, is an important contributor to modern International Relations theory. He drew on the Italian tradition of politics and counterpoise, and formulated a keen balance-of-power analysis which, in turn, greatly influenced English social theorists (Raab 1964, p. 237; Hirschman 1981, p. 37).

A final important reason for the improved clarity in the political theories of this age lies in a tighter grasp on the concept of the state. After the Peace of Westphalia, the kings of Europe replaced the old, volatile arrangements of military entrepreneurs with a new, centrally-direct system of military command and control. The monarchs became commanders-in-chief of their countries' armed forces. By the same token they expanded their powers over their civil societies. The reins of political power were collected and concentrated in the hands of the monarch. Around the king evolved the characteristic features of the absolutist court. And around the court emerged the streamlined structures of the modern state. During the second half of the seventeenth century the states of (Western) Europe became conceived of as independent communities whose court-led government asserted full authority over a specific portion of the earth's surface. The territorial nature of statehood was clarified. The delineation of an 'internal' and an 'external' realm of politics – domestic politics vs. foreign affairs – was emphasized. The state was individuated as a political actor and became a more clearly observed analytic unit. The classic concept of sovereignty was completed (Bartelson 1995, pp. 137ff). The concept was also irreversibly removed from the realm of the divine and the universal and planted in the province of the secular and specific – as a result of which political actors like the pope and the emperor, whose authority rested on divine and universal principles, were eclipsed by the great monarchs of Europe (Hertz 1957).

5

Enlightenment politics: the eighteenth century and the rise of popular sovereignty

Europe entered the eighteenth century through a wave of great wars which stimulated the growth of the modern state. Political power was concentrated, military command was centralized, and the wolf-packs of the Thirty Years War were transformed into the trained baroque poodles of the wars of Louis XIV. The evolving institutions of government became 'a means of securing order and safety at home, and of raising, supporting and controlling armies for use against other states' (Palmer 1951, p. 162). Interstate interactions were regulated according to precise protocol by professional diplomats and scholars in international law. Wars were conducted according to well-defined rules by professional soldiers. Each state explicitly acknowledged the legitimacy of others' territories; none had the right to universalize its own regime or its own laws at the expense of others (Howard 1984, p. 75).

Most European rulers in this period were absolute sovereigns. France's Louis XIV was the most absolute and powerful of them all. His machinations kept Europe in a fever of wars (1672–1713). They exhausted France. They shook and ultimately undermined her absolute monarchy. In the last years of his reign, Louis' life work was undone. A grand alliance led by Britain defeated him. England emerged from the wars of Louis XIV as the greatest winner and, improbably, as the dominant actor in eighteenth-century international politics.

England stood apart from the states on the European continent in one important respect: the country was not an absolute monarchy. The Glorious Revolution (1688) had forced the English king to accept that Parliament imposed specific checks on his freedom of action – no citizen could be arrested and detained without legal process, no law could be suspended by the king alone, no taxes could be levied and no army maintained without Parliamentary consent. Thus, by the end of the wars of Louis XIV, European politics encompassed two different doctrines of sovereignty. On the one hand was the old doctrine of the Divine Right of Kings which supported the absolute regimes on the Continent.

On the other was a new doctrine of popular sovereignty which had emerged in the wealthier, mercantile sea-powers of the North-Atlantic rim.

This difference brought about a political division in eighteenth-century Europe between the Continental regimes, with absolutist states and centralized politics, and the trading states of the North-Atlantic rim, with relatively weak state bureaucracies and growing market economies. During the course of the century, the latter would constitute an increasing ideological challenge to the former.

Changes in the use of power and in acquisition of wealth

England emerged as a formidable land-power during the wars of Louis XIV, its superiority gained by virtue of technological pre-eminence and great wealth and by the country's immense sea power: the Royal Navy both protected English trade and projected the country's power wherever in the world it was deemed necessary.

In the international struggle for power and prestige the national navies played a decisive role in this busy age of growing global commerce and trade. The eighteenth century was the age of mature mercantilism, and it was in England that the mercantilist doctrines had been theoretically elaborated and most consciously applied: in order to discourage imports, certain foreign goods were prohibited or discouraged by heavy duties; in order to promote domestic production, the state intervened heavily to improve communication and to encourage private enterprise. The economic doctrine of mercantilism was attended by the political doctrine of absolutism. And the two continued to dominate European politics after the wars of Louis XIV. But the relationship between them changed during the course of the century. While they had been mutually supporting doctrines at its beginning, they became riddled by internal contradictions and mutual oppositions by its end.

Absolutism went through a marked evolution during the long reign of Louis XIV (1661–1715). On the Continent, the centralization of power evolved towards enlightened despotism. This evolution was spurred not so much by the monarch as by his ministerial entourage. Through the needs of recruitment and taxation, the kings' ministers forged the state structures ever more solid and tight. From within absolutism itself emerged new structures and processes of production, procurement and allocation. At first, these structures represented the monarch and reflected the lustre and the authority of the Crown. Soon, they assumed authority in their own right. In the hands of the kings' powerful ministers, the absolute sovereignty of the monarch was incrementally superseded by its own institutional product. Absolutist theory was supplemented by doctrines of divine right, and the person of the monarch became such an intense focus of sovereignty that he was rendered impersonal, abstract and half-divine – as exemplified by Louis XIV, 'the Sun King'. With much of the official work being done by a growing corps of administrators, the actual monarch became more and more a figurehead. The impersonality of the State was beginning to take over.

Mercantilism, too, changed during the eighteenth century. It was streamlined and perfected in regions where the development of manufacturers and industrial wealth was slow. But among the wealthiest industrializing sea-powers of the North-Atlantic rim, mercantilism and absolutism were, in fact, eroded from below. Here the growing merchant and manufacturing middle classes had challenged the key principles of absolutism as early as the end of the seventeenth century. In England, for example, mercantilism had enriched the nation, but it had also boosted the growth of citizens' wealth beneath and outside the royal entourage. It had fuelled the evolution of new and independent social groups and forces. First it had spurred the transformation of the country's landholding élite; then it had fuelled the growth of new entrepreneurial classes.

During the course of the eighteenth century England's landowning nobles consolidated their power over British society. More and more of the country's common pastures were enclosed into private landholdings. These enclosures hurt the smaller freeholding farmers, who depended on the commons to feed their animals; but they consolidated the economic and political base of a narrow landholding élite from which most government officials were recruited. England's wealthy landowners dominated Parliament, passed enclosure acts, and conducted foreign policies which suited their interests. Unlike the nobility on the Continent, they did not depend upon the Crown for wealth or influence, and would therefore, at times, feel free to oppose their king if his proposals hurt their interests.

Hand in hand with the enclosure movement, British networks of communication and commerce were greatly expanded. Roads and canals were improved and extended. Transportation costs were greatly reduced. Markets expanded for bulk goods (foodstuffs as well as iron and coal) and finished products (agricultural and industrial, both). Such developments stimulated the growth of new, intermediate social groups – manufacturers, merchants, financiers, engineers. These were generally not represented in Parliament. But as the eighteenth century progressed, they clamoured for inclusion in the political process with mounting insistence.

The new groups tended to express a highly individualistic view of social life. They often argued that everyone was the architect of his own fortunes – which of course implied that those who held high office and great wealth held them because of personal talent, ingenuity, skill and diligence. They tended to resent the hereditary privileges of the old nobility, but they defended the right to inherit economic wealth – which obviously gave their own heirs great advantages. Their arguments tended to be rationalistic and optimistic. They were propagated through new channels of communications, notably the emerging popular press. During the eighteenth century, these groups began to oppose the prevailing mercantilist views. They claimed that a real increase in the wealth of the nation could be achieved if all hindrances to their rational self-interested plans were removed.

At first the members of these groups made no attempt to interfere with the king's prerogative to make foreign policy. However, they soon came to protest at the direct consequences of his foreign-policy entanglements. These entanglements meant war, and as war grew more global it also grew more expensive and disruptive. The wealthier groups of the public objected increasingly to its consequences: heavy taxation, interference with trade and industry, arbitrary justice and control of consciences by the monarch. It was around such issues that the Dutch and, later, the English organized opposition against the institutions and principles of absolutism.

Symmetry, sovereignty and the cult of reason

England emerged as a Great Power during the wars of Louis XIV. And as British wealth and force dominated interstate affairs in the post-war period, so British ideas influenced the study of international relations during this Age of Enlightenment.[1]

The sentiment of the age was marked by a confidence in the powers of human reason and a firm conviction of the regularity of nature. This sentiment had emerged during the seventeenth century; by the eighteenth, it had matured into a pervasive vision. Scientists and philosophers sought to capture the symmetry and regularity of nature and to express it in intellectual terms – through flow-charts, taxonomies or mechanical models. This obsession with balance and symmetry unified the contributions to science and philosophy of the age. Its most famous representation is Isaac Newton's vision of the universe; his *Mathematical Principles of Natural Philosophy* of 1687 expressed perfectly the vision of repeated movement in space. Newton's orderly universe dovetailed nicely with the ordered psychology of John Locke (1632–1704); his *Essay Concerning Human Understanding* of 1690 portrayed the human mind as a blank slate inscribed by experience – experience, obviously, of the physical universe. Locke expressed a new philosophy of knowledge. He provided a theory of sense-impressions, and this destroyed Descartes' assumption of innate ideas. He also rendered knowledge subjective, as it was made relative to the perceptions of the individual.

By mid-eighteenth century, Locke's argument had become a commonplace epistemological companion to Newtonian physics. What Newton did for humanity's view of nature, John Locke did for humanity's view of itself. Newton and Locke, with their belief in reason, their visions of a law-abiding universe and their mechanistic approach to nature, provided the basis for an empiricist approach to knowledge. Locke also provided the basis for a doctrine of popular sovereignty which suited the emerging middle classes of the North-Atlantic trading states. The British ideas would exercise a great influence on political theorizing in France – significantly mediated through the popular interpretations of

Voltaire (1980, pp. 68ff).

The most famous expression of this new doctrine of politics was Locke's *Two Treatises of Government* (1960 [1689]). The first treatise has a title which describes its content well: *The False Principles and Foundation of Sir Robert Filmer, and his Followers, are Detected and Overthrown.* The title is cumbersome. The argument is not. It is a resounding attack on Robert Filmer and authors like him who 'flatter princes with an Opinion, that they have a Divine Right to absolute Power' (Locke 1960, p. 176).

With his first treatise, Locke refuted the doctrine of the Divine Right of Kings. With his second, he formulated an alternative. The *Second Treatise of Government: An Essay Concerning the True Originals, Extent, and End of Civil Government*, mollifies Hobbes' state of nature into a condition in which human beings live in perfect freedom and equality. Indeed, whereas Hobbes described the state of nature as the worst possible condition, Locke sees it as quite happy. The main reason for this happiness lies in Locke's description of man as a reasonable creature who has a God–given law of nature to govern him. Locke's state of nature is governed by a law of nature which gives all humans certain Natural Rights: the rights to life, liberty and property. Since people are rational, most of them will obey the law of nature, argues Locke. They will be content to enjoy their own Natural Rights and will not violate the Rights of their fellows. Most people are reasonable. However, there are always some who are not. Some people disregard the law of nature and knowingly invade the Rights of others. They steal other people's property, enslave their liberty and destroy their lives.

Locke's state of nature appears benign when compared to Hobbes' ruthless scenario of 'perpetuall warre'.[2] However, Locke's state of nature, too, contains elements of conflict and war. The existence of a few people who knowingly violate the Rights of their fellows, prods Locke to explore the necessity of self-defence. In Locke's view, any person has a right to protect his or her own Natural Rights in the state of nature. Locke's basic idea is the same as Crucé's (1972, p. 29). But the new notion of a state of nature and the new concept of Natural Rights greatly refined the old argument: anyone who violates the Natural Rights of others, forfeits his or her own Natural Rights. By committing acts of theft, slavery or murder, people set themselves outside the realm of reason and law. They render themselves law-less. They declare war on others, and anyone has the right to pursue and punish them. Indeed, anyone has the right to hunt and destroy them, just as one would hunt and destroy a wolf or a lion: 'because such Men are not under the ties of the Common Law of Reason, have no rule, but that of Force and Violence, and so may be treated as Beasts of Prey' (p. 321).

The main problem with the state of nature is that those who have had their rights violated are rarely fair and impartial in their pursuit of revenge. So, in order to prevent excessive revenge meted out in affect, people agree to set up a government to enforce the observance of the Natural Rights of all persons. The conflicts and wars which occur in the state of nature, then, drive rational people to establish government.

Did Locke understand the state of nature literally? Did it correspond to any actual social condition? Locke's discussion is not exactly a paragon of clarity on this point. However there is ample evidence in his Second Treatise of Government to suggest that he would answer both questions in the affirmative. First of all, he suggests (in Chapter 2) that the state of nature describes an actual condition in humankind's distant past. Second, he claims that the state of nature exists in two places in his contemporary world: among savages in other lands (for instance the natives in America), and among '*Princes* and Rulers of *Independent* Governments all through the World' (Locke 1960, p. 317). However, he does not elaborate on the point.

Locke acknowledges that a state of nature exists among the sovereign states of the world (and that there is an essential difference between politics within commonwealths and politics between them[3]) ... However, he never actually discusses international relations at length in the light of this analogy. But as the eighteenth century unfolded, other authors did. Jean Barbeyrac's *L'histoire des anciens traités* of 1739 was greatly influenced by Locke's doctrines of right (Derathé 1979; Tully 1993). Christian Wolff's *Jus gentium* ('The Law of Nations', 1749) applied Locke's ideas to International Relations. Wolff's gifted Swiss pupil, Emmerich de Vattel (1714–67) wrote a Lockean analysis of International Relations: the *Droit des gens* ('The Law of Nations', 1916 [1758]).

Vattel's argument was so influential that it deserves a brief comment. It portrayed the relations among states as analogous to Locke's description of human beings in the state of nature (Tully 1993, pp. 109ff, 168ff). Vattel acknowledged that each state is a sovereign actor, yet he did not believe that interstate relations exhibit the vicious Hobbesian scenario of a perpetual war of all against all. In Vattel's analysis, interstate relations are governed by a natural law which obligates all states to respect each other's Rights. 'From this indispensable obligation ... results the right of every state not to suffer any of her Rights to be taken away, or any thing which lawfully belongs to her' writes Vattel (1863, p. 160) in Book II of his *Droit des Gens*. This right is fundamental; 'that is to say, it is accompanied with the right of using force in order to assert it'. And from this right arise two corollaries:

first, the right of a just defence, which belongs to every nation – or the right of making use of force against whoever attacks her and her Rights. This is the foundation of defensive war. Secondly, the right to obtain justice by force, if we cannot obtain it otherwise, or to pursue our right by force of arms. This is the foundation of offensive war (p. 161).

Vattel repeats an ancient proposition when he notes that states have a natural right to wage defensive war – that if one state should violate the Rights of another, then the offended state would have the right to protect itself by armed force. Also, Vattel echoes an old argument when he claims that states, under certain circumstances have a right to wage an offensive war. But he gave this old 'just-war' argument an epoch-making (Lockean) formulation. By knowingly violating the Rights of another, an offensive state forfeits its own Rights. By 'trampling justice under foot', the offensive state sets itself outside the realm of natural law. In such cases, explains Vattel, any state may pursue and punish it. And he adds, in an argument which amounts to nothing less than an early formulation of the idea of collective security, that other states defend natural law and pursue their own common interest if they agree to do so.

If there were a people who made open profession of trampling justice under foot, ... the interests of human society would authorize all the other nations to form a confederacy in order to humble and chastise the delinquents ... [I]f, by her constant maxims, and by the whole tenor of her conduct, a nation evidently proves herself to be actuated by that mischievous disposition, – if she regards no right sacred, – the safety of the human race requires that she should be repressed. To form and support an unjust pretension, is only doing an injury to the party whose interests are affected by that pretension; but, to despise justice in general, is doing an injury to all nations (p. 161).

Vattel had a great impact on subsequent developments in international law. He particularly influenced scholars in America,[4] where *Droit de gens* rapidly became the standard text on international law (Wiltse 1960).[5]

Speculation about interstate relations

The basic unit of eighteenth-century international relations was the impenetrable, unitary, territorial state, whose professional élite acted on reasoned calculations about states' material capabilities. The dominant focus of International-Relations analysis was the territorial state. States' interests, capabilities and power played as important a role for speculation about international relations as the concepts of velocity, mass and gravity played in Newtonian physics. And the conception of a natural balance between states of unequal capabilities provided the foundation for early eighteenth-century theories of international relations. This idea is clearly present in the balance-of-power theories of the period. It is also evident in the century's theories of international economics, most of which were variations on the theme of a balance of trade.

Both political and economic speculations hinged on the mechanical assumption that power and wealth exist as fixed quantities: when one country increases its share, other countries suffer a corresponding loss. The Newtonian themes of mechanics and equilibrium dominated the century, and were extended to new levels of analysis. The empirical orientation – with its mechanical logic, its demand for parsimony, its vision of equilibrium and its individualist theories of sense perception – was soon applied to domestic and international politics alike. And as it was extended from political relations among states to economic relations within states, new arguments would emerge and undermine the old, dominant balance-of-power model. This development is apparent among British social theorists.

Some British theorists

David Hume (1711–76) discussed international relations in traditional Newtonian terms – as titles like 'Of the balance of trade' and 'Of the balance of power' (written in 1752) suggest. His formidable *History of England* of 1754–62 includes scattered speculations on international relations that are couched in terms of maintaining equilibrium. Hume always claims that a balance-of-power principle regulates international politics. However, he does not really explain how it operates – only in an aside in his *Enquiry Concerning the Principles of Morals* of 1748 does he approach a theory: adjacent states resemble individuals; they regulate their interactions by rules of conduct and formalize these rules into diplomatic codes and laws of nations.

Among the many other British observers who commented on European politics in the light of balance-of-power theory, Daniel Defoe (1660–1731) deserves a closer scrutiny. Although Defoe is best known for his fiction, he was also an astute political essayist and published regular commentaries on world politics in his journal *Review* (Roosen 1986). Defoe admired William of Orange, an early master of balance-of-power politics, who had assumed the English throne in 1689. Defoe observed that although the balance of power was 'something we have made much ado about in the World,' it was still 'little understood' (Defoe 1938, p. 263). He devoted many pages of his *Review* to the European balance, but without producing convincing elucidation as to its basic principles. A similar verdict may apply to Henry St John (later Viscount Bolingbroke, 1678–1751). He had been Secretary of War under Queen Anne and chief architect of the Peace of Utrecht (1713). So when he collected his observations in *Letters on the Study and Use of History* in 1738 he drew on much personal experience; and in any case he discussed European affairs with instinctive acuity. But he did not develop anything like a parsimonious theory of international relations.[6]

William Godwin (1756–1836) did. His argument was developed at the end of the century, and differs sharply from Britain's traditional International-Relations theorists. Godwin's *Enquiry Concerning Political Justice* (1985 [1793]) is not a book on international affairs. It is a resounding critique of contemporary social thought in the name of individual freedom; it is a vitriolic *tour d'horizon* of Enlightenment theorizing during the course of which Godwin finds occasion to criticize the traditional approaches to international relations.[7] He very much doubts the existence of a balance-of-power principle which provides order and stability to the society of states. Indeed, he doubts that there is any substance at all behind the notion of a balance of power. 'The pretence of the balance of power has, in a multitude of instances, served as a veil to the intrigue of courts', writes Godwin (1985, p. 516). International relations is, in Godwin's opinion, largely an activity of kings. And every king in Europe surrounded himself with a court of fawning ministers and secretaries – 'voluntary prostitutes' he calls them (p. 435). They play games of deception and power among themselves and against foreign rivals. And in the process they produce injustices and wars for the world outside. If man should have any hope of establishing peaceful international relations, the corrupt courts must be removed from all the states of Europe and be replaced with democratic systems of government. For whereas monarchies and aristocracies are aggressive and warlike by nature, democracies are inherently peaceful, argues Godwin.

Democracies are inherently peaceful because the vast majority of common people will always strive to avoid war. Kings may believe that war is a glorious and profitable venture; however, common people know that wars bring death and destruction and that, ultimately, it is they who will have to pay their cost in blood and taxes. Thus 'war will be foreign to the character of any people in proportion as their democracy becomes simple and unalloyed' (p. 507).

This argument for the peaceful nature of democracy was a common and a characteristic argument of late-Enlightenment theorizing. This was an age densely populated with extraordinary intellects. And Godwin stands head and shoulders above most International Relations theorists because he refused to leave this argument alone. He observed the international scene and found that democracies and non-democracies appeared to be equally belligerent. He then adds that in practice it will always be difficult directly to observe the peaceful nature of democracies, because they will regularly fight with non-democracies. However, the peaceful nature of democracies would be apparent in cases where democratic states shared common boundaries. From this simple observation, Godwin derives two important implications. First, that the peaceful nature of democracies can only be observed in democracies' behaviour towards one another.[8] Second, that several adjacent democracies in the world would constitute a zone of peace in the international community.

Some French theorists
The many brilliant theorists of Enlightenment Europe makes it difficult to select a single writer to represent the International Relations theory of the age. Even the shortest list of authors who might be considered 'the voice of the eighteenth century' must include William Godwin. He was one of the most original and influential thinkers of the age. But Godwin stood on the shoulders of giants. Most of his heroes were French. France, too, applied balance-of-power theory to practical politics – as is readily apparent in Louis XIV's *Memoirs for the Instruction of the Dauphin* of 1668. In France balance-of-power theory was also systematically probed. It is quietly assumed in François de Callières' (1645–1717) famous text on *The Art of Diplomacy* (1983 [1716]). It is explicitly evaluated by François Fénelon (1815, pp. 766ff), who sought to base it on principles of natural law. It is criticized by Baron Montesquieu (1689–1755) and others, who fear that stability may be purchased at the cost of an arms race –

that as soon as one king augments his military forces in the name of peace and stability, 'the others suddenly increase, so that nothing is gained thereby but the public ruin' (Montesquieu 1990, p. 224).

Montesquieu made spectacular contributions to the political theories of the Enlightenment, and the twin themes of mechanics and equilibrium, which marked his age, are apparent in his famous *Spirit of the Laws* (1990 [1748]). Although Montesquieu does not explicitly address international politics, he has made spectacular contributions to the study of International Relations. First, because other authors have allowed his general arguments to illuminate their analyses of interstate relations. Antoine Pecquet is an important case in point. His *Spirit of Political Maxims* (1757) was an analysis of international politics pretentiously conceived as a sequel to Montesquieu's masterpiece. And although Pecquet falls short of this ultimate ambition, he nevertheless provides a masterful discussion of 'the Equilibrium of Europe' – Chapter 12 (pp. 191–207) of Pecquet's 1757 book, for example, rivals any of the best analyses written in English.

Also, Montesquieu often drew learned connections between international issues and the study of Law, Government, Economics, History, etc. One such connection is his claim that war is associated with regime type. 'The spirit of monarchy is war and expansion; the spirit of republics is peace and moderation', writes Montesquieu (1990, p. 132). His argument is that monarchies are driven to conquest by their very nature. Republics, on the other hand, are largely preoccupied with defending themselves. And if the republics are small, Montesquieu continues, they cannot defend themselves without alliances; and since monarchies are expansionist, small republics must seek protection through alliances with other republics, argues Montesquieu (1990, pp. 60ff). This line of reasoning adumbrates a point which is later elaborated by others: that from relations among popularly governed states a peaceful international community can be constructed.

Montesquieu draws a related connection between republics, peace and commerce. 'The natural effect of commerce is to lead to peace', he submits on one occasion (p. 338). And the logic which underlies this claim is that commerce has an enlightening effect on those who engage in it. Commerce spreads knowledge. It deepens insight into other peoples' customs and mores. It increases understanding and diminishes fear of others. 'Commerce has spread knowledge of the mores of all nations everywhere; they have been compared to each other, and good things have resulted from this'. Commerce cultivates tolerance by diluting 'destructive prejudices', and this encourages peaceful international relations, argues Montesquieu.[9]

A third connection is drawn by Montesquieu from monarchies and war to slavery and colonialism. He notes that the quest for security which drive monarchies towards expansion and conquest in Europe also apply to their behaviour in the extra-European world. He notes how the Spaniards arrived in the Americas, declared war on the natives and enslaved them. He also notes how the Europeans exterminated the native Americans but found new slaves in Africa so that they could clear land, establish plantations and supply Europe with sugar (p. 250).

This distinction between masters and slaves which is found in Montesquieu's political discussions is paralleled by a distinction between northern and southern nations which is drawn in his economic discussions: the nations of the North have 'many needs and few comforts of life', whereas those of the South have 'all sorts of comforts of life and very few needs'. Peoples of the North are obliged to work hard, lest 'they should lack everything and become barbarians'; peoples of the South, by contrast, have developed a lazy disposition, argues Montesquieu (1990, p. 355). These differences in industry have political consequences, for the nations of the South remain poor and weak and easily fall under the domination of the more entrepreneurial nations of the North. Montesquieu concludes with a sweeping, macro-historical claim:

What has naturalized servitude among the southern peoples is that, as they can easily do without wealth, they can do even better without liberty. But the northern peoples need liberty, which procures for them more of the means of satisfying all the needs nature has given them. The northern peoples are, therefore, in a forced state unless they are either free or barbarians; almost all the southern peoples are, in some fashion, in a violent state unless they are slaves (1990, p. 355).

Many of Montesquieu's ideas reverberated through French discussions of international politics for the remainder of the century.[10] The idea which associates monarchy with war was revolutionary in its implications: if monarchs cause war, then peace can be achieved by replacing monarchies with democratic republics. Voltaire (1694–1778), drew the revolutionary implications of the argument quite explicitly. He includes war, along with pestilence and famine, as among the worst scourges of humanity, and blames them on 'the imagination of three or four hundred persons scattered over the surface of the globe under the name of princes and ministers'. Voltaire, then, stripped the rhetoric of monarchs of pretence and patriotism and disclosed eighteenth-century wars for what they were: dynastic squabbles (Voltaire 1967). Voltaire's discussions on international politics constitute a tiny part of his prolific production. But his opinions on war and peace are unmistakable and firm, and reverberate with the revolutionary arguments of Montesquieu.

Some German theorists

In Britain and France Enlightenment theories triggered social revolutions. In Germany they sparked elaborate speculations. The key ideas of the Enlightenment never struck root in Germany; they were discussed, but in a socio-political vacuum. Germany was fragmented into hundreds of tiny states and principalities. Apart from Prussia, which was ruled by the iron-fisted Frederick the Great, there existed no central government as in Paris or London; the middle class was small and powerless; political reform was unthinkable. The British extracted from the Enlightenment ideas, political agendas and practical hard-headed demands for social change. The Germans extracted from the Enlightenment abstract ideas and universal (or cosmopolitan) formulations. Theirs was an Enlightenment of the spirit only.

German International Relations theorizing reflects this stark duality: the discussions were either abstractly idealistic or highly practical. This duality is evident in the international relations commentaries of Kant. On the face of it, Kant's description of interstate relations is pessimistic. He writes about the readiness with which states go to war and how this 'is exhibited without disguise in the unrestrained relations of the Nations to each other'. He notes how war requires 'no special motive', 'how it appears to be ingrafted in human nature' (Kant 1970b, pp. 220f). However, below the surface of Kant's argument, there are veins of rich ore from which Kant mines one of the most optimistic doctrines in the tradition of International Relations theory: humanity also possesses reason; and as human rationality inevitably evolves, all people will increasingly recognize the evils of international strife, and will work to put an end to all wars.

Kant recognized that a balance-of-power mechanism existed in interstate relations. However, he found it mechanically unsound. He did not for a minute believe that it possessed any natural, self-equilibrating properties. 'A lasting Universal Peace on the basis of the so-called Balance of Power in Europe is a mere chimera', he argues. 'It is like the house which was built by an architect so perfectly in accordance with all the laws of equilibrium, that when a sparrow lighted upon it, it immediately fell' (1970a, p. 198). Consequently, he refused to accept the argument, which was embraced by so many British authors, that an extra-human principle could be trusted to produce peace automatically through interstate equilibrium. Peace among states could only be established through human reason and political will. Paradoxically, such a will would inevitably emerge as humanity discovers new and more bestial forms of war: frightened by the growth of their own destructive capabilities, they will increasingly realize the pressing need to abolish war and to establish and keep peace (1970a, p. 198). In the long run, Kant concluded, Eternal Peace is inevitable.

This odd juxtaposition of aloofness and hard-headed practicality which marked Teutonic theorizing is hardly more interestingly expressed than in a little book written by Crown Prince Frederick (later Federick II) of Prussia: *Anti-Machiavel* (1981 [1740]). In this curious little volume on statesmanship, Frederick musters the major authorities of the Enlightenment to refute the pernicious doctrines set out in Machiavelli's *The Prince*. On one level, *Anti-Machiavel* is a seductively simple book; its intended message is clear, and its composition is straightforward. 'I dare come to the defense of humanity against this monster who would destroy it,' writes the young crown prince. 'I dare to oppose reason and justice to iniquity and crime, and I have ventured my reflections on Machiavelli's *Prince* following each chapter, so that the antidote may be found right next to the poison' (Frederick II 1981, p. 31).

On another level, *Anti-Machiavel* is a complex and enigmatic articulation of the contradictions which tormented Enlightenment statesmen. The author appears caught in a dilemma between the Enlightenment theories that he professes (but which he may not accept) and the Machiavellian practices that he despises (but may not yet fully understand). In the end, he 'falls into considerably greater contradictions than those he claims to find in his *bête noire*, and utterly misses the glaring similarity between Machiavelli and himself' (Sonnino 1981, p. 15). Frederick wrote his treatise in 1740, upon considerable encouragement from Voltaire – and Voltaire's Enlightenment ideals are very much present in its pages.

It is worth noting that, when Frederick succeeded to the Prussian throne in 1740, inheriting one of the most centralized states and one of the most disciplined armies in Europe, he suddenly displayed a very different image. As King Frederick II, he was an enlightened monarch – he liberalized laws regarding censorship, religion and torture. But he was hardly an Enlightenment monarch. He was an absolutist ruler, and soon emerged as one of the most astute and unscrupulous princes of the age. He threw Europe into turmoil for more than two decades, exploited the political confusion in a series of brilliantly conceived stratagems, and greatly enlarged Prussia's territories. Crown Prince Frederick became King Frederick 'the Great', a *Machtmensch* who made Prussia the foremost military power in eighteenth-century Europe – paving the way for German unification and dealing Europe's traditional balance of power its first major blow (Airas 1978, pp. 14ff). When he again found the time to write a book on statecraft, it was entitled *Military Instructions of the King of Prussia for His Generals*. This little volume – replete with information about the treatment of weapons, the training of horses and the organization of armies – is in essential respects similar to Machiavelli's *Art of War*. Frederick's *Politisches Testament* of 1768, however, is more similar to *The Prince*. This little book, which was intended as a 'foreign-policy handbook' for Frederick's successor, opens with the following bald claim: 'In international politics you should have no special predilections for one people, nor aversion to another. You must follow the interests of the state blindly, allying yourself with the power whose interests at the time match the interests of Prussia' (Luard 1992, p. 162). It then proceeds to discuss Prussia's position in European politics – in terms which would have earned him the most profound admiration of Machiavelli and Guicciardini:

The greatest error one can fall into is to believe that kings and ministers are interested in our fate. These people only love themselves; their own self-interest is their god. Their manner becomes flattering and insinuating only in so far as they have need of you. They will swear, with shameless falsehood, that your interests are as dear to them as their own. But do not believe them; block your ears to their siren calls ... (Luard 1992, p. 162).

Jean-Jacques Rousseau: prophet and paradox

The eighteenth century has been called by many names: the Age of the Old Regime, the Age of Cosmopolitanism, the Era of Democratic Revolution, the Age of Enlightenment. Few thinkers are as representative of this rich, complex century as Jean-Jacques Rousseau (1712–78). He wrote on astonishingly varied themes – including novels, operas and beautiful essays on botany. His analyses of international politics amount to only a minor part of his production. But what a part! Rousseau discussed war and peace, colonialism and wars of liberation (Knutsen 1994). All from a unique, sceptical perspective and with a penetration which singles him out as perhaps the major contributor to International Relations theory of this Age of Enlightenment.

Always a champion of individual freedom and self-reliance, Rousseau was a delinquent youth. He ran away from home several times, and periodically led the unsettled life of a penniless wanderer. He tramped around Southern Europe and earned his living as a tutor of music, a copyist, a writer of operas, a confidence trickster and a secretary to the French ambassador in Venice. At the age of 16, he encountered Mme de Warens at Annecy in Savoy. She would play for him the role of the mother he had never had. She would also become his protector, his teacher and his mistress (Cranston, 1991).

Rousseau's first major essay was his *Discourse on the Arts and Sciences* of 1749, which won first price in a competition announced by the Academy of Dijon. Much encouraged, Rousseau launched a career as a writer. Within a dozen years he had written most of his major works, including the *Discourse on the Origin and Basis of Inequality among Men* (1950a [1755]) and the *Social Contract* (1950b [1762]).

Rousseau was one of the first of the modern intellectuals; one of the first 'angry young men'. His penetrating intellect and his considerable charm earned Rousseau admirers all over Europe. His unorthodox clothing and his calculated scandals made him the darling of the Parisian salons. Here he became the principal voice of the essential claim of the Enlightenment: that human beings were fully capable of comprehending social reality and of manipulating their physical and social environment. Among the first social theorists in history, he claimed that humanity could devise formulae by which the structure of society and the fundamental human habits could be described.

Although he died a decade before the French Revolution, many contemporaries held him responsible for it – indeed, this was one of the few things on which Louis XVI and Robespierre agreed. During the Revolution, the National Convention voted to have his ashes transferred to the Pantheon. In the decades which followed this transfer, public opinion grew increasingly divided on his place in history. He attained the status of a saint to some, and favourite villain to others. To Shelley he was 'a sublime genius'. To Schiller he was 'a Christ-like soul for whom only Heaven's angels are fit company'. People who had met him usually begged to differ. Diderot, after long acquaintance, characterized him as 'vain as Satan, ungrateful, cruel, hypocritical and full of malice' (Crocker 1974, Vol. I, p. 356). But on one point has there been full agreement: Rousseau was a momentous contributor to International Relations theory.

To put Rousseau's International Relations analysis into perspective, it is necessary to begin with Charles Castel, Abbé de Saint-Pierre (1658–1743). Like other peace projects of the age, Saint-Pierre's *Project for Making Peace Perpetual in Europe* of 1713 is founded on the Enlightenment anthropology that men are endowed with reason. He had studied Hobbes, and he found in Hobbes' description of the state of nature a powerful analogy to the condition of war which existed among states. His solution to the problem of war was similar to Hobbes' – except that whereas Hobbes wrote about all humanity, Saint-Pierre only wrote about princes. The rulers of Europe will sooner or later be forced by reason to realize that their interests are better served by peace and order than by war, he argued. This realization would drive them into closer co-operation and, finally, into a 'confederal government' – a council or diet on which the ruling princes of all member states would be represented. Saint-Pierre is, like Crucé, an advocate of the integration of the states of Europe into a confederate union. He devised a variety of bureaux which should handle different matters of common interest to the member states; thus, one important bureau should work out a code of commercial jurisprudence to regulate commerce between the subjects of different states; another should standardize weights, measures and the currency of the member states. Saint-Pierre is, like Crucé (and also like Montesquieu and other Enlightenment authors), preoccupied with the characteristic Enlightenment belief that trade furthers peace (Perkins 1959; Russell 1936, p. 191).

Saint-Pierre's simple, appealing and important message was obstructed by his unattractively repetitive and rhapsodic style. After Saint-Pierre's death, his friends and family searched for a sympathetic scholar who could make the Abbé's voluminous writings on war and peace accessible to the princes and peoples of Europe. In 1754, they asked Jean-Jacques Rousseau to edit and abridge Saint-Pierre's grand Project. This request would spark one of the most unique and penetrating analyses in the history of International Relations theory – although not necessarily one which met with the approval of the Abbé's heirs. The work kept Rousseau busy for several years. But it was never completed. He only finished a long introduction to the planned work. This was issued separately as the *Project for a Perpetual Peace* of 1760 (Hoffmann and Fidler 1991, p. xxii).[11]

Rousseau was too impatient and imaginative to reproduce faithfully the thoughts of another man. His *Project* is a brilliant essay. But it contains more of Rousseau than of Saint-Pierre. Indeed Rousseau could scarcely hide his opinion that the Abbé's argument was 'superficial' and 'impractical owing to one idea from which the author could never escape: that men are motivated by their intelligence rather than by their passions' (Rousseau 1978, p. 393). He ends this abridgement, with the remark that the Abbé's case rests on the unproven assumption that kings have enough reason to see what is useful for society at large (1964a). He then wrote a detailed criticism in a separate commentary, *Judgement on Perpetual Peace* (1964b [1782]) – which he did not dare to publish.[12]

Where Hobbes, Crucé, Grotius, Hume, Kant, Voltaire and Saint-Pierre reduce the dynamics of international politics to human nature, Rousseau introduces other elements as well. Whereas Hobbes, for example, portrays humanity as proud and covetous, Rousseau portrays it as peaceful and kind. There is nothing inherent in human nature that predisposes people to aggression, Rousseau claims. People become fighters and warriors only when they are moved from the state of nature to civil society (Rousseau 1964c). War is a *social* undertaking; it is a product of human civilization. It is the *citizen* who is most eager to become a soldier, not the human being in a state of nature. Armies and wars do not exist until societies exist with states which organize their citizens into armies and march them off to further the interest of their rulers. At this point Rousseau is at odds with all other contract thinkers: for them, the social contract ends conflict among people; but for Rousseau it creates the preconditions for war.

Rousseau argued (like Locke) that human beings are endowed with natural reason and with a natural right to freedom; but he also claimed that, in actuality, humanity is enslaved. This apparent paradox appear in several of Rousseau's writings – for example in the opening line of *The Social Contract*: 'Man is born free; and everywhere he is in chains' (Rousseau 1950b, p. 3). His major social treatises all address this apparent paradox of liberty and rationality on the one hand and enslavement on the other.

If people are rational, why aren't they capable of seeing that they are being enslaved and exploited by the existing social order? Rousseau's answer is that humanity has been corrupted by this order. Society is corrupt, and as individuals are born into this corrupt society they become corrupted in turn. People, then, are malleable. They are shaped by the society they inhabit. If they are born into a good society, they will develop their reason and become good people; if they are born into a corrupt society, their reason will be stunted and warped and their natural liberty will be replaced with vanity, contempt, shame, envy and other dismal factors. In a corrupt society, people will be alienated from their original liberty, happiness and innocence.

Two important corollaries flow from this line of reasoning. First, the corruption and alienation of humanity cannot be explained as an outcome of human nature; it must be explained as a result of an intolerable social situation. Second, humanity is rational, but only potentially so. People are not born with reason; they *develop* reason.

This raises another question: if people were originally free, good, happy and innocent, how did society come to be so corrupt? Rousseau's answer to this question hinges on two intimately intertwined components: a historical analysis and a theory of a division of labour.

Evolution of the State: the loss of natural innocence

Rousseau's account of the historical evolution of civil society provides a convenient entry into his International Relations theory. This account describes an evolution which has alienated people from their original free, happy and innocent selves. It is most clearly set out in *A Discourse on the Origin and Basis of Inequality Among Men* (1950a [1755].) Like so many of his contemporaries, Rousseau, too, uses a state of nature as his vantage point. Before state and civil society existed, Rousseau claims, man lived in total freedom and innocence: 'I see him satisfying his hunger at the first oak, and slaking his thirst at the first brook; finding his bed at the foot of the tree which afforded him a repast; and, with that, all his wants are supplied' (Rousseau 1950a, p. 200).

From this initial condition of innocence, human history has been driven forward by an emerging division of labour. This division first evolved in response to demographic and geographic circumstances, Rousseau argues, and it removed humanity from its happy state of nature through stages of historical evolution.

In the initial stages, co-operation among people stimulated the growth of reason and language. People accumulated knowledge, and the more they were enlightened, the more they improved their efficiency of production. Then, as industry improved, people developed a sense of the advantages of mutual undertakings. Instructed by experience, they learnt that love of one's own well-being is the most powerful motive of human action. So an individual grew selfish; but he also learnt to acknowledge the selfishness in others, and to identify situations 'in which mutual interest might justify him in relying upon the assistance of his fellows'. So 'he joined in the same herd with them, or at most in some kind of loose association'. This was no lasting union, Rousseau, explains; it was strictly an *ad hoc* affair, for these men

were perfect strangers to foresight, and were so far from troubling themselves about the distant future, that they hardly thought of the morrow. If a deer was to be taken, every one saw that, in order to succeed, he must abide faithfully by his post: but if a hare happened to come within the reach of any one of them, it is not to be doubted that he pursued it without scruple, and, having seized his prey, cared very little, if by so doing he caused his companions to miss theirs (p. 238).

In later stages of human development, people were more permanently united by communalities which had evolved among many of them: language, customs, common ways of living and eating. And as co-operation became more systematic, the division of labour became more formalized and human relationships became more governed by laws or involved work and responsibilities. A decisive stage was reached in human evolution when metallurgy was introduced. This meant that some people had to specialize in the smelting and forging of iron; and others had to provide food for them as well as for themselves. Because no one could survive without the others, work became compulsory.

Rousseau realized that, on the one hand, a social division of labour meant increased efficiency in production and the creation of wealth which made life more abundant and comfortable. But on the other hand, the division of labour also meant the advent of compulsory labour, civil obligations and the dependence of each upon everyone. The more Rousseau considered the notion of interdependence, the more he grew convinced that a conflict existed between affluence and freedom; and that social wealth was purchased at the cost of human liberty. As long as people were content with their rustic huts and their primitive clothes made from animal skins, they were happy and free; 'but from the moment one man began to stand in need of the help of another ... work became indispensable, and vast forests became smiling fields which man had to water with the sweat of his brow, where slavery and misery were soon seen to germinate and grow up with the crops' (pp. 243f). Matters developed rapidly for the worse when private property was introduced:

The first man who, having enclosed a piece of ground, bethought himself of saying 'This is mine,' and found people simple enough to believe him, was the real founder of civil society. From how many crimes, wars and murders, from how many horrors and misfortunes might not any one have saved mankind, by pulling up the stakes, or filling up the ditch, and crying to his fellows: 'Beware of listening to this impostor; you are undone if you once forget that the fruits of the earth belong to all of us, and the earth itself to nobody!' (pp. 234f).

On this paragraph, undergirded by a vision of historical evolution and a theory of a division of labour, hinges Rousseau's vision of international politics.

The international system: 'the law of the strongest'
The social division of labour enhanced the material well-being of humanity. However, it also created conflict and inequality. It robbed all the individual participants of their natural liberty. This signalled a fatal turn of events in human history. As humanity evolved, social interdependence was exacerbated by private property, which released an insatiable quest in humankind for selfish economic advantages. 'Those who have nothing have limited desires, those who do not rule have limited ambitions', Rousseau writes. However, as society evolves, it imposes upon humanity both property and responsibilities. Material possessions have their own needs, the satisfaction of which stimulates the quest for more possessions and awakens the vanity and cupidity of humankind. 'The more one has, the more one wants. Whoever has much wants everything', writes Rousseau (1964c, p. 610).

Ever since the advent of private property, all human qualities have been tainted with a possessive element – infusing strength with a tinge of vanity, skill with competitiveness, love with jealousy. This development has robbed people of their ability to distinguish between good and evil, between real and apparent interest. History testifies to how the advent of property exacerbated the inequalities which nature had placed in humankind, rendering them more clearly seen and more deeply felt. It shows how the gap between the haves and the have-nots has widened. In the midst of growing misery and strife and the further weakening of the weak, humanity was driven to develop social hierarchies and orders (Rousseau 1950a, p. 244).

Finally, humanity developed political institutions backed by law. These institutions consolidated the principle of private property, sanctioned social inequality, protected the wealth and the power of the ruling élite, oppressed the poor majority of mankind and alienated them all in the process.

The foundation of the commonwealth marks the final stage of this long historical process. The commonwealth imposes order upon the growing anarchy among individuals. However, the same act which solves the problem of anarchy among individuals, creates a condition of anarchy among states. In Rousseau's mind, humanity has left one state of nature, characterized by liberty and peace, and entered another state of nature, marked by oppression and war. It is not difficult to see

that each of us is in the civil state with regard to our fellow citizens, but in the state of nature as regards the rest of the world; that we have taken all kinds of precautions against private wars only to kindle national wars which are a thousand times more terrible; that in joining a particular group of men, we have in reality become the enemy of mankind (Rousseau 1964a, p. 654).

Out of his depiction of rulers' greed and citizens' misery and everyone's alienation, Rousseau formulates a vision whose nightmarish qualities rival even those of Hobbes' state of nature. The rulers are greedy and animated solely by two desires: to extend their territorial power and to achieve a more absolute rule over their subjects. The citizens are alienated, and enthusiastically contribute money and men to support wars of conquest and the subjection of conquered peoples; and they do not realize that they thereby deepen their own misery. Rulers' greed and citizens' alienation feed on each other.

Anyone can understand that war and conquest without and the encroachments of despotism within give each other mutual support; that money and men are habitually taken at pleasure from a people of slaves, to bring others beneath the same yoke; and that conversely war furnishes a pretext for exactions of money and another ... for keeping large armies constantly on foot, to hold the people in awe. In a word, anyone can see that aggressive princes wage war at least as much on their subjects as on their enemies, and that the conquering nation is left no better off than the conquered (Rousseau 1964b, p. 592).

Rousseau depicts domestic society in gloomy terms, but his vision of international society is far bleaker. For whereas civil society at least is regulated by law (albeit the law of the ruling élite), the society of states, in effect, obeys no law but 'the law of the strongest' (Rousseau 1964d, p. 1013). In his description of this 'law', Rousseau is true to the sentiment of the age: he describes it in explicit, balance-of-power terms, and he does this with a sophistication and a concreteness which was scarcely superseded by other eighteenth-century authors.

In his *Project for a Perpetual Peace*, (1964a [1760]) Rousseau introduces a discussion of the European balance of power by a description of Europe's cultural geography. 'The powers of Europe constitute a kind of system, united by the same religion, international law and moral standards; by letters, by commerce and by a kind of equilibrium which is the inevitable outcome of all these ties' (1964a, p. 565). This equilibrium is in Rousseau's mind more a product of nature than the work of any human hand. 'The lie of the mountains, seas, and rivers which serve as frontiers for the various nations who inhabit it, seems to have fixed forever their number and their size' (p. 570). This equilibrium brings a semblance of order to the relations between European states, Rousseau explains. And although the rulers of individual states always act to extend their dominions, the balance still obtains. 'It is there; and men who do not feel themselves strong enough to break it conceal the selfishness of their designs under the pretext of preserving it' (p. 570). Rousseau articulates the sentiment of the age when he depicts the European balance of power as self-equilibrating:

Whether we are aware of it or not, the equilibrium continues to support itself without the aid of any special intervention. If it breaks for a moment on one side, it soon restores itself on another; so that, if princes who are accused of aspiring to universal monarchy were in reality guilty of any such venture, they displayed more evidence of ambition than of genius. How could any man look such a project in the face without instantly perceiving its absurdity? without realizing that there is not a single potentate in Europe so much stronger than the others as ever to have a chance of making himself their master (p. 570).

This self-sustaining balance prevents any one state from attaining mastery over all Europe. For whenever a ruler seeks to extend his country's territory by military means, other rulers will unite against him at every step. Every once in a while, a ruler may be lucky, and conquer an uncommonly large territory. However, Rousseau writes, even such lucky breaks are bound to fail over the longer haul: 'the resistance is in the long run as strong as the attack; and time soon repairs the sudden accidents of fortune, if not for each prince individually, at least for the general balance of the whole' (p. 571).

This self-regulating balance of power imposes a principle of order on the interaction between states. But it does not bring peace. Although the European balance of power blocks major conquests over the longer haul, in day-to-day politics it merely perpetuates instability and irritation. Indeed, Europe is plagued by perpetual conflict – quarrels, robberies, usurpations, revolts and wars 'which bring daily desolation to this venerable home of philosophy, this brilliant sanctuary of art and science' (p. 568).

The integration of the states of Europe has made the continent wealthier than other regions of the world and forged a historic 'fellowship far closer than is found elsewhere'. However, since their cruel conflicts occur not in spite of interdependence, but *because* of it, tighter integration only renders these plagues and conflicts more frequent, more intense and more deadly. Explains Rousseau:

The historic union of the nations of Europe has entangled their rights and interests in a thousand complications; they touch each other at so many points that the smallest move-ment of one of them gives a jolt to all the rest; their differences are all the more deadly, as their ties are more intimately woven; their frequent quarrels are almost as savage as civil wars.

Let us admit then that the powers of Europe stand to each other strictly in a state of war, and that all the separate treaties between them are in the nature rather of a tempo-rary truce than a real peace (p. 568).

The origins and nature of the state system.
The 'law of the strongest' only partly accounts for the relative order of the Euro-pean interstate system; balance-of-power dynamics only explains the mechanical workings of the system. In order to understand the origins of European politics, Rousseau adds a historical argument: the stability of the system hinges on his-torically formed preconditions which allow the balance-of-power dynamics to operate. Europe's interstate system is a temporal arrangement. It had a begin-ning, which can be distinctly determined by the historical formation of the pre-conditions upon which it depends – and consequently, it is likely to meet its historical end once these preconditions are removed.

The most important of these historical preconditions is the complex 'German Body', the Holy Roman Empire. Rousseau identifies several unique attributes which contribute to the stabilising role of the German Empire. First, its geo-graphical position; the German Body 'lies nearly at the centre of Europe and holds all the other parts in their place'. Second, its size; Germany covers a vast area and appears as 'a body formidable to all by its size and by the number and valour of its component peoples'. Third, its fragmented nature; Germany con-sists of over 300 states, and constitutes an exceptionally complex and stable bal-ance-of-power system in its own right. The constitution of the Holy Roman Empire, which deprived it 'both of the means and the will to conquer, makes it a rock on which all schemes of conquest are doomed infallibly to falter'. What Rousseau refers to as the 'constitution' of the German Body was established at the Peace of Westphalia (1648). Concludes Rousseau:

In spite of all its defects, it is certain that, so long as that constitution endures, the equi-librium of Europe will never be broken; that no potentate need fear to be cast from his throne by any of its rivals; and that the Treaty of Westphalia will perhaps forever remain the foundation of our international system (p. 572).

By identifying the Treaty of Westphalia as 'the foundation of our international system', Rousseau pinpoints the fountainhead of Europe's interstate order: the general acceptance of the principle of the sovereignty of states. The Treaty of Westphalia recognized the right of princes to act solely on the calculus of their own interest. While the brute power of these rulers *within* states keeps in check greedy individuals, who are constantly at each others' throats in pursuit of their personal gains, the relations *among* states are characterized by permanent conflict, since there is no higher system to regulate their interaction.

If war is the product of interdependent relationships among sovereign states, then war can be abolished by removing the states' sovereign attributes. Peace can be secured only if the states of Europe give up their sovereignty and invest it in a higher, federal body. War can be abolished if the states establish a social contract between them – i.e., if they establish 'such a form of federal government as shall unite nations by bonds similar to those which already unite their individual members and place the one no less than the other under the authority of the law' (p. 564).

Virtually all social contract philosophers who have addressed questions of war and peace have arrived at this conclusion. Rousseau, however, is distinct in that he goes further. Other Enlightenment thinkers build on the assumption that reason is a universal human property and that freedom and right are universal political values. Abbé Saint-Pierre, for example, argued that since all possess the faculties of reason and all strive to realize their freedom and right, it should be possible to replicate the social contract established among individuals within a state and form another contract among states. Most particularly, this should be possible in Europe, whose states possess so many common traits in customs, religion, letters, language, laws and trade. This contract would remove the states from the bellicose state of nature in which they presently find themselves, and establish a world federation.

Rousseau did not disagree with this proposal. He did not doubt that once it was implemented, the princes and peoples of Europe would immediately find its advantages 'immense, manifest, incontestable'. Realize 'this commonwealth of Europe for a single day', he wrote, 'and you may be sure that it will last forever; so fully would experience convince men that their own gain is to be found in the good of all' (1964b, p. 591). Rousseau did, however, protest at the proposal's basic assumption about human rationality. For him, humans are only *potentially* rational. *Actually* they are so alienated by the corrupt society they inhabit, that they can no longer recognize their own best interests.

Saint-Pierre believed that once the kings of Europe had considered his reasoned argument, they would agree to it. Rousseau doubts this – not because the Abbé's scheme is not good enough, but because it is so good and so sensible that alienated humanity 'will know no other way to react to it than with ridicule'. The Abbé's project will remain unrealized because the kings no longer know their true interest; they will not recognize a reasonable argument when they see one. Rather than follow the voice of reason, they will habitually act according to passion. In the corrupt environment of contemporary politics, alienation has robbed humanity of its ability to distinguish, 'in politics as in morals, between real and apparent interest' (p. 592). If the Abbé's project remains unrealized, 'it is not because it is utopian; it is because men are crazy, and to be sane in a world of madmen is itself a kind of madness' (1964a, p. 589).

In a world of alienated individuals, a federation of Europe would never come about through a spontaneous agreement. If it were to be established, this could only be done through force. A federation of Europe could be established only if one single state managed to conquer the entire continent militarily and rob all other important states of their sovereignty by the force of arms. Once this was achieved, the victor must replace these disparate sovereignties with a single, supranational legislative body with such immense powers that it could compel every other state to obey its common resolves.

To prove that this is not inconceivable, Rousseau recalls an earlier attempt to establish a lasting peace through a European federation. The French King Henry IV and his trusted minister, the Duc de Sully, had conceived of a plan for a Christian Commonwealth around the turn of the seventeenth century. They had made immense, protracted and detailed preparations to implement this plan when Henry IV was assassinated in 1610.

The Abbé de Saint-Pierre sought to revive the policy of Henry IV, and create a Christian Commonwealth through peaceful means, Rousseau argues. The Abbé, however, made two mistakes. First, he had no theory of alienation; he was therefore so naive as to believe that the kings of Europe would accept his proposal voluntarily. Second, he had no theory of History; he did not therefore realize that European politics have evolved since the times of Henry IV, and that the unification of Europe (admittedly through force), which was so close to success before Westphalia, would be met with failure after it.[13] Even if a strong ruler should emerge who understood the merits of the Abbé's proposal, who followed the example of Henry IV and who launched an effort to unify Europe through force, he would be defeated. He would be prevented by the balance-of-power principle which was consolidated at Westphalia in 1648. Instead of establishing a universal monarchy, he would – given the immensity of the force required to establish a federation of Europe and given the high likelihood of failure – launch a war of such unprecedented magnitude, that Europe might be destroyed in the effort. Rousseau wonders, at the end 'whether the League of Europe is a thing more desired or feared? It would perhaps do more harm in the moment than it would guard against for ages' (1964b, p. 600).

The sentiment of the century

During the seventeenth century, the natural world became an object systematically scrutinized by the human mind. Bacon, Galileo, Descartes, Hobbes and others had devised methods by which the world could be known and mastered. This 'scientific revolution' was the womb of the Enlightenment. The seventeenth-century scientific project was cultivated by eighteenth-century *philosophes*. They stressed the unlimited potentials of human reason (Kant 1949a). They were sceptical toward tradition, confident in the powers of science,

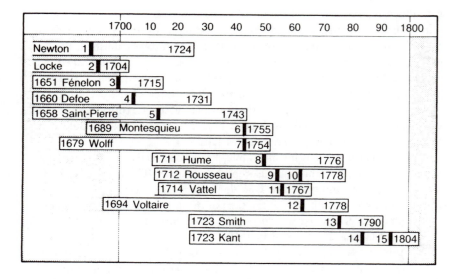

1. *Mathematical Principles of Natural Philosophy* [1687]
2. *Two Treatises of Government* [1689]
3. 'On the necessity of forming alliances' [1700]
4. *Review* [1704–13]
5. *Project for Making Peace Perpetual in Europe* [1713]
6. *The Spirit of the Laws* [1748]
7. *The Law of Nations* [1749]
8. 'Of the balance of power' [1752]
9. *Discourse on the Origin and Basis of Inequality among Men* [1755]
10. *Project towards a Perpetual Peace* [1760]
11. *The Law of Nations* [1758]
12. 'War' [1764]
13. *The Wealth of Nations* [1776]
14. 'Idea for a universal history with cosmopolitan intent' [1784]
15. 'Perpetual peace' [1795]

Figure 3 Some eighteenth–century authors and their works

convinced of the regularity of nature. They saw themselves no longer as servants and interpreters of the gods, but as challengers, even substitutes. Their heroes were Prometheus, who stole the celestial fire and brought it to earth, or Faust, who pursued knowledge, truth and power at the peril of his soul.

The Enlightenment vision
The scientists and theorists of the Enlightenment retained the seventeenth-century predilection for classificatory tables and taxonomies, the culminating

expression of which was the mechanical universe of Isaac Newton. But the eighteenth-century vision of symmetry transcended the material realms of astronomy and physics; it permeated all sectors of art, thought and human knowledge. This vision of symmetry is apparent in the architecture of the century's grand estates – in Louis XIV's Versailles as well as in Marlborough's Blenheim. It was visible in the splendid geometry of the estate gardens. It was audible in eighteenth-century music, in the fugues of Johann Sebastian Bach as well as in the sonatas of Joseph Haydn. It provided the organizing principle of the paintings of Reynolds, the novels of Defoe, Swift and Fielding. It blazed through the 'tree of knowledge' which organized the *Cyclopaedia* of Ephraim Chambers and the *Encyclopaedia* of d'Alembert. The hierarchical symmetry which organized the binary taxonomies of Swedish botanist Karl von Linnae is also found in new structures which Western nations began to impose upon armed forces – each army was divided into army corps, each corps into two or three divisions, each division into brigades, each brigade into regiments, each regiment into battalions.

In Britain, the notion of a natural harmony is apparent in several works on economics. It emerged during a debate about corn laws which Parliament passed during the wars of Louis XIV (Grampp 1965, p. 78). One notably influential argument for the natural harmony of free individual interaction was written at the outbreak of the wars by Richard Cumberland. He argued that a society of rational individuals contains natural rewards for virtuous behaviour and that all citizens will consequently act with benevolence and tolerance towards each other. Another famous argument for the natural harmony of free interaction was written at the end of the wars by Bernhard de Mandeville (1670–1733). In his *Fable of the Bees: or Private Vices, Publick Benefits* (1924 [1714]), Mandeville argued that the vices which were most despised in the older moral code would, if practised by all individuals, result in the greatest public good. Selfishness, individual greed and acquisitive behaviour were all properties which contributed to industriousness, to a thriving economy and to national wealth. Mandeville's point, of course, was that in view of the new moral and economic philosophies of the age, these motives should no longer be considered vices. Notions of a natural harmony also inform the anarchism of William Godwin (1985).

Social thinkers on the Continent developed variations on this eighteenth-century theme. The vision of the harmony of free individual interaction is evident in the writings of French economist François Quesnay (1694–1774). Jean-Baptiste Say (1767–1832) developed a theorem of market equilibrium, arguing that the very process of production creates a market for the commodities produced – that supply creates its own demand – and that any productive economy would remain in equilibrium. A theory of market equilibrium was also developed by James Steuart (1712–80). However, the classic formulation of the vision of a self-harmonizing economy was penned by Adam Smith (1723–90) (Winch 1996). He wrote in his *Wealth of Nations*, (1976 [1776]):

As every individual endeavours as much as he can both to employ his capital in the support of domestick industry, and so to direct that industry that its produce may be of the greatest value; every individual necessarily labours to render the annual revenue of the society as great as he can. He generally, indeed, neither intends to promote the publick interest, nor knows how much he is promoting it ... he intends only his own gain, and he is in this, as in many other cases, led by an invisible hand to promote an end which was no part of his intention (Smith 1976, p. 456).

This vision of a natural harmony of free, individual interaction was not restricted to economics; it also made its imprint on discussions of politics. It is evident in Jean-Jacques Burlamaqui's argument for a separation of powers in government; an argument which is more famously elaborated in Montesquieu's *The Spirit of the Laws* (1990 [1748]). Montesquieu argued that if a state intends to promote liberty, it ought to divide its supreme political authority into three branches of government: the legislative, the executive and the judiciary. If these three branches act independently of each other, then each one will act as a check upon the political authority of the others and thus guarantee the overall harmony of society and maximize the liberty of its citizens (Montesquieu, 1990, pp. 68–75). The authors of the American Constitution embraced Montesquieu's theory, and founded the new nation upon its principles of checks and balances. 'Ambition must be made to counteract ambition', writes the author of No. 51 of *The Federalist* in 1788, 'only by so contriving the interior structure of the government as that its several constituent parts may, by their mutual relations, be the means of keeping each other in their proper places.' That this doctrine reflects a larger law of nature, is obvious to the author; he contends that 'this policy of supplying, by opposite and rival interests, the defect of better motives, might be traced through the whole system of human affairs, private as well as public' (Hamilton *et al.*, 1937, p. 337).

Enlightenment International Relations theory
The themes of symmetry, balance and self-equilibrium are also apparent in eighteenth-century speculations about international affairs. Hume, Defoe, Fénelon, Hamilton, Kant, Rousseau and others articulated this dominant sentiment of the age in their discussions of the balance-of-power principle (Sheehan 1995).

This vision of social balance which characterizes eighteenth-century social thought, differs from that of earlier ages. In the seventeenth century, the balance of power among states was seen as a policy which benefited a particular country – the vision of balance was interpreted through the notion of individual interest. Thus, when Francis Bacon recommended that Britain throw its weight where it was most needed, his aim was to protect England's own sovereignty and enhance its freedom of action. His assessment of the relative strengths of the European countries, conjures up the image of a pair of balancing scales. Bacon referred to this image as a policy of counterpoise, 'whose object is the security and well-being of a particular state'.

In the eighteenth-century, by contrast, the vision of social balance was seen as a policy which benefited the whole society. The balance of power, for example, was seen in terms of an entire self-equilibrating social system. An early articulation of this is found in Fénelon (1815, p. 767), who argues that a country conducts a balance-of-power policy in order 'to preserve itself and its neighbours from servitude; 'tis to contend for the liberty, tranquillity, and happiness of all in general: For the over-increase of power in any one influences the general system of all the surrounding nations'. A balance-of-power policy, then, was a policy which benefited the entire system of states – and therefore also all the system's individual members. In this notion, the primary purpose of an eighteenth-century balance-of-power politics was not to preserve the sovereignty and independence of individual states – although it did accomplish this. Rather, it was to preserve the order of the interstate system itself. In the eighteenth century, the international balance of power was seen as the essential stabilizing factor in the society of sovereign states. It also became an end in itself.

From Rousseau to Kant

Vattel depicted a society of states living together in peace and equilibrium under the morally binding prescriptions of natural law. Comparable 'cosmopolitan' arguments were formulated by several German writers such as Lessing, Goethe and Schiller. A most influential conception for international interaction was formulated by Immanuel Kant in an essay entitled 'What is Enlightenment?' (1949a [1784]). Kant began by defining the Enlightenment as a stage in a larger historical process through which humanity acquired the ability and courage to use its own reason rather than submit to external authorities – be they books, priests, physicians or absolute rulers: 'Enlightenment is man's leaving his self-caused immaturity,' Kant writes. 'Such immaturity is self-caused if it is not caused by the lack of intelligence, but by lack of determination or courage to use one's intelligence without being guided by another. Sapere Aude! Have the courage to use your own intelligence! is therefore the motto of the Enlightenment' (Kant 1949a, p. 132; Foucault 1984a).

From the assumptions that human beings possess reason and are fully conscious of their true interest, and that they have a will to realize that interest, Kant develops an optimistic vision of international politics. The development proceeds through three analytic steps. The first step takes the argument from its assumption about human rationality to a claim about the rational individual response to war: all rational individuals know that it is always they, rather than their rulers, who will bear the hardships of war. It is, ultimately, they who have to pay the cost of war in blood and taxes. Therefore they are unlikely to bring the calamities of war upon themselves voluntarily.

The second step extends the argument from the response of the rational individual to a political universe inhabited by rational individuals: all rational people understand that it is always the rulers who gain from war, and the citizens who lose (Kant 1970a, p. 197; 1970b, pp. 208–10). This understanding divides human society into two camps. On the one hand are the many citizens whose interests are best served by peace; on the other are the few dynastic rulers who drive the citizens to war. This division has revolutionary implications. It suggests that the citizens of all countries are, in fact, united through a reason-based, transnational consensus of interest which is served by peace, whereas conflicts of interest exist only among the ruling cliques. Kant, in effect, agrees with Montesquieu, Voltaire and Godwin: that the most expedient way to abolish war is to abolish dynastic politics and to impose popular sovereignty and democratic rule on all the world's nations.

The third step follows naturally from the second: international politics is only *apparently* the relationship among states. The real and consequential theme is, in the final instance, made up of relations among all people in the community of humankind. Properly understood, the interests of all peoples are the same. Consequently, the study of world politics should not focus on the distributive quarrels of states; it should really debate the international society which is produced through the interaction of individuals. For when push comes to shove, Kant explains,

International society is none other than mankind, encumbered and thwarted by the archaic fiction of an international society composed of sovereign states. States are not persons, they have no wills but the wills of the individuals who manage their affairs, and behind the legal facade of the fictitious Society of Nations is the true international society composed of men (Wright 1987, p. 223).

To students of politics, Kant's gives the advice that they must first understand the rational nature of humanity, and then derive from the properties of human reason the common interests of humankind. Their primary task is to explore the nature of the universal moral imperatives which, in international relations, limit the actions of tyrants and states. For Kant, then, the study of world politics not only hinges on the claim that the community of humankind is the central reality in international affairs, it also means that the community of humankind is the end or object of human's highest social endeavour – in Kant's own words, 'a perfectly *just civic constitution*, must be the supreme task nature has set for mankind' (Kant 1949b, p. 122).

To students of history, Kant explains that a true community of humankind does not yet exist; that it exists not in actuality but as a potentiality. For humanity does not yet live in an enlightened age; only in an age of enlightenment. However, as human history progresses, and human reason attains greater self-consciousness, a world society of enlightened self-interest, harmony and peace will emerge. The primary task of the universal historian is to trace this evolution of history as it is driven by the emergence of human reason! The primary focus of the universal historian should not be individual people, irrespective of their greatness, but the evolutionary trend of humanity. 'Thus, that which appears to be complicated and accidental in individuals, may yet be understood as a steady, progressive, though slow, evolution of the original endowments of the entire species' (p. 116).

Order-in-space, progress-through-time and the Enlightenment paradox
Enlightenment contributions to International Relations theory included a shift in focus from the individual state to the state system. This also implied a shift in logic. It implied a general acceptance of – if not a profound faith in – a principle of natural harmony. And in this faith lies the major paradox of the Age of Enlightenment. This age, which emphasized so insistently the primacy of human reason, built its most characteristic social vision on an irrational, extra-human principle of self-adjustment.

Some authors sensed this paradox and wrestled with it. Kant and Rousseau, for example, took part in the century's characteristic discourse of mechanical self-adjustment; yet neither fully accepted the claim that self-regulation would be an automatic outcome of the free exercise of human reason. Both discussed interstate relations in balance-of-power terms. Both suggested that human societies are governed by immutable laws. Yet neither were willing to derive these laws from the rational workings-together of individual minds. 'Individual human beings, each pursuing his own ends according to his inclination and often one against another (and even one entire people against another) rarely unintentionally promote, as if it were their guide, an end of nature which is unknown to them,' writes Kant. 'They thus work to promote that which they would care little for if they knew about it' (1949b, p. 117f).

There is in Kant and Rousseau a notion that reason alone cannot explain the regularities of human behaviour. Rousseau insists on this point, since he believes that humanity is potentially rational but actually alienated. If millions of people are given the liberty to pursue their individual interests while still in this alienated condition, they are likely to produce chaos and conflict rather than harmony. Kant seems to agree: 'Man is an animal who, if he lives among others of his kind, *needs a master*, for man certainly misuses his freedom in regard to others of his kind. ... Man therefore *needs* a master who can break man's will and compel him to obey a general will under which every man could be free' (p. 122). Social harmony cannot be an assured outcome of the free exercise of warped reason. International peace cannot occur until human reason is transformed, educated, un-alienated, liberated by a good society and developed to its fullest potential.

Both Kant and Rousseau explored ways in which reason may be so transformed. They did this in terms of political will and human history. Instead of embracing the faith in reason and self-equilibration, which was expressed by so many Atlantic authors, they stressed the role played by political will. This emphasis on the volitional side of human nature had long characterized Europe's humanist tradition. Rousseau re-emphasized it, elaborated it and expressed it in his doctrine of the General Will – which is what each individual would will if alienation were removed and man could see his real interests. This doctrine had a formative impact on Continental political philosophy (Talmon 1952; 1960).

Kant and Rousseau also stressed the effect which history had on human society. They cast their discussions in evolutionary terms, thereby foreshadowing a major new theme which would characterize the social-scientific discourse of the nineteenth century. They held the notion that individual human beings are actors in a play whose plot they do not fully understand, and, however much they consult their individual reason, they help bring about some inevitable end. Kant's and Rousseau's discussions of reason, will and historical progress signalled a new conception of social order; they adumbrated the transition from the static eighteenth-century vision, according to which social order is depicted in terms of symmetry in space, to a dynamic nineteenth-century vision, where social order is captured through the notion of evolution through time. This emphasis on reason/will and History/progress would later provide a vantage point for Hegel's philosophical system.

Rousseau made historical investigation a key component of International Relations theory. Building on Rousseau, Kant broke with the mechanical, eighteenth-century vision of order-as-symmetry-in-space, and introduced an organic vision of order-as-progress-through-time. Both Rousseau and Kant saw this progress in terms of a dialectical relationship between man and nature: nature imposes afflictions and hardships upon man, who, in overcoming these, is gradually guided towards his moral destiny. This dialectic, which reverberates through Rousseau's and Kant's entire conception of politics, would later inform Karl Marx, for whom politics involved transformation not only of society, but of the political actors as well.

The belief that it is possible to discern in the course of human history some general scheme or design is very old. However, around 1800 there emerged a distinctly new version of historical evolution of which Rousseau provided an early foreshadowing. This 'new historiography' implied, first of all, a view of steady progress in human affairs. Second, it argued that this progress was a result of humanity's conquering the natural environment by means of human reason. Third, it divided the progress of human civilization into phases or ages. Rousseau and Kant are not the only representatives of this 'new historiography' – Adam Smith's account of the economic progress of humanity (1976 [1776]) divided human evolution into four historical phases; Condorcet's sketch of the progress of the human mind (1798 [1794]) divided human history into nine periods, each starting with some great invention; Fichte, Schlegel, Görres (Batscha and Saage 1979) and, above all, George W. F. Hegel (1980) subsumed all human history under a reason-driven progress. But Rousseau and Kant were among the first thinkers who also allowed this vision to undergird their International Relations theories.

6

Ideological politics: the nineteenth century and the rise of mass participation

Two revolutions convulsed the Old Regime: the political revolution in France and the industrial revolution in England. They occurred with rough simultaneity. Together they created new conduits for political and economic mass participation: large-scale armies, mass parties, mass production of consumer goods and rapid growth of consumer markets.

The triumphant growth of industry and man's power over the physical world gave nineteenth-century men new confidence in reason and science. Scholars applied novel scientific techniques and logic to society, feeding the rapid growth of the social sciences. The study of International Relations broke away from its narrow confines of diplomatic law and military science.

The Enlightenment had been populated with an astonishing number of men of genius. Ironically, as their emphasis on individual rights and liberties met with greater acceptance, individual theorists were increasingly overtaken by systems of thought – by schools, traditions, approaches and ideologies. Such new systems flourished in the post-Napoleonic age, which became an era of 'isms'. The word 'liberalism' appeared in the English language in 1819; 'radicalism' appeared in 1820, 'socialism' in 1832, 'conservatism' in 1835; in the 1830s came 'individualism' and 'constitutionalism'. The proliferation of systems of ideas at first overwhelmed the explorers of international relations; they were expelled from a garden carefully tended by a few legal and historical authorities into a new, uneven terrain of dense theoretical foliage.

Yet the spread of 'isms' did not always mean the dissemination of new ideas. Rather, the appearance of 'isms' marked the beginning of the systematic exploration, re-evaluation and arrangement of many existing ideas in the fresh context of a rapidly changing society. One of the most important novelties of this busy age, then, was not so much the discussion of the ideas themselves; rather it was their synthesizing into *systems* of ideas and the self-conscious placement of these systems in a social context. The early nineteenth century elaborated upon the Enlightenment discovery of 'society' as something which was both *more than* the mere sum of its constituent individuals and *different from* the state in which it was constituted. The political thinkers of the age began to search for the 'natural laws' which governed this new human arena. This search is reflected in the evolution of political economy, sociology, demography and other disciplines. Speculation about international political relations followed suit, and soon moved beyond the traditional domains of international law, political philosophy and diplomatic investigations of diplomats, generals and kings.

This chapter emphasizes the first half of the nineteenth century; the major changes wrought in the century's final decades are addressed more systematically in Chapter 7.

Revolutions in politics and economy

Earlier thinkers had viewed the state as an approximation to a divinely sanctioned order. The Enlightenment portrayed it as a man-made artefact – as a mutually beneficial, voluntary arrangement created by free and rational human beings to protect their natural rights and self-interest. This idea that the state originated in a voluntary social contract clashed conspicuously with the rhetoric of absolutist monarchies of the Old Regime, and fuelled criticism of the status quo. John Locke – and, later, Sidney and Bentham in Britain, Voltaire, Montesquieu and Rousseau in France, Jefferson in America – contributed to the mounting critique of the absolutist state and to the advocacy of alternative reason-based forms of rule. In the final quarter of the eighteenth century, this evolution climaxed in sweeping reforms in England and in Revolution in America (1776) and France (1789). The celebrations of abstract reason and the excesses of social revolution would, in turn, provoke reactions and mutations in Conservatism and Romanticism.

The American and the French revolutions transformed politics *within* states. They removed sovereignty from the monarch and lodged it in institutions which claimed to represent the people. Countries throughout Europe were compelled to confront the intoxicating notion of popular sovereignty. Some statesmen (like Russia's Tsar Alexander I and Austria's Chancellor Metternich) sought to contain and combat the revolutionary ideal; others (like Britain's Lord Liverpool and Latin-America's Bolivar) sought to adjust old political structures to new demands – to secularize, rationalize and reform existing institutions in the light of new democratic principles.

These changes which occurred within states would, in turn, alter the political relations *among* states. This is readily visible in the case of France. When foreign enemies threatened France in 1793, the revolutionary regime issued a general call to arms, a *levée en masse*, as an emergency measure to defend the new nation and its revolutionary ideals. This appeal to the patriotism of millions of free and equal citizens of France raised enough soldiers to fend off enemy assaults. Later, Napoleon transformed the revolutionary regime's last-resort appeal to popular sentiment into armies infused with such ardour that they conquered much of Continental Europe.

Other European states could not withstand France's armies without emulating their radically new organization. The novel emphasis on merit and mobility in the French army mirrored the new moral equality and openness in French society; Napoleon's rational sub-division of the army into specialized branches reflected its new spirit of rational planning and political engineering. Popular ideological and patriotic passions whipped up by the French whirlwind had to be guided by techniques of propaganda and mass mobilization. The language, rationale and style of politics were transformed.

Great changes also occurred in the economic realm. The productive forces of countries were harnessed to the engine of mass mobilization and transformed into political power. Carried on a wave of unprecedented industrial expansion, Britain emerged from the Napoleonic Wars of 1792–1815 economically strengthened and socially changed. Industrial expansion vastly increased Britain's national wealth: between 1800 and 1850 the value of Britain's exports tripled and the value of imports more than quadrupled (Hobsbawm 1969; Kennedy 1987).

The economic changes amounted to a veritable revolution in their own right. They altered the structures and relations within states.[1] They also changed the relations among states. In England, the rise of new middle and working classes eroded the old institutions of the great landowners who controlled Parliament. The rise of new occupations drove the new technology deep into the fabric of British society, and then outward into the rest of the world, stimulating trade and interaction of unprecedented scope. Groups of industrialists, financiers, shippers and shopkeepers increasingly opposed the chief obstacles to their mercantile activities – Corn Laws, Navigation Acts and aristocratic privileges at home; the forces of feudal and monarchic reaction abroad. They soon universalsed their position and claimed that policies which had brought them wealth would similarly benefit others: the free movement of labour, capital and commodities would contribute to the emergence of a fairer, wealthier and more peaceful world. The Holy Alliance of European Emperors, which had united the traditional monarchies of Europe against the rising revolutionary tide, struck them as repugnant. The first among the victors of the Napoleonic Wars, Britain broke with the Alliance, pursuing instead a more independent policy of national interest tailored to suit its dynamic economy.

Along with new means of production came new means of destruction. Prussia was one of the first states to adapt its armed forces to the new industrial culture. The introduction of rifled barrels enhanced Prussian artillery; the packaging of ball and charge into standard cartridges increased the rate of fire; the construction of guns and cartridges out of lighter material improved military mobility. Also, railways moved Prussian troops rapidly across Europe; the telegraph produced a new, centralized system of instantaneous communication and military co-ordination around which was built the famous German general-staff system. During the 1860s, these improvements were instrumental in unifying the divided German people through a string of quick, successful wars. Prussia's crowning achievement was its rapid mobilization of over a million soldiers in 1871 and its quick victory over France. This success led almost all other states in Europe to emulate Prussian military organization.

The application of science and technology to warfare tied the national security of states intimately to the nation's economic health and rate of development, setting the stage for a new phase of military history characterized by a self-reinforcing armaments spiral. Whereas past arms races had varied greatly in intensity and duration, they now became part and parcel of industrial nations' economic institutions.

Revolutions in social thought

The pre-revolutionary mind was permeated by visions of natural order – regimentation, symmetry and balance. Post-revolutionary thinkers were thrust into a disorderly world in which the dominant theme was not constancy, but change. Despite the turbulence of the age, new scientific discoveries, applications and methods gave rise to robust confidence. Now scholars began to insist that scientific methods could be transferred from the study of nature to the study of society. Just as the political and economic revolutions coincided and intertwined at the very end of the eighteenth century, the growth of the new social sciences and the evolution of political ideologies converged and intertwined throughout the nineteenth.

The evolution of social thought displayed two contradictory tendencies: unification and differentiation. On the one hand, there was an optimistic drive towards grand theory, i.e., a single, unified master science. Hegel, Comte and others argued that society was indivisible, and so likewise the study of society must be holistic and indivisible. On the other hand, there was a tendency towards greater differentiation and a deeper specialization of individual sciences.

Economics was the first to single itself out as a separate social science. 'Political Economy', as it was called, addressed the key issues raised by the Industrial Revolution (Winch 1996). Elaborating on old conceptions synthesized by Adam Smith and the physiocrats, the new science explored the creation of wealth and its social distribution in terms of a self-regulating process. Political Economy analysed the social and economic aspects of the new methods of producing ever greater economic surplus, and it addressed the resulting critical question of its just distribution among society's various classes. 'The produce of the earth – all that is derived from its surface by the united application of labour, machinery, and capital, is divided among three classes of the community,' wrote David Ricardo – viz., the proprietor of land, the owner of the capital and the workers. 'To determine the laws which regulate this distribution is the principal problem in Political Economy' (Ricardo 1984, p. 3). Students of International Relations, notably diplomats and officers at first, came under the spell of the new science of Political Economy and the arguments of Ricardo and Malthus.

The application of scientific modes of thought to human affairs led scholars to search for some hidden principle which governed their apparent chaos. The two themes which dominated these efforts were 'competition' and 'progress'. Nineteenth-century theories understood competition as a natural feature of human society, but infused the term with at least three different meanings: First, there were the liberal authors, for whom competition was beneficial for society: it was society's dynamic and creative force. They adopted Adam Smith's position that man's competitive nature is regulated by some natural law which applies equally to civil society and to the society of nations.

Second, there were conservative authors, who conceived of competition as a mortal struggle. Theorists like Burke, Malthus, Metternich and Bismarck maintained that this struggle characterizes relations among individuals and states alike.

Finally, there were radical theorists, like Marx and Engels, who shared this position. However, whereas the conservatives saw the struggle as an unalterable outcome of human nature, the radicals viewed it as a curable illness, as a temporary human condition.

A large and varied panopticon of political economists maintained that the struggle for existence pertains to one type of political relations but not to others. Ricardo, for example, painted a gloomy picture of domestic society as a vicious struggle between social classes; yet he drew an optimistic sketch of interstate relations as a system of free competition harmonized by the law of 'comparative advantage'. More common was the argument proposed by Kant (1970b) and Hegel that domestic society is harmonious, whereas the interstate system is conflictual. Some thinkers refined this argument further. Mill and Mazzini claimed that only democratic society is harmonious. Godwin agreed, but added that democracies also behave peacefully on the international scene; that despotic regimes are belligerent by nature, whereas democracies do not initiate war – at least not on each other (Godwin 1985, pp. 506f, 529ff).

If nineteenth-century theorists differed as to the first theme (competition), they largely agreed about the second (progress). They reconceptualized the old vision of order-as-movement-in-space into a new vision of order-as-progress-through-time. They saw social change as the uni-directional improvement of human existence. They captured progress in terms like 'development' and 'history' (Foucault 1973; Eckstein 1982; Tilly 1984).

Ideologies and world politics

Around the turn of the nineteenth century, the discussion of social change yielded three major secular systems of thought in the West. It fragmented the tradition of Western political thought into the three ideologies of liberalism, radicalism and conservatism. An 'ideology' is a systematic body of beliefs about the structures and processes of society; it includes a comprehensive theory of human nature that sustains a programme of practical politics. The liberal and the radical ideologies can be seen as continuations of the Enlightenment project; conservatism, by contrast, as a reaction against it. In practice, these three ideologies were never sharply demarcated; they interacted and overlapped. Especially in the early decades of the nineteenth century, it was often difficult to determine where radicalism ended and where liberalism or conservatism began. This section sketches the three ideologies as ideal types, distinguishing them with excessive clarity to isolate their distinctive cores.

Liberalism and the bliss of the world economy
Liberalism has its firmest foundations in the socio-political culture of the North-Atlantic rim. The 'classic' version of liberal ideology is a continuation and elaboration of the major themes of the Enlightenment, nourished by changes wrought by the political and industrial revolutions and articulated by members of the emerging middle classes in the Atlantic world.

As the new industrial and commercial entrepreneurs hastened to build their mills and factories, they found their way blocked by the traditional privileges of the aristocracy, the institutions of the established Church and the State, and the restrictive mercantilist policies of the seventeenth and eighteenth centuries, These obstacles forced them to systematize their outlook as they struggled to construct institutions and policies more congenial to their needs.

The liberal outlook can be summed up in the four concepts of 'equality', 'rationality', 'liberty' and 'property'. Eighteenth-century *philosophes* re-formulated the old idea of the moral equality of man into more abstract social, economic and human rights. This reformulation lies at the core of John Locke's political philosophy. It also informs the American *Declaration of Independence* (1776), which holds 'that all men are created equal, that they are endowed by their Creator with certain inalienable rights, that among these are life, liberty and the pursuit of happiness'. Equality of opportunity – not the equal distribution of material and social goods among all citizens – is the first cornerstone of nineteenth-century liberalism.

The second cornerstone is an optimistic view of man as able to satisfy his natural needs and wants in rational ways. Man is fully capable of comprehending and mastering the social and physical reality which surrounds him. He has the capacity for self-improvement and self-reliance and should therefore be given the opportunity to realize his right freely to pursue his happiness according to his own life-plan.

Liberalism's fundamental commitment is to the rational individual rather than

150

to society. For the liberal, the proper goal of social policy is to maximize the autonomy and the freedom of the individual. The best society allows the rational individual the greatest liberty. The individual could be allowed great autonomy largely for reasons set forth by political economists like Adam Smith: their particular interests would fit together harmoniously, producing a wealthy, happy and peaceful society. In the context of the eighteenth and nineteenth centuries, liberty meant freedom from tradition, from hierarchical authority and from any concentration of political power. This demand for citizens' liberty to seek private ends is the third cornerstone of liberalism.

The fourth cornerstone is private property. Through private property, man can seek private ends and thus realize his individuality and his happiness. Property gives man an incentive to work; and through his labour, man will not only enrich himself, he will enrich society as well.

Of the many theorists who contributed to the development of nineteenth-century liberalism, few have exerted more influence than Jeremy Bentham (1748–1832). To the basic liberal themes of equality, rationality, liberty and property, Bentham adds the concepts of economic utility and harmony of interests. Bentham's confidence in an open society, the common man, the value of popular democracy and the general harmonizing effect of free trade stems from his identification of the ancient concept of 'the Good' with 'Happiness,' and the definition of Happiness as an outcome of man's habit of 'maximizing pleasure and minimizing pain'. As each man strives to obtain Happiness through this rational 'calculus of felicity', he automatically does the Good. The common man will 'infallibly conform to the moral law of nature once its content had been rationally determined' (Carr 1964, p. 23). If every man were free to maximize pleasure and minimize pain, 'the greatest happiness for the greatest number' would result.

Adam Smith postulated a connection between the self-interest of the individual and the Good of society. Bentham provided a simple and logical connection between the two – in a sense, Bentham laid bare the social mechanism which governed the operation of Smith's 'invisible hand'. By making Happiness the criterion for goodness, the only requirement for separating good from bad was to understand where one's Happiness lay. This made Goodness 'not a matter of abstruse philosophical speculation, but of simple common sense' (p. 24).

Bentham also distinguishes between the realm of economics and the realm of politics. For Bentham, the economic order is the realm of private activities of production, procurement, distribution and consumption of goods and services. It is a realm of open access operating under natural laws and a fundamental harmony of nature. It allows human society to self-equilibrate and operates best and to the benefit of all when political authority interferes least with the system's automatic operation. In contrast, the political order is the realm of public decision-making, influence and the exercise of power. Politics does not obey natural laws: it is a closed realm in which social control is maintained through manipulation, corruption, conflict, strife and, occasionally, by forceful repression (Spero 1990, pp. 1–20).[2]

The liberal view on international affairs undergirds Bentham's 'Plan for a Universal and Perpetual Peace' (1843 [*c*.1794]).[3] It is largely an economic tract, and argues that colonialism is the major impediment to free trade and, therefore, to international stability and peace as well. Colonialism forces states to maintain strong navies in order to defend their colonies and to protect their trade. Since trade is limited by the amount of capital available at any given moment, the more national capital is tied up in naval forces, the less there is available for productive investments. If the nations of Europe divested themselves of their overseas possessions, they would reduce conflict at home as well as in their colonies. They could reduce the size of their military forces and government, freeing national capital for investment in domestic industries and overseas trade. In sum, a Europe without its overseas dependencies would be a more peaceful and richer Europe. Its colonies would similarly prosper (Bentham 1843, pp. 546–9; Airas 1978, pp. 432 ff).

The dismantlement of empires would restore European politics to its pre-colonial condition, argues Bentham. In the absence of colonial struggles, international conflict could easily be reduced to manageable proportions. Of the four basic causes of international conflict, feudalism is 'happily extinct everywhere'. Religious conflict and the passion for conquest are extinct 'almost everywhere', and where they still persist, they might be easily managed by a Common Court of Judicature or a Congress of States. The uncertainties of succession are also largely removed from civilized politics, and should they on flare up, they, too, might be easily managed by a Congress of States, writes Bentham. Only the fourth cause of conflict, colonialism, remains. But if the colonial empires were dismantled, global peace would be within the realm of the possible for the first time in human history (p. 552).

The idea of a Congress of States is discussed by many earlier authors – by Dubois, Crucé, Sully, Saint-Pierre, to mention but a few. But Bentham adds a new dimension to the discussion. He claims that punitive force is dispensable in orderly interstate relations. His Congress of States would not 'be armed with any coercive powers', but would operate by the force of human reason alone. The most powerful instrument for the sanction of the Congress' resolutions was, he insisted, 'the tribunal of public opinion'. In order for the world's public to judge fairly and reasonably, the citizens of the world must have free and constant access to full information about disputes among states. Consequently, the Congress of States must not only report widely upon all matters presented before it, it must also operate under 'a clause guaranteeing the liberty of the Press in each State'.

This recognition of the key role which liberty of the Press plays in the free workings of human reason and the sustenance of world peace leads Bentham to formulate his famous argument for the abolition of secret diplomacy. The veil of secrecy makes it possible for monarchs, ministers and military men to exploit foreign negotiations for their own enrichment, he argues. In the process, they corrupt the nation's politics and plunge the world into wars which serve only a minuscule élite. 'Under the present system of secrecy, ministers have ... every seduction to lead them into misconduct, while they have no check to keep them out of it' (p. 556).

Bentham influenced the study of International Relations in important ways. First, he made an indelible mark upon its discourse. He coined the term 'international law', thus distinguishing between laws designed for government internal to states on the one hand, and those created for transactions of Sovereigns on the other. This drew the boundaries of the study of 'international relations' – a term he was also the first to use.

Also, Bentham deeply affected the liberal view of international politics by distinguishing between politics and economics. In domestic society, the liberal wants government to stay out of economic affairs; he largely restricts the role of government to legislation, law enforcement and adjudication. In the society of states, by contrast, no over-arching government exists, nor is there an economic order to obey the self-equilibrating laws of nature. The countries of the world exist in a state of nature in which politics and economics have not yet evolved into differentiated activities. The liberal statesman, then, must *make* this differentiation. His task is to set up some kind of Court or Congress of States in which the functions of legislation, law enforcement and adjudication can be carried out on an international scale. The main function of this Congress is to promote the operation of the world economy according to the principles of natural law – in a word, to replace colonial and protectionist practices with free trade.

Radicalism and the global class struggle
Critics took issue with the liberal axiom that man is a rational creature. Both conservatives and radicals agreed that man is *passionate* as well as rational; that he is part of a larger society which shapes him in its image; that this society, in turn, is an organic product of a historical evolution.

Radicals generally perceived themselves to be members of an international movement and accordingly developed concepts and theories of international interaction. They seized upon the need for revolution against the existing system of government to achieve the transformation of society required for the perfection of man. The French Revolution of 1789 swiftly became the signal modern event for left-wing radical theorists.

In France, radical ideas were formulated by authors like Saint-Simon and Fourier. In England, they were expressed by Godwin, Price, Owen and members of radical organizations like the Chartist Movement. These early radicals developed the continuing theme that war is a function of the vast accumulation of private property, blaming the social and economic systems which made such accumulation possible. Radical internationalism was spurred by the Continental upheavals of 1830 and 1848. The age's most influential radical theorists, Karl Marx and Friederich Engels, added and expanded upon Rousseau's insights, arguing that social inequality and human alienation are the outcomes of a social division of labour.

The Enlightenment was the fundamental source of radical ideology. The dual revolution in politics and economics boosted and redirected the energies of the Enlightenment project into an oppositional mode. The left-wing radicalism of the age is perhaps more correctly dubbed an 'insurgent creed' or an 'oppositional state of mind' than an ideology, although it does possess a clear philosophical core from which emerge distinct blueprints for 'the good society'. Radicalism's central aspects are: 'rationalism', 'critical analysis' of the status quo (including a hostile attitude towards private property), 'political activism' and a belief in 'historical progress'.

The first and most fundamental radical assumption is the Enlightenment premiss that human beings are essentially good, that they are endowed with natural reason and accordingly have a natural right to freedom. Human beings have the ability to comprehend their social and material environment and the potential to construct a new, good and just society.

But if individuals are good and rational, what can account for the wretched condition in which mankind finds itself? Rousseau formulated the two essential elements in the radical response to this question in the 1750s, and they need to be noted before the second cornerstone of radicalism can be addressed. First, people are not endowed with fully developed powers of reason at birth; they have the potential for developing reason, but this development is dependent on the nature of the society in which they find themselves. Second, society is corrupt; and when individuals are born into a corrupt society, their natural goodness is thwarted and the growth of their rational faculties is stunted. Radical theory singles out private property as the most insidious of society's corrupting influences. Rousseau (1950a, p. 279) claims that under the impact of property people's souls and passions 'gradually deteriorate until they can almost be said to have changed their nature'. Godwin (1985, p. 436) writes that the accumulation of property is always attended by abuse of power, capricious politics, personal convenience and pecuniary corruption. Marx and Engels argue that under the influence of private property, people becomes alienated from their true selves (Mészáros 1970). In sum, people are only potentially rational, and their potentialities for reason can be fully realized only within the context of a good society – i.e. a society in which the unlimited accumulation of private property is abolished.

The second cornerstone of left-wing radicalism flows from this logic: a critical analysis of the existing social order – an analysis which seeks to disclose the intimate relationship between relations of property and political power. The existing order serves the narrow property interests of a small, privileged élite at the expense of the interests of the vast majority of humanity. Existing socio-political institutions, broadly designed, support the élite while they enslave the majority and deny people the ability to develop to their full human potential.

Because the prevailing order is oppressive for most people, it must be changed if their lives are to improve. Political action is the third cornerstone of radicalism. Radicals are not satisfied with merely understanding the world; they want to better it. In its last instance, this argument becomes an advocacy for the overthrow of the existing regime – for revolution. It becomes a plea for 'the dissolution of political government, which has been the perennial cause of the vices of mankind' (Godwin 1985, p. 16). Marx and Engels advocated such a revolution on a global scale in the famous closing command of the *Communist Manifesto* (1974 [1848]):

> The Communists everywhere support every revolutionary movement against the existing social and political order of things. In all these movements they bring to the front, as the leading question of each, the property question ... They openly declare that their ends can be attained only by the forcible overthrow of all existing social conditions. Let the ruling classes tremble at a Communist revolution. The proletarians have nothing to lose but their chains. They have a world to win.

The fourth cornerstone of left-wing radicalism is the vision that history evolves in such a way that the material wealth of humanity improves over time. Nineteenth-century liberals nurtured a comparable claim, but the radical vision is distinctive in two ways. First, the radicals observe that material wealth is unequally and unfairly distributed among social classes. Although the wealthiest classes of society note considerable improvement over time, the poorest classes do not share in the improvement. Second, the radicals maintain that History is of decisive importance in the study of politics and society. Whether a specific event implies a betterment or a worsening of the condition of the working masses of the world depends upon the historical context of the event. It depends upon where in the *Stufengang*, or stage of Historical Evolution, the event occurs.

Marx and Engels furnished radicalism with a new, crisp, historically self-conscious formulation which spread across the west after 1850, replacing the 'utopian socialism' of the first half of the century with the 'scientific socialism' of the second. The *Communist Manifesto* expresses a new, internationalist vision of politics. It holds that the exploitative and alienating regime of capitalism is challenged by a self-aware, defiant and global working class. It sees international politics not in terms of sovereign states, but of global classes. It argues that the capitalist economy constitutes a new, truly international system, an essential aspect of which 'is the internationalization of communications and commerce, the development of a global division of labour and the emergence of a class struggle on a world scale' (Marx and Engels 1974, p. 73). It describes human society as sharply divided between rich and poor, between those who rule and those who are ruled. This division results in a perpetual struggle between two classes. This struggle is the force which drives the evolution of History (p. 67).

This vision of the historical evolution which undergirds 'scientific socialism,' was built on the social theories of Rousseau and Hegel and fortified by the new Political Economy of Mill and Ricardo. The struggle between classes is a material, essentially economic, struggle; it inevitably ends in a revolution which destroys the old social order (or mode of production) and erects a new order in its place. 'At a certain stage of development, the material productive forces of society come into conflict with the existing relations of production', explains Marx. 'From forms of development of the productive forces these relations turn into their fetters. Then begins an era of social revolution' (Marx 1975b, pp. 425f).

Marx dubbed this vision of social evolution 'dialectical materialism'. He argued that the rapid development of productive forces which took place in the West in the modern ages inaugurated a new stage in History. As the new productive forces evolved, they destroyed the old industries and the traditional relationships of production which sustained them. In this light, the discoveries of the long sixteenth-century opened up fresh ground for a new entrepreneurial class, the bourgeoisie.

The East Indian and Chinese markets, the colonization of America, trade with the colonies, the increase in the means of exchange and in commodities generally, gave to commerce, to navigation, to industry, an impulse never before known. The feudal system of industry, under which industrial production was monopolized by guilds, now no longer sufficed for the growing wants of the new markets. The manufacturing system took its place ... Thereupon, steam and machinery revolutionized industrial production. The place of manufacture was taken by the giant, modern industry, the place of the industrial middle class, by industrial millionaires, the leaders of whole industrial armies, the modern bourgeois (Marx and Engels 1974, pp. 68f).

The bourgeoisie evolved during the seventeenth and eighteenth centuries, and accomplished several feats. First, it fuelled a string of social revolutions which marked the transition from the feudal age dominated by the old nobility to a capitalist age dominated by the new bourgeoisie. The first of these revolutions took place in the United Provinces, followed by the revolutions in England and France; the era which followed was marked by the rise of Dutch and British colonialism (Marx 1977, pp. 914–20). Second, the bourgeoisie instituted wage-labour; separating the workers from the means of production, making labour a commodity and creating a propertyless class or proletariat. Third, it conquered the governing institutions of the modern state – indeed, the 'executive of the modern state is but a committee for managing the common affairs of the whole bourgeoisie' (Marx and Engels 1974, p. 69).

Finally, the bourgeoisie, helped by the means of organization and oppression which the modern state put at its disposal, spread its capital, its political influence and its interests all over the world:

The need for a constantly expanding market for its products chases the bourgeoisie over the whole surface of the globe. It must nestle everywhere, settle everywhere, establish connections everywhere ... The bourgeoisie, by the immensely facilitated means of communication, draws all, even the most barbarian, nations into civilization ... It compels all nations, on pain of extinction, to adopt the bourgeois mode of production (p. 71).

However, by creating the world in its own image, the new global capitalist class is also sowing the seeds of its own destruction. For by exporting the capitalist mode of production to all corners of the earth, the bourgeoisie also calls into existence its own *antithesis* – an international class of wage labourers. For a time, the global proletarians 'do not fight their enemies, but the enemies of their enemies, the remnants of absolute monarchy, the landowners, the non-industrial bourgeois, the petty bourgeoisie' (p. 75). However, as the old classes decline in strength, and the proletariat increases in number, it becomes concentrated in greater masses, its strength and its political self-consciousness grow. Thus:

the unceasing improvement of machinery, ever more rapidly developing, makes their livelihood more and more precarious; the collisions between individual workmen and individual bourgeois take more and more the character of collisions between two classes. Thereupon the workers begin to form combinations (trade unions) against the bourgeoisie (Marx and Engels 1974, p. 75).

Marx and Engels understood all politics in the light on an expansionist, global economy characterized by a growing antagonism between a dominant (bourgeois) and a dominated (proletarian) class. These two classes are international in scope; they are both creations of a global economy.

Although classes and class struggles exist within individual states, the overriding struggle is that which exists between a global bourgeoisie and a global proletariat (p. 78). The nation is not the primary social actor for Marx and Engels, the class is; the primary social struggle is not expressed in war between states, but in war between global classes.

Sooner or later, a global revolution will usher in a socialist mode of production: the working class will sweep away the remnants of bourgeois society – including the state, and the bourgeois ideology of nationalism – by means of a social revolution, for which the French Revolution was a prototype (pp. 85–7). The bourgeoisie will then dissolve as a class, and the traditional bourgeois mechanisms of oppression will 'be thrown in the dustbin of History'. The State itself will ultimately wither away. The Great Proletarian Revolution will first triumph in the most advanced capitalist countries. Then war will liberate those peoples who are still unjustly oppressed by their own ruling classes or by colonialist occupiers.

The early nineteenth-century radical view of world politics is little more than a magnified version of domestic politics. In this respect, radicalism and liberalism have much in common. Both envision peace and harmony as the natural state of properly managed human affairs; both maintain that conflict and war are caused by ruling classes who intervene to protect and further their vested interests. This similarity between the two Enlightenment traditions was most visible in the early decades of the century, when liberal democracy and utopian socialism stood shoulder to shoulder in opposition to the status quo. However, its utopian streak ran far into 'scientific socialism'. When the International Working Men's Association – the 'First International,' founded by Karl Marx in 1864 – debated foreign policy, national defence and the causes of war, the recurring arguments tended to be as vague as they were simplistic: war was caused by capitalism; peace would come with socialism.

This initial naïveté changed with the founding of the Second International (1889). This organization was intended as a kind of international parliament of socialist movements, rather than as the doctrinally pure organization that the First International sought to be. The German Social Democratic Party (SPD) dominated the Second International. The SPD provided, on the eve of World War I, a radical environment within which modern radicalism transcended both Rousseau and Marx and sponsored several sophisticated and influential radical discussions of international politics (Semmel 1981).

Conservatism and the defence of the Old Order
The conservative ideology arose in response to the rapid evolution of industrialists, entrepreneurs, merchants, labourers, mass movements and progressive authors. Conservatism repudiated the advocacy of the equal rights of man, and denounced the new faith in reason, science, and historical progress. In opposition to the concepts of equality and individual freedom, conservatives posed the primacy of community; against the rhetoric of improvement and change, they emphasized traditional social order and responsibility. The French Revolution, which so inspired the radicals, haunted the conservatives. They adopted a defensive mission: to provide the philosophical basis of opposition to the progress which liberals and radicals championed.

Edmund Burke (1729–97) laid the foundations for this mission in his *Reflections on the Revolution in France* (1988 [1790]). Its cornerstones are 'communalism and traditional authority', a 'pessimistic anthropology', 'hierarchy' and 'private property'. For Burke, the community is prior to and above the individual. On this claim Burke constructs a conception of the individual's proper relationship to the social order in staunch opposition to the rational individual of the Enlightenment project. A society is more than the mere sum of its constituent individuals, argues Burke. It is a network of social obligations, historical in origin, fashioned by generations of social interaction. From this argument emerges the first cornerstone of conservatism: a deep respect for tradition and established authority. Traditional authority governs the dynamic web of familiarity and respect, duty and allegiance that obviates the need for administrative bureaucracy, political repression and military force to maintain the well-ordered society. The conservative fear of progress rests on the belief that the Enlightenment project was unravelling traditional community and authority by stressing individualism and rationalizing economic and social relations. The destruction of accustomed points of social reference – the patriarchal family, the guild, the village and the church – left people bereft of direction, prey to their own whims and the manipulation of demagogues. 'A certain *quantum* of power must always exist in the community, in some hands, and under some appellation,' lest social order be irreparably undone by human frailty and vice, Burke (1988, p. 248) insists. To a member of the revolutionary National Assembly in France in 1791, Burke wrote:

I doubt much, very much indeed, whether France is at all ripe for liberty at any standard. Men are qualified for civil liberty in exact proportion to their disposition to put moral chains upon their appetites ... Society cannot exist unless a controlling power upon will and appetite be placed somewhere, and the less of it there is within, the more there must be without (Burke 1866, pp. 51f).

This grim estimate of human capabilities is the second cornerstone of the conservative tradition. Burke expressed a profound scepticism about the intellectual capabilities of man, and rejected the concept of the autonomous and rational individual. He distrusted the human intellect with 'all its defects, redundancies and errors,' its pride, 'personal self-sufficiency and arrogance' (Burke 1988, p. 193). The study of history confirms the frailties, follies and infirmities of mankind, Burke maintained. 'History consists of the miseries brought upon the world by pride, ambition, avarice, revenge, lust, sedition, hypocrisy, ungoverned zeal, and all the train of disorderly appetites' (1988, p. 247). Religion, morals, laws and other supposedly universal principles upon which men claim to base their actions are in reality mere 'pretexts' or reflections of particular interests. The conflict of interests among competing groups constitutes the essence of human existence, which politics must master.

Burke's ideal society is founded on social hierarchy and differentiated status – the third conservative cornerstone. Conservatism distrusts the 'masses'. Burke displayed a paternalistic attitude towards them. He recommended that leadership be entrusted to those groups that have already demonstrated their ability to lead – i.e., to the rich, the well-born, and the able. Only under such leaders can a people find the freedom to act and to live in accordance with their own traditions. Properly placed and held within the gravitational field of community and tradition (nation, Church and family), the ordinary person is protected from his own vices and freed from fear and disorder.

The need for an élite within society leads to the final cornerstone of conservatism: private property. Ownership and management of property, primarily landed estates, have an ennobling effect on man, argues Burke. Ownership provides a unique social experience which instils responsibility, skill and practical reason, and which tempers man's passionate nature. It is among the largest property owners and the most successful managers of industry and institutions that the nation should recruit its leaders. The wealth and status of these men guarantee their dispassionate pursuit of the common good; their property allows them leisure, which is the prerequisite for knowledge and independence. Private property is therefore the necessary precondition for a good government, and the large-scale destruction of property is the most heinous of all crimes. Burke's attack on the French Revolution obsessively stresses its destruction of property (p. 260ff).

Burke's outlook is summed up in his view that only a strong state can produce the social stability and political order necessary for human freedom (p. 196). Conservatives do not conceive of a 'strong state' in terms of forceful bureaucratic institutions. Rather, the state is an imagined corporation produced by distinct geography and shared historical experiences; it is a spiritual community founded as a partnership and seasoned by history. 'As the end of such a partnership cannot be obtained in many generations', Burke notes, 'it becomes a partnership not only between those who are living, but between those who are living, those who are dead and those who are to be born' (p. 194f). A state is a collectivity, not a collection of individuals. It is the product of history. The movement of a people through time results in a collective memory and heritage which cannot be consciously altered or designed.

For conservative thinkers, the primary task of government is to maintain order. They do this best by resisting the natural tendency of man towards conflict and war. Around a central core of power, governments establish institutions which can defend the physical safety of the nation, the property rights of its citizens and the wealth and welfare of the population against external and internal enemies. As important as defending its territory against physical enemies is the preservation of the historical partnership, traditions and communal values. Such conservative maxims sustain Burke's *Reflections on the Revolution in France*. That they also inform his observations of foreign and international relations is apparent in his contributions to the *Annual Register*, a yearly survey of world affairs which he edited (unacknowledged) from 1758 to about 1776. For Burke, governments must help maintain international (as well as domestic) order. States must co-ordinate their capabilities and manage their interests. And always within a balance-of-power framework.

Burke praises the balance of power as the main stabilizing institution in international politics. He claims that the prudent management of Europe's balance of power preserves interstate order and international peace. This management is facilitated by several factors. One of these is the set of rules specified by international law – that 'great ligament of mankind'. Another decisive factor is the set of communal values which inform European states. These create an underlying sense of unity among the states of Europe and a collective commitment to maintaining order. Burke emphasizes the common factors which contribute to 'similitude' throughout Europe – Christian religion, monarchical principles of government and a common Roman-law heritage foremost among them. At one point he even goes so far as to portray Europe as one great state whose unity is only marred by a few trifling diversities in provincial customs and local establishments. For Burke, Europe owes its relative order and superior wealth to a balance-of-power system which is regulated by the common norms, rules and law embedded in (European) society. While other civilizations have perished 'for want of any union or system of policy of this nature', the Western world has acquired an astonishing 'superiority over the rest of the globe'. Whereas other regions have been torn apart by strife or folded under the weight of excessive conquest, Europe has emerged pre-eminent in the world owing to the vigilant maintenance of the balance of power (Burke 1772, p. 2).

The conservative approach to International Relations is informed by the two modern notions of state interest and necessity – by *raison d'état* (the phrase that comprehends both). The conservative statesman maintains, with Guicciardini and Rohan, that the interest of the state is the mainspring of political action; he agrees with Spinoza that the necessities of policy arise from the anarchical inter-state context in which states are forced to operate. The theoretical implications which flow from these notions contradict the liberal doctrine of a general harmony of social interests. Rather, conflict of interest is the normal state of human affairs, and war is the normal condition of interstate relations. No universal principles exist on to which a new world order can be grafted. Each state – each culture, religion and nation – defines its own truth.

Conservative thinkers belittle the importance of theoretical blueprints. They are often pragmatists who stress experience over speculation. They treat politics as a practical activity, and react to events as they occur, rather than follow any long-term master plan. They treat international politics not as a science but as an art. And since they consciously adopt an a-theoretical posture, it is difficult to find a clear exponent of a conservative International Relations theory. To the extent that the conservative statesman theorizes, he examines the past with a pronounced empirical disposition, guided by his 'ear for history', and draws careful lessons from concrete events. Conservative theorizing is characteristically a carefully delineated, empirically based 'conversation with tradition'. It focuses on the complex interconnectedness of past events; the lasting properties of 'tradition' as well as the constellation of forces of a particular moment. Still, the challenges presented by liberalism and radicalism and the social and economic changes of the dual revolution forced conservative paladins consciously to defend their traditions and to justify that defence.

One of the most theoretically explicit conservative commentators of the age was Friedrich Gentz (1764–1832). As secretary and foreign policy adviser to the powerful Austrian statesman Klement von Metternich (1773–1859), he was also one of the most influential. Gentz translated Burke's *Reflections* into German in 1793, and adopted many of Burke's ideas. A constant theme in his writings on international politics is the idea of a coalition of like-minded peoples to act as a stabilizing body in peace and war (Gentz 1953). He argued that an alliance between Russia, Austria and Prussia was necessary to minimize the influence of radical French and English ideas and to contain the expansion of revolutionary French power (Gentz 1806).

Gentz placed his faith in the post-Napoleonic Holy Alliance as the coalition which would preserve the old order. As the Holy Alliance disintegrated, he championed the notion of a Continental Order, an idealized version of the eighteenth-century Concert, to defend against the unfolding of the nineteenth century. For Gentz, the balance of power was the international counterpart of domestic traditional authority, which preserved the social order. If the existing balance were disturbed, he maintained, then the challenging force must be blunted, co-opted and absorbed and a new but essentially similar *status quo* established. Whether commenting on the Greek rebellion against the Turks, the Spanish liberals' opposition to Bourbon absolutism, the Latin Americans' declaration of war on Spain or German students battling the Prussian police, Gentz invariably supported Metternich's policy of opposing the forces of liberalism and democratization and defending the old order.

Metternich, too, was an advocate of a balance-of-power system; he, too, excluded all illusory ethical considerations from the conduct of international politics. After Napoleon's fall, he opposed proposals from his more morally-minded colleagues to punish France severely for its belligerence. If a stable order were to be imposed upon the Continent, France must be retained as one of the major actors in a balanced system. If too severely penalized, France would be weakened and Europe would find itself at the mercy of Russia. Europe could not have order without balance nor justice without restraint.

Among the conservative International Relations theorists, Carl Philipp Gottlieb von Clausewitz (1780–1831) ranks among the most sophisticated. He once stated his view of international politics in a credo which summarizes the conservative sentiment well: 'never relax vigilance, expect nothing from the magnanimity of others; never abandon a purpose until it has become impossible, beyond doubt, to attain it; hold the honour of the state sacred' (Clausewitz 1962, p. 304).

Clausewitz experienced the Battle of Jena (1806), where Napoleon soundly defeated the Prussians, as an intellectual awakening. As an officer of Prussia's defeated army, Clausewitz grasped that the French victory stemmed from Napoleon's ability to mobilize the entire French nation for war and fire it with nationalist ardour (Clausewitz 1976, p. 593). He realized that the future would belong to spiritually unified nations (*Völker*). Napoleon showed him that armies which were not founded on a *Volk* would be destroyed.

In internment in France, Clausewitz brooded on the Prussian defeat and on the fate of the fragmented German nation. The task which faced Prussia, he resolved, was not just military reform, but also spiritual renewal. Confronted with the real danger of annihilation, it was essential that Prussia's ruling Hohenzollern dynasty articulate and cultivate a patriotic sentiment, place itself at the helm of a popular nationalist movement, and create what would in effect be a modern nation-state.[4]

Clausewitz saw humanity as naturally divided into nations (*Völker*), each of which has its own characteristics and qualities. He argued that a *Volk* forms a state in order to express its national identity and to maintain its freedom (Clausewitz 1922). This vision has a democratic aspect, because it acknowledges that state policies must somehow reflect the popular will. Yet Clausewitz' brand of democracy is quite different from the Enlightenment notion of popular participation. He was doubtful of the potential of human reason, which he saw as limited by passion and chance; he feared that a system based on broad participation would 'not allow citizens to sleep at night for worry of what the government did yesterday, does today and will do tomorrow' (H. Smith 1990, p. 43). His distrust in the democratic ideas of the Atlantic states fits perfectly the paternalistic vision of Continental conservatism.

Clausewitz develops a theory of war on the conservative premiss that conflict of interest is inherent in human society. 'War is part of man's social existence. War is a clash between major interests, which is resolved in bloodshed – that is the only way in which it differs from other conflicts,' writes Clausewitz (1976, p. 78ff). War is the supreme manifestation of human conflict; it is politics concentrated in a single point.

From this premiss, Clausewitz develops the argument that war is embedded in society and history. War is never an isolated act. It occurs in a distinct social and historical context which affects the nature of its outbreak, its conduct and its outcome. War is shaped by the intentions of the belligerents, the nature of their military forces, the geography of the battlefield, the pre-war relationship of the participants and the international environment. In the modern age, states are so closely integrated that 'no cannon could be fired in Europe without every government feeling its interest affected' (p. 590). Attuned to the natural propensity for man to feud and to the immense complexity of interstate interaction, Clausewitz does not harbour any illusions about man's ability to impose lasting order upon his social environment. He has little admiration for the intellect of the citizen; instead, he invests his faith in the genius of the exceptional leader–the skill of the general, the wisdom of the statesman–and in the historically sanctioned, collective reason of the *Volk*.

Although war is a natural feature in international relations, it cannot be separated from politics; it is part of politics, a mode of it, a continuation of political intercourse with the addition of other means. 'We deliberately use the phrase "with the addition of other means"', he explains,

because we also want to make it clear that war in itself does not suspend political intercourse or change it into something entirely different ... War cannot be divorced from political life; and whenever this occurs in our thinking about war, the many links that connect the two elements are destroyed and we are left with something pointless and devoid of sense (p. 605).

The overriding, formative concern of statesmen and strategists must be the political objectives specific to their own states. The political interests and objectives of sovereign nation-states constitute, at each moment in history, an intricate political field. They are fashioned by the character of the states, the perceptions of national leaders and their (usually limited) aims: territorial annexation, regional domination or maintenance of the existent relations of forces among states.

States monitor their position in this dynamic diplomatico-strategic field, and adapt to its incessantly changing matrix of interests (Aron 1966, pp. 4–16, 437–58; 1986). Emphasizing the role of force, Clausewitz repeats Thucydides' insight that law and justice play a role in international politics only in so far as the states involved are of equal power. Otherwise, the strong do what they will and the weak suffer what they must.

The purpose of the war is always 'to compel our enemy to do our will' (p. 75). In order to achieve this purpose, it is necessary either to destroy the enemy's armed forces so that he is rendered defenceless, or to place him in 'a position that is even more unpleasant than the sacrifice you call on him to make' (p. 77). Clausewitz devotes most of his book to various techniques by which a state can produce these outcomes, either of which will put the victorious state in a position to dictate the terms of peace. But it is not this exposition of the techniques of battle which is Clausewitz' main concern; it is the political purpose and the goals that they must serve.

Nation-states do not resort to war in their everyday efforts to secure or further their objectives. They are, however, always exposed to the risk of war and they always remain under arms. Their environment is one of change and uncertainty, in which no absolute equilibrium of force is possible. The strength of states continually waxes and wanes, causing the balance of forces to fluctuate. Consequently, long periods of peace between two armed, hostile states 'cannot be explained by the concept of balance. The only explanation is that both are waiting for a better time to act' (p. 82). Peace, then, has no higher meaning than the temporary absence of war.

Also, Clausewitz recognizes that war has a meaning beyond the strictly and obviously political. For some reason, states have tacitly agreed to accept limited war as at least a temporary arbiter in their clash of interests. He suggests two reasons for this. First, war is accepted because the use of physical force is a common occurrence among individuals or groups that have a clash of interests. Second, there are two factors which give war and battle a special quality: war is conducted in the name of the state and on behalf of the nation, infusing it with a larger political purpose; also, war transcends politics – it is a conflict of interest 'resolved by bloodshed' (p.149).

When Clausewitz refers to 'bloodshed' in the very definition of war, he alludes to acts of universal significance. The shedding of blood has a deep symbolic meaning and a powerful mythic appeal in human affairs. A variety of myths and religions use blood as a symbol of both life and death in rites of atonement, purification and renewal – Christianity included. Blood is associated with a broad variety of social relationships and political objectives. References to battles, and blood as a symbol of the ultimate heroic sacrifice and as the ultimate signifier of ownership or membership, evoke powerful emotions. In Clausewitz' words:

I believe and profess that a people never must value anything higher than the dignity and freedom of its existence; that it must defend these with the last drop of blood; ... that shame of a cowardly submission can never be wiped out; that the poison of submission in the bloodstream of a people will be transmitted to its children, and paralyse and under- mine the strength of later generations; ... that a bloody and honorable fight assures the rebirth of the people even if freedom were lost; and that such a struggle is the seed of life from which a new tree inevitably will blossom (Clausewitz 1962, p. 301).

The last great synthesizer

As the three ideological tendencies evolved and the nineteenth century span itself out, their development echoed the prevailing themes of the age – frag- mentation and unity on the one hand and competition and progress on the other. As proponents of each tendency clarified their views, they produced universally applicable systems of thought.

In practical politics these competing systems of thought were not starkly delineated; adherents of the three ideologies of liberalism, radicalism and con- servatism often formed expedient alliances in which a common interest would temporarily unify two ideologies against the third. In theory, however, while the three ideologies share some assumptions, they are, in their totality, fundamen- tally at odds with one another.[5] The liberal ideology was born of the struggle to throw off the confining social, political and economic institutions that conserva- tives understood to be the heart, soul, and connective tissue of society. Radical- ism developed as a critique of both the comfortable world of the *ancien régime* and of self-congratulatory liberalism. Conservatism defined its essence in oppo- sition to radicalism and liberalism. In terms of theory, the West fragmented into three competing political approaches.

At the heart of the conflict lay questions which radiated out from the notions of 'progress' and 'competition'. The states of the Atlantic rim which embraced liberalism also embraced industrialization, agrarian reform and political democ- ratization. Their economies were dynamic and aggressive and they came to embody and define the idea of 'progress'. The peoples in Central and Eastern Europe perceived themselves as competing with the economic and political power of the West and as wrestling with the mesmerizing idea of progress. The Prussian philosopher Georg Wilhelm Friedrich Hegel (1770–1831) not only expressed this anti-liberal *Angst*, he also combined the most typical themes of his age into a complex and abstract system which has provided one of the richest ores of anti-liberal theorizing ever devised (Airas 1978, pp. 472ff; Chanteur 1992).

Hegel is a suitable representative for the sentiment (or in his case, the 'spirit') of the age. At the core of Hegel's political theory, the century's distinctive themes of progress and competition intertwine – it even embraces the two different views of competition: the harmonious as well as the conflictual. For Hegel, history is the progressive realization of the ultimate Truth or Idea. The Idea evolves through a dialectical struggle towards an Absolute End.

In the Hegelian approach, history must be understood in terms of *ideas* rather than events. History is the evolutionary process through which the Absolute Idea attains full consciousness of itself as spirit (*Geist*) and realizes itself in the form of a new world spirit (or *Weltgeist*) of Reason, Freedom and Equality. For Hegel, this process is not linear, but dialectical: a given thought will always contain inherent contradictory aspects and will produce its own negation. Thus, a given state of affairs (the 'thesis') will inevitably produce a conception of an opposite state of affairs (the 'antithesis'). The contest between the two will, in turn, be resolved in an *Aufhebung*: a reconciliation and a fusion (a 'synthesis') which includes the key elements of the original thesis as well as the antithesis, but which is more than and different from both.

Hegel first set out his system in *The Phenomenology of Spirit* in 1807. He saw in the French Revolution the irresistible rise of progressive values, and he saw in the Napoleonic Wars the triumphant dissemination of these values throughout the world. Like Clausewitz, he saw Napoleon as the agent of history, advancing its ultimate development by acting to universalize the progressive ideas of Freedom and Equality throughout Europe, by force when necessary.

After the fall of Napoleon and the triumph of reaction in central and eastern Europe, Hegel shifted his emphasis to the necessary competition and struggle which accompanies progress. His new analysis is set forth in Hegel's last, major work, *The Philosophy of Right* (1980 [1821]). It discusses how the *Geist* articulates itself through a rationally organized (and therefore genuinely free) nation or *Volk* and its state. The *Volk* is the basic spiritual unit in Hegel's later works. Each free *Volk* possesses its own proper spirit. This *Volksgeist* is the supra-individual Reason, or 'spirit objectified' of a nation, expressed in the institutions of its state. A people without a state is merely a vulnerable 'formless mass' (Hegel 1980, p. 183).

Politics internal to states is harmonious; since the state is *Volksgeist* objectified, it is only as a member of the state 'that the individual himself has objectivity, genuine individuality and an ethical life' (p. 156). Politics among states, by contrast, is marked by extreme conflict. In Hegel's earlier works, the *Volksgeist* is only a subordinate, historically specific part of the *Weltgeist* – ultimately, the *Weltgeist* will prevail and provide the final context within which the individual *Volksgeist* (and its state) will find self-consciousness and Freedom. After the defeat of Napoleon, however, Hegel's long-term optimism dampened. The synthesis which promised to remove the contradiction between *Volksgeist* and *Welt-geist* fades from view; the violent competition between nation-states emerges as a permanent feature of international politics.

Hegel agreed with Clausewitz that a state articulates the sovereign will of a *Volk* and that 'if states disagree, and their particular wills cannot be harmonized, the matter can only be settled by war' (p. 214). Such 'war is not to be regarded as an absolute evil and as a purely external accident'. Rather, for Hegel, war has constructive, even progressive, functions. It promotes national unity. It stimulates the growth of states. It contributes to the progress of History. War also prevents established nation-states from deteriorating; peace makes men and states grow soft – 'corruption in nations would be the product of prolonged, let alone "perpetual" peace', writes Hegel (p. 209f). War keeps states fit and alert.

Hegel was enormously influential – partly because he included all the major early-nineteenth century themes in his vast synthesis; partly because his arguments were so abstract that adherents of all ideologies found some support in his works. He provided philosophical support to the stage-theories of historic evolution which marked the age. This initially attracted liberals, who held the view that human history had passed from primitive tribal life to higher stages of evolution in which increasing differentiation meant social advance. However, it soon grew obvious that Hegel's definitions of 'liberty' and 'equality' and his elevation of a strong state were quite incompatible with the liberal outlook. When Darwin's theory of evolution offered an alternative (and, by liberal standards, a more 'scientific') vision of historical progress in the final decades of the century, Hegel's spell was broken in the liberal cultures around the Atlantic rim.[6]

It was on the Continent that Hegelian thought struck its firmest roots. It provided Continental conservatives with a set of concepts and a sense of purpose which allowed them to comprehend the dramatic social changes they couldn't prevent. Also, conservatives who were frustrated by the fragmented nature of German politics found in Hegel a conception of the nation-state as an 'imagined community' – as *Geist*, or a set of spiritual common values which had evolved historically and had articulated themselves through a people to form a consensual community and a nation. Hegel's arguments constituted a Teutonic counterpart to Burke's conservative view of the British state as an organic, historically created whole and a necessary precondition for social order and individual freedom.

Hegel also transfixed Continental radicals. He provided philosophical support particularly suited to their doctrines of progress and the dialectical method they favoured. When Hegel renovated the old, radical theme of human alienation in the light of the concept of human labour, he exerted a immediate impact on radical theorizing. From the early nineteenth century on, radical theorists placed the concept of 'labour' at the heart of their social critique (Marx 1975a; Mészáros 1970).

After his death in 1831, Hegel's works remained popular, especially in Germany, whose traditional industries were under strain owing to a flood of inexpensive British imports. Anti-British and anti-liberal sentiments intertwined with economic patriotism and romantic empathy for German craftsmen, and fuelled new applications of Hegel's arguments. Hegel's interpreters divided into two camps. The conservative Right Hegelians emphasized the older, somewhat disillusioned Hegel. They argued that through the dialectical progress of History, the disunity of Germany would produce the idea of unity and *Volk* and would inevitably bring about the creation of a German state. Hegel's emphasis on *Volk*, war and History and his advocacy of monarchism as the best form of state endeared him to the Prussian state.

Radical Left Hegelians saw in the early Hegelian dialectic a revolutionary international force. They claimed that History would soon transcend the Prussian state. Their analysis soon proceeded to study of the destiny of historical evolution and its necessary preconditions – as evinced in the works of Karl Marx.

The sentiment(s) of the century

The spread of industrialism, the increase in commercial interaction and the rise of democratic ideals of freedom and equality eroded the old order. The growth of the social sciences, too, were powerful solvents – the rapid growth of Political Economy, most notably, had a profound effect on nineteenth-century social speculation. These events contributed to the fragmentation of social theorizing in the West. After Hegel's death, they boosted divisions among different ideologies and between the eastern and the western regions of the Western world.

The nineteenth century witnessed a rapid development of the political ideologies into distinct systems of social thought. These ideologies did not develop or take root uniformly throughout western Europe, but separated into two distinctive political traditions, which roughly correspond to distinctive economic and social systems.

The two Western traditions

In the most general of terms the origins of this division can be traced back to the split of the Roman Empire (Szücs 1990; Geiss 1993). The split was re-enforced in the Middle Ages and consolidated in the long sixteenth century – Western Europe evolved urban, seawards centres (Amsterdam, England and North-western France) which specialized in trade and manufacturing, whereas Eastern Europe specialized in rural production of raw materials (Moore 1966; Wallerstein 1974; Hall 1986). In the seventeenth and eighteenth centuries the division was accentuated as several countries in the West (the United Provinces, England, America, France) experienced political revolution, agrarian reform, and the advent of wage labour. These countries spread their ideas along the north-Atlantic rim. In the largely land-locked regions east of the Elbe River, by con-

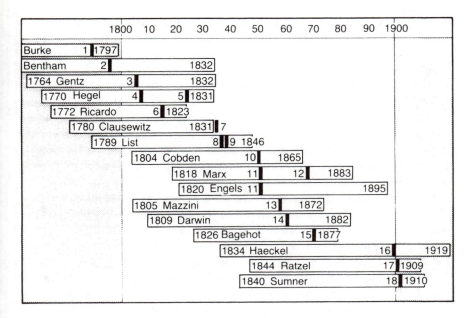

1. *Reflections on the Revolution in France* [1790]
2. 'A plan for a universal and perpetual peace' [1794]
3. *Fragments upon the Present State of the Political Balance of Europe* [1806]
4. *The Phenomenology of Spirit* [1807]
5. *The Philosophy of Right* [1821]
6. *Principles of Political Economy and Taxation* [1817]
7. *On War* [1832]
8. *The Natural System of Political Economy* [1837]
9. *The National System of Political Economy* [1841]
10. *Speeches on Peace, Financial Reform, Colonial Reform and Other Subjects during 1849*
11. *Communist Manifesto* [1848]
12. *Capital 1* [1867]
13. 'People's war' [1855]
14. *On the Origin of Species* [1859]
15. *Physics and Politics* [1872]
16. *The Riddle of the Universe* [1899]
17. *Political Geography* [1903]
18. 'War' [1903]

Figure 4 Some nineteenth-century authors and their works

trast, the Old Regimes retrenched their traditional social and political positions. By 1800, a politico-economic division of the Western world was drawn quite clearly between the market- and trade-oriented nation-states along the north-

Atlantic rim, which professed democratic, Enlightenment-derived political ideals, and the agriculturally-based, authoritarian states east of the Elbe.

Liberal Enlightenment values had origins deep in British history. Notions of human rights and individual freedom were, for example, present in the Magna Carta (1215). In the rapid economic and political evolution in the eighteenth and nineteenth centuries, the expanding middle classes embraced the values of social equality, individual freedom and the right to unencumbered accumulation of private property. A rapid succession of political and constitutional Reform Bills passed during the 1830s transformed Britain into the most liberal country in Europe. By mid-century, most British thinkers had rejected mercantilist thought in favour of Bentham's vision of free trade.

In post-Napoleonic France, the liberal ideology was only reluctantly embraced – domestic politics were a tense tug-of-war between democrats of various hues and a counter-revolutionary reaction, which first gained the upper hand but then collapsed. In July 1830, workers, intellectuals and members of the bourgeoisie in Paris toppled the reactionary Charles X and replaced him with the progressive Louis-Philippe. The Paris parliament passed a series of reforms which liberalized the French political economy. Yet the conservative tendency (which in the French context became reactionary) remained an important presence in French politics. The radical tradition fired by Rousseau and the Revolution also remained a permanent fixture of French political life.

The social and political differences between the Atlantic rim and the Continent were accentuated by the policies of the conservative Austrian statesman Klement von Metternich. After Napoleon's defeat, Metternich was the architect of the Congress of Vienna (1814–15), which provided Europe with a comprehensive peace treaty. His intention was to manage post-war policies through a system of regular congresses, later known as the Concert of Europe, which would facilitate the settlement of disputes between the European powers and work to repress revolution on the Continent.

Metternich's Concert of Europe was an effort to reconstruct the Europe of the Absolutist age. It rested on a pre-revolutionary vision of world politics and was supported by Europe's most autocratic regimes. Britain was a member of the Concert at the outset, but soon clashed with its conservative scheme. Britain wanted to preserve her ability to conduct free trade and to support the spread of liberal values to the rest of the world. In 1822 she left the Concert in a huff and proceeded to defend the South-American nations in their revolt against Spain, and the Greek insurgents' struggle for independence from Turkey.

By leaving the Concert, England deflated Metternich's influence in western and in southern Europe. But by the same token, England also surrendered her opportunity to mitigate Metternich's anti-liberal policies in central and eastern Europe. In the absence of both British and French meddling, Metternich's scheme remained unchallenged there.

The purpose of the Concert was to contain liberalism. This policy was successful in the short run.[7] However, despite the best efforts of Metternich and the Holy Alliance, the Enlightenment project and its attendant visions of progress, industrialism and mass participation gradually emerged as the dominant vision of the century. In 1848, a wave of upheavals washed across the Continent and swept away both Metternich and his reactionary system. This collapse of the anti-Enlightenment bulwark of the reactionaries did not result in the clear victory of liberalism. Rather, it produced throughout Europe a fragmented political scene of kaleidoscopic complexity. On the Atlantic rim, liberalism broke up into a 'classic' and a 'revisionist' interpretation, as the key themes of equality, reason, freedom and property became subject to various interpretations. On the Continent, scholars and statesmen elaborated their ideological reactions to west-coast individualism into a variety of conservative and radical approaches.

Atlantic Theories: Cobden and Mazzini

In France, the revolution of 1848 produced a half-way house between the Atlantic and the Continental traditions. The upheavals introduced more liberal measures in some areas (e.g. universal suffrage); at the same time it established a unique kind of mass-dictatorship under Emperor Louis Napoleon.[8]

In Britain, a split in liberalism became evident as Bentham's classic doctrines were challenged by new, reformist arguments. This mid-century split between a 'classic' and a 'reformist' interpretation of liberalism hinged on a debate about the proper function of the State. The classic doctrine distinguished sharply between politics and economics, claimed that the economic sphere obeyed natural laws and that the state disturbed the natural, harmonious properties of social life if it intruded in the economic realm. Reformist liberals disagreed, and argued for an active role for the State in certain economic activities. Their argument hinged on a distinction drawn (e.g. by Mill 1866) between productive and distributive activities. The realm of production is subject to immutable natural laws which are fixed by nature and technology, it was argued. Distributive activities, by contrast, are socially determined and subject to human control. The reformist liberals argued that the laws of the free market can be trusted to stimulate the social division of labour and to enhance the efficiency of production. However, they cannot be trusted to allocate the goods produced in a fair and just manner. The state had an important role to play in the allocation of values in society, they claimed. State intervention was necessary to prevent social inequalities which would erode social justice and equality, and to provide conditions under which free economic competition could operate most efficiently.

The reformist argument influenced liberal approaches to international politics. A more active State in the domestic realm implied a more active role in foreign affairs as well. In domestic politics, the role of the State is to maintain justice and order in ways sanctioned by popular consensus through democratic channels. In the anarchical environment of international politics, by contrast, the State can maintain justice and order only if it can overcome the opposition of other states. When a democratic state assumes the role of judge and executor in the realm of international politics, it must be prepared to back its adjudications by force. The reformist liberal would agree with the conservative that war is the ultimate means of settling disputes among states. By this acknowledgement State intervention in domestic politics would find a functional equivalent of war in interstate relations. British foreign minister Sir Edward Grey (1925, p. 286), reflecting in his memoirs upon the experiences of a liberal statesman, resolved that force must be available to uphold law among states as within states. Herbert Spencer put the point most succinctly: 'policemen are soldiers who act alone; soldiers are policemen who act in concert' (Spencer 1897, p. 118).

Bentham had argued that peace and order are best guaranteed by the principles of utility, free trade and non-intervention. His followers argued that the streams of goods and ideas which flowed unhindered across borders had peaceful effects on world affairs. Nations would grow richer through commerce than through conquest. According to Richard Cobden, man could best combat conflict and war by continuing to develop new means of communications which would, ultimately, spin humanity into a web of wealth and understanding – parliaments, international conferences, the popular press, compulsory education, the public reading room, the penny postage stamp, railways, submarine telegraphs, three-funnelled ocean liners, and the Manchester cotton exchange were all forces for understanding, peace and harmony (Blainey 1973, pp. 18–32).

But how should democratic states behave towards assertive, intolerant and aggressive autocracies? Cobden was among the first liberal theorists to wrestle with the difficult question of whether a democratic state should tolerate states which rejected democratic principles. He noted that the lawless international environment 'corrupts [domestic] society; exhausts its wealth, raises up false gods for hero-worship, and fixes before the eyes of the rising generation a spurious if glittering standard of glory' (Morley 1881, p. 276). Faced with such contaminating international forces, should democratic societies retain their non-interventionist policies? Or should they actively combat despotism and the ignorance which sustains it?

In 1846, Cobden concluded that liberal democracies must not risk their ideals by exposing them to power politics. Democratic states should limit themselves to economic transactions and shun war. They should put their faith in free trade and in the steady progress of Reason and Freedom through history. Sooner or later, the inhabitants of autocracies, too, would realize that their true interests lie in Bentham's greatest happiness principle, in free trade, democracy and tolerance. The popular masses would then rise up, throw off the yoke of despotism and join the ranks of the open, enlightened and democratic societies (Cobden 1973).

The Italian patriot Giuseppe Mazzini disagreed. He countered Cobden's 'optimistic non-interventionism' with a doctrine of 'messianic interventionism' (Waltz 1959, p. 103). If democratic states do not contain despotic states, they will in effect allow those states to expand their influence, argued Mazzini. Such a passive stance would ultimately endanger the very existence of democracy. In 1853, Mazzini used this argument to convince the British government to support Turkish and Italian nationalists in a war to stop the westward expansion of autocratic Russia. He insisted that such a war would be unlike any war waged by despotic states; it would be a war for Progress, Peace, Liberty and Justice (Mazzini 1945, p. 91).[9]

Continental reaction: List and Bismarck

As Metternich's stable order eroded during the 1840s, several Continental states felt increasingly threatened by the political ideals of popular participation and by the increasing flood of low-cost British products. In the wake of the revolutionary upheavals of 1848, many states evolved their own ideological responses to the North-Atlantic doctrines of social order.

Put on the political defensive, conservative rulers sought to stave off Atlantic influences through appeals to national communalism and the nation-state. Neither institution was fully established on the Continent; yet the concept of a *Staat* which articulated the will of a *Volk* was immensely seductive. Without it, as Clausewitz and Hegel had observed at Jena, the fragmented central region of Europe would easily become the prey to either the military power of France or the industrial power of England. During the Napoleonic Wars, German scholars had attacked the Enlightenment project's claim to universality and developed an alternative doctrine of cultural relativism. Herder, Hegel, Clausewitz and others argued that each people possessed not only a unique collective spirit, but also an inherent right to preserve its identity and independence.

Fichte (1979a) developed an important, concrete foreign-policy theory which reflected these concerns. He delivered an emphatic attack on the free-market ideology of Great Britain and proposed a mercantilistic policy based on a doctrine of strict protectionism as the obvious German response. Similar arguments were pursued by Friedrich List.[10] He denounced the liberal economic theory as 'pure ideology' – by which he meant the universalization of the special interests of a dominant state. Free trade was no universal doctrine, it was a body of ideas developed to suit a specific country at a certain stage in History. It was designed to make England the world's industrial centre by keeping other countries in the dependent role of suppliers of raw materials and food (List 1927).

Like Fichte, List emphasized the value of the national community. Individuals come and go, the nation has a continual life. The nation-state represents continuity, whereas individuals are its temporary inhabitants, and the concerns of the individual must be subordinated to those of the *Volk*. It is only 'right and proper that the individual should be ready to sacrifice his own interests for the benefit of the nation to which he belongs,' writes List (1927, pp. 181–9).

The security and the stability of a nation-state must be judged in terms of the harmonious development of its three major productive sectors, List continues

(1930): agriculture, industry and commerce. This sectoral division of the national economy provides him with a stage theory of history as well as a strategy for industrialization. The first and most primitive stage is based on agricultural production. In an agricultural society, people work the land for subsistence and remain isolated from the international economy. Here, 'the whole range of intellectual and moral powers is virtually non-existent and sheer physical strength is all that can be expected from those who work the land' (List 1927, pp. 239f; also 1930, p. 214).

The second stage of development introduces trade. Agriculture is complemented by trade and by some manufacturing, which 'promotes the growth of intellectual and moral forces of every kind' (List 1927, p. 243). Enterprising citizens emulate foreign means of production, elaborate domestic manufactures into fledgling industries. These budding domestic ventures will, however, inevitably reach a point at which further development is impossible, argues List. For when local entrepreneurs begin to master elementary industrial techniques, they will encounter competition from cheap, high-quality foreign imports and be undercut by them. Consequently, the nation's development will stall at a relatively low level of industrialization.

This stagnation can be overcome by state intervention. The state can bring a nation to the third stage of economic development by a policy of protectionism – the state can, in a manner of speaking, de-couple the nation from the world economy and temporarily isolate it behind a tariff wall. Tariffs and state planning will 'revive the spirit of enterprise in a country' and propel the nation on to a higher, more competitive stage of economic development, argues List (1930, p. 357).

During this period of temporary isolation, the nation has an opportunity to combine the sectors of agriculture, industry and commerce into a mutually-supporting, self-reliant whole (p. 257). When the domestic economy is harmonious and domestic industries strong enough to compete with foreign producers, the state must dismantle its protective tariff wall and re-enter the world economy. Now that it can participate in the international economic competition from a position of strength, a country has everything to gain from a free-trade world economy.

List did not provide a general theory of economic development. Only countries which possessed a certain 'völkish' unity of spirit, an inordinate political discipline and a strong state could bear the temporary cost of a strategy which would sacrifice the gains and enjoyments of an entire generation of citizens (1927, pp. 181–9). It fell to Otto von Bismarck to provide Germany with the final prerequisite in List's strategy, a strong nation-state – thus ensuring the success of the Continental response to Atlantic liberalism.

It was not immediately apparent that Bismarck's aim was to contain liberalism. He first advocated German unity at a time when this idea was identified with the liberal cause of an all-German parliamentary democracy. But it soon became clear that, while Bismarck supported German unity, he did not support the cause of parliamentarism. Nor did he believe that democratic reform and greater economic co-operation would achieve German unification as German liberals argued. In Bismarck's view, Germany could only be united through war. 'It is not by speeches and resolutions that the great questions of the time are decided,' he insisted, 'but by iron and blood' (Taylor 1967, p. 56). He saw international relations as a struggle between conflicting state interests. And he understood that in the age of modern, powerful nation-states, Prussia's interests could be maintained either through a close association with Austria or through unification with other, smaller German states, thus building Prussia into a substantial nation-state in its own right.

Bismarck is a significant contributor to International Relations theory. But his fame rests not so much on his writings as on his example. It rests on his remarkable practice of balance-of-power politics – through which he managed to unify Germany (Bismarck 1898).[11] Once he had attained this goal, the old 'white revolutionary' suddenly distinguished himself by his moderation, insisting that Germany be content with the frontiers he had given her. Illustrating Goethe's words, which everyone quotes: 'In der Begrenzung zeight sich der Meister', Bismarck invested his considerable acumen in the service of interstate stability. He became an honest broker for peace, and his shrewd system of alliances compelled every country on the Continent, whatever its will, to follow a peaceful course (Kissinger 1968; 1994).

Beyond Europe

The upsurge of industrialism and democracy spread the new confidence in science and the new visions of society throughout Europe and beyond. The Western concepts of 'industrialism', 'nationalism', 'democracy,' 'liberty' and 'equality' proved irresistible to extra-European areas. So did the interconnected, capitalist world economy which emerged from the Atlantic rim, and remained centred there. This involved a dual revolution 'of the economies and states in a particular geographical region of the world (part of Europe and a few patches of North America), whose centre was the neighbouring and rival states of Great Britain and France' (Hobsbawm 1962, pp. 17f).

Western institutions, ideology and techniques thence spread across the world. The economic and military power displayed by the Western countries as they conquered other regions made their ideological visions extraordinarily potent far beyond their point of origin. These new ideologies appealed to mass audiences throughout the world and stirred them to action. Statesmen, soldiers and charlatans soon developed tools of mass propaganda and organization through which they could bring mass action to bear in their intra-élite quarrels or to mobilize societies to meet the economic, technological and military threats from the West.

The nineteenth-century Prussian response to the onslaught of investments, armies and Enlightenment doctrines from the West foreshadowed the twentieth-century dilemma which would face non-European areas: the assault from the West could only be beaten by adopting Western ideas and institutions. Prussia's response proved particularly attractive. Prussia adopted several Western ideas and institutions as it built a new, strong state. But at the same time, it rejected the liberal ethos upon which these ideas and institutions were originally based. The Prussian example suggested that particular elements of the Western outlook could be successfully extracted from the Enlightenment package of liberal modernism and then turned against it. In particular, industrialism, the strong state and a mass-mobilizing political programme could be adopted with minimum threat to local élites (Barraclough 1976, pp. 153–99; Laue 1987).

It is vital to bear in mind the indigenous roots of the nationalism which drove extra-European societies towards independence in the twentieth century. However, it is also important to recall that the first successful defences against the free-market liberalism of the Atlantic rim were not erected in Asia or Africa, but in the heart of Europe (Veblen 1939). Bismarck successfully contained the liberal influence from the West – informed by a nationalist doctrine expressed by Fichte and a centre-periphery theory developed by List, Bismarck provided the economic basis for a strong and viable state; he constructed a modern state bureaucracy, a rationalized military force, progressive voting laws and a social legislation which foreshadowed the twentieth-century welfare state. It appears paradoxical on the face of it, but the paternalist conservatism of nineteenth-century Prussians exerted a profound influence on radical twentieth-century national-liberation movements in the extra-European world.

Part 3

The Contemporary Age

7

Intermezzo: becoming contemporary

International Relations theorizing has varied wildly since the long sixteenth century. The first stumbling decades that followed the Italian Wars were particularly turbulent. During the 'scientific revolution' of the seventeenth century there emerged clear, modern themes. The eighteenth century introduced a new, secular confidence in the symmetry of the universe and the self-regulating properties of human action. The nineteenth century developed a preoccupation with history and with the progress of mankind.

Each of these three centuries was characterized by a clear theme. Also, it is possible to identify a distinct 'voice' which has articulated this theme – Hobbes, Rousseau, Hegel. The contemporary age is different. It has not been marked by a clear unifying theme, but rather by a cacophony of voices. The twentieth century resembles the sixteenth in that it has been torn between irreconcilable modes of thought. This fragmentation began with the Enlightenment and the growth of the distinct ideologies of liberalism, radicalism and conservatism. It continued through the Industrial Revolution and the Napoleonic Wars, during which these ideologies were torn and pummelled by several intellectual forces.

The four most important of these forces are nationalism, industrialism, imperialism and Darwinism. These are presented in this chapter. Unlike previous chapters, it does not discuss the speculations of a particular century; it retraces the transition from modern to contemporary theorizing.

Nationalism

The idea of the 'nation' emerged as a notable political force in eighteenth-century Europe. It spread to the Americas and, in the wake of the revolutionary upheavals of 1848, to central Europe. The 1860s saw the emergence of several new self-titled nation-states: a unified kingdom in Italy, a new empire in Germany, a Dual Monarchy in Austria-Hungary and a political reorganization in

179

tsarist Russia. This age also witnessed the creation of a central authority in the United States and a united Dominon of Canada. In the last decades of the century, nationalism spread beyond Europe and America as well. In Asia, for example, arose the new 'Westernized' Empire of Japan.

The word 'nation' can be traced back to medieval universities, where it signified groups of students of a distinct, common origin. From the beginning of its modern usage, then, the word denoted a group of people, and it concerned their common geographical origin. Soon it would also denote their allegiance.

In medieval and early modern times people gave their allegiance to the city state, the feudal fief, the town, the region or the religious group. The rise of nationalism implied an important change of allegiance: it forged strong bonds of loyalty between people and state. At the core of the concept lies the idea that all citzens owe their supreme loyalty to the nation and its representative state institutions. Patriotism has long been present in the Western political tradition – as is evident in the concluding chapter of Machiavelli's *The Prince* and in several texts of Rousseau and Herder. Nationalism, however, was created in late eighteenth-century Europe to reinforce the cultural, linguistic and ethnic oneness of a people (Gellner 1983; Hobsbawm 1991; Smith 1991; Viroli 1995).

Benedict Anderson (1983) sees nations as 'imagined communities'. He traces the emergence of nations back to the growth of standardized languages, and singles out the printing press as one of the most significant of its encouraging factors. The advent of printing dissolved ancient allegiances: it fuelled the Reformation and broke the unifying power of the Pope. But print also constructed new social ties: by shattering the illusion of Christian unity it broke the dominance of Latin as a universal language and stimulated the rise of local languages. These local languages were encouraged all over Europe by the evolution of capitalist markets for cheap editions of printed venacular texts – bibles, practical handbooks, almanacks, novels, leaflets, news-sheets. These markets were limited by linguistic boundaries, and contributed to the standardization of market-specific print-vernaculars. Soon such standardization was encouraged by princes and kings, who used print-vernaculars as languages-of-state-power.[1]

In Anderson's account, the growth of capitalist markets for cheap, vernacular prints provided a decisively important precondition for the emergence in Europe of various nations unified by common language and by linguistically-specific stories, myths and norms. For Anderson, then, a nation is 'an imagined political community – and imagined as both inherently limited and sovereign' (Anderson 1983, p. 6). But there is more to the story. With the advent of industrialism, for example, the unifying impact of print-vernaculars was intensified. For hand in hand with the growth of industry and commerce went a new secularization of life, new social theories, modern school systems, mass literacy and the rise, for the first time in history, of a truly mass readership and a popular literature within everybody's reach (Fébvre and Martin 1976, p. 295; Eisenstein 1993). By the end of the eighteenth century, Enlightenment ideas of popular sovereignty and the rights of man spread throughout the industrializing regions of Europe. As industrialism waxed, the power of the absolute monarchs waned. By the nineteenth century, the monarch embodied neither the nation nor the state; the state became a people's state, a national state, a *patrie* or a *Vaterland*. And with this rapid spread of the Enlightenment ideas of the self-determination of the nation and the general participation of all its members ('citzens') in the politics of the state, nationalism emerged as an irresistible political force (Hobsbawm 1991).

The ideas of self-determination and mass-participation had their twin sources in the French conception of popular sovereignty and in the German notion of political romanticism. These two strands of Western thought were early articulated by Rousseau and Herder. Jean-Jacques Rousseau wished to restore the close togetherness of the ancient city-state. He devised the potent concept of the 'general will' to capture this togetherness, based on an active 'consent of the governed'. He followed the example of Sparta in regarding love of the *patrie* as the most heroic of human passions. However, whereas the Spartans praised the values of the urban, educated élite and the warrior noblemen, Rousseau extolled the virtues of the rural population and the common man (Rousseau 1950b, 1964d). Johann Gottfried von Herder expressed a similar admiration for the common people. But his arguments were more romantic than even Rousseau's. All true culture must rise from the native roots of the natural, rural masses, claimed Herder. He criticized the evils of pride and lust and bellicosity, which he attributed to the artificial, educated upper classes, whereas he glorified the virtues of the *Volk*. He stressed the collectivist themes of the Romantic movement, and conceived of the national community as a creative, genetic, almost organically developing unit.

Rousseau expressed a democratic nationalism which informed the revolutions in western Europe. Rousseau's arguments were revived in the French Revolution, during which they merged into the potent new forces of mass-mobilization. The confluence is evident in the *levée en masse*. This ordinance invoked the values and the *gloire* of *la patrie* to mobilize the French population and place all Frenchmen at the disposal of the army.

Herder expressed a romantic nationalism which informed the political struggles of eastern Europe. Using the revolutionary principle of the *levée en masse*, Napoleon transformed the limited wars of the eighteenth century into the total wars of the nineteenth. He conquered central and eastern Europe. And when he imposed the Western, democratic Enlightenment ideals upon the conquered peoples, his efforts were opposed. Opposition to the French invaders implied opposition to the Enlightenment theories they represented, and drove the occupied peoples deeper into the embrace of Herder's Romanticism. In the eastern regions of Europe, then, anti-Westernism, Romanticism and nationalism became intertwined concepts. When Prussian scholars countered the universalist faith in human reason and popular participation which were inherent in the French

Enlightenment, they drew upon Herder's particularist claim that each people possessed a unique collective spirit. Herder's emphasis on language, culture and spirit was glorified, and his concept of the *Volk* was idealized. During the nine-teenth century, Herder-type arguments gathered strength. These ideas attained a notably pitched intensity in Germany, where the notions of *Volksgeist* and *Volkstum* emerged as explosive political ideas.

In a self-conscious reaction against the threats of French militarism and British mercantilism, Prussian political theorists searched busily for the distinc-tive qualities of their own *Volksgeist*. In their eagerness they created a 'German ideology' according to which Germans possessed greater spiritual depth – more music – than the materialist or cerebral Western imports (Laue 1987, p. 38). Hegel claimed that the servant, knowing both his own role and that of his master, is wiser than the master, who knows only his own. Hegel and Clause-witz noted that whereas eighteenth-century monarchs had found it hard to gen-erate popular enthusiasm for diplomacy or war, nineteenth-century kings had discovered how to use the concept of the *Volk* to mobilize mass support. Clause-witz found it significant that whereas eighteenth-century armies had counted between 10,000 and 70,000 men, Napoleon had managed to mobilize over a mil-lion soldiers. He also observed that the mobilization of popular masses affected the traditional system of international politics.

In the eighteenth century, international interaction had largely been dynastic. The kings of Europe had traded territories with relative ease according to rules of marriage and war – the two most important tools of dynastic diplomacy – and they had paid little attention to the inhabitants of the territories traded. In the nineteenth century, by contrast, nationalist leaders insisted that the will of the inhabitants constituted the only acceptable criterion for drawing state bound-aries. The new leaders argued that people who belonged to the same distinct ethnic or linguistic group should inhabit the same territory. From this argument, movements of national independence spread throughout Europe and the Amer-icas. They were driven, not by kings' concerns for territory, but by peoples' quest for self-determination. The stakes of international politics transcended the limited concerns of dynastic diplomacy. They 'became the business of the people', in Clausewitz's words. From now on, the outcome of wars depended not only on the wealth of the monarch, but also on the will of the nation (Clause-witz 1976).

The observations which Clausewitz made at the beginning of the century were echoed by Leopold von Ranke by the century's end (Meinecke 1957, pp. 377ff). But Ranke, stung by disillusioned experiences as a youthful political activist, cautioned against the emotional energies which could be mobilized by the abstract ideals of nationhood and self-determination. He also warned that the self-conscious emergence of nations was stimulated by the industrialization and the creation of skilled labour forces through compulsory education. Reading, writing, religion and history were introduced as major subjects in schools. And all subjects introduced pupils to a standardized print-language, shared cultural values and a common History.[2]

Mass education had an obvious socializing effect on the inhabitants of a nation. Chairs of 'national' literature and history were established at European universities, where dissertations were now written in the vernacular rather than in Latin or Greek. This initiated a golden age for European philologists, grammarians, lexicographers and litterateurs (Hobsbawm 1962, p. 166). There was also the related effect of the expanding market for cheap, vernacular texts. Encouraged by growing literacy, cheap paper and the rotary press, commercial printed matter proliferated all over Europe and people were socialized into key national legends and myths through mass-produced texts. Elementary readers and patriotic history books were efficient means of socialization, by means of which each new generation of citizens was introduced into a collective imagination and identity (Anderson 1983, p. 39).

Early nineteenth-century nationalism had a progressive character. The movement was built around the idea that all citizens owe their supreme secular loyalty to the nation and its representative institutions – often with an emphasis on the institutions. This idea implies, in turn, both the development of strong emotional attachments between citizens and a central state and the involvement of the citizens in the political life of the state. Late nineteenth-century nationalism, by contrast, was largely associated with conservatism if not reaction. This shift in nationalism from the political left to the right was more marked on the Continent than along the Atlantic rim.

In the Atlantic tradition, a 'nation' was politically defined – often in liberal-democratic terms – by reference to a state and its representative institutions. A nation, wrote the French ideologist the Abbé Sieyès in 1789, is 'a union of individuals governed by *one* law, and represented by the same law-giving assembly'. Thus defined, a nation's unity and identity derive from political organization, and the state would be logically prior to the nation. In the central regions of Europe, however, a nation tended to be defined in terms of culture and language. According to this definition, the nation was logically prior to the state. For the French revolutionaries a nation was a group of individuals subject to a single political order, but for the Germans nations were distinguished from one another by God and nature. For the French *philosophes*, the nation was expressed through the state, for the Germans the nation was expressed through the *Volk*, which articulated a distinct *Geist* that was expressed in its language.

The liberal nationalists of the Atlantic tradition possessed no elaborate notion of how a world of nation-states would interact. They commonly entertained the simple faith that once all nations established their own states, international conflict would no longer occur. The nationalists who did conceive of more elaborate and more realistic visions of international relations, ceased being liberals. In the fragmented central regions of Europe, nationalism fuelled wars of national liberation or unification. In the 1860s, Cavour united Italy in a series of remarkable military operations. In the 1870s, Bismarck united Germany through a succession of masterfully contained wars. Such exploits produced profound changes in the nationalist movements. Fuelled by a sentimental mix of historical myths and romantic philosophy and fortified by industrial expansionism, nationalism became a right-wing cause. By 1900, the extreme nationalists had often become reactionaries and opponents of democracy. Bismarck introduced democratic reforms solely to draw their sting and to use them for his own, Prussian purposes. Garibaldi's Red Shirts of the 1870s became Mussolini's Blackshirts of the 1920s.

Industrialism

The spread of nationalism was related to the great changes brought about by railroads, steamships, telegraphs, industrial production and mass markets of consumer goods. These products of industrialism made communication of ideas, exchange of goods and transport of people easier than ever before. The last quarter of the nineteenth century marked a particularly intense and turbulent phase in the evolution of industrialism. It implied not just the expansion to the rest of the world of the industrializing process that had altered England so dramatically during the Napoleonic Wars (the 'first industrial revolution'). It was in many respects so different in nature and pace that it deserves to be seen as a phenomenon in its own right (the 'second industrial revolution'). For whereas the first industrial revolution had involved incremental change, the second was sudden. It was quicker in its pace and more immediately prodigious in its impact.[3]

Industrial expansion effected a rapid growth in the size of enterprises and necessitated new modes of economic and social organization. In all sectors of industry, factories were built in gigantic dimensions which required the cooperation of hundreds of workers. This meant that the old enterprises which employed a dozen workmen were rendered anachronistic. The new factories hired armies of workers who came from far away to live in rapidly growing urban agglomerations.

The trends towards greater concentration of capital, growth in factory-size and urbanization of labour gathered pace during the last quarter of the century. This was a period of unprecedented triumphs; it was also an age of spectacular failures. But most of all it was a period of rapid transformation, and it acted as a solvent of the old order and a catalyst of the new. The rapid pace of industrialism upset the old, domestic order of the Western nation-states. As it spread across Europe, converting the rural labourers of the traditional village into the workers of the new industrial regions. This development fuelled the rise of new middle classes. However, it also prepared a fertile soil for anti-liberal mass movements on both the left and the right – and as a rule, the more rapid the industrialization, the stronger the anti-liberal reaction (Bull 1948; Moore 1978). The creation of new industrial societies encouraged the growth of workers' unions, labour parties, class consciousness and radical politics. Also, the destruction of the traditional social order stimulated the rise of conservative-romantic movements which resisted the new trends of urbanization and social *anomie*.

The pace of industrialization also upset the old order among states. The faster nations industrialized, the more their power grew. When the nations of the West improved their school systems, they not only enhanced the quality of the work force, they also improved the quality of their soldiers. When they improved the methods of steel-production, they also increased their ability to build better weapons. When they improved their roads and railways, they also improved their ability to project their military power. When they replaced their wooden ships with steel vessels, they increased the speed and capacity of their navies and boosted their ability to transport vast numbers of men rapidly to any port or bay on the globe.

Different Western countries industrialized at different rates. This uneven industrial growth translated into uneven growth of nations' military potentials. During the final quarter of the nineteenth century, some medium-size states in Europe (like Germany) expanded their industrial capabilities and their military potentials at a breakneck rate. By contrast, some traditionally great powers (like Britain) grew at a slower rate, and were, by 1900, not as superior as before. The old interstate balance of power became unclear, and the hierarchy of military force and political prestige became uncertain.

These developments created turbulence in world affairs. First, the uneven growth of state capabilities tore apart the last remainders of the relatively stable Concert system. Second, Europe's own monopoly of modern production was broken by the dissemination of industrialism to other continents.[4] During the final quarter of the century, the mounting uncertainty of world politics was accentuated by great economic fluctuations. The first serious downswing occurred in 1873, when major US ventures defaulted on their bonds. This triggered a panic which immediately swept the capitals of Europe. Waves of booms and busts followed for the next twenty-odd years, earning the period 1873–96 the sobriquet 'the Great Depression'.

The depression accentuated the speed with which capital concentrated and centralized. The main casualty of the panic was the old small-scale family business. Small ventures, which had typically emerged during the first industrial revolution, were too narrowly based and too inefficiently run to withstand the birth-pains of the second. The more diversified and rationally run enterprises did better. The panic, in effect, favoured the large-scale concern. It stimulated diversification and combination, and encouraged the formation of trusts and cartels.

Germany and the United States were hardest hit. Both were new states, which were thrown from domestic war and nation-building into financial panic. Both saw an inordinate amount of bankruptcies and small businesses going under, large ones growing larger, and capital concentrating in large combines (Barra-clough 1976, p. 51). By 1900, the economies of Germany and the USA were dominated by a small number of huge combines. The credit requirements for these companies were gigantic, and the banks and credit institutions involved in their financing insisted on membership of their boards of directors in order to safeguard their loans and investments. In this way, great financiers came to exert a great influence on the management of the behemoths of business.

Britain and France, older and established nation-states, escaped more easily from the 1873 panic. In both countries the small-scale, family venture remained a common feature in the economic landscape. But here, too, the concentration of capital produced giant combines in steel and chemicals – in Britain, firms like Brunner-Mond and Vickers-Armstrong grew to giant proportions during the final quarter of the century, and in France the Schneider-Creusot company grew rapidly.

In 1880, Britain was the world's leading industrial power; 25 years later she was second to the United States, and was also challenged by Germany, which industrialized at a more rapid rate. By 1914, Germany had acquired the world's second-largest industrial potential, relegating Britain to third place. Germany took the lead in the newer, more important industries of chemicals and machine-tools. German engineers like Diesel, Daimler and Benz ignited a revolution in transportation when they, in the 1880s and 1890s, developed small, efficient engines which ran on the light, volatile fractions of petroleum. The swift spread of the new engines sparked the creation of ventures for the exploration, drilling, transport and refinement of oil. Around the turn of the century, large oil companies were drilling in Europe, the United States, the Middle East and Asia (Yergin 1991).

The quest for petroleum altered the political economies of the world. For although most European countries initially could find the oil they needed on their own territories, the largest reserves were found at great distances from the major consumer countries. Great discoveries in Pennsylvania, Texas and California made the United States self-sufficient in oil. Europe, however, realized that its future needs for petroleum could be secured only by safeguarding access to foreign wells.

At the turn of the century, this reliance on extra-European oil increased the geopolitical importance of the Near and the Middle East. This development intruded upon the concerns of Britain, whose leaders had long propped up the tottering Ottoman Empire so that it could serve to contain the interference of other European powers in the Near East, notably Russia – indeed, defeating Russian designs in Asia Minor was an obsessive goal of British officials. At first, concerns for oil supplies were minimal – although oil companies were scrambling for concessions in areas controlled by the drowsy and negligent Ottomans, it was not yet known that astonishing quantities of oil existed in the area. But by the end of World War I, when the Ottoman Empire had finally collapsed,

Mid-Eastern oil began to emerge as a complicating and divisive factor in the politics of the region.

The diffusion of modern instruments of industry and the world-wide quest for fossil fuels illustrate a final difference between the first industrial revolution and the second. Whereas the first revolution had largely concerned England and Europe near the Channel, the second involved the entire world.

Imperialism

The second industrial revolution unleashed an unprecedented dissemination of Western-style capital, products and modes of economic and political organization to all parts of the globe. And just as the second industrial revolution was different from the first, this nineteenth-century wave of Western expansionism was different from previous waves. To denote the unique character of this expansionism, many scholars refer to it as 'imperialism', so as to distinguish it from the 'colonialism' of earlier ages.

Old-style colonialism was a product of mercantilism. It retained its mercantile base and involved competition and quarrels between colonial powers. Through the use of military force, the old-style colonists simply took or purchased wares brought to them by native merchants, who procured them by native methods. Precious metals, tropical products and slave labour were acquired through a kind of cash-and-carry mercantilism. By 1775, this old-style colonial system was withering.

Colonialism and imperialism were two different things. And imperialist activities were often accompanied by a staunch anti-colonial rhetoric. Several arguments supported this anti-colonial stance. First, colonialism meant wars.

Second, industrialism changed the needs and the trading patterns of Europe and dictated a shift in colonial policy. It transformed the West from primarily a buyer of colonial goods to an exporter of capital and a seller of machine-made products. Countries which, in the past, had frequently been under strain to offer their colonies sufficient goods to balance out the products they imported, were now brimming with products and frantically searching for markets. Also, industrialism altered the composition of European demand. Spices, sugar and slaves diminished in relative importance, whereas there was an increasing demand for raw materials for Western factories and food for the swelling legions of Western factory workers.

Removed from its liberal context of free trade, this second anti-colonial argument, which stressed industrial evolution and growing economic interdependence, was easily turned around. From 1870, the liberal emphasis on economic interdependence was re-evaluated in the light of a new, conservative brand of nationalism. This re-evaluation was undoubtedly fortified by the turmoil of rapid industrialization and of the uncertainties of the Great Depression, and it altered the perceptions and the foreign-policy orientations of the European states. As the old, progressive spirit of nationalism was replaced by a new patriotic-chauvinist sentiment, the notion of 'Empire' attained a new lustre. Suddenly, the term 'imperialism' was informed by visions of greatness, duty, and prestige.

The economic dimension of imperialism

This change was sustained by several interacting factors. But the second industrial revolution was the most decisive of these, because it altered the relationship between the Western nation-states and the rest of the world.

Under the new 'imperialism,' the Westerners were not content to purchase solely what native merchants provided. Westerners demanded products for their growing industries. The natives could not always supply these goods. As the nineteenth century evolved, the Westerners began to take over these supply efforts themselves. They moved into the interior of distant countries and organized the production themselves. They built harbours, docks, warehouses, roads, railways, river steamship companies, mines, plantations, refineries, factories, offices, homes, banks and hotels.

During the final quarter of the nineteenth century, Western agents took over the productive life of large regions of the world, and in doing so Westernized them. They overhauled the existing land-claims and property arrangements – introducing the concept of private property to areas where it had not previously existed. They transformed large populations into wage employees, levied taxes upon them, introduced the market exchange of commodities and spread the use of money. They lent money to native rulers – the Khedive of Egypt, the Shah of Persia, the Emperor of China were all indebted to Western financiers – and developed financial stakes in the continuation of their regimes. In a word, the industrial countries of the West were no longer mere importers of colonial goods, they were major exporters of capital.

Economic and normative dimensions of imperialism

Western imperialists realized that they had a profound effect on non-European societies. But they did not consider this a bad thing. They saw the world in terms of the dominant nineteenth-century vision of historical progress. It was commonly held that the progressive nation-states in the West did the 'backward' nations of the world a favour by bringing them Christianity, education, wealth and the values of European civilization; by including them in the historical evolution of Reason and Freedom.

This faith in the inevitable evolution of history made liberal and radical theorists in the West anti-colonialist in rhetoric, but imperialist in practice. Many liberals associated 'colonialism' with mercantilism, conflict and war. War meant taxes, which depleted a nation's capital. It also meant blockades and enmities, which kept a country from its markets. 'Imperialism', on the other hand, was associated with progress and development; it meant the inclusion of all the world's peoples into the harmonizing embrace of an international division of labour marked by interdependent transactions, a self-regulating world order, knowledge and wealth.

In the radical ideology, colonialism meant looting, enslavement and murder. Also, colonialism involved mercantile wars between colonial nations. It implied press gangs, forced conscription and depletion of the labour force in the mother country. Although imperialism, too, was predatory and repressive, the radicals admitted that it nevertheless served a progressive function by pulling 'non-historical' and 'barbarian' societies out of their 'Asian mode of production' and into the cog-wheels of historical evolution (Molnar 1975). Karl Marx put this radical paradox succinctly: 'England has to fulfill a double mission in India: one destructive, the other regenerating – the annihilation of old Asiatic society, and the laying of the material foundations of Western society in Asia' (Marx 1972, p. 82; 1977, pp. 931–41; also Said 1978, pp. 153ff).

Economic, normative and political dimensions of imperialism
The last quarter of the nineteenth century saw a transition from an age in which imperialist practice went hand in hand with anti-colonial rhetoric to one in which imperialism assumed a clear purpose of territorial acquisition.[5] This change was abrupt: it can be precisely dated to 1872, when Prime Minister Disraeli suddenly abandoned Britain's earlier anti-colonial stance and adopted an aggressive policy of imperial expansion and consolidation. The suddenness of Disraeli's conversion, and the willingness with which other statesmen in Europe followed suit, makes it particularly necessary to find the special reasons for the wave of expansionism which followed.

The second industrial revolution helps explain the wave of overseas expansion. For, as the European powers industrialized, they went further abroad for raw materials and foodstuffs, developing new modes of communication and transport and extending the global division of labor. In the last quarter of the nineteenth century Western imports included growing amounts of raw materials for Europe's expanding industries (cotton, wool, timber, ore, hemp, jute, dyes, vegetable oils and, increasingly, petroleum) and important food staples (wheat and meat).

Political economists discussed this development in terms of interdependence among nations. Liberal theorists saw this as a reassuring extension of the global division of labour, and argued that interdependence both increased the wealth of all participants and reduced the danger of conflict among them. Anti-liberal theorists, by contrast, saw interdependence as dependence of each upon all, and claimed that it meant greater vulnerability, as a dependent nation would be susceptible to suppliers' exercise of political power. This concern with power politics was enhanced by the economic panic of 1873 and by the 'Great Depression' which followed.

Radical theorists associated interdependence with inequality, class struggle and exploitation. This association had as a long tradition in German scholarship.

Hegel (1980, p. 150) had argued that, as industrialism progressed, countries would divide into two major classes: a wealthy élite on the one hand, and a 'rabble of paupers' on the other. However, statesmen could delay or diminish such a division by resorting to colonialism Hegal argued. Foreign expansion would soften the class struggle and mitigate the inequality between the poor and the rich. But just as the poor are exploited and alienated as a class at home, they will continue to be so when they settle abroad as colonists. This argument, which was curiously overlooked by Marx, was elaborated by Engels, Bebel, Kautsky and other German socialists in the final years of the nineteenth century.

Conservative theorists argued that interdependence undermined the self-sufficiency of the nation-state and rendered it vulnerable to foreign influences. To enhance their security, the states had to improve domestic industries and consolidate and protect those overseas territories with which they had forged their closest ties. Again, it was German theorists who elaborated the anti-liberal argument. Fichte (1979) had submitted that excessive trade and interdependence threatened the pure spirit of the *Volk*. Friedrich List argued that in an international economy which was based on the doctrine of *laissez-faire*, the strongest countries would always win and the weakest countries would be perpetually dependent. He saw the doctrine of the free market as 'pure ideology' – as a justification of practices which benefited the wealthy. While free trade was the correct policy for an industrially dominant nation like Great Britain, a policy of protectionism would enable weaker nations to break the British stranglehold.

List was confident that his strategy of protectionist industrialization would ensure Germany's industrial growth and shelter it from British influences (Carr 1964, p. 47). However, he did not think that all countries could follow this path. Only nations which possessed a *völkisch* unity and an inordinate political discipline could carry the temporary cost of a strategy which would sacrifice the gains and enjoyments of an entire generation of citizens (List 1927, pp. 181–9).

Pursuing this point, List (like Hegel and, before him, Montequieu) divided the world into two economic/spiritual zones: one temperate, creative and wealthy; the other torrid, lethargic and poor. Only the world's temperate zones are likely to attain the spiritual unity necessary to build a nation-state and attain the final stage of economic development and political independence, List claimed. The torrid regions of the globe are naturally predisposed towards agriculture, and therefore unlikely to evolve any 'intellectual and moral powers'. As the nation-states in the temperate zones evolved industrial, urban-based economies, a natural division of labour would spontaneously emerge between the northern and the southern nations of the world.

List (like Hegel) depicted the relationship between the world's northern and southern zones in terms of inequality of spirit and unequal exchange. However, whereas the radical interpreters of Hegel often criticized such inequalities, List accepted them as natural and inevitable, and saw in them an invitation to colonialism: 'the countries of the temperate zone, since they are destined by nature for industrial production, should seek to develop their major markets in the countries of the torrid zone, which supply them with products in return', he recommended (List 1930, p. 223).

List expressed the sentiment of many Western thinkers of his time. Three or four decades after his death, List's arguments were revived. In Germany, Bismarck relied on List to create the economic foundation of a modern state. In the rest of Europe, List's vision of international trade gathered momentum during the Great Depression – not as self-equilibrating exchange, but as interstate struggle and power politics. In the capitals of Europe, scholars, soldiers and statesmen increasingly stressed that a far-flung empire was the source of a nation's might. To continue their industrial development and acquire a 'place in the sun', it was necessary to acquire a colonial empire and make it economically and politically self-reliant.

After 1873, the world market prices for industrial goods declined. This intensified competition among industrial nations. They raised tariffs to keep out each other's products; also, they began to invest more heavily in 'backward' countries, which now brought a higher rate of return. Under the impact of nationalism, the concept of a global division of labour was reinterpreted along List's lines. In the final quarter of the century, the global division of labour was no longer seen as the automatic outcome of a self-regulating, free world market. In fact, the old 'free market' was replaced by the notion of 'sheltered markets'. Its central image was that of a unified family of nations, in which a northern home country would supply manufactured goods to its less developed colonies in the south and receive foodstuffs and raw material in return. The idea was for the home country to maximize its independence by creating a large, self-sufficient trading unit, embracing various climates and types of resources. It would be protected from external competition by tariffs; it would guarantee an internal market for all its members as well as wealth and prosperity.

The Fin-de-siècle *paradox*

Around 1875, Europe saw imperialism both as a key to wealth and glory and as a service to mankind. By 1900, however, the promises of imperialism were badly disappointed. The profits were elusive; the costs were higher and the conflicts it triggered more enduring and violent than anticipated.

Also, the interests of the home country and the colonists began to diverge. The idea of imperialism had been that the colonies and the mother country should co-operate for mutual benefit. But once the overseas dominions began to develop, the white settlers grew unwilling to surrender the powers essential to economic and political maturity. They protested the surrender of their budding national interest to a vast supernationalism which claimed for itself the coercive equipment of a sovereign state (Hancock 1937, p. 39). Fired by the new doctrines of nationalism, the colonists sought instead to wrestle themselves free from

191

imperial constraint. 'It was the paradox of the new imperialism that it released pressures which made its own tenets unworkable', comments Barraclough. 'By stirring the outer world into activity, it loosened the ties of Empire just as it undermined the preeminent position of Europe, which was its most cherished belief' (Barraclough 1976, p. 75).

Darwin's revolution

In the nineteenth century, history, change and evolution were dominant themes in economic and political theorizing. They blaze through most debates in International Relations theory – the liberal view was infused with an optimistic notion of steady progress; the radical view invested its faith in the iron laws of history and in the *Stufengang* which would produce a final, liberating revolution; the conservatives trusted that a close reading of history could produce lessons for statesmen.

The age was obsessed with the idea that lessons and laws could be drawn from human events and be applied by politicians and statesmen. This obsession was evident towards the end of the eighteenth century – in Smith's law of the market, in Lasalle's iron law of wages, in Burke's laws of commerce, in Malthus' law of population ... In the first half of the nineteenth century, this quest for laws finds its most influential expression in the works of Hegel. In the second half, its most influential articulator is Charles Darwin – whose work combines these characteristic themes of the age with an image which has reverberated through International Relations theories since their earliest times: the notion that social order emerges from an initially anarchic condition as a result of unrestrained competition between free agents (Crook, 1994).

Darwin's theory of evolution has its roots back in the early 1830s, in the experiences he had on a voyage to South America. The observations he made on the Galapagos Islands, 600 miles off the coast of Chile, particularly stimulated Darwin's curiosity and imagination. Here he discovered birds and animals which 'bear the unmistakable stamp of the American continent'; yet many of them were so distinct that they could rank as separate species. Darwin found it strange that the Galapagos birds were unafraid of man, and that the iguana was less afraid of man than of the sea, where its natural predators lived. It struck Darwin that this anomalous behaviour could be the outcome of a long-term conditioning; the animals and birds on these islands differed from those of the South-American mainland because they had been left to themselves for a long stretch of time and slowly adapted to the peculiar circumstances of these isolated isles. The species, then, had attained their characteristic attributes by adapting to their natural environment.

On 35 pages of notes, Darwin immediately pencilled out questions which he would ponder for subsequent decades. He wondered why some species adapt successfully to their environment whereas others do not, and therefore die out.

He speculated whether the successful adaptation of species to natural circumstances describes a teleological path – i.e. whether there is a direction in the evolution of species (Darwin 1958, Ch. 27; 1962, Ch. 13).

Darwin could think of no general answer to these questions. It was only when, in 1838, he read Malthus' *Essay on the Principle of Population* (1982 [1798]) that he found a general proposition which ordered his thought. Malthus argues that the human population always tends to increase at a higher rate than agricultural crops. Population would always outgrow food supply, and man is destined to always compete for scarce resources. Darwin reviewed his questions in the light of Malthus' argument. The guiding principle that governs the evolution of the species is a struggle for scarce resources, he resolved. In this struggle for survival only the strongest, the cleverest and the most adaptable will make it, and they will in turn pass their strength and cleverness on to their children. Survival, Darwin contended, will always be a matter of constant competition for limited resources. 'A struggle for existence inevitably follows from the high rate at which all organic beings tend to increase. It is the doctrine of Malthus applied with manifold force to the whole animal and vegetable kingdoms,' he wrote (1958, p. 376).

In a universal struggle for existence, the right of the strongest prevails. This principle, which Herbert Spencer summarized as the 'survival of the fittest', gave Darwin the answer to why some species were successful and others became extinct. Only those best equipped to command the available food supply would survive the struggle for existence.

Darwin published his theory in the *Origin of Species* in 1859. It hit the scholarly world like a bombshell. It unleashed a ferocious debate which closed the circle on Malthusian political economy and profoundly transformed the three political ideologies of liberalism, radicalism and conservatism.

Darwinian influences I: Marx and Marxism

Darwin provided radicalism with a new scientific term: 'adaptation'. Through adaptation living organisms fit themselves to the distinct features of their environment – partly by modifying their own behavior, partly by labouring to change their environment. Those organisms which adapt well to their environment, flourish; whereas those which do not, might perish.

Marx recognized immediately that Darwin's argument could be used to identify 'the laws of capitalist production', and explain how these laws worked 'with iron necessity towards inevitable results' (Marx 1977, pp. 91f). Marx was writing *Capital* at the time Darwin published his *Origin of Species*, and he found that Darwin's concept of adaptation suited the major themes which guided his own research. It fitted perfectly with the claim that mankind transforms its natural environment through its labour and is, in turn, transformed by it. In addition, it echoed the Hegelian claim that nothing was real but 'the whole' and that History was a series of advances from the less to the more perfect. Marx noted that although *The Origin of Species* was 'developed in the crude English style, this is the book which contains the basis in natural history for our view' (Marx 1964a, p. 131).

The nineteenth-century idea of progress-through-struggle, which reverberated through the theories of Hegel and Darwin, also guided the writings of Marx and Engels. The dialectical method, through which Marx sought to discover 'the natural laws' which drove History through successively more advanced stages of development, parallels Darwin's theory of evolution. In Marx's vision, humanity forges ahead towards a new society with the weight and momentum of all human history behind it. Society, like nature, progresses over time, driven by an inherent struggle among its members. Darwin's claim that evolution was general and inevitable echoes through Marx and Engels' notion of the inevitable victory of the new, proletarian society.

After Marx's death, some of his followers attempted to bring the doctrines of 'scientific socialism' into greater harmony with Darwinism. Such efforts were quite explicit in the writings of prominent socialist theorists like August Bebel (1893). Other Marxists, however, warned against too close an identification between Darwinism and Marxism. Darwin discussed the animal world, whereas Marx discussed human history, and although humanity belongs to the animal world, it also transcends it, wrote Anton Pannekoek. In contrast to the rapacious animals which Darwin discusses, human beings are social animals. In human society, it is neither brute strength or individual cleverness which determines an individual's survival; it is the size of the individual's property. 'The competitive struggle between men does not bring forth the best and the most qualified, but destroys many strong and healthy ones because of their poverty; while those who are rich, even if they are weak and sick, survive', writes Pannekoek (1912, p. 33).

Darwinian influences II: Spencer, Sumner and Social-Darwinism
From the early 1800s, liberal thinkers had sought to develop a theory of social evolution. Herbert Spencer made a celebrated effort in his *Principles of Biology* (1846). This book gave an influential definition of evolution as 'a change from an indefinite, incoherent heterogeneity, through continuous differentiations and integrations'. Such change, he wrote, came about through a struggle for survival in which only the fittest will survive. In the 1850s, Spencer applied his definition to issues of political economy and history. He saw the evolution of human civilization in terms of an increasing division of labour from primitive, undifferentiated tribes into complex civilizations, which allow for greater and greater individual freedom.

Darwin's theory assisted Spencer greatly. Where Darwin saw that a struggle for existence brought evolutionary change in plants and animals, Spencer argued that in human society, too, the struggle for existence was a progressive force. A principle of natural selection would weed out society's weaker members; the poor, the incapable, the imprudent, the stupid, the disease-ridden and the idle would succumb in the keen competition for survival. This would allow the healthiest and strongest members of society to mature and procreate. Spencer argued that this principle benefited the good of the greater community. Any effort to help the weakest elements in society would only make everyone worse off in the longer haul. Any interference by the state to provide housing, education and poor-relief to society's poorest members would only stimulate their procreation, to the detriment of the community.

In the last quarter of the nineteenth century, the influential British journalist and editor Walter Bagehot relied on Darwin and Spencer in a sweeping attempt to explain the principles of human history in the light of a few general laws:

First, in every particular state of the world, those nations which are strongest tend to prevail over the others; and in certain marked peculiarities the strongest tend to be the best.

Secondly, within every particular nation the type or types of character then and there most attractive tend to prevail; and the most attractive, though with exceptions, is what we call the best character.

Thirdly, neither of these competitions is in most historic conditions intensified by extrinsic forces; but in some conditions ... both are so intensified.

These are the sort of doctrines with which, under the name of 'natural selection' in physical science, we have become familiar (Bagehot 1889, pp. 457f).

Bagehot's *Physics and Politics* (1889 [1872]) contains an early, sustained discussion of nation-building. The book explores at great length the 'first law of politics'. Foreshadowing Ratzel and Gumplowicz, Bagehot explains how civilization progresses through time because of man's innate propensity to emulate all behaviour which proves most advantageous in the 'competition between nation and nation'.

Bagehot's argument is rephrased by Benjamin Kidd and William Sumner – American advocates of Spencer who discussed historical and international issues in a Darwinian light. Kidd builds a theory of human civilization, according to which 'states are cradled and nurtured in continuous war, and grow up by a kind of natural selection, having worsted and subordinated their competitors in the long-drawn-out rivalry through which they survive' (Kidd 1894, pp. 43f). Sumner agrees, but retains a more Malthusian attitude. Conflicts arise among men because there are not enough natural resources to satify everybody's demand, argues Sumner (1954; 1965). Resource scarcity drives men 'into rivalry and a collision of interest with each other'. In prehistoric times, men organized in groups in order to ensure their survival in an environment of scarcity; partly to divide social tasks and produce more effectively, and partly to defend themselves against other groups. With echoes of Bagehot, Ratzel, Gumplowitz and Kidd, Sumner writes:

Such a group, therefore, has a common interest. It must have control over a certain area of land; here it comes into collision with every other group. The competition of life, therefore, arises between groups, not between individuals, and we see that the members of the in-group are allies and joint-partners in one interest while they are brought into antagonism of interest with all outsiders. It is the competition of life, therefore which makes war, and that is why war always has existed and always will. It is the condition of human existence (Sumner 1965, p. 206).

As groups fought each another, they acquired greater discipline and efficiency inward; through war 'they were learning cooperation, perseverance, fortitude, and patience'. The more cohesive and efficient a group was within, the greater chances it had to emerge victorious in the struggle without. War is 'the iron spur of the nature process', for it is through war that human groups have evolved institutions of domestic order; laws and rights, political bodies, social classes, division of labour – even the nation-state itself and the economic base upon which its rests are products of war (pp. 229, 211, 225).

This does not mean that Sumner glorifies war. Far from it. He argues that war is an evil. However, it is part of the human condition, and 'like other evils, it must be met when it is unavoidable, and such gain as can be got from it must be won' (p. 230). The struggle for survival which had characterized world politics in the past would, in Sumner's mind, also mark international relations in the future. On the threshold of a new century Sumner foreshadows the coming of a new wave of disastrous wars. He observed how the Great Powers of his time were building ever-large navies and carving up overseas territories into colonies. On the eve of World War I, he commented that as the Great Powers 'prepare for war they certainly will have war, and their methods of colonization and exploitation will destroy the aborigines. In this way the human race will be civilized – but by the extermination of the uncivilized (p. 229).

The German general and military author Friedrich von Bernhardi agreed with the main tenets of Sumner's International Relations theory. But whereas Sumner was essentially an American liberal, who saw war as a frightful 'waste of life and and waste of capital' (p. 230), von Bernhardi was a German reactionary who saw war as a force for the further evolution of humanity towards ever higher levels of moral and spiritual perfection. And in a book entitled *Germany and the Next War* (1912), he argued that 'the law of the strongest' is a general principle of nature and that it governs the behaviour of both animals and humans, individually and in groups. War is a central phenomenon in nature and in history. Indeed:

War is a biological necessity of the first importance, a regulative element in the life of mankind which cannot be dispensed with, since without it an unhealthy development will follow, which excludes every advancement of race, and therefore all real civilization. 'War is the father of all things.' The sages of antiquity long before Darwin recognized this (Bernhardi 1912, p. 18).

Von Bernhardi did not fear the coming war. He welcomed it. A good world war would once and for all reveal the weak and cowardly nature of the peaceloving and corrupt Anglo-Saxons and finally demonstrate the spiritual superiority of the German nation, he argued.

Darwinian influences III: Haeckel and Continental Nationalism
Von Bernhardi's arguments were not the ravings of a lunatic. They were entertained by militaristic and imperialistic circles in Germany. Indeed, they reflected the mood at the imperial court of Wilhelm II, and they expressed the sentiments of patriotic German youth movements whose members often portrayed Marxism and Liberalism as intertwined faiths, and opposed both of them in the same breath.

The Prussian zoologist Ernest Haeckel (1834–1919), for example, wrote a lengthy essay to rescue Darwinism from the clutches of the revolutionaries. He argued that socialism and liberalism are theories which assume that people are naturally equal; Darwinism, on the contrary, advocates social *in*equality. Darwin's theories corroborate the fact that animals evolve in the direction of ever greater differentiation; the higher or more perfect the animal, the greater the inequality existing. The same principle holds good for the human animal, Haeckel continued. Human society, too, is marked by a great divide between social classes and nations; the more developed a human society is, the more specialized the social division of labour and the stronger and abler are its ruling members.

Darwinism shows that the struggle for survival is not only unavoidable, but a law of nature. Indeed, the struggle fuels social evolution. Those members of society who are unfit for competition will perish, whereas those who are best qualified for it will survive. Consequently, the struggle for survival is accompanied by an ever greater perfection of society. This may be lamentable – just as it is lamentable that all men must die. However, it is a fact of human existence, which it would be foolish to deny and disastrous to alter. 'Darwinism, or the theory of selection, is thoroughly aristocratic', Haeckel wrote:

it is based upon the survival of the best. The division of labour brought about by development causes an ever greater variation in character, an ever greater inequality among the individuals, in their activity, education and condition. The higher the advance of human culture, the greater the difference and gulf between the various classes existing (quoted in Pannekoek 1912, pp. 29f).

Haeckel extended this Darwinian logic to international politics. In his view, states relate to each other in a lawless environment, in a state of nature, where competition is naked and absolute and where only the fittest of states would survive and the unfit would be conquered. Actions of states could therefore not be judged according to legal or moral standards. Each state should act solely according to its own interest.

Seen in isolation, Haeckel's arguments did not bring new insights to International Relations theory. Seen in the context of the age, however, this old axiom evolved into a distinct political doctrine. It got caught in the complex, intellectual maelstroms which swept the Continent, such as the romantic movement, whose influence attained a torrential force in central Europe in the mid-nineteenth century. In Germany romanticism transcended the narrow boundaries of literature and art; it emerged as an irresistible political force, intimately intertwined with nationalism, Hegelianism and frustrations about the political fragmentation of the German *Volk*.

Early in the nineteenth century, Hegelian dialectics explained that the disunity of Germany would produce the idea of unity, which would, with historical necessity, bring about the creation of a German state. Conservative Hegelians argued that this idea would find its supreme articulation in the Prussian state. However, by mid-century, the Hegelians no longer possessed the only theory of political evolution; they were challenged by the Darwinists, who expressed the same themes in a more concrete, materialist discourse. In 1860, Haeckel began to dress the right-wing Hegelian message in Darwinian terms. At a sports camp in Coburg, he conceived of the idea of a 'single people of brothers', living a healthy life in accordance with the laws of nature. He elaborated this notion in a doctrine of 'monism' – Haeckel used the term to differentiate himself from west-European 'dualism', a view which drew a distinction between humanity and nature. To the monist, humans were part of nature, animals who were distinguished from other animals only by a superior degree of development. Darwin had united the natural and the social worlds: humanity was part of nature and had, according to laws of natural selection, evolved from the animal kingdom.

Haeckel used Darwinism as the scientific basis for a new, cosmic philosophy of history and politics. Human history must be re-examined in terms of humanity's biological nature, Haeckel claimed. This will show that human society is ruled by the laws of competition. Nowhere is this more evident than in world politics. Nations are living organisms, which must fight to survive.

In 1862, Haeckel began to present his monist philosophy on lecture tours all over Germany. His ideas were well received in a fragmented nation which was in the throes of an industrializing process of unparalleled scope and pace. Haeckel's theories reverberate with the strong, romantic chauvinism and the unprecedented socio-economic turbulence of the age; they both reflected the rapid social change of the era and fuelled its growing demands for economic integration and political unification.

The Germans were a superior *Volk*, Haeckel argued. But they could only remain so by ensuring the survival of their distinct Aryan features. They must minimize the influence of alien elements; they must remove foreign doctrines, such as liberalism, which praise equality and harmony, from the German educational system. Such ideas were false, and had a corrupting influence on German youth. The encouragement of reason and free will must also be discouraged, Haeckel argued, because organisms did not triumph by reason but, as Darwin had shown, by struggle and purity. 'The human will has no more freedom than that of the higher animals, from which it differs in degree and not in kind.' Humanity can experience freedom only in the context of an ordered society; and 'the greater the freedom, the stronger must be the order'. Thus, he made liberty a consequence of submission to the authority of the group and the primacy of the group's survival. In the interest of the State, the individual was unimportant. In order for an individual biological organism to survive 'thousands, indeed millions of cells are sacrificed'. And just as cells die to save the organism, so individuals might be sacrificed for the greater good of the State (Gasman 1971).

Haeckel stirred the imagination of his colleague Friedrich Ratzel (1844–1909) who also applied Darwin's theory to human history and society. Ratzel, whose chief interest lay in the dialectics between man and his physical environment, made important contributions to several social sciences. He made an indelible impression on International Relations theory with his concept of *Lebensraum* (or 'living space'). It elaborated on the territorial nature of the state, explaining that a close relationship exists between a *Volk* and the geographical space in which it has historically evolved. Ratzel viewed the nation–state as an organism, which expanded and contracted its boundaries according to the quality and the capabilities of its inhabitants (Ratzel 1896; Haushofer 1928). Comparable arguments were formulated by several other social theorists (Weikart 1993) – starkly by Ludwig Gumplowicz (1883), more subtly by the young Max Weber (1994, pp. 2, 5, 16, 84, 134).

In 1899, Haeckel published *Das Welträtsel* ('The Riddle of the Universe'). An immediate best seller, it spread the ideas about an evolutionary process driven by struggle between social groups founded on force and maintained by power. It evoked Germany's pagan past and extolled the virtues of the German nation. In 1906, Haeckel founded the Monist League, a youth movement, dedicated to sports and national virtues. Within five years, the League had become an international movement.

In the decade which preceded World War I, the Monist League introduced a generation of German teenagers to an intense German nationalism. The political importance of the League lies in the long-term effects its ideas exerted on the generation of Germans who were born in the 1890s. This generation became soldiers in World War I, in which they suffered a costly defeat. The Monist League was dissolved after 1918, but other youth organizations were organized along the same lines and stressed the same explosive mix of Social-Darwinist doctrines and the romantic myths of a pagan past. The Thule Society, the Artamanen League and other organizations contributed to the rise of bio-political patriotism in the Weimar Republic. They advocated the creation of a racially pure Germanic peasantry through the cultivation of the nobility inherent in German blood. They argued that Poles should be removed from the territories east of Germany in order to give the expanding German population *Lebensraum*. This land should be resettled by racially acceptable Germans rescued from the alienating slums of the new industrial zones of the Ruhr and the Saar. Among the individuals who received their ideological and political training in the Arta-manen League were Walter Darré, Rudolf Höss and Heinrich Himmler – all of whom later joined the Nazi movement and became officers and leaders of Hitler's SS (Gasman 1971, pp. 152f).

Modernity and beyond

History, change and evolution were dominant themes in nineteenth-century International Relations theorizing. These themes reflect an idea which had marked the entire modern age: the idea that lessons could be drawn from human events, expressed in terms of maxims and laws and applied by politicians and statesmen. This idea evolved into an obsession at the end of the eighteenth century and the beginning of the nineteenth.

During the middle of the nineteenth century a reaction developed in the form of a mounting critique of the very idea of material and moral progress. This critique was, in some respects, foreshadowed by Darwin. Although he expresses some of the most characteristic properties of modern, nineteenth-century scholarship, he also represents a rupture. He excludes rational and moral considerations from his theories. Darwin's theory of organic evolution relies on biological and environmental variables alone.

Darwin's disregard for human reason was emulated by other theorists. One of them was Karl Marx, who developed one of the most significant criticisms of modern society. Drawing on German methodology, French politics and British Political Economy, Marx developed a bitter critique of modern society, whose inhuman mode of production alienated individuals. But in the final acount, Marx' castigation of the capitalist mode of production was an argument from within the tradition of Western modernity. It was a limited critique in the sense that the Marxists proposed to replace one vision of modernity (capitalism) with another (socialism). The analyses of Marx amounted to a less stinging critique of modern society than that of Nietzsche, who mocked the idea (shared by materialist liberals and radicals alike) that each individual is an infinite reservoir of possibilities and that these possibilities will prevail once society is rearranged.

Nietzsche entertained a deep scepticism about human reason and morality. He turned the human faculty of reason against rationality itself in order to disclose its flimsy nature. He doubted man's ability to find truth and moral universals, and sought to reveal the contingent nature of man's moral standards. He attacked the moral pretensions of liberals and radicals alike. He argued that 'good' and 'bad' are inappropriate terms in historical and social analysis. He doubted the ability of human language to describe any real or true thing, and held moral rhetoric to be just one more political tool in the hands of those hungry for power. He insisted on revealing the power structure which moral discourse concealed and which the entire social order was built on. 'Seek ye a name for this world? A solution for all its puzzles? ... This world is the will to power – and nothing else', he affirmed (Nietzsche 1960, p. 917). Nietzsche rejected the facile contemporary belief in progress. And this rejection was a frontal attack on the values and assumptions on which modern Western society was based (Chanteur 1992, pp. 83ff).

Similar arguments were touched upon by others. Nietzsche had noted that human beings were prey to unconscious drives that operated in hidden and devious ways, but Sigmund Freud laid bare the alleged mechanisms of those operations. Nietzsche had argued that the human language was a haphazard construct, but Ferdinand de Saussure showed how language is a socially maintained unity whose distinct rules of syntax and semantics are quietly adopted by human individuals who are born into its structures and forced to observe the world and formulate thoughts through them.

Around the turn of the century, then, social theories were developed according to which human behaviour may be driven by concerns other than material interest and rational calculation. Their effect was to splinter the modern image of man as a coherent individual who responds rationally and intelligently to events. The new theories adumbrated an epistemological rupture with a kind of representational reasoning which had held sway in the West since the Renaissance. They indicated the coming of an abstract trend which would soon engulf writing, poetry, music no less than social theory, and which would bring artists and scientists self-consciously to reject old, accepted forms and traditional preoccupations with causality, natural symmetry and three-dimensional space.[6] They sounded early warnings of the dangers which attended the modern quest for wealth and power in Europe in general and in Germany and Russia in particular.

They were made and launched during the first decade of the twentieth century, but they detonated much later. They were torpedoes with delayed charges. They struck the modern image of man as a coherent individual who responds rationally and intelligently to events around the turn of the century, but their impact was not really felt until after World War I.

8

Interwar politics: the twenty years' crisis

In August 1914, war broke out in Europe. It came as no surprise. Industrialism, nationalism and imperialism had already undermined the old order. Tense rivalries contributed a nervous atmosphere to European diplomacy. The assassination on 28 June 1914 of Austrian Crown Prince Franz Ferdinand was the jolt which finally broke the log-jam of European politics. His murder, in the remote Balkan town of Sarajevo, pulled all of Europe into war.

Enraged by the assassination, the Austrian emperor secured Germany's support to punish Serbia and repress nationalism in the Balkans. Russia, by contrast, had no interest in punishing Balkan nationalists, for they provided Russia with an excuse for gaining control over the Bosporus and access to the Mediterranean. Russia had allied itself with Serbia. And as soon as Austria began to shell the Serbian capital, tsar Nicholas II ordered military mobilization to defend his ally.

Since Germany's Kaiser had promised to support Austria, and since Russia was allied with Germany's arch-enemy France, he felt compelled to mobilize as well. This mobilization was the single most important step towards World War. The Germans were not prepared for a war in the Balkans. They had made a detailed plan of mobilization around one single inflexible precept: Germany must avoid being caught in a two-front war between Russia and France. The Germans had only one crisis plan: if war came, they would first defeat France by a massive invasion through Belgium; then they would quickly move their troops east through Poland to face the Russian onslaught.

Consequently, when the Kaiser gave the order to mobilize, Germany's momentous military machine executed a response which had no relation to the Serbian crisis: it quickly transported two million men into the fields of Flanders. Immediately, nationalist issues which were at the heart of the Balkan crisis were relegated to secondary importance. The war became an all-European struggle to contain an expanding Germany. The major states of Europe found themselves locked in a deadly struggle of two equipollent alliances, pummelling each other senseless. The interstate violence lasted for three years. The nations of Europe bled each other dry at the rate of over 100,000 young men per week. Over fifteen million deaths later, the stalemate was broken by events beyond the traditional cockpit of European politics: by the Russian revolution in March 1917, and by America's entry in April. These two events and the international ripple effects they created will be the primary focus of this chapter.

There is a close conceptual connection between Russia's exit from the war and America's entry into it. This connection, which is often overlooked despite its major effect on twentieth-century international politics, will be discussed first. Then the chapter will examine the consequences of the Great War; one of which was the evolution of a new academic discipline dedicated to understanding the causes of war and to their elimination.

This fledgling discipline emerged along the north-Atlantic rim – with the nominal but disillusioned victors of the War. Its members rejected the conservative view of world politics, arguing that it had contributed to the outbreak of War in 1914; and they shunned the vigorous anti-establishment writings of communists and fascists. They adopted a rather narrow, liberal, view of war and peace, much informed by the tradition of International Law and by the idealistic peace visions of the north-Atlantic states. The discipline developed just as new threats to peace and order were born on the Continent and in the colonies, but it was not equipped to deal with them.

Two visions of a lasting peace

When war broke out in Europe, US President Woodrow Wilson believed that America's national interest was best served by a policy of isolation. By remaining aloof from the war, Wilson thought that the United States could play the role of a neutral broker in Europe's suicidal conflict. When his efforts to mediate failed, the president was faced with a dilemma. In his mind, the worst possible outcome of the war would be the victory of the anti-liberal Central Powers; this would mean the triumph of German militarism on the Continent and a blow to democracy and free trade. However, if the Allies won, autocratic Russia would see in the German defeat an opportunity to expand into eastern and central Europe.

In May 1916, Wilson's political arithmetic was complicated by an Allied conference in which Britain, France, Russia and Italy drafted a programme for a new post-war order. The Allies realized that Europe would be weakened by the war and that the USA would emerge as the world's strongest economic power. They made a plan to use high tariffs, government subsidies and controlled markets to shield Europe from the effects of that power. But this added new fears to Wilson's concerns. The post-war order was being defined without US participation – and in direct contradiction to America's liberal national interests.

Continued US neutrality would erode his chances to wield any influence over the post-war world order.

Wilson became torn between his belief that only as a neutral actor could he mediate a just peace and his fear that only as a belligerent could he obtain a seat at the conference which would define the post-war order. In his re-election campaign he repeated his pledge to keep the United States out of the war. But at the same time, he began to consider his own post-war plans more carefully.

Wilson's dilemma ran through a speech he made to Congress on 22 January 1917. He urged the belligerents to accept a 'peace without victory', to simply end the war without bring either victory or defeat upon Germany. It pleased no one. Wilson attacked the old, European balance of power for having failed to prevent world war; he criticized the Europeans for now relying upon power politics to secure the peace. 'There must be, not a balance of power, but a community of power', he warned; 'not organized rivalries, but an organized common peace.' Such a peace could only be founded on peoples' full freedom to travel and trade. 'The freedom of the seas is the *sine qua non* of peace, equality and cooperation', he said. 'The free, constant, unthreatened intercourse of nations is an essential part of the process of peace and development' (D. M. Smith 1966, pp. 165, 167).

The claim that man has a natural right to travel and trade goes back to the earliest International Relations theorists. Wilson could have referred to a number of legal authorities, like Vitoria or Grotius, to substantiate his proposal. But he chose to rely on a narrower formulation: 'I am proposing', he concluded, 'that the nations should with one accord adopt the doctrine of President Monroe as the doctrine of the world' (D. M. Smith 1966, pp. 165, 167).

The reference to the Monroe Doctrine was a diplomatic *faux pas*. It enraged European statesmen, who saw Wilson as provincial and chauvinistic. 'The man is the quintessence of a prig'; he dares to come after three years of terrible war to ask us to put down our arms and meekly agree to American principles, commented a British observer. A French writer called Wilson's comments 'fetid, ignominious, obscene, fistulous and hemorrhoidal' (Link 1967, pp. 273f). The most significant reaction came from the German Kaiser, who attacked the *sine qua non* of Wilson's proposal: six days after the president's speech, the Kaiser implemented a policy of total submarine warfare against neutral or enemy vessels.

In February and March 1917 Wilson was forced to make up his mind. The Russian tsar was replaced by a Provisional Government led by Alexandr Kerensky. British intelligence reports announced (falsely) that Germany was forging an aggressive alliance with Mexico with the intention of expanding into Texas. German U-boats began to sink American merchant ships. If Wilson wanted to protect the freedom of the seas he could only do so by becoming a full belligerent against Germany.

On 2 April, Wilson declared war on the Kaiser. German submarines were destroying American property and American lives, he angrily argued before Congress. But Wilson did not insist on the necessity of revenge. Rather, he appealed to universal principles of decency and to Lockean arguments of natural law. From the theories of Locke and Vatell, Wilson inferred that the German attacks were not only crimes against the United States, but violated the very rules by which civilized humanity lives. It amounted to war on all humankind, and America must punish Germany in the name of the rights of all humankind.

Wilson's close adviser, Edward House, feared the consequences of Wilson's sweeping logic. US Secretary of State Robert Lansing had similar reservations. In addition, he feared what would happen if Kerensky lost control of the Russian revolution and the vast tsarist empire was plunged into a 'hideous state of disorder' and undermined the Allied war effort on the eastern front (Lansing 1935, p. 337).

The Bolshevik challenge

On 7 November 1917, Lansing's worst fears materialized. The Bolsheviks seized power in Petrograd. To placate the war-weary workers, peasants and soldiers, they confiscated the country's means of production, distributed land to the peasants and pulled Russia out of the war. They immediately called upon all belligerent peoples to follow the Bolshevik example and start 'negotiations for a just, democratic peace.' On 9 November Lenin announced a 'Decree of Peace':

The [new Soviet] government considers it the greatest of crimes against humanity to continue this war over the issue of how to divide among the strong and rich the weak nationalities they have conquered, and solemnly announces its determination immediately to sign terms of peace to stop this war ...

The government abolishes secret diplomacy, and, for its part, announces its firm intention to conduct all negotiations quite openly in the full view of the whole people. It will proceed immediately with the full publication of the secret treaties endorsed or concluded by [Kerensky's] government of landowners and capitalists from February to October 25, 1917 (Lenin 1975a, p. 541).

Lenin's initiative put Wilson in a diplomatic squeeze. First, Lenin levied against the peoples of the entire world a similar argument to that which Wilson had launched against Germany: that the people are inherently peaceful, but that their leaders are a dictatorial, self-serving and corrupt clique of militant oppressors.

Second, Lenin carried out his pledge and made public all the duplicitous deals that the European governments had secretly made during the war. These made it obvious that Britain and France had no intention of supporting Wilson's war aims; they were fighting a costly war to maintain their overseas possessions.

Finally, Lenin offered a radical alternative to Wilson's liberal theories of a new world order. Lenin not only withdrew Russia from the Allied war effort, he incited workers and soldiers of all countries to turn their weapons on their capitalist and imperialist oppressors and begin a world revolution. Only revolution, Lenin argued, could end the war and bring self-determination for all nations.

On 4 December 1917, the day after Russia began separate peace negotiations with Germany at Brest-Litovsk, Wilson called for a 'very grave scrutiny' of America's war aims; he was worried that the Bolsheviks were using rhetoric – '"no annexations, no contributions, no punitive indemnities" – to lead the people of Russia astray' (Walworth 1969, p. 144). Lenin had become a chief competitor for conceptual leadership in the post-war world. He had 'absconded with the biggest piece of liberal theory: the principle of self-determination' (Gardner 1984). For the next 75 years, the liberals could not compete with the Leninist doctrine of national liberation. Little wonder Wilson sweated blood over Russia (Fromkin 1995, pp. 150–64).

Wilson's Fourteen Points

The negotiations at Brest-Litovsk were conducted openly and gave Lenin an important rostrum for revolutionary propaganda. The concomitant armistice enabled Germany to transfer troops from the Eastern to the Western front. News of the transfers fuelled disillusion in France and England; revolutionary propaganda incited mutiny in both French and British armies. Wilson met the challenge of Bolshevik propaganda and the crisis in Allied morale by a major address on the American war aims and the post-war order. This address was destined to be 'democracy's answer in its first full-dress debate with international communism' (Link 1971, p. 108).

On 18 January 1918, Wilson outlined his peace programme. He began by carefully discussing the situation in Russia. Commending Lenin's insistence on open negotiations, 'in the true spirit of modern democracy', Wilson adopted this principle as the first of Fourteen Points for peace. He denounced the 'secret covenants' of old diplomatic practices; he called for 'open covenants of peace, openly arrived at, after which there shall be no private international understandings of any kind but diplomacy shall proceed always frankly and in public view' (Walworth 1969, p. 148).

Next, Wilson reiterated his old *sine qua non* of peace: 'absolute freedom of navigation upon the seas, outside territorial waters, alike in peace and war' (Point II). He called for 'the removal, so far as possible, of all economic barriers and the establishment of an equality of trade conditions among all the nations concenting to the peace ...' (Point III). He insisted on 'a free, open-minded, and absolutely impartial adjustment of all colonial claims' (Point IV). After several specific proposals for redrawing contested boundaries in Europe, Wilson finally proposed the establishment of a League of Nations: 'A general association of nations must be formed under specific covenants for the purpose of affording mutual guarantees of political independence and territorial integrity to great and small states alike' (Walworth 1969, p. 148).

The Fourteen Points got mixed reviews in Europe. The bereaved, war-tired masses leapt at Wilson's blueprint for a lasting peace. They eagerly embraced the idea of an international organization designed to guarantee open diplomacy and arbitration of international disputes. When Wilson arrived in Europe in January 1919 to attend the Peace Conference, the populations in several European capitals greeted him as the sole visionary statesman of of the age. It is a measure of his popularity that he was awarded the Nobel Peace Prize that year.

Diplomats and statesmen, by contrast, were reserved about this projection of America's liberal philosophy into world affairs. However, they recognized Wilson's popularity and did not publicly reject his proposals. After much bickering, Wilson's ideas were included in the Versailles Peace Treaty. On the face of it, the Treaty was a triumph of reason; but behind the scenes, delegates agreed that the Treaty was badly flawed (Keynes 1920). First, neither Germany nor Russia had attended the Peace Conference. Not surprisingly, both of them refused to sign the Treaty and to accept the League of Nations, whose covenant the Treaty guaranteed. The League suffered another irreparable blow when the US Senate refused to ratify it – thus denying the United States League membership.

Second, the Treaty's recognition of the right to national self-determination paved the way for insoluble ethnic strife in central Europe and the Near East. The Treaty dismembered the multi-ethnic Ottoman and Austrian empires. It separated Austria from Hungary, adjusted central-European borders to fit national configurations, and created seven new independent states – Czechoslovakia, Finland, Estonia, Latvia, Lithuania, Poland and Yugoslavia. Also, the Conference carved Syria and Lebanon out of the Ottoman Empire and gave them to France as mandates of the League of Nations. Palestine and Iraq were given to Britain on the same basis. These actions angered leaders of the non-European world, and fuelled the fires of nationalism and anti-liberalism in the Middle East and Asia.

Third, the Peace Conference infused Western politics with acrimony. It bound Germany to pay $32 billion for damages inflicted by the war and ceded to France the rich iron and coal deposits of the Ruhr. With Germany impoverished and robbed of its industrial base, the country would be unable to muster a military threat in the future. These measures were made both to punish Germany and to replenish the exhausted Allied economies. The war had destroyed land, labour and capital and disrupted international exchange. During the war, England and France had purchased weapons from the United States on credit, and had borrowed to finance their post-war reconstruction. After the war, they needed money to pay the Americans back.

The decision to make Germany pay exorbitant reparations paved the way for the post-war Depression. The political economy of the 1920s come to hinge on a web of American financing, German reparations and European reconstruction: US investors made large dollar loans to Germany; the Germans used the loans to pay reparations to the Allies; the Allies used the reparations payments to pay their war debts to the United States.

The post-war world economy consisted, in effect, of the United States paying itself. The Allies could not pay the American loans without German reparations; Germany could not pay reparations to the Allies without American loans, for the Versailles Treaty had stripped Germany of its industrial and commercial resources. Germany's economy wobbled under the burden. Unprecedented inflation struck the German currency. Between 1921 and 1923, the mark became practically worthless.[1] It soon became obvious that the Versailles Treaty had failed and that the League of Nations could not guarantee a lasting peace. Wilson's idea of an open world economy consisting of democratic states was being eroded by the Great Depression. Market economies were replaced by principles of plan and command. Many democracies were replaced by dictatorships. The euphoric hopes of 1919 plunged into into deep and dark depression. The result was a sustained political crisis, about which Edward H. Carr writes:

The characteristic feature of the crisis of the twenty years between 1919 and 1939 was the abrupt descent from the visionary hopes of the first decade to the grim despair of the second, from a utopia which took little account of reality to a reality from which every element of utopia was rigorously excluded (Carr 1964, p. 224).

The twenty years' crisis

Wilson's visionary hopes dominated the new discipline of International Relations in its first years. Wilson's approach to world affairs was very much informed by the eighteenth-century confidence in reason, equality, liberty and property.

The United States attained independence at the end of the eighteenth century, when Enlightenment ideals were in full bloom. The American confidence in equality, in divinely-inspired human rights like 'life, liberty and the pursuit of happiness', in representative government and in popular sovereignty blazed through Wilson's political career – as governor of New Jersey, he conducted a dynamic and fearless campaign against the élitist authority of the entrenched politicians of the state and their closed political practices; as president of the United States, he hurled the same charges at the Austrian Emperor and the German Kaiser. He repeatedly emphasized that the war was fought against the autocrats of the world; not against the people of Germany:

We have no quarrel with the German people. We have no feeling towards them but one of sympathy and friendship. It was not upon their impulse that their government acted in entering this war. It was not with their previous knowledge or approval. It was a war determined upon as wars used to be determined upon in the old, unhappy days when peoples were nowhere consulted by their rulers and wars were provoked and waged in the interest of dynasties or of little groups of ambitious men who were accustomed to use their fellow men as pawns and tools ... Such designs can be successfully worked out only under cover and where no one has the right to ask questions ... They are happily impossible where public opinion commands and insists upon full information concerning all the nation's affairs. (D. M. Smith, 1966, pp. 194ff).

The Americans never seemed to understand that Wilson's declaration of war was informed by a peculiar understanding of world affairs. In was in fact a wholesale application of Locke's liberal, social–contract philosophy (on which America itself was founded) to interstate affairs. In Wilson's mind, the German Kaiser had knowingly violated the Law of Nature. This law would apply to the German Kaiser as it would apply to all other 'Rulers of Independent Governments all through the World, [who] are in a State of Nature' (Locke 1960, p. 317). The Kaiser had shown by his acts that he had chosen to live by other rules than those inherent in the Law of Nature. By violating those rules, the Kaiser had declared war on all law-abiding rulers. He had thus placed himself outside the Law, and could no longer claim to be protected by the Law (Locke 1960, p. 320). Thus, anyone had the right to pursue and punish him – not for his own sake, but for the sake of the Law itself. The German Kaiser had violated the very rules by which civilized humanity lives, argued Wilson. His violations amounted to a declaration of war on all mankind, and America must punish Germany in the name of the rights of all mankind.

Wilson, then, declared war on Germany, motivated not by 'revenge or the victorious assertion of the physical might of the nation, but only the vindication of right, of human right, of which we are only a single champion' (D. M. Smith 1966, p. 191). America should fight for 'the ultimate peace of the world and for the liberation of its peoples, the German people included: for the rights of nations great and small and the privilege of men everywhere to choose their way of life'. The United States sought no selfish ends, Wilson insisted. 'We desire no conquest, no domination. We seek no indemnities for ourselves, no material compensation for the sacrifices we shall freely make.' America's war aim was only to defeat 'autocratic governments backed by organized force which is controlled wholly by [the autocrats'] will, not by the will of the people'. All peoples naturally want democracy. If the autocrats were destroyed, then the peoples of the world could create the democratic, peaceful governments they naturally sought, join the 'partnership of democratic nations' and help cement a 'steadfast concert for peace' (pp. 194ff).

Wilson's declaration of war and his proposal for peace were anchored in a liberal, social–contract tradition which emphasized individual liberty, social openness, human progress and a self-adjusting political order. The tradition had its roots in the trading states along the north-Atlantic rim. And as Wilson's proposals spread to other regions of the world, they met opposition. The strongest political reactions to the Wilsonian vision of a liberal/free-market world were mounted by Continental proponents of old, aristocratic orders and by new groups and classes of agricultural and industrial workers. Important challenges to the liberal faith in the rational individual and in the freedom of human agency, on which the Wilsonian vision hinged, had emerged among Continental intellectuals before the turn of the century (Marx, Haeckel, Nietzsche, Freud and others).

By 1900, these challenges were restricted to small groups of philosophers and scientists, and had little political impact. After World War I, however, the new ideas were popularized and widely disseminated.[2] As the economic bases of Western democracies began to falter, anti-liberal ideas were exploited by doomsayers, demagogues and populist organizers who wooed the vast, marginalized groups of Western societies with simplified, often vulgar renditions of Marx, Darwin and Freud. During the traumatic uncertainties of the 1930s, the old Enlightenment notions of reason, freedom and natural law were attacked by anti-rationalist, anti-liberal arguments. Often with great effect.

The sad irony of the liberal crisis is that it was to some degree fuelled by the spread of liberal ideals. As suffrage was extended and mass markets grew, whole populations were integrated into national politics and global economics. They grew conscious of their economic interests and their political power; they defined themselves as members of distinct groups or classes; they filled the traditional institutions with new demands and burst them asunder.

The new political groups consisted predominantly of farmers and working-class males. In interwar Europe, a substantial number were veterans of World War I. They were disillusioned, hardened men who had risked their lives for statesmen's follies and received few rewards in return. They had little trust in politicians and little faith in old social values. Nor did they share the idealism of the industrialists and the academic liberals (Drucker 1939). The veterans of the Great War constituted a pool from which evolved a generation of defiant pleasure-seekers, a 'lost generation', typically portrayed with glass in hand and cigarette dangling from the lips.

The financial panic of 1929 was the final straw. The Great Depression upset the world's commodity and labour markets. It tossed manufacturers and labourers helplessly about in unpredictable ups and downs. These fluctuations were beyond reason; they defied any larger order which the human mind could discover; they did not describe a unidirectional evolution of skills and wealth and power. In these chaotic circumstances, appeals to the natural laws of the free market sounded like renunciations of social responsibilities.

The combined force of mass mobilization and of economic and socio–psychological depression poisoned the soils in which liberalism was striking its newest roots. Mobilization and disillusion interacted to create a distinct political climate. When the disillusioned men of the lost generation were stirred to action in the 1930s, they tended to shun liberal ideals, and instead embraced hard-and-fast solutions to complex problems. The disillusion of the intellectuals and the cynicism of the masses reinforced the ideological division of the world between dictatorial and democratic politics; between market economies and command economies; between liberal politics on the one hand and communism and fascism on the other.

International Relations: the infancy of the discipline

International Relations emerged as a discipline in its own right after World War I. However, the subject-matters discussed in these first formative years were curiously out of touch with the political realities of the age. Many of the courses taught were theoretically barren; many of the books written were ideologically myopic. Early students of world affairs confined themselves to the Wilsonian vision of world politics, and rarely ventured to explore the many non-liberal theories which swept the streets outside their ivory towers.

Why did the infant discipline of International Relations remain so strangely aloof from the diverse, intense and polarized debate of the interwar period? The answer, writes Edward Carr, is that every new scholarly discipline has come into being in response to some social or technical need. It first identifies a need, and then thinks of ways to address and alleviate this need. Only then will it focus its attention on reality. The need to promote health created medical science; the desire to build bridges created the engineering sciences; 'the desire to cure the sickness of the body politic has given the impulse and its inspiration to political science. Purpose, whether we are conscious of it or not, is a condition of thought' (Carr 1964, p. 3). After World War I, the common need and most sincerely felt wish to avoid another world war provided the main impulse for the new science of International Relations. 'The passionate desire to prevent war determined the whole initial course and direction of the study. Like other infant sciences, the science of international politics has been markedly and frankly utopian' (Carr 1964, p. 8).

In order to appreciate the nature of the utopianism which characterized International Relations in its infant years, it is important to recall that the new discipline primarily was an Atlantic phenomenon, infused with the Enlightenment ideals of the Atlantic tradition. When new courses in International Relations emerged after World War I like mushrooms after rain, the zone of scholarly growth was limited to the north-Atlantic academic culture. Its language was English. Its theoretical tradition was that of liberalism. Its visions of war, wealth, peace and power were those of the Enlightenment project. Continental scholars also studied world affairs, but they did so within the traditional confines of Law, Sociology, History, Geography and other established disciplines.

The emerging study of International Relations was informed by the ideals of the anti-war societies which grew up during World War I. These societies had deep roots in Western political thought,[3] and had by 1900 engendered an international peace movement and a considerable body of theoretical literature. Most peace theories involved the development of new international institutions and new legal codes for interstate behavour. Norman Angell's book *The Great Illu-*

sion (1909) did not. Indeed, the book marked a theoretical turning-point for peace theory. Many Europeans laboured under the illusion that war was a useful foreign-policy tool, argued Angell, who drew on theory from the social sciences and facts from contemporary history to demonstrate the dangerous hollowness of this view.[4]

The peace movement was given a great boost by active politicians around the turn of the century – Tsar Nicholas II issued a call for an international conference on disarmament in 1899,[5] and Woodrow Wilson was a member of the liberal American Peace Society. The movement was also stimulated by intellectuals, who developed a keen interest in techniques of political order and 'social control'.[6] Also, philanthropists supported the early peace movement: Alfred Nobel established through his will a wealthy fund to support the cause of peace; in 1910 Andrew Carnegie put up the money for the Carnegie Endowment for International Peace; and in 1912 Sir Richard Garton gave a generous donation to establish the Garton Foundation – whose aim was 'to promote and develop the science of International Polity and economics as indicated in the published writings of Mr. Norman Angell' (Angell 1951, p. 164). However, the more common attitude towards the peace movement was one of uninterest, or even mild amusement: one observer characterized von Suttner's Peace Society as 'a comical sewing bee composed of sentimental aunts of both sexes' (Chickering 1975, pp. 327f).

As a rule, the attitudes and actions of the early peaceniks did not impress turn-of-the-century statesmen. The many commendable efforts on behalf of international peace proceeded simultaneously with Great Powers pursuit of what were, whether so intended or otherwise, preparations for World War I. In 1913 the voice of the peace societies was scarcely heard over the din of innocent clamour for the inevitable clash of national wills that would quickly and dramatically settle old scores. When the war finally erupted in 1914, the warnings and protests drowned in the common din of patriotic jubilation.

After a few weeks of battle, it was apparent that the military experts who had insisted that the new weapons favoured the offensive were mistaken. Armies were immediately contained by impenetrable defences. In the fields of Flanders new powerful howitzers transformed the battlefield to a moon landscape in which advancing infantry had every disadvantage. Trees and rocks were destroyed by shelling and the ground was transformed into loose soil or knee-deep mud. Infantry offensives were reduced to slow crawls in which the advancing soldiers were easy victims of enemy fire. Massive deployments of barbed wire converted even the most unpromising defensive positions into fortresses more resilient than those made of brick and mortar. Crawling men on open ground, heavy with mud and entangled in barbed wire, were sitting ducks for enemy machine-guns. They were killed in tens or hundreds of thousands at a time, and soon realized that their most effective life insurance was not the rifle, but the spade. So they shielded themselves with the vast networks of trenches and tunnels by which World War I is best remembered.

One year of resultless, mechanized slaughter changed the attitudes of Western peoples towards war and peace. By 1916, discontent and disillusion had spread through the trenches. In 1917, the Bolshevik Party was carried to power in Russia on army mutinies. In 1918, the widespread bitterness and revulsion was only contained by America's entry with fresh, optimistic troops. But clearly the anti-war societies, once a ridiculed minority, by now represented an influential view which found war immoral, uncivilized, repulsive and futile.

During the war, peace groups had revived the old idea that a lasting, just peace could be guaranteed by a body of international arbitration. In 1917, Jacob ter Meulen published the first volume of an encyclopedic trilogy which traced the idea of a league of nations from the High Middle Ages through modern history. Ter Meulen discussed 29 peace projects in detail, and concluded by supporting Kant's argument that peace is a natural condition in a world of democratic states. In the years which followed, several such works were published (York 1919; Marriott 1937). When President Wilson proposed the establishment of a League of Nations, public opinion cheered him as the man who would forgive a corrupt Continent its past sins and lead civilization out of its wasteland.

War-tired, bereaved and confused, the masses of the West found emotional release in Wilson's liberal vision. During the 1920s, specialized journals emerged on both sides of the Atlantic in response to this renewed interest in world politics – the American *Foreign Affairs* and the British *International Affairs* were both established in these years. These journals tended to focus on current events; their articles usually explained the nature of specific problems in historical and legal terms. In Europe, governments funded scholarly projects designed to uncover the 'causes' or 'origins' of war, and to explore the legal, political and economic relationships between modern states; in the United States, similar projects were endowed by wealthy philanthropists like Andrew Carnegie.

The first chair in International Relations was established at the University of Wales at Aberystwyth in 1919. Other universities followed suit. Courses in International Relations rapidly became among the most popular courses taught. In British universities, the very first courses tended to discuss the historical roots and the diplomatic implications of international events; in the United States, these early courses were marked by a focus on current events and by a preoccupation with International Law. The heavy American legal emphasis tended to stress discrepancies between the formal obligations and the actual conduct of states – which, on occasion, lent support to chauvinist myths of US isolationism and exceptionalism. Emerging from these initial foci, the infant discipline did not beat itself any new paths; but it did promote some appreciation of the geography and some understanding of the diversity of the world. It did not rely as much on social science methodology as on historical investigations and on jurisprudence.[7]

Interwar approaches to international politics

During its first, formative years, the study of international relations was dominated by legalistic arguments heavily informed by the liberal tradition of political theory. This bias is evident in the titles of early textbooks – among these
were *International Law*, *The Law of Nations*, *International Government*, *The Function of Law in International Community* and *The League of Nations and the Rule
of Law*.[8] An array of perspectives existed outside these liberal parameters, but
were rarely represented on the early reading lists of the international-studies
community. The most important alternative approach was the old doctrine of
Realpolitik. It was usually expressed by conservative statesmen who found
Wilson's Fourteen Points dangerously naive – but, as statesmen, they were too
busy to engage in scholarly debate; and, as conservatives, they were disinclined
to theorize. The conservative, state-centred arguments of diplomats and old
statesmen were hardly included on the syllabi of the first courses in International
Relations.

Two additional approaches emerged during the course of the 1920s, and they
were not included in the syllabuses of International Relations either. The first
of these was the radical socialism of the revolutionary socialist movement.
Although their basic doctrines could be traced back to social theorists of the
Enlightenment and in spite of their having a great impact on political events
after World War I, the theories of revolutionary socialism did not influence the
scholars of International Relations. The internationalist doctrines which were
seductively refined by the cosmopolitan intellectuals of Russia's Bolshevik
revolution remained oddly quarantined by members of the academic international-studies community. The second approach which emerged during the
interwar period was fascism. But this was largely an anti-intellectual movement,
and exerted only slight influence on the study of International Relations.

At least four perspectives of world politics, then, existed side by side in the
interwar period – liberal legalism, *Realpolitik*, communism and fascism. The last
three were curiously excluded from the discipline of International Relations. If
mentioned at all, they were regularly rejected as unhelpful, if not destructive.
However, when the world was hit by a deep and lasting depression in the 1930s,
the dominant liberal approach found itself seriously challenged from three sides.

Utopianism and Woodrow Wilson

President Wilson became the world's most influential statesman in the immediate aftermath of World War I. His arguments dominated the new discipline of
International Relations. They drew heavily (and often unselfconsciously) on a
liberal social-contract tradition, and were expressed in tight, legislative arguments which strongly echoed those which Jeremy Bentham had formulated a
century before.

Wilson and Bentham both emphasized a strong faith in human reason, individual liberty, public opinion and social openness; both built on the liberal principles of enlightened self-interest and individual utility. Bentham's faith in reason and public opinion dominated social thought in both England and America after Waterloo. After 1850, however, it was increasingly criticized in Europe. At the turn of the century, the belief that human reason alone was sufficient to promote right conduct was challenged by psychologists; the identification of virtue with enlightened self-interest was refuted resoundingly by political economists. 'After 1900, it would have been difficult to find, either in Great Britain or in any other European country, any serious political thinker who accepted the Benthamite assumptions without qualification' (Carr 1964, p. 26).

In the United States, by contrast, the early-nineteenth-century assumptions survived the critique of the 1860s and the economic upheavals of the 1870s. Indeed, Bentham's utilitarian argument was fortified by the tonic of American Social Darwinism around the turn of the century, and re-emerged in American politics in the nineteen-tens. It was launched into the realm of international politics during World War I, and became a formative force in the new Anglo-American discipline of International Relations in the 1920s. Comments Carr:

By one of the ironies of history, these half-discarded nineteenth-century assumptions reappeared, in the second and third decades of the twentieth century, in the special field of international politics, and there became the foundation-stones for a new utopian edifice ... Just as Bentham, a century earlier, had taken the eighteenth-century doctrine of reason and refashioned it to the needs of the coming age, so now Woodrow Wilson ... transplanted the nineteenth-century rationalist faith to the almost virgin soil of international politics and, bringing it back with him to Europe, gave it a new lease on life (Carr 1964, p. 26).

The new discipline of International Relations, can thus be seen as a reflection, viewed in an American mirror, of early nineteenth-century liberal thought.

The influence of social thinkers like Locke and Bentham is most apparent in the idea of a League of Nations. The League was portrayed as an organization which could sustain itself simply on openness and freedom of information, without resort to force. This idea expressed a repudiation of *Realpolitik*, which Americans associated with the corrupt and sinful ways of European politics. Many US intellectuals claimed that war was a product of ignorant, prejudiced or self-serving autocrats and manipulative politicians. They disclaimed balance-of-power diplomacy. Above all, they rejected the conduct of secret diplomacy and advocated as its alternative a system of 'open covenants openly arrived at'. Open debate and proper education would dispel ignorance; international contact and co-operation would eliminate prejudice; popular democracy would prevent self-serving, evil and egotistical leaders from assuming autocratic power. And the democratic institutions which prevented violence within each enlightened nation would be recreated at the world level to resolve disputes in non-violent ways.

The liberal legal logic of Locke, Bentham and Wilson informed the most

important introductory texts in the emerging field of International Relations –
texts by Satow (1917), Heatley (1919) and Allen (1920). Pitman Potter (1922)
stands out as a notably comprehensive presentation of the history of interstate
relations and the diplomatic procedures of international relations – including a
definition of the key concept of sovereignty, an introduction to the nature and
role of conferences, arbitration and treaties, and a lengthy explanation of the
League of Nations. Such themes also mark the texts by Lawrence (1919), Muir
(1919), Brown (1923), Brierly (1928), Mitrany (1933) and Zimmern (1936).

Clyde Eagleton formulated a tight, time-typical argument in his admirable
little book *Analysis of the Problem of War* (1937). Eagleton rejects the assumption held by fascists and many realists 'that war results from the innate desire
of human beings to fight'. Instead he extols the Enlightenment assumption that
man is endowed with desires and with reason, and will strive to satisfy his desires
in rational ways:

Force has always been called upon because it is the ultimate method by which peoples,
whether individually or in rational groups, have been able to achieve their desires. It is
not war which is desired, but other things, good or bad, which it is hoped can be attained
through the use of war. It is logical to believe that, if a more effective method could be
discovered for accomplishing these ends, that method would be employed rather than war
(Eagleton 1937, p. 117).

The utopian approach to International Relations was preoccupied with finding
reason-based substitutes for war. It claimed that if there had been a chance to
bring grievances out in the open before the Balkan conflict erupted into war in
1914, if there had existed a forum in which national leaders could talk things
out, the escalation towards war might have been avoided.

Realism and Winston Churchill
The utopianism of Woodrow Wilson relied on concepts derived from the social
philosophy of the Enlightenment. Wilsonism totally dominated the infant discipline of International Relations. Opponents of the utopian view were to be found
among Western statesmen and diplomats. Georges Clemenceau, for example,
had already in 1918 juxtaposed Wilsonism with Leninism and brushed off both
as 'pure ideology' (Clemenceau 1930, p. 140). In the aftermath of the World
War, his was a minority view. But it was soon embraced by other statesmen.
And during the 1930s it was embraced by scholars as well. Hodges (1931)
announced that he expected his students to transcend the orthodoxy of legal idealism and study international events in the light of history and interstate relations. Davies (1932) sought to show that international politics has always been
rife with conflict and the use of power. In *Moral Man, Immoral Society* (1932)
Reinhold Niebuhr warned that the study of international affairs was dominated
by naive idealists who approached the relations among states through a mis-
placed moralism based on individual-rights philosophy. He argued that these

utopians have occasioned 'considerable moral and political confusion' because they have 'completely disregarded the political necessities' in their naive struggle for justice (p. xii). Hersh Lauterpacht (1933) authored a similar critique, but along more subdued lines. He reminded the advocates of the League that although law is essential for a peaceful world, it is no panacea. He argued that there are limits to the authority of law, and in his *Function of Law in the International Community* (1933) he sought to identify them.

Several books appeared during the the the 1930s that were deeply concerned about the increasing disorder in contemporary international relations (Schmitt 1932; Muir 1933; Schuman 1933; Simonds and Emeny 1935; Shotwell 1936; Mantoux *et al.* 1938). The most consequential critic of the utopian approach to international politics may have been Winston S. Churchill. He thought that the most notable characteristic of those 'well-meaning, loyal-hearted people' who support the League, was their 'long-suffering and inexhaustible gullibility' (Churchill 1938, p. 36). Churchill did not expound his approach to international politics in clear theoretical terms. His insights were not derived from the study of Enlightenment *philosophes*, but from the reading of history and from practical experiences as a soldier and a statesman. Churchill admired the works of Gibbon and Macaulay, and he wrote several books himself on historical topics; he took part in several colonial expeditions, both as a soldier and as a correspondent; he held several important Cabinet posts and wielded substantial influence on world politics during and after World War I – indeed, he was a formative force behind the division of the Ottoman Empire between England and France, the creation of the nations of Jordan and Iraq, and the selection of their rulers (Fromkin 1989).

After years of war and high politics, Churchill grew rapidly conservative in his political views. Increasingly out of step with the reformist sentiment of the post-war years, he was a poor tribune of popular passions and lost his seat in Parliament in the 1922 elections. During his subsequent 'years in the wilderness' Churchill wrote *The World Crisis*, his inside account of World War I. The multivolume discussion is historically rich; the style is erudite, with a romantic patina of a by-gone age of imperial grandeur and larger-than-life statesmen. It is informed by the key tenets of conservatism – although these are, typically, never explicitly identified. The tale is guided by a sceptical anthropology which doubts the Enlightenment axiom that human action is guided by reason. Churchill sees human reason as limited or flawed, and he sees human interaction in terms of conflict rather than harmony. He depicts international relations as a contest in which war is a frequent, inevitable occurrence.

Churchill sees international politics as relations between nation-states. His account's '*dramatis personae* [are] the great States and Empires and its theme is their world-wide balance and combinations' (Churchill 1923, p. 19). Following the example of historians since Thucydides, Churchill describes these relations in anthropomorphic terms – he animates the states of Europe with human characteristics. His text abounds with expressions like 'Italy saw ...,' 'Russia thought ...,' and 'Austria decided ....'. He portrays Germany as 'obstinate,' 'reckless' and 'ambitious'; France as 'brooding' and England as 'entirely unconscious of the approaching danger'. Thus, he discusses the interaction between states in terms of interaction between egotistical individuals of different psychological dispositions. All states seek to maximize their own security. Each state does so according to its own situation and sentiment – each state analyses international events in the light of its own distinctive interests and acts according to its own national predisposition and its own assessment of its relative military strength.

When Churchill discusses the perceptions and actions of states, he initially neglects complicating domestic dynamics. In his account 'the Government', 'the Cabinet' or, quite often, a single statesman tend to speak on behalf of the entire state and to express the national interest. The states, then, are unitary actors, speaking with one voice in foreign affairs. Churchill's portrayal is replete with imagery from the Absolutist Age, when interstate relations were largely the business of kings and their close advisers. Under such circumstances, the personality of the monarch was often reflected in the policies of the nation. It is the image of absolutist politics, then, which is reflected in Churchill's conception of world affairs.

The first volume in Churchill's five-book opus delineates the causes of World War I; it is therefore the most theoretically interesting book in the series. It explains how the Franco-Prussian War (1871) created a unified Germany in the centre of Europe, altering the Continent's traditional state system. France was stunned by its defeat – 'beaten, impoverished, divided and alone ... [she] fell back to ponder in shade and isolation on her departed glories' (p. 7). Germany was apprehensive about her victory: Bismarck realized that to avoid the abiding enmity of the rest of Europe, he must conduct a policy of extreme moderation; he had to avoid any act which could alienate Britain or draw France and Russia together in an anti-German collusion. For twenty years, Bismarck maintained an orderly balance in Europe by a cautious, complex diplomacy of alliance management.

This era of calm ended in 1890 with the fall of Bismarck. The new German Kaiser, Wilhelm II, had no understanding of the Chancellor's keen sense of limits, and he foolishly assailed the system which Bismarck had so carefully maintained. The Kaiser made no effort to smooth the enmity with France, he neglected his friendly relations with Russia and he launched a naval rivalry with England. Writes Churchill:

In 1892 the event against which the whole policy of Bismarck had been directed came to pass. The Dual Alliance was signed between Russia and France. Although the effects were not immediately visible, the European situation was in fact transformed. Henceforth, for the undisputed but soberly exercised predominance of Germany, there was substituted a balance of power. Two vast combinations, each disposing of enormous military resources, dwelt together at first side by side but gradually face to face (p. 9).

At the turn of the century, these 'two vast combinations' congealed into an inflexible opposition. In the years prior to 1914, Europe possessed no statesman wise enough to reinject diplomatic fluidity into this brittle, titanic constellation.

Churchill condemns the reckless Kaiser for this breakdown of flexibility. But he also places great blame on the other statesmen of Europe, faulting them for their ignorance and inability to transcend the narrow confines of their own petty ambitions. 'Far more than their vices,' Churchill writes, 'the nations ill-directed and mis-directed by their rulers, became the cause of their own undoing and of the general catastrophe.'

With the conservative's appreciation for irony and for the complex interplay in human affairs between reason and passion, Churchill portrays the *fin-de-siècle* confidence in reason and liberty as illusory. Intoxicated by material progress, man put his trust in science, democracy, decency and education – in the spread of these values to millions of ordinary men and women. But hand in hand with this expansion, Churchill notes, went the growth of nationalisms and patriotic passions. Ill-guided by their naive rulers, ordinary men only had to do their duty for the catastrophe to erupt. Finally, when disaster descended on Europe in 1914, people greeted it with ignorant enthusiasm. Comments Churchill:

One rises from the study of the causes of the Great War with a prevailing sense of the defective control of individuals upon world fortunes. It has been well said, 'there is always more error than design in human affairs.' The limited minds of even of the ablest men, their disputed authority, the climate of opinion in which they dwell, their transient and partial contributions to the mighty problem, that problem itself so far beyond their compass, so vast in scale and detail, so changing in its aspect – all this must surely be considered before the complete condemnation of the vanquished or the complete acquittal of the victors can be pronounced (pp. 5f).

Communism and Vladimir Lenin

The third interwar approach to international politics was also informed by the Enlightenment project. Lenin, like Wilson, subscribed to the precepts of rationality, equality, liberty and human power over nature. However, Lenin followed not the liberal but the radical interpretation of the Enlightenment *philosophes*. He subscribed to the nineteenth-century, Continental reaction to liberalism; notably to Marx' and Engels' vision of a historical *Stufengang*. Lenin based his theories on the claim that man interacts dialectically with nature and propels human history from one evolutionary stage, or 'mode of production', to another – from the 'Asian mode of production', through slavery, feudalism and capitalism to socialism. Each mode of production is characterized by distinct economic relationships, Marx had argued. Each such mode, Engels had continued, is also characterized by a distinct mode of warfare. Not only do the different modes of production determine man's economic and military behaviour at distinct stages of historical evolution, they also suggest that each historical epoch is characterized by a specific relationship between economic and military structures.

Austrian economist Rudolf Hilferding pursued this argument. In *Das Finanzkapital* (1955 [1910]), Hilferding draws a rigorous connection between capitalism and militarism. He saw that in the final years of the nineteenth century a tendency for capital to centralize and concentrate transformed capitalism from its old mode of free competition to a new mode in which a few gigantic financial institutions exercised tight control over industry. Relying on Marx and on liberal economist John A. Hobson (1902), Hilferding claimed that capitalism had entered a new stage of 'finance-capitalism' which forced Western states on to a course of imperial expansion and war. In this latest phase of capitalist development, finance-capital – 'capital controlled by banks and employed by industrialists' – needs new markets and new supplies of raw materials to expand (Hilferding 1955).

Other Marxists (Luxemburg 1951; Kautsky 1970) elaborated on the connection between capitalism and militarism. A most significant contribution was made by Nikolai Bukharin, who, in *Imperialism and World Economy* (1973 [1915]), anchors Hilferding solidly in Marx' axiom that capitalism naturally tends to concentrate and centralize. Eventually, capitalist competition will concentrate production into vast, monopolistic combines and centralize financial power in the hands of a narrow oligarchy of industrialists and financiers. To ensure their own survival, the combines will be forced to expand beyond the boundaries of their nation for continued supplies of raw materials and new markets. The combines of different countries will then begin to compete. Again, capital will concentrate and centralize; only this time on a global scale, and with governments backing the economic interests of the financial oligarchs with military might. The world will divide along class lines between wealthy industrial regions and poor colonies. Gigantic combines will form, divide the poorer regions of the world among themselves and incorporate them into a gigantic, global division of labour. In the end, the combines will reach the limits of further expansion. At that point, when no nation can expand except at the expense of another, begins a phase of violent competition for world markets and natural resources. 'Capitalist society is unthinkable without armaments, as it is unthinkable without wars, 'concluded Bukharin (1973, pp. 139f).

Whereas Bukharin's book on imperialism is the most theoretically interesting of these Marxist arguments, Lenin's has been the most influential – indeed, Lenin's *Imperialism: the Highest Stage of Capitalism* (1975b [1917]) may be the single most influential book on international politics of the century. Lenin gave Hilferding's and Bukharin's arguments a popular, accessible form and an impressive empirical base. According to Lenin, World War I must be understood as a 'territorial division of the whole world among the greatest capitalist powers'. The war, he insisted, was 'an annexationist, predatory war of plunder', fuelled by the imperialist powers' need for markets and raw materials. Lenin, echoing the geopolitical thesis of Halford Mackinder (1904), argued that, with little of the world left to conquer, international competition would grow more intense and erupt in a war 'for the division of the world, for the partition and repartition of colonies and spheres of influence ...' (Lenin 1975b, p. 206). For Lenin, war is the weapon that capitalist classes apply against a double enemy: against the capitalist classes of other territorial states and against the proletariat of their own country.

Lenin's theory had a strong political appeal in Europe – after the Russian Revolution virtually all Europe's labour parties split into a reformist (or social democratic) and a revolutionary (Leninist or communist) wing. The reformist wing gained most adherents, but the revolutionary wing gathered immense force under the impact of the Great Depression.

Fascism, Mussolini and Hitler

Fascism, like conservatism, is rooted in a reaction to the optimistic values of the Enlightenment project. Both reject the doctrines of liberalism and socialism; both maintain that man is a passionate rather than a rational creature; both emphasize that human society is marked by conflict, struggle and war.

In the 1920s it was not easy to distinguish the most doctrinaire conservatives from the emerging fascists – a complication which clearly contributed to the neglect of considerable interwar theorists like Carl Schmitt (1932). However, whereas conservatism was a creation of the ailing, landowning nobility of the eighteenth century, fascism was a function of the crisis-ridden, illiberal, industrial mass-societies of the twentieth. And as Continental scholars elaborated the ills of modern industrial societies, fascism attained a distinct ideological profile. Three Italians contributed greatly to this discussion: Wilfredo Pareto, Gaetano Mosca and Benito Mussolini. There was also the brilliant young Russian emigré sociologist Pitrim Sorokin, who, after the Russian Revolution, feared that Western civilization was descending into chaos – a theme pursued by Oswald Spengler's massive study *The Decline of the West* of 1918–22.

Fascism soon distinguished itself on two points. First, whereas conservatism prefers the popular masses to be passive, even docile, fascism envisions a mobilized, dynamic population which actively supports an omnipotent State. 'The fascist conception of the State is all-embracing,' argued Mussolini, 'outside of it no human or spiritual values can exist, much less have value. Thus understood the fascist State is totalitarian' (Mussolini 1933, p. 3).

Second, whereas the conservative merely sees conflict as inevitable, the fascist attributes positive values to struggle and ennobling qualities to war. This vision of struggle justified a fascist foreign policy of imperial expansion. Mussolini argued that Italy should conquer North Africa and make the Mediterranean 'an Italian lake'. Adolf Hitler insisted, in his rambling manifesto *Mein Kampf* (1943 [1925]), that Germany needed *Lebensraum*. He recognized that this meant conflict with Germany's neighbours; however, he continued, Germany was largely surrounded by inferior peoples like Slavs and Jews. The soil of Europe 'exists for the people which possesses the force to take it', he wrote; and if the present possessor objects, 'then the law of self-preservation goes into effect; and what is refused to amicable methods, it is up to the fist to take' (Hitler 1943, pp. 138f). With reference to the geopolitical theories of Friedrich Ratzel, Rudolf Kjellén and Karl Haushofer, Hitler claimed that Germany deserves to expand eastwards – first into the fragmented inferior 'Slavic lands' of eastern Europe, then onwards into Bolshevik Russia. 'The giant empire in the East is ripe for collapse. And the end of Jewish rule in Russia will also be the end of Russia as a state', he wrote (p. 654), suggesting that communism is a Jewish conspiracy.

This vision was anchored in a generation of German philosophers who saw History as the conflictual unfolding of a divine plan by which superior forms of civilization will replace primitive forms. These thinkers formulated their doctrine not in a Hegelian discourse but in a pseudo-scientific racial terminology developed by some of Darwin's Continental followers. In the 1870s, the German historian Henrich von Treitschke surpassed Hegel's elevation of the State and struggle by glorifying the Prussian state and proclaiming war the highest expression of man. In the 1880s, Ernest Haeckel reformulated Hegel's and Treitschke's basic visions in atheistic, racial terms. In the 1890s, Houston S. Chamberlain – British by birth but Prussian by choice and the son-in-law of the German composer Richard Wagner – rewrote Western history as a struggle between the 'two pure races', the Germans and the Jews. According to Chamberlain, societies, like biological species, evolve and advance through competition, which ensures the survival of the fittest and eliminates the weak. In this conception, international politics essentially involve combat between *Völker* over territories, political rank and, ultimately, the destiny of the world. Chamberlain defined these peoples in terms of blood-lines, and saw the struggle between them as a struggle between races. Hitler was much influenced by the theories of Chamberlain – he adopted the view that world politics was a struggle between *Völker*; he portrayed the German *Volk* as having a distinct historic destiny, and focused the intense chauvinism of his Nationalist Socialist (Nazi) Party against the Jews; he elaborated this ethnic vision into a peculiar International Relations theory in which both Marxism and capitalism were reduced to Jewish-led, anti-German movements (Shirer 1983, pp. 120–66).

There was, however, more to German fascism than racial theories. The admiration for a *völkisch* community, an omnipotent State, a martial code of civic virtues and an imperialist foreign policy show that German fascism derived much of its appeal from a political exploitation of ethnic mythologies (Shirer 1983). Whereas liberal and radical theories provide plans and blueprints for action, fascism usually began with action and theorized afterwards. As a political theory, Hitler's fascism was barren. When fascism nevertheless evolved into an irresistible mass movement in interwar Germany, it was not because of its intellectual appeal – fascism largely ridiculed theorizing and emphasized action. Rather, the appeal lies in the Nazi promise to restore the wealth and the pride of the nation. By applying the emerging mass media in systematically propagandistic ways, the Nazi Party transformed ethnic mythology into a political message which spellbound an entire nation and led it into a new, ruinous world war. It is a sobering recollection that this mythological seduction did not occur in a 'primitive' and 'superstitious' region of the world; rather, the spell was cast upon a nation which was generally admired as one of the most technologically developed, spiritually advanced and well educated nations in the Christian world.

East, West, North, South: the contours of a new era

The classic evaluation of the birth of the discipline of International Relations is Edward Carr's book on *The Twenty-Years' Crisis* (1964 [1939]). Carr explains that a utopian orientation is normal for any new science. Whenever the human mind begins to exercise itself in some fresh field, it will always first concentrate on the needs it wishes to address and on its own goal and purpose. Only when these initial projects are disillusioned will the investigators begin to adopt a more realistic attitude; they will temper their ideal wishes and utopian goals with empirical descriptions of reality (Carr 1964, p. 5).[9]

This tension between utopianism and realism, Carr continues, runs parallel with a set of social-scientific contradictions – between utopia and reality, prescription and description, free will and determinism, theory and practice, morality and pragmatism, the political left and the political right:

The antithesis of utopia and reality can in some respects be identified with the antithesis of Free Will and Determinism. The utopian is necessarily a voluntarist: he believes in the possibility of more or less radically rejecting reality, and substituting his utopia for it by an act of will. The realist analyses a predetermined course of development which he is powerless to change ... The utopian fixes his eyes on the future, thinks in terms of creative spontaneity: the realist, rooted in the past, in terms of causality (p. 11).

Broadening the utopian-realist antithesis

In order to draw a broader road-map of international-relations theories of the interwar years – in order to include observations and ideas from the rest of the world – it is necessary to expand the utopianism-realism antithesis. Carr's discussion of Free Will and Determinism provides a vantage point for such an expansion. It draws a broad, basic distinction which has blazed through modern thought since the Renaissance. This is the distinction between the Enlightenment project and its anti-Enlightenment reaction.

In this larger picture, Lenin and Wilson are placed together as the primary heirs of the Enlightenment project. Both are informed by an optimistic anthropology – although the radical theory of alienation makes Lenin's anthropology more complex than Wilson's. Both discuss the human condition in terms of reason, justice, freedom, progress and, ultimately, harmony of interests. Enlightenment theorists insist, first and foremost, that people are endowed with reason and that they can both understand and control theeir natural and social environment. Second, since norms of justice are knowable only through reason, all just acts are rational acts; consequently, they hold that the interests of all humanity are served by rational behaviour, and the interests of individuals as well as of states are, in the final instance, complementary. Third, Enlightenment theorists believe that people can identify a just political order through their reason – including an international order. By relying only upon mind and will, humanity can find a course of action which will change the world. Also, Enlightenment theorists view society in terms of evolution or progress; they assert that human reason and human society can be understood in terms not of immutable facts but of potentialities which are progressively actualized in the course of history. Finally, Enlightenment theorists entertain a materialist vision of an industrialized, mass-producing society of wealthy, educated inhabitants as the precondition for a good life, a just society and a peaceful world.

Proponents of the anti-Enlightenment reaction, however, are informed by a pessimistic anthropology. When they discuss the human condition, anti-Enlightenment theorists emphasize passion, power, determinism, constancy and conflict of interest. First, they consider human reason as limited and untrustworthy; human beings never act on reason alone, they are primarily creatures of passion. Second, they insist that all politics is, ultimately, power politics; and that in politics among states, which is marked by the absence of any supreme authority, this is particularly true. Third, the argument of the anti-Enlightenment reaction hinges on a static notion of human history; on an insistence that throughout human record, interstate politics has always been power politics and that there is no reason to assume or expect that this feature will suddenly change or disappear. This position is related to the denial of the Enlightenment assumptions of progress and justice. Both the conservatives and the fascists, for example, reject the materialist conception of History: they insist that humanity has spiritual needs and they see human society as a spritual community. Moreover, they tend to reject doctrines of spiritual absolutism: the principles which human reflection so often extols as absolute and universal, are, for them, little else but unconscious reflections of national policy based upon a particular interpretation of national interest. There are, in their view, no universal principles upon which a new world order can be grafted. Each culture, religion and nation expresses its own truth, and each state insists on securing its own, specific national interest.

The rise of the Enlightenment project

During the Middle Ages, Western thought rested on a universal ethic and a universal political system based on divine authority. The precursors of realism first emerged during the Renaissance, when humanists like Guicciardini and Machiavelli made their onslaughts on the primacy of divine ethics and 'propounded a view of politics which made ethics an instrument of politics, the authority of the state being thus substituted for the authority of the church as the arbiter of morality' (Carr 1964, p. 22).

In the eighteenth century, Renaissance realism was challenged by the emergence of a doctrine of natural law derived from empirical observation of nature and from individual human reason. 'In science, the laws of nature were deduced by a process of reasoning from observed facts about the nature of matter. By an easy analogy, the Newtonian principles were now applied to the ethical problems' (Carr 1964, p. 22). The claim that a moral law of nature could be scientifically established, found its final expression in the Enlightenment project. At the end of the eighteenth century, this project divided into two major interpretations. Adam Smith and Jeremy Bentham were major exponents of one; Jean-Jacques Rousseau and Karl Marx were key representatives of the other.

Towards the end of World War I, these two major tenets of the Enlightenment tradition emerged as ideological rivals on a world scale. President Woodrow Wilson assumed the liberal mantle of Smith and Bentham; Vladimir Lenin took up the radical heritage of Rousseau and Marx. Both Lenin and Wilson blamed the statesmen and soldiers of the pre-war era for having caused World War I. Both condemned the old, élitist approach of *Realpolitik* and its secret alliance managements; both demanded that henceforth international diplomacy be conducted in full public view. Both Wilson and Lenin were, in turn, criticized by the realists and fascists alike for being either naive or duplicitous.

The rise of the East–West conflict
At the end of the nineteenth century, the contours of twentieth-century international politics were drawn by the emergence of the extra-European expansionism of Russia and the United States. World War I sharpened these contours: it brought the old, European system to the cusp of collapse, thus accentuating the dwarfing of Europe between the neo-liberal, economically dynamic USA in the West and the revolutionary, ideologically intense USSR in the East. World War II would later pave the way for the extreme expression of this constellation: the Cold War, in which a prostrate Europe was militarily overshadowed and politically divided by two dynamic, mutually antagonistic superpowers.

This twentieth-century division of international politics between a Western bloc, represented by the United States, and an Eastern bloc, represented by the Soviet Union, was foreshadowed by geopolitical thrusts which few observers noted in the late nineteenth century. When Europe was preoccupied with imperialist expansionism in the tropics, both the United States and Russia expanded rapidly towards the Pacific. The United States expanded westwards, across the great plains to Texas and California. Russia expanded eastwards, across the Siberian steppe and to the vast new territories of the Amur basin and Sakhalin. The demographic and economic growth of Los Angeles and Vladivostok expresses this parallel evolution, which was stimulated by the opening of transcontinental railroad lines. In the United States, a sentiment of 'manifest destiny' fuelled the expansion, and the Monroe Doctrine legitimized political and economic interventions in Central and South America. In Russia, the tsar used Christianity and pan-Slavism to hasten the break-up of the Ottoman Empire and to expand towards the Straits of Bosporus.

Moreover, the contours of the twentieth-century world were foreshadowed by the emergence of cockpits of consequential conflicts and wars outside the purview of European control. At the turn of the century, Asia emerged as a vital arena of great-power conflicts; here the states of Western Europe were no longer the superior actors. Spain, France and England were all challenged by the United States and by Russia, and also by native states like Japan. America provoked conflicts in the Pacific and on the Asian rim – cf. America's first war in Korea (1871) and the occupation of the Philippines and annexation of Hawaii (1898) – the debates about Admiral Mahan's treatise on *The Influence of Sea-Power upon History* of 1890 and John Hay's Open Door policy (1899) reflect America's introduction to world affairs. Russia was also engaged in several Asian conflicts. The most fatal of these was was the war with Japan (1904), in which Russia lost a major share of her fleet.

The Russo-Japanese War marks the transition to twentieth-century international politics in two ways. First, by fuelling the East–West conflict: it ignited a Soviet Revolution in Petrograd (1905) which was in many respects a dress rehearsal for the Revolution of 1917. With the Bolshevik Revolution, radical interpreters of the Enlightenment project first attained power over a territorial state, thus giving Marxism-Leninism a 'homeland', a territorial headquarters from which it could defend its doctrines with mass armies and military force. As the Russian Revolution evolved, a new communist state was constructed. Thirty years prior to the onset of the Cold War, Wilson and Lenin were in 1918 competing for the political attention of the peoples of the world; and both were greeted eagerly by them. Also, both experienced the same abrupt descent from visionary hopes to grim despair; both were plunged into the same long interwar crisis. Wilson's ideals were brought crashing down by the rise of fascist dictatorships on the Continent and by the Great Depression. Lenin's were shaken by the Russian Civil War, by the institution of repressive 'war communism', and by the rise of the ruthless Josef Stalin.

The rise of the North–South conflict

The Russo-Japanese war marks the transition to twentieth-century international politics in a second way as well: Japan's victory over Russia signalled the emergence of emancipatory movements all over the extra-European world (Spector 1962). The relationships between the European colonial powers and their colonies were further shaken by World War I, which brought a flurry of native nationalist and anti-colonialist activities in the Near, Middle and Far East. And just as Wilsonian liberalism and Leninist radicalism experienced an abrupt descent from hopes to dark despair after the Great War, so were the nationalisms of non-European theorists also disillusioned in its aftermath.

Some leaders of colonial independence movements had invested their faith in the quick dismemberment of Europe's empires after the war. They were deeply deceived when the colonial powers reneged on their wartime pledges. Instead of dismantling their overseas empires, they tried to redraw the colonial boundaries and consolidate their imperial footholds (Fromkin 1989, pp. 188–200, 286–301). Such efforts were often met by anti-imperialist rebellions. In its weakened post-war state, Europe could not prevent the east–west division of the world between two actors, each of whom entertained a distinct interpretation of the Enlightenment project. Furthermore, Europeans could not entirely contain the erosion of colonialism either. Their inability to manage this erosion gracefully contributed to a widening north–south conflict, which would erupt into a torrent of decolonization half a century later (Hobsbawm 1994, pp. 199ff).

The theoretical awakening of the East
World War I affected the colonial regions of the world in three ways. First, the wasteful rivalries of the war impoverished the European powers and weakened their colonial grip. It reduced their ability to project their power and defend their interests and authority in far-off corners of the globe. Second, the war stimulated industrialization and development in the colonies. It helped disseminate the Enlightenment ideals in whose name the Allies fought the war. Finally, the weakening of colonialism and the growth of Western values fuelled a world-wide sentiment of anti-colonialism and national liberation. Thus, the twenty-years' crisis which shook Europe was closely tied in with the emergence of emancipatory movements in the extra-European world.

Upon the collapse of the Ottoman Empire, the valleys of the Euphrates and the Tigris became riddled with tribal revolts – mainly directed against British military rule, though several national groups in the area also turned against each other. In Lebanon, the dissident Druze Muslims fought French attempts to impose stricter administrative control. In nearby Palestine, Arab nationalists revolted against Jewish immigration. The Jews, for their part, agitated for increased immigration as conditions for Jews in central Europe grew intolerable in the 1930s.

These conflicts in the Near and Middle East spilled over to other regions. In Cyrenaica, the Arab Sanusi brotherhood resisted Italian occupation in several rebellions throughout the 1920s. Berber tribesmen of Abd el-Krim in the Rif mountains of north-western Sahara demanded independence and fought both Spanish and French troops. In Afghanistan, the Third Anglo-Afghan War erupted when the British government refused to recognize King Amanullah's proclamation of Afghan independence.

Further east, too, European failures to honour wartime pledges also ignited nationalist revolts. Britain's refusal to consider national independence for India provoked a major uprising in Amritsar in 1919. In Bengal, nationalist resistance was marked by intermittent terrorist activity between 1923 and 1932.

Extra-European nationalists often found fascist doctrines unattractive. These were selectively embraced to a modest degree among militant leaders in North Africa and the Middle East; also, in Japan, a strong militarist tradition and the mythical stature of the Emperor as the embodiment of the national will and identity facilitated the evolution of a fascist movement in the 1930s. With these exceptions, the most effective movements were those which managed to adapt the Enlightenment ideals of liberty, democracy and mass participation to a native national purpose. In 1919, the Wafd party was founded in Egypt and the Destour party in Tunisia. The Sarekat Islam movement grew into a mass movement for national independence in Indonesia. The Congress Party in India was reorganized into a mass party by the Nagpur constitution in 1920 under the leadership of Mahatma Gandhi. In China, the Fourth of May movement stimulated the creation of several mass parties, most importantly the reorganization of the nationalist Kuomintang (1919) under the old Sun Yat-sen and the Chinese Communist Party (1924).

In many cases, Enlightenment ideals had been carried to the colonies by intellectuals who had studied or worked in the West. Mahatma Gandhi, for example, had studied in England and practised law in the British colonies and dominions before he returned to India in 1919 to reform the Congress Party into a tool of national independence; the nationalist movement in Indonesia had its origins in the foreign students' union in Holland. However, World War I was the decisive agent of dissemination. Quite often, the ideals of national independence and popular sovereignty were spread by European powers who sought to distract their enemies by encouraging national movements in enemy colonies – the Germans, for example, incited the populations of the Maghreb to take up arms against France; similarly, the French and the British stirred up Arab nationalism in Syria, Mesopotamia and on the Arabian Peninsula against the Turks (Fischer 1961; Lenczowski 1952).

Moreover, the independence movements on the subcontinent and in South-East Asia were deeply influenced by natives who had been recruited to Western armies. Both France and Britain recruited able-bodied men from India and Vietnam and sent them to Europe, where they were exposed to the Allies' wartime propaganda. In 1916, these Asian soldiers learnt that they fought for freedom, democracy and the protection of national independence. In 1917 they followed the fate of the Russian Revolution. In 1918 they read and discussed President Wilson's Fourteen Points and Lloyd George's declaration that the principle of national self-determination applied to the colonies just as much as it applied to European countries. In 1919 they heard of Lenin's denunciation of imperialism and the revolutionary proclamation that the subject peoples of the tsarist empire were free to secede.

Asians who had been to Europe as students, workers or soldiers 'returned home with new notions of democracy, self-government, and national independence, and a firm resolve no longer to accept the old status of inferiority' (Barraclough 1976, p. 156; Pannikar 1953, pp. 259–66). Among the most influential Asians who returned in the immediate post-war period were Ho Chi Minh (to Vietnam) and Zhu De and Zhou En-lai (to China). They had all joined the Communist Party while in Europe; they all returned to Asia after the World War as ardent anti-imperialists, and proceeded to build Communist Parties in their homelands – Ho founded Vietnam's Communist Party; Zhu and Zhou became the trusted collaborators of Mao Zedong, possibly the most influential non-European political theorist of the twentieth century.

Forced out of China's major industrial centres by strong opponents, the Chinese communists fled to the countryside, where, after years in the wilderness, they developed a sizeable army. In 1935, they organized a communist republic in Yanan in the north-west of China. Here, Mao finally found the time to study the communist classics. When Mao committed his thoughts to paper, it was not Marx' theory of History he emphasized – there are hardly any substantial references to Marx or Engels in Mao's voluminous *Works*. Rather, it was the underlying dialectical method which appealed to him. Furthermore, although Lenin's theories helped Mao understand the forces which drove Western nations to meddle in Chinese affairs, it was Lenin's commentaries on war and the Soviet *example* which impressed him. Mao's writings on war are seasoned with the dialectics of Clausewitz whom Lenin admired; his writings on politics are much preoccupied with the Leninist doctrine of a tightly organized political apparatus which expresses the will of the proletariat; soon he embraced Stalin's interpretation that the communist party is 'an organism living its own separate life' (Stalin 1953, p. 199; Mao 1965a).

Mao freely interpreted the Soviet experience and tailored it to the conditions in China. He defied Soviet theory by insisting that China was a semi-feudal society, in which the term 'proletariat' did not refer to a class of urban wage labourers but to the rural peasant masses. As is apparent from Mao's treatises from Yanan – and from Soviet opinions about them (Ch'en 1953) – this theoretical amendment had major implications for subsequent political practice. It meant that in China the 'proletarian vanguard party' was a peasant organization and that the 'people's army' was a peasant-based guerrilla force. The army is more than a mere fighting force, Mao insisted, it is also 'an army of labour', which engages in productive activities, and a 'cultural army', which educates the masses (Mao 1964; 1965b; 1965c).

Mao's reflections illustrate an important point: many Asian leaders were attracted to Leninism in the 1920s, and not only because of the Enlightenment values which infused them. They embraced Leninism partly because of the self-understanding they derived from Lenin's theory of imperialism and partly because of the promise of liberation inherent in the communist doctrine of revolution. But the decisive appeal was that of Lenin's example. Lenin had demonstrated that a small party can, through organizational discipline and superior political techniques, seize power in a backward society and hold on to it in the face of the West's best efforts to bring it to its knees. To many national liberation movements in the 1920s, 'it appeared as if the communists were in possession of some magic political and organization formulas that until then had eluded the Asian reformers' (Ulam 1974, p. 173; also Hobsbawm 1994, pp. 70ff).

9

Cold War politics: international relations after World War II

In the aftermath of World War II, the study of International Relations grew more self-conscious and academically assured. Yet scholars retained the ambition of advising statesmen. And as the United States dominated the Western world politically, its peculiar tradition of social theorizing soon come to dominate the field it had helped establish. At the outset of the Cold War, when an overwhelmingly powerful United States confronted Soviet hostility, idealism gave way to realism – a peculiarly American brand of power politics.

As the excesses of Cold War abroad and McCarthyism at home became evident, the realist approach was challenged by behaviouralism. This laid the foundation for approaches more in keeping with traditional liberal US values. As Vietnam and other events demonstrated the limits of power and its use, rational theories began to explore alternative forms of power and order in the international system. Regime analysis subsequently emerged to explain order in a world in which no state was demonstrably in charge, thus restoring the field to its original organizing problem of making and maintaining order in an anarchic world system.

Colonial wars attracted the attention of International Relations scholars. This shifted the attention of scholarship towards the special problems of the Third World – to wars of national liberation and problems of political modernization and economic development in non-Western regions. It also brought attention to non-Western theories of world affairs. Having no theoretical tradition of their own, Third-World theorists were forced to borrow heavily from the Western canon. And since they were generally sceptical of the liberal theories of the colonial powers, Third-World voices often ended up drawing heavily on anti-liberal, Continental ideas. Radical theories of a Hegelian–Marxist tenor were notably popular – and emerged during the 1960s as a legitimate theory perspective in theit own right. During the second half of the Cold War, then, International

Relations theories multiplied quickly. But the succession of perspectives tended to match the ebb and flow of American fortunes.

From World War to Cold War

The Cold War was long foreshadowed by the territorial ambitions of the Russian tsars and the Western responses to them. In the nineteenth century, a combination of Western powers contained Russian expansion in Europe, while Japan performed the same task in Asia. World War II destroyed German and Japanese power and exhausted France and Great Britain, removing these traditional impediments to Russian expansionism. Most importantly, by the end of the war Britain, which since the nineteenth century had also contained Russian expansion in the Middle and Near East with a belt of buffer states from Greece through Turkey and Persia to Afghanistan, was too exhausted to continue 'the Great Game'.

The United States shunned such geo-strategies, serenely unaware at the outset of the new need to fill the power vacuums which appeared on either side of Soviet Russia. Stalin, by contrast, was a ruthless power politician; although the Soviet Union was impoverished and exhausted by the war, Stalin acted quickly and decisively and, by bold bluff, managed to exploit the geo-strategic opportunities afforded by the war.

British preoccupations

In 1945, Great Britain found itself exhausted and its empire on the edge of collapse. When that summer's victory exuberance subsided, Britain's traditional, liberal outlook did not reassert itself. A Labour government led by Clement Attlee replaced Winston Churchill's Conservative wartime cabinet. After much debate within the Labour Party about Britain's new role in the world, the new government continued the essentially realist foreign-policy course Churchill defined during the war.

The short-term aim of Churchill's wartime Cabinet was to dissuade Hitler from dominating the Continent. To this end, he signed a pragmatic, anti-Nazi alliance with Stalin in July 1941. Churchill's long-term aim, however, was to deter Stalin from dominating the Continent once Hitler was defeated. Since the nineteenth century, Britain and Russia had been locked in a 'Great Game' in which England had sought to contain Russian access to the Mediterranean by supporting Turkey and Greece. In Churchill's view, Stalin simply added to traditional Russian expansionism an aggressive world-view derived from Lenin's theories of International Relations.

Towards the end of the war, Churchill warned the Americans against trusting Stalin.[1] He advised Roosevelt against withdrawing US troops from Europe, as this would leave a power vacuum on the Continent and enable Stalin to consolidate the position of the Red Army over eastern Europe. Churchill sought to formalize a continued US presence in an Anglo-American alliance.

When the war was finally over in Europe, however, Churchill was no longer in office. It fell to Attlee's Labour Cabinet to convince the Americans of the potency of the Soviet threat. Britain's Socialist foreign secretary Ernest Bevin conceptualized the geopolitical difficulties which faced Europe in realist terms. 'Instead of world co-operation we are rapidly drifting into spheres of influence, or what can better be described as three great Monroes', wrote Bevin (1945). The United States would emerge strengthened from the war, with dominance over Latin America, Japan and China. The Soviet Union had already extended its territory to large parts of Eastern Europe. Stuck between these two giants, Western Europe would be reduced to a weak conglomerate of nations – a 'scattered Monroe'. If Europe was pressured by one or both of these extra-European blocs, Bevin feared, it would be unable to hold out for very long. Given this pessimistic scenario, Bevin saw Churchill's Anglo-American alliance as the least of all post-war evils.

Soviet preoccupations
Before the war, Stalin had seen no real difference in the policies of Chamberlain, Roosevelt and Hitler. After the war, he continued to deny any substantial difference between liberal America and Nazi Germany. To him, both were imperialist countries led by capitalist oppressors set on expansion. In his view, the world was starkly divided into a socialist and a capitalist camp.

Early in 1946, Stalin expressed his 'two-camp theory' of international politics. It was necessary to prepare for war against an Anglo-American onslaught, he insisted. He told the Soviet people that they must sacrifice and accept the continuation of the economic policies of the 1930s: the development of the country's heavy industry rather than its consumer goods in 'three or more Five-Year Plans' (Stalin 1946).

Stalin implemented his vision by a three-pronged strategy of geopolitics, bluff and a divide-and-conquer diplomacy. He consolidated a buffer-zone in Eastern Europe by establishing Soviet-controlled regimes in Eastern European countries and tying these regimes to the USSR partly by military presence, partly through the communist party structure and, later, through a 'socialist division of labour.'

Second, to muster a credible deterrence, Stalin concealed the real extent of Soviet poverty and destitution. He closed the USSR firmly off from the rest of the world, and allowed only the friendliest of supporters to visit the country. This deprived the West of reliable knowledge of Soviet conditions, and provided a decisive precondition for Stalin's successful propaganda offensive of subsequent years. Western anti-Stalinists became victims of the *generalissimo*'s exaggerations of Soviet military strength and economic health. Left-wing sympathizers, on the other hand, became victims of Stalin's empty appeals to liberty, human solidarity and the brotherhood of the dispossessed. Under a blanket of tight secrecy, propaganda and bluff, Stalin sought to rearm and reconstruct the Soviet Union as rapidly as possible. He exploited the occupied territories in Eastern Europe, transferring capital and entire factories into Soviet Russia.

Finally, to postpone the inevitable Anglo–American collusion, Stalin sought to maximize the political divisions between the two capitalist countries. He negotiated with American foreign-policy-makers while harshly attacking British imperialism and belligerence.

US preoccupations: the dawn of the American Age

America's approach to world affairs was also ideologically informed. In 1941, Roosevelt had sought to obtain Churchill's signature on a joint Anglo–American declaration of war aims. His version of what became the Atlantic Charter bore the unmistakable marks of traditional liberalism. It asserted that the war should be fought to protect the sovereignty of all nations, and to maintain the freedom of the seas. It promised to establish a 'general security' system and a fair world economy; to guarantee equal access to the world's wealth for 'all states, great or small, victor or vanquished'. Only when it was substantially diluted did Churchill sign it (LaFeber 1989, p. 381).

Henry Luce, publisher of *Life* magazine, quickly emerged as an influential spokesman of the new American postwar order. The vision he revealed was derived from the old precepts of liberalism, but it articulated twentieth-century American concerns. Echoing Woodrow Wilson, Luce insisted that the United States must assume an active role in creating 'a vital international economy' and 'an international moral order'. America's postwar policies must transcend narrow, materialistic and nationalistic concerns. The nation must instead help create an open world which embodied the ideals of freedom, justice and opportunity. This would not only ensure the survival of democracy in America itself, it would bring wealth and a stable peace to peoples all over the world. Every American was called, 'each in the widest horizon of his own vision, to create the first great American century' (LaFeber 1989, p. 380).

Most American observers agreed with Luce. State Department analysts adopted the position that 'unhampered trade dovetailed with peace; high tariffs, trade barriers, and unfair economic competition with war' (Hull 1948, p. 81). They saw the wartime alliance as the promise of a new age of great-power co-operation. They saw in the new United Nations (UN) a fledgling interstate government; they saw in the International Monetary Fund (IMF) and the World Bank the foundations of a stable post-war world economy: a postwar depression could be averted only if a free-market world economy was established.

Through 1945, American scholars and politicians sounded Wilson's old utopian themes. But their liberal visions were soon frustrated. First, the great-power conferences between America, Britain and the USSR at Yalta and Potsdam (in February and July 1945) revealed deep conflicts of interest between the Soviet Union and the Western powers – notably over the post-war status of Soviet-occupied Poland. Instead of supporting America's vision of a new world order, Stalin worked to consolidate Soviet power in Eastern Europe.

Second, the atomic bomb changed world diplomacy. The American bombs which levelled the Japanese cities of Hiroshima and Nagasaki in August 1945 also sent political shock waves through the rest of the world. These atomic blasts destroyed the postwar plans of Britain and the Soviet Union, forcing them to redraft their postwar designs. With a monopoly on the new atomic weapon, the Americans were in position to dictate the terms of the post-war order and tailor it to suit America's interests. The economy-centred US politicians, however, were slow to recognize the immensity of the political power which had fallen into American hands. Once they awoke to the new world order, they were quite uncertain whether to withdraw into isolationism or play a leading role in its management.

Third, Roosevelt died unexpectedly in the spring of 1945. His successor, Harry S. Truman, had little knowledge of foreign affairs, and his inexperience was evident in the lack of a guiding theoretical vision in America's foreign policy in the vital post-war months. It is often argued that Roosevelt's death marked a shift from an essentially utopian, economic vision of world affairs to a realist foreign policy attuned to power analysis and geo-strategy. But Truman at first assumed Roosevelt's idealist mantle. As late as October 1945, he enumerated the principles of America's postwar policy in twelve points. Echoing Wilson's Fourteen Points, Roosevelt's Atlantic Charter and Luce's vision of the 'American century', the president extolled the virtues of freedom of the seas, emphasized all nations' right to self-determination, to freedom of expression, religion and commerce, and urged all nations to support the United Nations. Lacking Roosevelt's deeply engrained world vision, however, Truman quickly adopted new policies which reflected the unique postwar world order, America's unprecedented place in it, and Soviet empire-building in Eastern Europe.

International relations in a divided world

In the immediate aftermath of World War II, students of International Relations avidly discussed the institutional, legal and educational prerequisites for a lasting peace (Eagleton and Wilcox 1945). This debate was nipped in the bud. Many scholars were reminded of the idealism of the 1920s, and feared that the study of world affairs might again become mired in naive and dangerous utopianism. They insisted that the study of world politics build on 'ascertainable facts' (Dunn 1949, p. 67).

The idealist fixation on the legal and educational prerequisites for peace was further shaken by a rapid succession of disillusioning events. The 1945 summit meetings at Yalta and Potsdam exuded none of the amity that had marked former wartime conferences. Common cause had yielded to concerns of national interest; good will had given way to suspicion.

Cold War statesmanship

In February 1946, after months of confusion in Washington about the future of the wartime collaboration, exasperated officials at the State Department sent a cable to the US Embassy in Moscow seeking explanations for the Russians' unexpected behaviour. Chargé d'affaires George F. Kennan, who had long deplored the utopian fantasies of US policy-makers, responded with an 8,000-word telegram which explained Soviet foreign policy in realist terms (Kennan 1967, p. 288).

By Kennan's account, the Soviets saw the world as divided between a capitalist and a communist camp, between which there could be no peaceful coexistence. Capitalism was, according to the Soviet view, fraught with internal contradictions and would, in time, collapse. Socialism would then rise to take its place. In the meantime, the Soviets would exploit any opportunity to weaken America's power and prestige by using a world-wide network of communist parties.

Under such circumstances, only two courses of US action existed, Kennan argued: either to wait for changes within the Soviet Union to produce changes in Russian policy; or to resist as effectively as possible Soviet attempts to undermine Western institutions. Kennan recommended the second course. He emphasized that the Soviet theory of International Relations was not the product of an objective study of world politics; rather, it stemmed from the Soviet leaders' need to justify their autocratic rule by ideological means 'without which they did not know how to rule'. Marxism-Leninism, he wrote, is the 'fig leaf of their moral and intellectual respectability' (Kennan 1946, p. 700). The Soviets are bold, he continued, but not reckless. Echoing old theories of counterpoise, Kennan wrote:

[The Soviet Union is] impervious to [the] logic of reason, and it is highly sensitive to [the] logic of force. For this reason it can easily withdraw – and usually does – when strong resistance is encountered at any point. Thus, if the adversary has sufficient force and makes clear his readiness to use it, he rarely has to do so. If situations are properly handled there need be no prestige-engaging showdowns (p. 707).

Churchill reinforced Kennan's portrayal of Stalin's policies in a celebrated speech he made in America in March. 'From Stettin in the Baltic to Trieste in the Adriatic, an iron curtain has descended across the Continent', he began. It would make matters worse if the West sought to placate Stalin, he continued. 'From what I have seen of our Russian friends, I am convinced that there is nothing they admire so much as strength, and there is nothing for which they have less respect than for military weakness.' He warned Americans that the UN would remain ineffective unless Britain and America united in a 'fraternal association of the English-speaking peoples' (Harbutt 1988, pp. 186ff).

Kennan and Churchill expressed the unravelling of an uneasy wartime alliance. Kennan's 'long telegram' provided the conceptual basis for an active American foreign policy of containing Soviet expansionism in Europe and the Near East. Churchill's 'iron-curtain speech' provided the idea for an economic understanding and a military alliance between the Atlantic states as a bulwark against the Soviet Union. In the autumn of 1946, the unravelling of wartime co-operation erupted into open antagonism between Soviet Russia and the West. This 'Cold War' intensified in 1947, when the Soviet Union installed commu-nist regimes in most East European nations and the United States responded with an immense economic aid programme which sustained the liberal-demo-cratic polities and the open, capitalist economies in Western Europe.

The Cold War reached its most intense phase between 1948 and 1953. When the USSR blockaded the Western-held sectors of Berlin in the winter of 1948/9, the USA organized a gigantic, around-the-clock airlift which supplied the iso-lated city during the nine-month blockade; when Europe declared its fear of Soviet subversion, America entered into a military alliance with the Atlantic powers, the North Atlantic Treaty Organization (NATO); when the Soviets exploded their first atomic bomb, the Americans declared their intention to develop a hydrogen bomb; when Mao Zedong established a communist govern-ment in China, the United States made military alliances in the Near and Far East and in the Pacific. When North Korea invaded South Korea in June 1950, the United States fully committed itself to defending the small Asian country, in a war which took 5,000,000 lives – of which 30,000 were American. With the Korean War, the world was sharply divided between two atomic blocs, locked in a deadly political contest – 'like two scorpions trapped in a bottle' (Oppen-heimer 1953, p. 529).

Cold War scholarship and the emerging US centre

This 'cold snap' stunted the revival of the idealist approach. Influential com-mentators argued that the Cold War made it impossible for the United States to return to a foreign policy based on naive legalities and isolationism. Walter Lippmann (1943) and George Kennan (1950) claimed that idealist preoccupa-tions with legal appeals, moral duties and educational efforts were worse than useless; a revival of the woolly utopianism of the 1920s represented a diversion from the need to contain Soviet expansionism. Churchill drew a parallel between the failure of Western democracies to oppose Nazi Germany in the late 1930s and the idealist reluctance to contain Soviet Russia in the late 1940s. It was dis-graceful that Western leaders in 1939 at Munich had accepted Hitler's preda-tory designs on Czechoslovakia, said Churchill – who had been one of the few outspoken critics at the time. Munich demonstrated that a dictator who is set on expansion can be contained only by the threat of overwhelming military force.

This 'lesson of Munich' was widely embraced, and became a central tenet of the Cold War discourse, which emphasized the need for military preparedness and anti-communist security commitments.

This challenge to idealism also had a methodological side. Many scholars recalled the mistakes of the 1920s and insisted in 1945 that students explain more clearly the methods they relied on for dealing with questions about world affairs (Dunn 1949). The methodological introspection which followed this challenge was much informed by a debate which a circle of Viennese philosophers had initiated in the 1920s. Alfred Ayer's and Karl Popper's 'new look' of the 1930s (Popper 1959) now emerged to increase the methodological self-awareness of the International Relations theorizing and encourage greater rigour in analysis.

Popper's philosophy of science was based on the simple insight that human knowledge progresses through 'conjectures and refutations'. A theoretical claim is formulated and predictions are made about what, if the claim is true, should happen when empirical tests are conducted. Young students of politics quickly adopted Popper's approach of specifying the logical devices for arriving at hypotheses and for testing them against empirical reality. The problem was that Popper's philosophy of science was not entirely neutral. It had an anti-Continental bias, which was quite apparent in Popper's wartime books, which presented Hegel as the spiritual ancestor of both Hitler and Stalin. Popper lumped the two dictators and the modes of thought they represented together under the opprobious label of 'historicism' (Popper 1945; 1957). His argument suited the post-war climate of anti-communism very well. And although the 'new look' cleared much romantic metaphysics away from political theory, the ground was cleared at a price. Some scholars broadened Popper's concept of 'historicism' to include legal philosophy, grand theory and macro-historical investigation. This was singularly unfortunate for a discipline like International Relations, whose students had traditionally relied heavily on legal philosophy and on History as important auxiliary disciplines.

In the 1940s, several political theorists noted similarities between Hitler and Stalin (Hayek 1944). In the 1950s, several comparative studies emerged which presented Nazi Germany and Communist Russia as a new, anti-liberal and insidious form of dictatorship: *totalitarianism*. In an argument which harmonized with the thrust of Popper's philosophy of science, Hitler and Stalin were depicted as different from the run-of-the mill despots of previous ages. Both were seen as twentieth-century tyrants who exploited industrialism and modern technology to build a mass society tightly controlled by a centrally-directed, one-party state and an omnipresent apparatus of compulsion. Their formidable secret police enforced an ideological orthodoxy dictated by a single party with a constitutionally sanctioned 'leading role'. The party was at once the body from which the ruling élite recruited its members, the institution which monitored the tight economic and political planning of society, the instrument of social control and the primary vehicle for the negation of individuality through the ideological indoctrination of the citizens into the official ideology of the state.[2] Many Western scholars saw in Nazism and Communism the antithesis of representative democracy.

The debate about totalitarianism was closely related to the confrontations of the Cold War. Although many sceptics denounced 'totalitarianism' as a misleading ideological and polemical construct, the concept shaped the Atlantic categories of political perception, thought and decision-making into the 1950s and beyond. Together with the 'lesson of Munich' and the concept of 'containment', the notions of 'historicism' and 'totalitarianism' fueled an anti-communist hysteria which washed across the North-Atlantic nations after World War II. In the wake of the Chinese Revolution (1949) and the outbreak of war in Korea (1950) the West was gripped by a deep mass-anxiety which erupted in Joseph McCarthy's witchhunts in the early 1950s.

The rise of the Cold War in turn marked US military and economic leadership of the 'free world'. The war destroyed European capital and killed European labourers, but the United States actually prospered. Europe's GNP fell by about 25 per cent during World War II, but America's increased by over 50 per cent. After the war, the United States accounted for about 6 per cent of the world's population but produced nearly 60 per cent of the world's industrial goods. America's defence budget, sharply cut back in the late 1940s, nearly quadrupled during the Korean war, from about $15 billion in 1950, to $54 billion in 1953 (Kennedy 1987, pp. 367ff). These funds financed an unprecedented build-up of military might – armed forces, state-of-the-art weapons systems and a new, world-wide network of military readiness and combat. The funds also paid for the build-up of scientific infrastructure. Massive government grants supported the efforts of arms manufacturers, laboratories and universities to improve techniques and technologies of future weapons systems.

Finally, these funds fertilized a thicket of foreign-policy consulting firms and 'think tanks' which were devoted to public service through research and education in government and foreign policy. The US Air Force created and generously supported the RAND Corporation. Prodded by federal grants, the Hoover Institution on War, Revolution and Peace began to concentrate its research on communism. Department-of-Defense funds established institutions and centres for research and education in world affairs at several prestigious universities. The institutes for the study of Soviet Russia at Harvard and Columbia (Kluckhohn 1949; Orlans 1972; Dickson 1972) are examples.

These institutions for International Relations research were unusual, not in that they were created and sponsored by a government to benefit the security of the state; indeed, throughout history, the study of world affairs has, as a rule, been sponsored by governments. Rather, the unusual feature of the many American institutions for International Relations research was their open and democratic nature. In earlier ages, the study of International Relations was the 'sport of kings', the preserve of cabinets, the final domain of secrecy reserved for narrow castes of specialized diplomats and soldiers.[3] In the post-war USA, think tanks and the new university centres opened foreign-policy deliberations to the public through widely disseminated books, reports, conference papers and articles in a rapidly expanding number of academic journals.

In 1945/6, students of International Relations had struggled with the task of defining their field. They knew that it concerned 'the conflict, adjustment and agreement of national politics' (Dunn 1949, p. 144), but its agenda was impossibly vague. Students were frustrated by their inability to master the many 'influences that bear upon the shaping of foreign policy, the mechanisms to carry out policy, and the devices which have been developed for the pacific adjustment of policy conflicts' (Kirk 1949, p. 426). Their frustations were alleviated as the mounting tenseness of 1947/8 imposed upon the uniquely open American community a remarkable consensus as to the nature of the enemy, the enormity of the stakes involved and the clear, empirical focus of his research: the power of states (Hoffman 1987).

Between anarchy and (inter)dependence

On the threshold of the 1950s, scholars' interest in America's conduct merged with their temptation to offer expert advice to America's amateur foreign-policy-makers. The scholars offered precisely what the policy-makers wanted: commitment to an open and free society (but not a legalistic utopia); an empirical methodology which could expertly isolate salient 'facts' in the present and extract 'lessons' from the past (but which did not slide into woolly 'historicism'); theories which could justify the abandonment of isolationism, the sudden establishment of US-led alliances, the build-up of massive arsenals of conventional and nuclear weapons, the construction of hundreds of new military bases abroad and the costly involvement in distant wars. With idealism branded as naive and with fascism and Marxism shunned, students of International Relations embraced realism.

Post-war realism emerged out of a unique and fertile dialogue between American authors, who reviewed the tradition of US foreign policy, and European authors, who drew on a long tradition of Continental politics. This confluence did not produce any single, consistent theory. Post-war realism was a composite of approaches which rapidly grew more diverse and fragmented.

'Arch-Realism'
The prescient and respected Winston Churchill was an early, powerful advocate of realist foreign policy. His realism was expressed through practice rather than explained in theoretical terms. After the war, his tough, anti-communist prescriptions were enormously influential, even while his élitist conservative philosophy was quietly forgotten. George F. Kennan, a distinguished career diplomat and an acclaimed historian of Russian and American foreign policy, was

another key contributor to post-war realism (1950; 1956). Like Churchill, Kennan derived his world-view from studies of history and from diplomatic experience, and was more practitioner than theorist. Together they laid the foundation for realism in America.

Reinhold Niebuhr was a key formulator of post-war realist theory. Niebuhr was a Protestant theologian who formulated a forceful moral argument against utopianism in the 1930s, but was long neglected by the members of America's established International Relations community. But he greatly influenced a new generation of young, Continental scholars who arrived in the United States as refugees from Hitler's Germany – young men like Henry Kissinger, John Herz and Arnold Wolfers. They found in Niebuhr's *Moral Man and Immoral Society* (1932) the basis for a tight, critical approach to international politics. Foremost among these young emigré scholars was Hans J. Morgenthau. During the early years of the Cold War, Morgenthau emerged as the major synthesizer of the Atlantic and Continental approaches to world politics and as one of the most influential realist theoreticians in the world.

American realism rests on the works of these two men: on Niebuhr's several scattered writings on theology, history and world politics and on Morgenthau's *Politics Among Nations* (1978 [1948]). Niebuhr provided the moral foundation for the new realist approach. But his writings on world affairs are too scattered to add up to a complete international relations theory. Morgenthau drew out the International Relations implications of Niebuhr's writings.

Together, Niebuhr and Morgenthau defined the basis of post-war realism. First, they share the pessimistic anthropology of the conservative tradition (Niebuhr 1950a, 1955; Morgenthau 1978, p. 4). Morgenthau's vantage point is a minimalist capsule of Niebuhr's view of human nature: that the 'drives to live, to propagate and to dominate are common to all men'. Second, from their perspective, human beings confront one another as members of social groups, not as isolated individuals (Niebuhr 1932, pp. 83ff; Morgenthau 1978, pp. 10f). Third, they accept the view that conflict is endemic in group interaction (Niebuhr 1932, p. 19; Morgenthau 1978, p. 37). Finally, they see the State as the principal actor in modern international politics. They conceive of the state as an anthropomorphic unit which defends its boundaries to render its territory impenetrable. And in the systematic interrelations among such states, 'international politics, like all politics, is a struggle for power' (Morgenthau 1978, p. 138).

This perspective was well suited to the early phase of the Cold War. The power struggle between the world's two superpowers dominated international politics, and the United States sought to contain Soviet expansionism. The Chinese revolution and the outbreak of war in Korea reinforced the US containment doctrine: the idealist advocacy for a world government and an understanding with the Russians appeared naive and dangerous. A stark line was drawn between discredited idealism and tough-minded, 'realistic' realism. Perspectives which did not obviously fit the realist mould risked being lumped in the idealist category and rejected.

On the face of it, the dichotomy between idealism and realism recreated Edward Carr's categories from the previous decade. However, whereas Carr in the late 1930s had emphasized the dynamic interaction between idealism and realism, scholars of the late 1940s often saw the two in static opposition. Postwar students, unaccustomed to Carr's dialectics, simply considered idealism a naive alternative to realism; they treated it as a straw man which they could knock over in order better to portray the mature wisdom of the realist alternative. One of the early casualties of this Procrustean dichotomy was the complex conceptualization which theorists like Kennan, Niebuhr and Morgenthau entertained of the key realist concept of power.

Morgenthau defined power broadly as 'man's control over the minds and actions of other men ... [as] a psychological relation between those who exercise it and those over whom it is exercised' (Morgenthau 1978, p. 30). Kennan and Niebuhr, too, included a crucial psychological element in the concept (Kennan 1993). The 'arch-realists' saw power as a product of material and spiritual factors – as a product, not a sum, because, in the absence of either of its key factors, the product equals zero.

This broad concept of power is the basis for their sophisticated discussion of the 'national interest' – viz, those material and moral capabilities which sustain the impermeability of the national territory, the identity of its inhabitants and the integrity of its social institutions (Morgenthau 1978, pp. 417–29, 553). It is also the basis for Niebuhr's and Morgenthau's discussion of international order. For them, the interstate system is an anarchic society. The only principle which can lend it a semblance of order is the 'balance of power'. Such a balance is never the automatic outcome of military force alone; it is a function of 'moral conviction' and 'will' as well. Because power is a function of actors' perceptions of each other's spiritual and material capabilities, a balance of power implies more than a simple balance of forces. The international order is thus sustained by an underlying perceptual consensus – or 'a silent compact' (p. 226).

By 1949, American analyses of world politics were predominantly expressed in a state-oriented and power-focused discourse. In the scramble to enlist in the new community of realists, pretenders (who often had slight knowledge of its theoretical tradition) helped consolidate a vulgate version of the Realist approach. They often claimed that a connection existed from Thucydides through Hobbes to Morgenthau – in spite of the fact that about 2,000 years of Western history separate the two first authors. Many of them added the notion that the 'State' was a rational actor – in spite of the arch-realist discussions of how foreign-policy decisions are made on the basis of incomplete information by statesmen who are guided by intuition.[4] To pass as a realist, it sufficed to don a tough, anti-communist line, to assume that Soviet policies were intentional (and therefore rational), and to fortify one's arguments with the doctrine of 'containment', the theory of 'totalitarianism' and the 'lessons of Munich.'

Realist rivalries

Kennan, Morgenthau, Niebuhr and other 'arch-realists' deplored the shallow misconception that realism meant 'power politics' narrowly conceived in terms of military might. Already in 1947, columnist Walter Lippmann warned that excessive reliance on military might could wreck the American constitutional system (Lippmann 1947; Steel 1980, Chs. 34–5).

Kennan, appointed as an adviser to the US Department of State in 1949, had intense arguments with high-ranking officials, warning them of the dangers of a foreign policy based on military might. It would destroy diplomatic intercourse, provoke the superpowers into a deadly arms race and lock the world into a decades-long division, he argued (Kennan 1967).[5]

Niebuhr cut to the heart of the issue. He explained that political power 'is a compound of which physical force, whether economic or military, is only one ingredient'. Many American scholars and politicians 'do not fully appreciate that a proper regard for moral aspirations is a source of political prestige; and that this prestige is itself an indispensable source of power,' he wrote (1942, p. 4). In war, states rely on force, but in peace, they rely on 'prestige' – i.e., not on 'power' itself, but on their carefully constructed 'reputation for power' (1959, pp. 8, 35–47).

Niebuhr blamed the popular misunderstanding on the fashionable division between idealism and realism. This artificial dichotomy imparted to the public dangerous foreign-policy blinders which persisted 'in confronting us with two horns of a dilemma and beg us to choose between them'. Soon, the idealist position would become impossible to hold – as evinced by the rapid decline of Henry Wallace's Progressive Party. People let go the idealist horn because they 'could not keep a grip on it', Niebuhr wrote (1950b, p. 338).

Our realists are convinced that neither world government nor a a pragmatic understanding with the Russians is an attainable goal. They are therefore tempted to grasp the second horn of the dilemma. They accept the fact of an inevitable war. From the idea of an inevitable war it is only a short logical step to the concept of a preventive war. For if we must inevitably fight the Russians, why should we not have the right to choose the most opportune time for joining the issue? (Niebuhr 1950b, p. 338)

Niebuhr's critique of American realism was published immediately after the triumph of the revolution in China. The United States had just begun its support of the French colonial war in Indo-China. Fearing US entanglements in Asia, and pitting his own 'arch-realism' against the fashionable anti-communism of the policy-makers, Niebuhr castigated the 'counsels of desperation on our side which would tempt us to confront Communism in Asia primarily in military terms'. To neglect the psychological and moral factors of political power would both weaken America's prestige and enhance that of the Soviet Union, he argued. A military policy would 'play into the hands of the Communist political propaganda by which it would expand still further into Asia', and broaden

America's containment mission. Chinese patriots would conceal their grievances with the Russians, the Asian peoples would be driven into the arms of an apparently unified communist camp, and the United States would be locked into unwinnable wars in Asia, he cautioned (p. 344).

Morgenthau entertained similiar thoughts, and, when the US Government began to send its first 'advisers' to Vietnam in the mid-1960s, he inveighed against 'the futility of the search for abstract principles, the error of anti-communist intervention *per se*, the self-defeating character of anti-revolutionary intervention ...' (Morgenthau 1967, p. 430).

The reassertion of liberal theorizing

The conservative philosophy which undergirded Realism was essentially alien to mainstream American scholarship. Without the nourishment of a conservative tradition, the imported realist plant did not strike solid roots in American soil. The 'arch-realism' of Kennan, Niebuhr and Morgenthau met with one of two fates. Either, it was adopted in form only, in which case a line of discord was drawn between the arch-realists and the crusading anti-communists, or it was rejected altogether.

In Europe, scholars like Schwarzenberger (1951), Aron (1966) and H. Bull (1977) self-confidently elaborated on realism's subtleties and conservative precepts. In contrast, by the mid-1950s in the United States the liberal tradition of American politics and scholarship had reasserted itself as the paranoia of McCarthyism receded. This reassertion began as criticism of 'power politics', but soon plunged the study of International Relations into a double crisis.

A crisis in methods flowed from the insistent demand that students of politics apply strict, scientific reason in their work. The demand triggered an acrimonious debate between the realist (or 'traditional' or 'classical') approach on the one hand and the 'behaviouralist' approach on the other. The behaviouralists challenged the idea that realism was the sole 'realistic' approach to international politics. They argued that ostensibly objective and dispassionate realism was rhapsodic, a-scientific, and ideological; that it relied far too much on artistic sense and subjective intuition. They advocated the objectification of the field through the application of research methods inspired by the natural sciences: quantitative descriptions, Popperian hypothesis-testing, and new techniques of data processing (H. Bull 1966; Singer 1969). Their approach allowed the embrace of concepts more in tune with the essentially liberal orientation of the US, while its scientific discourse helped dispel charges that it was utopian and unrealistic.

A crisis in substance flowed from the notion that students could explain political events by investigating decision-makers' reasoning processes. This focus on individual decision-making directed attention away from politics and into neo-classical economics, psychology and systems engineering, all of which studied the rationality of choice. The renewed focus on human reason tied neatly in with the liberal claim that, if human reason is cultivated and refined, it strengthens the natural harmony of human society; it creates a co-operative order which encourages progress, affluence and peace. But whenever reason is stunted or subverted, the natural harmony of human society is distorted, and fuels injustice, violence, conflict and war.

Economics had elaborated these liberal precepts into a tight logical system. Theories of micro- and macroeconomics, international trade, development and modernization were a conceptual bonanza for many students of International Relations. They found in economic scholarship seductive discussions of rational decision-making and analogies to integrated systems and the tough-minded thinking of the aggressive business man.

Microeconomics focuses on individual decision-makers; it studies the economizing behaviour of rational producers, consumers, traders and company leaders. In the 1950s and 1960s, many students of world politics adopted microeconomic assumptions of human rationality; they emulated business men's advocacy of openness and communication as the key to progress and well-being. Analogies from *laissez-faire* economics, business communication and systems analysis reverberate through their writings.

Macroeconomics deals with the workings of entire economies in terms of the total amount of goods and services produced, total income earned, volume of employment, flows of investments and behaviour of prices; it studies a society's total employment of its productive resources in terms of a social system. Many analysts found systems analysis an exciting alternative to power theories.

From such ruminations emerged two new approaches (Wolfers 1959). The first approach placed individual human beings at the centre of the stage which had previously been reserved for nation-states. Sustained by the microeconomic assumption that irrational, violent and unjust behaviour will follow if human reason is corrupted, a number of psychological theories emerged in the 1950s. Each new theory of international conflict elaborated on a new phenomenon which might corrupt the reason of politicians – crisis situations (Holsti 1972), the sustained pressure of high office (Jervis 1976), the opportunities inherent in the exercise of power or the character or dynamics of the groups to which they belonged (Allison 1971; Janis 1972).

The other approach emphasized the existence, side by side with the State, of other corporate actors. It challenged realist assumptions about the primacy of the State in world politics and the anarchic nature of world society. Supported by systems analysis and theories of trade, post-war critics disputed both assumptions. Regular complex interactions among states required – and gave rise to – a degree of international order served by a variety of new transnational actors – international organizations like the UN, the EEC, NATO and the rapidly expanding global network of multinational corporations.

In the 1950s emerged a new rational perspective on world politics. Assumptions of impenetrable state boundaries gave way to studies of human transactions. Authors now investigated the nascent process of European integration and, relying on sociological theories of functionalism, argued that a high volume of transactions enhances the material interdependence of countries and facilitates the growth of economic and political integration (Deutsch 1953, 1957; Haas 1964; Mitrany 1966). They drew 'transactional maps' which depicted the flow of material goods and the transmission of knowledge and ideas attached to participation in decision-making. In such maps, the patterns of world politics appeared 'like a mass of cobwebs superimposed on one another,' or 'the type of a diagram an electrical engineer would draw showing the wiring links within the electrical system' (Burton 1972, p. 41).

Robert O. Keohane and Joseph S. Nye advanced the discussion on transactions in their *Power and Interdependence* (1977). They began with the simple point that whereas economists have discussed transactions, political scientists have been instead preoccupied with concepts of 'power' and 'influence'. Keohane and Nye introduced a concept of 'complex interdependence' and used it to discuss those aspects of the rational cobweb which are systematically unbalanced or asymmetrical – echoing the concerns of Rousseau and List that interdependence not only increases wealth but also dependence and vulnerability. In transcending the simple focus on economic co-operation, they linked their theories to the traditional concerns of international relations: insecurity, influence, and structural power.

The systems perspective

Power and Interdependence reflects a sea change in International Relations theorizing. The book reverberates with a new set of issues which emerged around 1970 – superpower parity, America's defeat in Vietnam, global recession, the quadrupling of oil prices, the spreading demand for a New International Economic Order. Such new issues led scholars to ask two related questions: were America's days as a dominant world power numbered? What would happen to the global system if the United States could no longer enforce the world economy's basic principles of operation?

The scholarly community was quick to recognize these questions, introducing in the process a new theory of 'hegemonic stability'. It holds that a dominant actor or 'hegemon' emerges in the international system under specific condictions to assume leadership and guarantee order in an international system. With respect to the contemporary scene, some argued that as America's relative power declined, international politics would assume a new and different character (Keohane 1984).

Other authors disagreed. They claim that a high volume of transactions triggers a learning process which produces common decision-making procedures, perceptions, norms, beliefs, rules and expectations – or 'international regimes'. They argue that although such regimes are often established by a single, hegemonic actor, they tend to persist even if that actor becomes too weak to enforce the basic rules upon which the system depends. 'Regimes, are maintained as long as the patterns of interest that gave rise to them remain' (Stein 1982, p. 299).

These debates about 'hegemonic stability' and 'regimes' reintroduced concepts like 'power' and 'national security' – regime theory, in particular, has a clear affinity with Morgenthau's notion of an ordering 'silent compact'. But the new participants in the debate viewed the old realist concepts in the new light of game theory, systems analysis and structural sociology. In so doing, they breathed new life into the tattered remains of American liberalism.

In the early 1950s, John Hertz contributed an influential reformulation of the realist assumption. He blunted realism's pessimistic edge by re-casting its key premiss in a simple, state-of-nature analogy. Whenever people 'live alongside each other without being organized into a higher unity', Hertz explained, there has always arisen 'what may be called the "security dilemma" of men, or groups, or their leaders'.

Groups or individuals living in such a constellation must be, and usually are, concerned about their security from being attacked, subjected, dominated, or annihilated by other groups or individuals. Striving to attain security from such attack, they are driven to acquire more and more power in order to escape the impact of the power of others. This, in turn, renders the others more insecure and compels them to prepare for the worst. Since none can ever feel entirely secure in such a world of competing units, power competition ensues, and the vicious circle of security and power accumulation is on.

Whether man is by nature peaceful and co-operative, or domineering and aggressive, is not the question. The condition that concerns us here is not a biological or anthropological but a social one (Hertz 1950, p. 9).

Hertz' security dilemma depicts the struggle among states as a function of the competitive character of their environment; not as an effect of the evil or flawed nature of man. It is a state-of-nature analogy which made the anarchic nature of the interstate system the new vantage point of a realist approach, thereby obviating realism's pessimistic anthropology.

This analogy was pursued by others. In his important book *Man, the State and War* (1959) Kenneth N. Waltz distinguishes between three 'images' (or levels) of International Relations analysis. The first level tries to explain international relations by reference to 'man' – either to the psychological make-up of individual decision-makers or to some abstract notion of the 'nature of man'. This is a futile effort, argued Waltz; studies of individual interaction are too specific to yield any theories about international relations, and discussions about flaws in human nature are too vague and general. The second level of analysis tries to explain international relations by reference to 'states' – e.g. by claiming that distinct regime types (democratic, capitalist, communist ...) are associated with particular patterns[5] of international behaviour. Such second-level efforts are also futile, argued Waltz; international relations cannot be reduced to the domestic structures of states. Only third-level explorations are worthwhile, argues

Waltz. Only through analyses of the systemic interaction of states can we hope to develop general theories of international relations, argues Waltz, who found in Rousseau's *Discourse on the Origin of Inequality* an analogy to interstate co-operation under the the the security dilemma (Rousseau 1950a, p. 238). Assume that five hungry men in the state of nature happen to meet. The hunger of each can be satisfied by one-fifth of a stag, so they agree to co-operate and trap one. However, the hunger of any one of them will also be satisfied by a hare. So, when a hare hops within reach, one of the hunters sets out after it, catches it and satifies his own hunger. However, in doing so, he condemns the stag hunt to failure and his companions to continued starvation.

'The story is simple; the implications are tremendous', concludes Waltz. 'In co-operative action, even where all agree on the goal and have an equal interest in the project, one cannot rely on others' (Waltz 1959, p. 168). In so far as the individual hunter is driven by hunger to co-operate with others, his intent is immediate and his act is one of passion. However, if he considers his position rationally, he would realise that his long-run interest depends on convincing all the hunters that co-operation will benefit them all. But reason also tells him, that if he forgoes the hare, the man next to him might leave his post to chase it, leaving the first man with nothing but food for thought on the folly of being loyal. Waltz concludes:

> If harmony is to exist in anarchy, not only must I be perfectly rational but I must be able to assume that everyone else is too. Otherwise there is no basis for rational calculation. To allow in my calculation for the irrational acts of others can lead to no determinate solutions, but to attempt to act on a rational calculation without making such an allowance may lead to my undoing (p. 169).

The first implication of Waltz' parable is that a person who acts with perfect means–end logic to maximize his personal utility in the short run, might in the long run damage the system on which he depends for survival. The traditional concept of 'rationality' must be amended: an act cannot be considered rational unless it includes long-term considerations.

The second implication is that the concept of 'rationality' not only pertains to individual decision-makers; it also pertains to *systems* of human interaction. Social systems can display irrational behaviour even though each of their members acts rationally. Therefore the rationality of the system is not a function of the rationality of its members. The system, in effect, has its own rationality.

States are members of a social system. Each state participates in an interactive process or 'game' whose rules are beyond its immediate power to alter. The outcome of this game depends on what *all* participants do, as all the players try to anticipate the probable choices of other players in order to determine their own best courses of action (p. 192). Since states are immovable territorial units, interstate games are never played only once; they are played over and over. As the game is repeated, the players evolve a history of interaction from which each can derive lessons and all can derive rules of interaction.

In the 1960s, this concept of systems rationality opened the door to new types of International Relations theorizing. Complex, high-stakes issues were converted into games concerning the life and death of the planet. Authors studied interaction of the superpowers in the new, systemic light. They concluded that, in a nuclear world, the major players have at least one interest in common: to continue the game. From this perspective, a state acts rationally if it contributes to the maintenance of the game – an act is rational if it turns out well in the long run. Thomas Schelling (1966) and others conceived of the nuclear balance of terror as a state of nature with two lethal but logical participants. His game-theoretical discussions of superpower strategies were highly influential. Pentagon advisers adopted Schelling's language, characterizing key properties of the new superpower constellation in game-theoretical analogies like 'Chicken' or 'Prisoners' Dilemma'.[6]

From international systems to interstate structures

It was a small conceptual step from the logic of systems rationality to the unwieldy terrain of structural theories. In the interest of brevity, a rough distinction may be drawn between two main areas of structural theorizing in International Relations: on the interstate system on the one hand and the world economy on the other.

Morton Kaplan broke new ground with his discussion of interstate structures in his *Systems and Process in International Politics* (1957). He discussed relations among states in terms of patterns of geopolitical power, and developed six structural models or shapes which the international system might assume: balance-of-power, tight bipolar, loose bipolar, universal, hierarchical and unit veto systems. Richard Rosecrance reconstructed 200 years of European history in structural terms in his *Action and Reaction in World Politics* (1963). He divided the period from 1740 to 1960 into nine epochs or systems, and discussed each in terms of its characteristic interstate structures.

Kenneth Waltz drew on his earlier work to produce an ambitious structural *Theory of International Relations* (1979). Following his own advice from *Man, the State and War*, Waltz excluded considerations about human nature and regime types (i.e. his old 'first' and 'second images') from the discussion, and riveted his focus on the systemic level of analysis (or his 'third image'). Different statesmen and different states often end up conducting similiar policies, Waltz observes. This suggests to him that something other than individuals and regime types affects interstate behaviour. He submits that that these 'other' influences are found at the level of the international system; that since states do not behave according to their inner dispositions, they must be influenced by external forces which are located in the structure of the international system. This structure cannot be directly observed. But as it works as a constraining force on state (inter)actions and produces 'a tendency towards sameness' in state behaviour (Waltz 1979, p. 127), its effects can be monitored.

In some respects Waltz' analysis does not deviate much from established realist arguments – the focus is still on state interaction and on the capabilities of power. But in other respects it breaks with Realism. Most significantly, Waltz turns away from the traditional realist philosophy of science. He embraces a more modern, Popperian stance by seeking to distil from the observation of interstate interactions a few basic axioms or 'laws' about International Relations. His *Theory* immediately triggered an intense debate, through which the approach of 'Neo-Realism' emerged during the early 1980s (Keohane 1986).

Structures in the world economy
The application of structural arguments to analysis of the world economy has constituted a large (controversial) sub-field in International Relations since the early 1960s. The approach was pioneered by authors from relatively poor, industrializing states. The UN Economic Commission on Latin America (ECLA) was a particularly fertile forum for their discussions of global equity and development. Frustrated by the insistent free-market liberalism of the USA, ECLA evolved an alternative strategy for industrial development. Analysts at ECLA argued that, in the initial phase of industrial growth, states must protect domestic producers from the competition of foreign imports by tariffs or quotas. Once domestic industry and commerce gained some momentum, they would stimulate the growth of a new bourgeois class which would then support national interests in the face of foreign penetration.

The logic of this strategy has parallels with the 'national political economy' of Friedrich List. The theorists at ECLA, too, divided the world economy into two regions: the wealthy, industrialized 'centre' region on the one hand and the poor, underdeveloped 'periphery' on the other. However, they adopted a structural argument which emphasized the systemic interaction between these two regions through history. They claimed that Europe's industrial development had not only produced capitalist growth and modernization; it had also perpetuated some of the primitive features of the previous pre-capitalist system. Wealth and poverty, development and underdevelopment did, in other words, exist side by side. Celso Furtado, Raul Prebisch and others used this insight to criticize the liberal economists for telling only half the story. There is no guarantee, they argued, that poor states will develop more rapidly if they become more closely integrated into the global division of labour. Rather, they run the risk of simply perpetuating their own position as the world's underdeveloped periphery. Consequently, ECLA analysts opposed poor states' integration into the world market and favoured a doctrine of autonomous development.

ECLA's analysts were not orthodox Marxists. Furtado, for example, was as sceptical of the Marxist doctrines of a command economy as of liberal theories of the free market. Marxist theories, however, harmonized closely with ECLA's structural argument, and gained access to International Relations theory and theoretical respectability through its discourse. Marxist theories had an immense appeal in many regions of the Third World. They sharpened ECLA's division of the world economy between a wealthy centre and an impoverished periphery and re-cast it in terms of a class struggle on the world scale; they embraced the duality thesis that developed and underdeveloped nations exist side by side, and grafted it on to a method of dialectics and a theory of imperialist exploitation; they re-inforced ECLA's critique of free-market economies with Lenin's theory of colonial wars; and they boosted the recommendation of autonomous development with anti-imperialist advocacy of wars of national liberation.

The last point contains a key to the appeal of revolutionary Marxism. Its emphasis on wars of national liberation addressed a problem which faced many Third-World nations after World War II: decolonization. Nearly 100 new countries emerged in the first 40 post-war years. Emancipation usually entailed conflict; often it involved long and bitter conflict – as in Algeria and Vietnam.

Free-market theorizing carried no credence in these poor, conflict-ridden regions of the world. The ECLA approach, tailored to the needs of relatively well-established actors in Europe and Latin America, had limited appeal. Marxism, by contrast, addressed problems of nations still mired in efforts to secure their statehood and define their national identity.

Intellectuals and activists in Europe and America observed the advent of a new, Third-World Marxism at a time when orthodox communism was in a deep crisis. Stalin's death had provoked rebellions and uncertainty in the Soviet Bloc. From the throes of the Sino–Soviet split and the Soviet invasion of Hungary emerged a vibrant and independent 'New Left' movement in the West. Beginning in the late 1950s, it was fed by hopes that a new kind of socialism would emerge from the mass-based revolutions in countries like China, Vietnam and Algeria. A potent myth of the noble *guerrillero* was given a decisive boost in 1960 by the radicalization of the Cuban revolution. Inspired by the figures of Ho Chi Minh, Frantz Fanon and 'Che' Guevara, Cuban leaders founded an organization which advocated a Tricontinental Revolution. The Tricontinental sponsored the spread of Guevara's treatise On *Guerrilla Warfare* (1961) and Fanon's inflammatory manifesto, *The Wretched of the Earth* (1961).

Marxist theory has two major components: a socio-economic aspect, plus a political–philosophical doctrine of liberation. First, Marxism is a rich structural theory. It possesses a conceptual coherence and a self-sufficiency which provides a comprehensive explanation of world events. Its plausibility was much enhanced by post-war globalization of the industrial economy. After World War II, decisions about capital investment and growth were made on a world scale; giant multinational corporations concentrated capital, centralized decision-making and believed in a global division of labour. Marxism explained these developments. In their influential *Monopoly Capital* (1966), Paul Baran and Paul Sweezy provide a theory of world affairs which is both elegant and comprehensive. André

Gunder Frank (1967) drew upon the Marxism of the New Left to explain precisely how the wealthy capitalist states in the 'centre' of the world economy exploit the poor nations in the 'periphery'. Immanuel Wallerstein's multi-volume work on *The Modern World System* (1974, 1980, 1989 and forthcoming) is a project of rare ambition. Wallerstein draws on Marxist theory and on French historiography in his impressive account of the history of the relationship between the 'centre' and the 'periphery' regions of the world economy. He argues that these regions are parts of a single world economy, that is driven by a capitalist dynamic and that has been expanding since the seventeenth century.

The elegant structural theory on which the Marxist argument rested offered Third-World nations a comforting explanation for the unequal distribution of global wealth. It placed the blame for underdevelopment on the structures of capitalism. These had siphoned wealth and resources away to the industrialized, European centre. In the process, native economies were distorted to serve the needs of the centre. In the Marxist argument, political oppression and economic poverty are two sides of the same global-historical process.

Secondly, Marxism is also a theory of liberation; it promises a release from the present conditions of exploitation, strife and alienation. Without this second dimension, it is doubtful whether its structural argument alone would have generated such an immense appeal in post-war political theory.

Marxism links political liberation and economic development. Through revolution, a poor nation can break out of the enslaving, global structures, harness the forces of History, telescope the process of evolution, and transform its poor, feudal-style societies into socialism without passing through the stage of capitalism. Marxism, in other words, offered a blueprint for development. The example of Soviet Russia's economic progress in the 1930s and its victories in World War II provided convincing evidence for the revolutionary model of development.[7]

Three basic International Relations paradigms

Since the 1970s it has been common to give an overview of contemporary International Relations theories through a presentation of three traditions (or images, perspectives or paradigms): Realism, Rationalism and Revolutionism.[8] This triptych emerged as a popular taxonomy in the 1980s. It is an appealing arrangement, because it is parsimonious and because it imposes a sensible order upon a complex body of theoretical literature. Also, it is appealing because it links the literature to three traditional social contexts of international-relations practice: the interstate system, the system of habitual intercourse and the realm of moral solidarity.

The three paradigms
The realist paradigm holds that the group is the primary actor in world politics

(Niebuhr 1932). In practical analysis of modern world affairs, Realism focuses on the state – a territorial entity which strives to surround itself by a hard impenetrable shell (Hertz 1957). Realism sees International Relations in terms of conflict among states, which interact in an integrated state system. Realist theories view the state as a unitary actor; they tend to disregard the internal dynamics of states.

Furthermore, the realists see international relations in terms of a hierarchy of issues, with national security concerns at the top the list. They tend to examine the achievement and maintenance of international stability – or how stability breaks down. Power is the key concept in the realist vocabulary: the utility of force as a means to solve disputes dominates the realist research agenda.

The rationalist paradigm sees the state not as a unitary actor, but as an interdependent system composed of a myriad of smaller parts – departments, offices, teams, interest groups, directors, secretaries. These parts, including the decision-makers and managers, can be analytically disaggregated, their complex interactions traced and their motivations scrutinized.

Although the rationalist paradigm recognizes that states are important actors in world politics, it contends that the dominance of states has diminished with the advent of other influential actors. Various types of international organizations have an immense independent impact on world politics – multinational corporations, for example, have considerable influence in an increasingly interdependent world economy. World politics, then, is an infinitely complex process, which involves both public and private actors of a wide variety, incessantly interacting on local, national and transnational levels.

Rationalist theories expand the range of interests and issues of international politics beyond state-centred issues of military security to a tangle of economic and social issues related to information, communication and welfare. One of the key concepts which help bring these diverse interactions under a common perspective is the notion of bargaining. In the complex web of interdependence, each actor seeks to further its interest or maximize its gain through bargaining involving a mixture of both conflict and co-operation. Many rationalists argue that, as the scope and the pace of human interaction increases and as the web of interdependence grows ever more intricate, international conflict decreases.

The revolutionist paradigm does not view the state as the basic unit of analysis; it focuses on the context within which state action takes place. Its unit of analysis, then, is the entire class-divided modern world system. The revolutionist approach thrives on historical investigation. For only by understanding the long-term, large-scale forces which have shaped the world system is it possible to capture its essential dynamics and, in turn, understand the present interaction of its constituent parts.

Revolutionist theories comprehend the world system primarily in economic terms. It is seen as capitalist in nature and composed of two major classes or regions – centre and periphery. These are separated by a gap in wealth. The states at the centre of the system are wealthy, whereas those at the periphery are poor. The relationships between centre and periphery are governed by a global division of labour which works to enrich the centre states and to impoverish the actors at the periphery. The essential feature of this world system, then, is its exploitative nature.

The rich centre states are rich (and the poor are poor) because of a transfer of wealth from peripheral to centre regions. In the revolutionist view, this unjust distribution of global wealth has existed as long as the world system itself: about 400 years. The ultimate preoccupation of the revolutionist approach is to liberate the impoverished and exploited masses of the world. Since its exploitative dynamics is built into the global division of labour, the system cannot be amended or reformed. In the interest of world freedom and justice, the entire system must be torn down and replaced.

The three spheres of international interaction
Realist theories address the interstate system. Their key theoretical preoccupation is the old question of how order can be maintained in a system of sovereign states. The first modern theorist to address this question was Thomas Hobbes. He was one of the first theorists to make an explicit analogy between international interaction and the state of nature. This analogy has subsequently been elaborated by others, and is now a key image in realist theories.

Rationalist theories emphasize arenas of habitual human interaction, particularly international diplomacy and relations among groups and organizations. They have a tendency to stress the importance of commerical interaction in world politics – an emphasis foreshadowed by authors like Crucé. Rationalist theories also draw on the analogy between international interaction and the state of nature. However, the rationalists do not express this analogy in Hobbes' nightmarish image of a war of all against all. Rather, their vision is more akin to Locke's state of nature, where 'men live according to reason,' good will and mutual assistance (Locke 1960, p. 321). Grotius, likewise, argued that, although sovereign states exist in a state of nature in so far as they obey no supreme government, they nevertheless form a society. States continually interact, regulated by special institutions established by habit and reason, such as commerce, diplomacy and alliances.

Revolutionist theories emphasize the moral solidarity of man. One of the characteristic features of revolutionist theories is their holistic perspective. They discuss all of humanity – hence they are often called 'globalist' theories (Viotti and Kauppi 1987). These theories discuss state as well as commercial interactions, but they portray both in a critical light. Rousseau emphasized the alienating and enslaving effects of the social division of labour and economic interaction. His discussion of interstate interaction is even more gloomy than Hobbes' state of nature. Revolutionist theorists are not satisfied with merely describing international relations. For them, description is a vantage point for prescription. They ultimately advocate revolutionary change – hence they are referred to as 'revolutionist' theories.

A second key feature of the revolutionist theories, then, is that they are not merely so many elaborate empirical systems of explanation; they are also bases for political action. Hume's old distinction between empirical and moral theories is often hazy in the globalist paradigm – indeed, it is often explicitly contested. Globalist theories rest on a normative base. They are informed by concerns about justice and fairness; their analysis of international relations is driven by a commitment to change the present reallocation of the world's resources to achieve greater equality in conditions of life. By appealing to humanity's natural sense of solidarity, they strive to educate and organize people around collective issues and, through mass action, to alleviate the greatest conditions of need.

The three ideological traditions
There is a final reason why this tripartition of post-war theories into realism, rationalism and revolutionism appears so sensible: it captures the three major ideological traditions which inform contemporary speculations about politics: liberalism, conservatism and left-wing radicalism.

The liberal ideology informs the rational approach. This ideology originated with the optimistic Enlightenment. Its most basic assumptions are that men are equal in their faculties, have natural needs and wants, are endowed with reason, and seek to satisfy their needs and wants in rational ways. The liberal tradition views man as basically decent and gregarious. Richard Cumberland summed up the liberal perspective in the 1670s when he explained that, in a world of equal and rational individuals, there are enough natural rewards for virtue and punishments for vice to maintain a peaceable social order without the aid of civil force.

As the liberal tradition is complex and ambiguous, so is the rationalist approach. At one extreme, some liberal theorists tend towards anarchism, believing that society benefits most where social actors are left unregulated. This position is echoed by rationalists, who believe that an open world economy increases wealth and diminishes war. On the other extreme are liberals who tend towards socialism, believing that the State must be used as an instrument to enhance the general welfare of society. This argument harmonizes with the position that strong states or (preferably) a world organization can guarantee the rules for international conduct, maintain order and help redistribute the resources and opportunities more justly among the rich and the poor nations.

The radical ideology blazes through a wide range of revolutionist approaches which made a big mark on the study of world politics in the 1970s. The characteristic anti-establishment sentiment of radicalism is already apparent in the opening line in Rousseau's *Social Contract* – that 'Man is born free, yet everywhere he is in chains.' It also informs Marx' and Engels' *Communist Manifesto*, and appears clearly in its famous closing appeal: 'Workers of the world, unite. You have nothing to lose but your chains.'

Rousseau and Marx developed a radical anthropology from a dialectical understanding of the relationship between humanity and Nature: human beings are what they are because of the way they produce the means to live. Human beings produce as a society, not individually. What distinguishes human society from a beehive or an anthill is that humans are endowed with reason: they have the capacity to reflect and, through reflection, to change the way they work on Nature. Humanity transforms Nature according to its own will in order to produce the means to live. Through labour, humanity transforms Nature into society, and is in turn transformed by the society it has created. To the extent that people have created an artificial, acquisitive, conflict-ridden society, labour has alienated them from nature and from their true Selves.

The radical ideology explains the economic origins of humanity's wretched lot in terms of capitalist appropriation, oppression and injustice. It offers a theodicy and a vision: through the repossession of the fruits of their labour, labourers could overcome their alienation. In one revolutionary sweep, humanity must do away with the old, enslaving capitalist mode of production; it must entirely rearrange the way it produces its means to live. This revolution will be initiated in those segments of society in which human beings are least alienated and least corrupted by affluence and property. According to Marx and Lenin, it is the impoverished masses of industrial workers who will carry the revolution to its world-wide triumph; according to Mao, Ho, 'Che' and Fanon, the revolution will originate with the poor, exploited masses of the Third World. Once the revolution has triumphed, and a new, socialist mode of production has been established, the preconditions are created for the evolution of a 'new man' (Guevara 1961).

The conservative ideology informs the realist approach. Conservatism emerged as a reaction to the turbulence of the industrial and democratic revolutions. Early Conservative authors feared the *hubris* of these revolutions. They rejected the Enlightenment axiom that man is governed by reason; for them, human life is a struggle for security and for control of scarce resources. They scoffed at the simple assumptions that all good things go together; that health, wealth, peace, development and democracy are interrelated; that man can engineer his natural and his social environment; and that change is easy. For the conservatives, change is always attended by uncertainty. And advocates of change are either fools or charlatans – 'mad-headed enthusiasts' or 'artful and designing knaves' who feel cramped by the status quo and preach ardent benevolence 'only the better to enable them to destroy the present establishments and to forward their own deep-laid schemes of ambition' (Malthus 1982, pp. 72, 68). If such agitators should succeed in arousing the multitudes, utter chaos would undoubtedly result (Burke 1988).

These old-fashioned conservatives insist that social order can best be maintained by preserving the existing political economy to the greatest extent possible. Whether they discuss domestic issues or world affairs, they take their bearings not from human reason but from experience; from traditions and institutions which have proved themselves through the test of time. They are less concerned with what is morally 'right' than with what is pragmatically possible. Burke, for example, acknowledged that the rights asserted by the French revolutionaries might well be 'metaphysically true'; however, he did not think that this should have any relevance for political practice. The rights of people, Burke claimed, are best guaranteed by the wisdom of their rulers, the well-being of their State and the soundness of the status quo. Comparable attitudes inform the 'arch-realism' of Churchill, Kennan, Morgenthau and Niebuhr. All of them warned against confusing 'the moral aspirations of a particular nation with the moral laws that govern the universe' (Morgenthau 1978, p. 11).

Summary

During the first few years after World War II, the study of International Relations was dominated by the realist paradigm. The 1960s saw the emergence of alternative approaches. The first sections of this chapter mentioned at least six different approaches to the study of international politics: (1) the 'arch-realism' of Morgenthau and Niebuhr; (2) the 'neo-realism' of Waltz; (3) decision-making approaches; (4) systems approaches; (5) self-reliance models for development; and (6) revolutionary anti-imperialist theories. In addition, several influential arguments were mentioned that do not fit easily into the taxonomy – the argument expressed in *NSC-68* (which dominated American foreign-policy-making circles for nearly a generation after 1950)[9] does not fit neatly, and might be considered in a category of its own. Also, the 'behavioural revolution' might be singled out as a distinct approach. Clearly, the ecological arguments which emerged during the 1960s and 1970s merit special attention.

The final quarter of the twentieth century has seen a proliferation of International Relations theories, and the simple triptych presented immediately above cannot possible contain them all. However, the purpose of this chapter is not to be exhaustive but to be reductive. And in order to identify briefly the most basic modes of thought in post-war International Relations theorizing, the many arguments can be summarized in the (admittedly procrustean) table 1, below.

Table 1 The three main paradigms of International Relations

	primary unit of analysis	*primary level of analysis*	*(key) explanatory factors*	*(main) topic or focus*	*ideological tradition*
Realism	human groups	(inter-)group/state level	military might/power, balance of power	conflict, order in anarchy	conservatism
Rationalism	rational actors	(inter-)individual level	bargaining, compromise, interests	rational co-operation	liberalism
Revolutionism	capitalist world system	world-systems level	structural power, repression, exploitation	economic development, political independence	radicalism

10

Leaving modernity?

When the Zapatista National Liberation Army (EZLN) rose up in Southern Mexico in January 1994, it marked a revolution in international politics. The EZLN was among the first political actors to exploit the global propaganda possibilities of the microelectronic web of world-wide communications. The rise of the EZLN coincided with the coming of a complex confederation of communications connections, 'the internet', which became a world-wide, multi-media phenomenon. Tens of thousands of people saw the masked countenance of the rebels' elusive leader, Subcomandante Marcos, on the 'EZLN home page'. They read his detailed explanation of how the Zapatistas fought for the rights of indigenous Maya Indians and for greater democracy in Mexico. It was reported that Marcos could be contacted by E-mail.

This development was ignited by a combination of new kinds of computer software and a new way of connecting distant documents that allowed users to travel 'the net' simply by pointing at images on the computer screen, clicking an electronic 'mouse' and instantaneously receiving signals converted into text, pictures, sound and video. The internet became a new medium. It was based on broadcasting and publishing, but with the new dimension of interactivity added. It became a place to visit. A virtual world. It spawned 'cyberspace'.

President Clinton is on the 'net'. Pope John Paul II, too. Thor Heyerdahl has his own home page. So do Niccolò Machiavelli, Harry P. Flashman, the UN, the Rolling Stones, the Library of Congress, the CIA, the Louvre, IBM, Greenpeace, Playboy, Zen Buddhists, White supremacists, Satanists and hundreds of thousands of ordinary men and women. Millions of people visit cyberspace daily to download documents and images and to add their own contributions. This development amounts to a communications revolution. It affects international relations and International Relations theory. Its impacts are often presented through terms like globalization, transnationalism, state erosion and structural transformation.

Changes in the world arena

Globalization, transnationalism and erosion of state sovereignty are recurrent themes in late-twentieth century discussions of International Relations. During the early 1990s, these terms were used with mounting frequency. What do they mean? 'Globalization' may be a new term, but it does not denote a particularly new phenomenon. Europe, America and Asia were interconnected already in the late Middle Ages when developments in the Far East and political conditions across central Asia affected the trading routes that linked the two areas to European traders and manufacturers. 'Transnationalism' has similarly been an integral part of the modern West – Renaissance Italy and sixteenth-century Iberia, the seventeenth-century United Provinces, and eighteenth-century England were all deeply involved in global trade and finance. Also, challenges to state authority have been constant companions to modern politics, sometimes as internal insurrections, sometimes in the shape of external invasions. Are the fundamental problems of international politics so enduring? Are the theoretical perspectives that we use to understand them – Realism, Rationalism and Revolutionism – really universal categories?

Changes in the world economy

Contemporary discussions of International Relations are rife with exaggerated claims about the newness of the post-Cold War world. Many things are not new. But, as Susan Strange (1994) points out, this does not mean that *nothing* is new. Among the changes that have occurred in world society in recent years, the technological revolution may be the most important one. Indeed, technological changes are a major factor – perhaps even the main factor – behind the much-talked about trends in globalization, transnationalism, state erosion and the transformation of political life. This revolution implies much more than quick access to the internet and many new TV stations. It has had instant and important consequences for world affairs.

The most immediate consequences are noticed in economic relations. First, new technology is altering old modes and relations of production. One important trend concerns the unravelling of the traditional factory system. Partly because robots and other kinds of automated equipment are replacing factory workers. Partly because the various tasks involved in the production process occur in different parts of the globe. Notions about 'commodity chains', 'comparative advantage' and a 'global division of labour' are not new (A. Smith 1976; Ricardo 1984). What is new is that the factory is unravelling – at least in the West. A factory used to be a hierarchical organization, with a managerial élite at the top and production workers at the bottom who were bent on producing high-volume goods. The more they produced, the better everyone did – from the rank-and-file worker to the chief executive officer. And what was good for the factory was good for the nation. But, with the globalization of production, the transnational corporation has replaced the local factory. Productivity has shifted from high-volume goods to high-value goods, and the old notion of a pyramid is replaced by the new image of a world-wide spider's web. The threads of the global web are fax machines, satellites, modems, computers and high-resolution monitors, which are linking designers, engineers, contractors, licensees, and dealers across national boundaries (Reich 1991).

Second, technological change has altered old modes of trade and finance. New modes of transportation – such as the container technology (a vast infrastructure designed to handle identical, sealable metal containers world-wide) – revolutionized global transport and trade. Computer technology, together with new software programmes and new systems of telecommunications, have revolutionized world finance.[1] The smooth flow of monies and goods has been greatly assisted by late-twentieth century trends of economic liberalization – as reflected in the establishment of customs unions, free-trade agreements and common markets in various parts of the world (EU, NAFTA, APEC), the progress of the GATT negotiations and the establishment of the World Trade Organization (WTO).

What are the world-political consequences of such changes? What really goes on when the production of an item is no longer limited to a specific country or region, but takes place globally? What will it do to the famous comparative-advantage argument in favour of free trade and specialization? What will happen in a world where 50 countries (with varying standards of wages) are equally capable of assembling parts into cars and computers? What will it do to the traditional idea of sovereignty? What will it do to the old legitimacy of states? What will it do to interstate relations?

Changes in interstate affairs
The accelerating change in technology has caused great changes in interstate relations. It has altered the modes of war and politics among nations. One of the most consequential changes in world affairs in this century is, undoubtedly the introduction of nuclear missiles – brought about by equipping nuclear-armed ballistic rocketry with miniaturized navigation systems. The advent of intercontinental ballistic missiles (ICBMs) mounted on hidden (and thus invulnerable) launchers altered the traditional logic of war.

In the pre-nuclear age, generals and statesmen could seriously discuss whether war might be a reasonable means to obtain specific political ends. In 1912, for example, Friedrich von Bernhardi argued that Germany would benefit from starting a European war – longer-term gains would offset the immediate costs and casualties, and the nation's war ledgers would ultimately show a pretty profit. With the advent of nuclear weapons, even von Bernhardi might calculate otherwise. Nuclear weapons represent such an overwhelming and indiscriminate destructive force, that the cost of war would always exceed the gain.

In the nuclear age, generals and statesmen agree that the use of nuclear weapons would run such an overwhelming risk of destroying everybody that the weapons can have no operational military purpose. However, they retain an old political purpose: they represent a deterrent, and therefore provide some security against enemy attacks. Thus the USA and the USSR (and other powers, too, in proportion to ambition and prestige) responded along familiar lines to the threat posed by others' weapons: they built up their nuclear strength because they saw this as the only way to balance the weapons of the enemy and deter their use. They claimed that only the threat of swift and assured retribution on a massive scale (with similar, hi-tech weapons) could provide a credible deterrent to their initial use.

It is one of the paradoxes of the hi-tech age that a lasting Great-Power peace may have been the sturdy child of nuclear terror. The Great Powers have agreed that atomic weapons cannot be used in actual warfare against a nuclear-armed enemy. Indeed, they have also felt constrained in their use of nuclear weapons against non-nuclear countries – even to the point of accepting defeat in conventional wars (as evinced by the many Third-World wars of liberation in general, and by the American defeats in Korea and Vietnam and the Soviet defeat in Afghanistan in particular).

This indicates another paradox of the high-technology age: that war is most prevalent in low-tech environments. The globally-televized images of the Gulf War contributed greatly to forming an incorrect, popular image of post-Cold War wars as hi-tech affairs. Empirical reality offers a very different picture: the six years from 1989 to 1994 counted 94 armed conflicts in 64 countries, most of which were civil wars fought with low-tech weapons. The incidence of such wars has been particularly high among poorer countries – of the world's 50 poorest countries, 38 were at war or suffering from particularly high levels of political violence in 1993 (Wallensteen and Sollenberg 1995). The connection between poverty and war is so striking in the post-Cold War world, that some authors argue that resource scarcity constitutes an important cause of war (Homer-Dixon 1994). Others argue that war today is a function of poverty and 'weakness', i.e. it is a problem of 'weak' states which are unable to sustain domestic legitimacy, order and peace (Buzan 1991; Holsti 1996).

The 1991, hi-tech Gulf War is not a typical post-Cold War operation. The weapons systems that have caused most casualties in the 1990s are neither the laser gun nor the guided missile; they are the old-fashioned mortar and the landmine. Yugoslavia's disintegration, Russia's campaigns in Chechnya, the unravelling of central power in Somalia and (the less widely broadcast) gruesome killings in Angola and Rwanda offer more representative examples of post-Cold War wars. They are representative in more ways than through their high rate of incidence. They are representative, first, because they occur in poor regions. Second, because their origins are unclear – most of them have a tangle of causes; many of them have causes that change over time. And third, because they erupt in regions where the nation-state is a relatively recent arrival. In such regions conflict and war have not been commonly perceived in interstate terms. Here, wars were often a domestic phenomenon, representing internal challenges to the legitimacy of specific regimes. With recent wars in the Middle East as the exception, Southern security threats have usually arisen not from outside aggression, but from the failure to integrate diverse domestic groups into the political process. A security concept cast in terms of interstate security dilemmas was never entirely convincing under such circumstances. Consequently, the notion of security as deterrence against attack from an enemy state would often have an alien air; it would often be seen as serving the local interests of US (or Soviet) hegemony, Western control, or the interests of world capitalism.

A final paradox of the age is that in the post-Cold War world, these 'un-Western' perspectives on conflicts and security threats have been increasingly embraced in the West. The collapse of the USSR seriously undermined the traditional security concept of the West and spurred discussions about a 'new security concept' of the post-Cold War era. Whereas the old notions of 'security' were captured in state-focused terms – in power rivalries, disputed boundaries or security dilemmas – the new notions focused on society. Whereas the old views were rooted in the dynamics of strategic interaction, the new ones are informed by social interpenetration, economic interdependence, 'weakness' and resource scarcity. Whereas the old views concentrated on 'high politics', the new ones focus on 'low politics' – and especially on the ecological preconditions of welfare and justice and on the socio-cultural arena of political interaction. Borrowing both from the Realist concept of interstate anarchy and from the Rationalist notion of complex interdependence, recent International Relations scholars have explored new definitions of 'threat' and 'security'. Barry Buzan (1991) for example, has introduced the notion of 'multidimensional security'. He has greatly subdued the traditional military dimension of 'security' and added new dimensions (for instance the 'social', the 'economic' and the 'ecological'), thus broadening the scope of analysis.

The accelerating change in communications technology has shaped these new notions of conflict, threat and security. The news media have become near-ubiquitous. During the 1991 Gulf War, CNN had news crews in Saudi Arabia that showed how sophisticated US rockets left their Saudi launchers with deafening roars trailing fire and smoke across the sky. The CNN also had a news crew on the receiving end. It traced the rockets as they approached Baghdad, sometimes filming the detonation. CNN would show, to TV-viewers all over the world, the destruction wrought on Iraqi civilians, cutting, between salvoes, to Washington, New York or Riyadh for comments on the ongoing operations by military experts.

For some observers, this development eroded the traditional role of intelligence agencies. The new media converted battlefield operations into public knowledge in a matter of minutes. By thus breaking governments' monopoly of knowledge and penetrating the old atmosphere of secrecy, the media have contributed greatly to diminishing the political power of governments. Even in the most secret recesses of the CIA, analysts followed the Gulf War on TV. However, for other observers, the Gulf War demonstrated that the battlefield realities of past wars had been replaced by mass media disinformation simulators. Der Derian (1992, p. 175) saw the Gulf War as the first 'cyberwar' – a 'televisually linked and strategically gamed form of violence that dominated the formulation as well as the representation of US policy in the Gulf'. Jean Baudrillard went a step further. For him, the Gulf War erased the line between soap-operatic computer simulations and the serious business of international relations, putting immense power in the hands of media and public-opinion managers. In a 'hyper-sceptical' observation, Baudrillard (1995) offered the hypothesis that the Gulf War was a simulation in its entirety. That it did not really take place.

Late-twentieth-century politics

The collapse of the Soviet Union around 1990 was a turning-point. It marked the end of a long-lasting era marked by tense ideological rivalry, and was accompanied by significant reconfigurations of interstate relations. The break-up of old interstate structures unravelled familiar geopolitical patterns. It sparked a world-wide uncertainty which was accentuated by new means of mass communication and deeply affected the development of the world's means of mass-destruction as well as the global means of mass-production. It spurred the evolution of a truly global market-place attended by multicultural eclecticism, where

one listens to reggae, watches a western, eats McDonald's food for lunch and local cuisine for dinner, wears Paris perfume in Tokyo and 'retro' clothes in Hong Kong; knowledge is a matter for TV games. It is easy to find a public for eclectic works. By becoming kitsch, art panders to the confusion which reigns in the 'taste' of the patrons. Artists, gallery owners, critics, and public wallow together in the 'anything goes' … (Lyotard 1983, p. 75).

Lyotard referred in the 1980s to this state of affairs as the 'post-modern condition'. The ideologically divided world of the post-war era was suddenly replaced by the global, mall-like reality of the post-Cold War era, in which time and space are suspended and where eclecticism passes for culture. What consequences does this development have for international relations? What imprints may it leave on International Relations theorizing? These are big and vague questions. More specific foci may emerge through the discussion of a single, big, concrete event: the disintegration of the old East Bloc.

Closures and openings

The disintegration of the East Bloc is a consequence of the unravelling of the Soviet Union. Together these events mark the end of the Cold War – the tense era which had its origins in the conclusion of World War II and in the expansion of a set of geopolitical lines of conflict which erupted in Europe during the late 1940s and rapidly spread from Berlin through Korea, Indo-China and the Middle East to encompass the entire globe. The end of the Cold War, in turn, marks more than the end of an era. Buzan (1995a) sees it as closing no less than *three* eras: the post-war era, the twentieth century and modern history.

The end of the Cold War – and post-Cold War questions
The Soviet Union was the big loser in the Cold War. Around 1990 the USSR acted the way losers have often done after major wars: surrendering its most recent conquests (its 'outer empire'); retreating to a core area designated by its pre-war boundaries; and shifting leadership (with the new leaders trying hard to build friendly relations with the former enemy – an effort involving the credible dismantlement of the old regime type, the public rejection of all that it stood for, and the blaming of the old regime for all that went wrong). It also involved a deep economic crisis.

The West, with the United States as the leading power, was the big winner. Many Westerners were euphoric when the USSR collapsed and the Cold War ended. Around 1990 (as in 1919 and 1946), Western observers of international affairs flirted with utopian theories which claimed that the victory of the liberal-democratic West would open the way to substantial arms reductions and an era of peace and prosperity (Huntington 1991; Fukuyama 1992). The United States, deprived of a defining crusade to inspire its hegemony, began to wind down its leadership and to play a more narrowly self-interested role in world affairs.

The Iraqi invasion of Kuwait, the violent unravelling of Yugoslavia, the eruption of chaos and war in the Caucasus and Rwanda threw disillusion and uncertainty into the camp of the post-Cold War optimists. These were cruel surprises, and they purged post-Cold War politics of its most utopian ideas. They exposed the inability of European states to take on any significant role in global management, and poured cold water on the excessive enthusiasm of European integration. They made it evident that the United States was still the preeminent actor in world affairs and that American leadership was needed to help maintain order in parts of a post-Cold War world. They demonstrated, that when the United States was willing to lead a coalition of sympathetic states, then the West could muster effective responses to international crises.

This acknowledgement broke the old America-in-decline arguments (which had influenced many International Relations scholars since the mid-1970s). It ushered in a new sentiment, according to which a new political climate existed that favoured international co-operation and UN interventions (in Cambodia, Somalia and Bosnia) in the interest of peace, democracy and human rights.

The end of the twentieth century – and twenty-first-century issues
The collapse of the USSR and the end of the Cold War also marked the end of the twentieth century. The century began with the carnage of World War I. Its

main features were mass production, mass education, mass media and mass mobilization. It was also an era of total war and of a world-wide ideological tension between (Atlantic-type) liberal-democratic regime types on the one hand and (Continental) authoritarian or totalitarian regime types on the other – most notably revolutionary communism in Russia and Nazism in Germany (Hobsbawm 1994). There was little doubt that the dominant social formation of the century would be some kind of mass society. But there was a lingering question about the nature of this society's economic base and its mode of political organization.

During the final quarter of the twentieth century it became apparent that the nature of mass society would be of a post-industrial kind. The arrival of new microelectronic means of production altered its economic base: they eroded the old factory system; they forced many factory workers to choose between retraining programmes, early retirement, and unemployment; they pulled the rug out from under traditional working–class-based ideas and ideologies. They stimulated the rise in transnational corporations, of international knowledge-workers, and of a new, multicultural political discourse. Also, it became apparent that the emergent mass society would be society-led and democratic rather than state-led and totalitarian.[2]

With both industrialism and totalitarianism eliminated, the old ideal of an enlightened bourgeois democracy emerged from the 1980s the sole victor. In the post-Cold War world, liberal democracy was the only coherent political aspiration that spanned different regions and cultures around the globe. Ideological speculation about first principles of political and social organization was at an end (Fukuyama 1992). The liberal democracies of the West had, in the end, proved themselves more effective in realizing the human potential of their populations and in harnessing their energies than did their totalitarian competitors. Liberal democracy, then,

has thus survived not just one severe challenge, but three, proving its superiority in both military and economic competition against imperial monarchies, and two types of totalitarian dictatorship. In perspective it becomes clear that a whole round of historic struggle has come to an end, and that Fukuyama's (1992) liberal triumphalism is not without quite impressive foundations (Buzan 1995a, p. 389).

The end of modernity – and post-modern concerns

The collapse of Soviet-style communism and the end of the Cold War also closed the age of modern history. This age began with Europe's maritime explorations of the late fifteenth century. It continued with the colonization of Africa, America and Asia, and with the growth of a new world economy which linked European markets to those of the outer world – to slaves and gold in Africa; to gold, silver and sugar in the Americas; to spices, textiles and gems in Asia (Wolf 1982). This age was also attended by the emergence of the territorial state and the modern state system – first in Europe and, later, in extra-European regions – and with balance-of-power politics.

In this macro-historical perspective, the first 400 years of modern history can be seen as a period during which Western states consolidated their domination of the entire planet. The twentieth century can be interpreted as a period of decline of Western control. This decline occurred in two phases. The first took place during World Wars I and II – which emerge, in this macro-historical portrayal, as European civil wars. Internecine wars which weakened the Europeans' grip of global power. They sapped Europe's economic and military strength, and undermined Western prestige – after the horrors of the Nazi extermination camps, Europe could never again credibly claim to represent a superior 'standard of civilization'; and after Japan's victories over Russian (1905) and American and British (1941/2) forces, white soldiers could no longer be credibly portrayed as invincible. In addition, the European civil wars speeded the democratization of European society at home and helped bring the ideals of mass mobilization, self-determination and industrialization to their extra-European empires, undermining them in the process.

The second phase occurred during the Cold War. From one perspective, this phase embodied the irreversible decline of Western dominance – it was marked by an epic confrontation between liberal democracy and communism that caused the final self-exhaustion of the West. From another perspective, the second phase concluded with the world-wide triumph of Western social ideals like statehood, democratization and industrialism – the territorial state was the dominant social formation in the twentieth-century world; mass mobilization of the state's citizenry through institutions of democratic participation became the main criterion for state legitimacy; industrialization emerged as the recognized basis for states' viability and development.

The Western ideals spread unevenly among the states and regions of the world. Their growth was slow and hesitant in much of Africa. But the ideals struck firm roots in Asia – indeed, many Asian countries (Japan, South Korea and other 'small dragons', India and China) emerged as centres of industrial production and power during the final quarter of the twentieth century. Overall, a more globally distributed and multiculturally-industrial order has replaced the old world order in which Western states were pre-eminent actors in economic and political affairs – in which Asia is playing an increasingly significant role. This development goes hand in hand with several other trends. Capital and industrial products are for example moved over the surface of the earth in larger quantities and with greater efficiency than earlier. Countries now import from abroad a larger share of what they consume than they did a few decades ago. These movements are increasingly controlled by multinational corporations operating smoothly across state boundaries. These developments in trade, interdependence and transnationalism have demolished traditional notions of self-sufficiency and independence. Indeed, they have chipped away at the very core of the sovereign nation state – and, according to some, endangered its continued survival.

The three paradigms transformed

The end of the Cold War introduced new issues in the study of international relations. It also introduced new ways of approaching the issues. Some assessments of International Relations theory emphasize the importance of historical continuities (Olson and Groom 1991; Chanteur 1992; Thompson 1994); others wriggle, quicksilver-like, between epochs and ideas as if time and space did not matter (Der Derian 1995). Some authors highlight the fragmented and fluid nature of events (Walker 1993); others emphasize the seamless whole of world affairs and the basic patterns of global governance (Rosenau 1995).

The old, familiar Cold-War world unravelled unexpectedly during the 1990s, forcing students of international politics to redirect their attention towards new questions and issues. Moreover, familiar concepts, through which the world was observed and understood, were corroded. To the question of *what* we should study was added a mounting uncertainty about *how* we should study. To a good number of observers, these questions poured new oil on old anti-positivist embers. Traditional approaches to International Relations encountered a barrage of criticism. Halliday (1994) warned against two major threats to post-Cold War International Relations: on the one hand factual accounts void of theoretical reflection, and on the other theorizing unanchored in historical analysis. Gaddis (1993) ridiculed the way in which students of international relations cling to antiquated methodological precepts imported from the natural sciences, stressing that they need to proceed along firmer, more historically informed, lines. Connolly (1993) agrees, but would add that the study of world affairs needs to be informed by a discourse analysis anchored in the arguments of Nietzsche and Wittgenstein. More radical authors insist on importing to the study of International Relations 'post-positivist' insights (Smith, Booth and Zalewski 1996, pp. 11ff) from semiotics, genealogy, psychoanalysis, feminism, intertextualism and deconstruction ...[3]

This section will assess some of these changes and arguments. It will use as a simple focusing device the question: what has become of the three familiar paradigms of Realism, Rationalism and Revolutionism in the post-Cold War era?

Neo-liberalism

The fate of the Rationalist paradigm is easily summarized. It met beautiful theories of co-operation, was swept off its feet, and eloped with a travelling band of economists.

Co-operation theory emerged from Economics around 1980. When an easy ideology of market liberalism swept the USA and England in the early 1980s, many economists shifted their attention away from old models of market equilibrium towards new theories about market breakdown. They explored new questions and built new, often historically-informed, theories of political economy. Under labels like 'institutional economics' (Buchanan and Tullock 1962) and 'constitutional economics' (Brennan and Buchanan 1985) they developed various kinds of co-operation theories to illuminate problems of market failure. Most of them drew heavily on social-contract theories to explain the preconditions for effective co-operation. On the one hand, these discussions put back on to the economists' agenda concerns which had long been dismissed by neoclassical approaches. On the other, they built bridges to other social sciences.

International Relations scholars quickly embraced such neo-institutional arguments, and imported them from the world of firms to that of states. The old question of why wars occur when all states involved in them want peace, could then be expressed in co-operation-theory terms: when rational, self-interested actors interrelate, they sometimes reach sub-optimal solutions and thus fail to maximize their utilities. International Relations scholars dressed their arguments up in the Nobel-Prize winning garb of Douglass North or James Buchanan. North (1981) resolved failures of co-operation between firms and states alike by creating institutional arrangements which provide information, monitoring and enforced solutions. Robert Keohane (1984) and Arthur Stein (1990) similarly 'resolved' world conflicts by establishing international organizations with comparable functions.

The decline of traditional market models and the rise of more complex, philosophically rich and historically self-conscious social theories built bridges among the social sciences. North (1990, p. 14) probed the nature of market exchanges by asking: 'Under what conditions can voluntary co-operation exist without the Hobbesian solution of the imposition of a coercive state to create co-operative solutions?' International Relations scholars immediately picked up their ears. This was a question about the behaviour of rational actors in anarchic societies – a problem which International Relations Realists have discussed for more than 300 years. 'Under what conditions can independent countries co-operate in the world political economy? In particular, can co-operation take place without hegemony and, if so, how?' asked Keohane (1984, p. 9). His answer became a prizewinning book about international co-operation – firmly founded in institutional economics.

Neo-Realism

The evolution of neo-liberalism was intimately associated with developments of the Realist paradigm, and cannot be properly appreciated without examining the fate of Realism more closely.

The Realist paradigm dominated the early post-war field of International Relations. During the late 1960s – during the age of superpower *détente* – Realism was challenged by an ascending wave of liberal theorists who scoffed at its 'billiard-ball world view' and advocated a 'cobweb model' as a more appropriate metaphor for international relations (Mitrany 1933, 1966; Burton 1972). In 1979, with the Soviet invasion of Afghanistan marking the final collapse of *détente*, the advocates of complex interdependence were caught off balance by the 'second Cold War'. Also in 1979, Kenneth Waltz published his *Theory of International Politics*, arguably the most influential International Relations text of the 1980s.

Waltz transcended the traditional limits of Realist analyses. In fact, he self-consciously and in full view entered the encampment of the economists, availed himself of useful concepts and theories (such as the microeconomic theory of the firm). When he returned, he had lost none of his basic Realist faith. Rather, he claimed to have found a more solid social-scientific foundation for Realist analysis, thereby contributing greatly to restoring the flagging fortunes of Realism. For example, he insisted that the effort to explain state behaviour is predicated on a focus on power and on a careful treatment of the level-of-analysis problem – that only by investigating the properties of the interstate system is it possible to understand the behaviour of states. At the same time, Waltz also transcended the Arch-Realist argument. Two such paths of transcendence are particularly noteworthy. First, Waltz is more 'scientific' than traditional Realists: he intends to distil from systematic observations of state behaviour a few general laws about interstate interaction and a few basic axioms about the structural properties of the international system.

Second, although Waltz insists on scientific rigour, he rejects mainstream social-science methods. These are useless because they are simple derivations from natural-science methods, which investigate 'parts' in order to draw conclusions about the 'whole'. Waltz, by contrast, intends to investigate the whole to explain the parts. His important point is that in international politics the whole (the interstate system) is more than the sum of the parts (the constituent states). He observes that different statesmen and different states regularly engage in similar behaviour, and he draws the conclusion that innate properties of states do not really determine their behaviour. Interstate behaviour is better explained in terms of the structure of the interstate system. The parts (the individual states) are determined by the whole (the interstate system), claimed Waltz, and in order to identify the determining agents (which are properties of the whole), he needs a more suitable method than that which is offered by traditional social sciences.

To define the structure of the international system (without referring to innate state properties), Waltz needs a structural method which can help him navigate between the Scylla of reductionism and the Charybdis of tautology. This method involves three stages. First, he consults writings (often outside the field of Political Science) where he finds a general definition of *structure*: 'Structure defines the arrangement, or the ordering, of the parts of a system' (p. 81).

He then delves into systems theory to explore *political structures*. He identifies three salient dimensions of political structures: (1) their ordering principles –

which means in practice that a social structure is either hierarchic or anarchic; (2) the extent of specialization (or functional differentiation) of the constituent parts; and (3) the relative capabilities of their parts.

Finally, he defines *international political structures* in terms of how they vary along their three salient dimensions. He concludes that (1) international political structures are ordered according to the principle of anarchy, that (2) their constituent parts are not functionally differentiated, but that (3) the relative capabilities of their parts vary in terms of power. Thus, through a rather lengthy and abstract discussion that draws heavily on Durkheim, Waltz arrives at the old, Realist chestnut that the international system is anarchic in nature. But he adds a controversial point: since the constituent units of the system are functionally similar, all concerns about their differentiation 'drop out'. All analysis of interstate relations, he concludes, can safely disregard the different functions performed by states. This means that structures of international systems differ only along the third dimension, that which concerns the distribution of power. Thus, when Waltz wants to explain the behaviour of states, he pays no attention to their internal properties (p. 99; cf. also Ruggie 1986, p. 142)!

Waltz retains many features of Realism – for example the focus on state relations and the preoccupation with anarchy and with power. But he also deviates from the Realist tradition in several respects – he takes on fundamental philosophy-of-science issues by discussing basic terms like 'laws' and 'theories'; he seeks to purge useless natural-science methods from the study of international politics; he draws on insights from outside the traditional province of politics. Such deviations, together with the high scientific ambitions of the project and the controversial implications which flow from its logic,[4] triggered an intense debate.

One critical charge has been levelled at Waltz repeatedly: his theory is static. Like most structural theories, it cannot adequately account for historical change. It cannot, for example, illuminate the transition from medieval to modern politics. John Ruggie (1986) notes that medieval and modern politics can both be described as international (and therefore anarchic) systems. But they are based on two different kinds of institutional frameworks. The modern system is a 'sovereignty-system'; it is composed of sovereign states separated by impermeable boundaries which distinguish between 'internal' and 'external' political realms. The medieval system, by contrast, was a 'heteronomous' system; no obvious boundaries separated one territory from the next and, consequently, no distinction could be made between 'internal' and external' politics. Ruggie's point is that Waltz has been too eager to eliminate the inherent characteristics of the system's constituent units. Some international events can only be properly addressed in terms of inherent characteristics, and the transition from medieval to modern politics is such an event. And it is not just any event. It is arguably the most important event in International Relations history of the last 1000 years.

Waltz' book is methodologically sophisticated and theoretically rich. Its grounding in social-science classics, contemporary systems theory, and rational-actor models, and its flirtation with structural anthropology and linguistics triggered immediate controversy. The debate which followed its publication transcended narrow preoccupations with states and power. It addressed the nature of theory-building, the relationship between methods and methodologies, the appropriate procedural designs for the study of International Relations and other abstract, philosophy-of-science related issues. Waltz' *Theory of International Politics* quickly became the centrepiece of a new approach which dominated International Relations theory during the 1980s: 'Neo-Realism'.

How has Waltz' *Theory* and its neo-Realist elaborations fared during this debate? Waltz' Popperian research agenda, his positivist method and his appeals to economic theory are in tatters. However, his structural research programme remains intact. This, at least, is the verdict of Barry Buzan, Richard Little and Charles Jones. Buzan (1995b), in particular, has re-examined Waltz' concept of 'structure'. He has ended up agreeing with Waltz' (first basic) proposition: that the international political system is composed of sovereign states whose interaction is ordered according to the principle of anarchy. But he disagrees with Waltz' (second basic) proposition that states are functionally undifferentiated and that concerns about the internal properties of states can, accordingly, be disregarded in systemic analysis.[5]

Buzan argues, like Ruggie (1986), that the international system has more levels than Waltz admits. He makes his point by adding a distinction between two kinds of international structures. On the one hand is the system's 'deep structure', which remains constant across centuries. On the other is the 'distributional structure', which ensures the allocation of capabilities among the units. This introduction leads Buzan to refine Waltz' (third basic) proposition: that the relative capabilities of states vary in terms of capabilities of power. States possess more than one kind of capability, argues Buzan. They have different kinds of capabilities in different areas, and they translate them into different kinds of power in different situations. Thus, Buzan introduces a new dimension to International Relations analysis: 'interaction capacity'. In theory, it concerns the 'types and intensities of interaction that are possible within any given unit/subsystem/system at the point of analysis' (Buzan 1995b, pp. 204f; also Ruggie 1986). In practice, it means the inclusion of technology – of 'the level of transportation, communication and organization capability' (Buzan 1995b, pp. 204f) of the various states. This inclusion allows for analyses of technology-driven change in the light of a structural-Realist theory. It permits the analyst to draw on new varieties of theories – on unequal-rate-of-development theories (Lenin 1975b; Kennedy 1987) and power-transition theories (Organski and Kugler 1980), among others.

Concrete results of these conceptual elaborations are apparent in *The Logic of Anarchy* (Buzan, Little and Jones 1993). In this book the authors revise the

Waltzian model in a way which meets Ruggie's (1986) critique and which enables them to analyse pre-modern as well as modern social formations. Richard Little, for example, discusses the Greek city-state system and also the Macedonian Empire. He even challenges the traditional historians by claiming that the Roman Empire did not fall as the result of barbarian invasions, but that it was eroded by increasingly divergent internal economic and social structures.

Buzan *et al.* have broadened the discussion which Waltz initiated. They have made sure that it has become less of a debate about interstate politics and more one of international relations. They have also reintroduced important Realist points, which were pushed aside by the Neo-Realist insistence on using rational-actor models, to the study of interstate relations – they have, for example, reintroduced History and the old insight that although states may be the most important actors in world affairs, states are man-made and contingent.[6] Thus they have brought notions of change and evolution back to the interstate system. But they have done so at the price of simplicity. Much like the Renaissance astronomers who scribbled cycles and epicycles all over Ptolemy's beautiful vision of the heavens, Buzan *et al.* have cluttered up the streamlined simplicity of Neo-Realism.

Post-Revolutionism
The Revolutionist paradigm transmuted during the 1980s (Linklater 1990), and all but collapsed in the wake of the Cold War.[7] But the radical spirit which it embodied was not quenched; it re-emerged in new, post-industrial, post-modern forms. And Kenneth Waltz played an unlikely, catalytic role in the development of new, radical approaches to International Relations theory. Waltz' Neo-Realist revolution produced a handful of clear and simple maxims which were easy to criticize, and he immediately became a favourite *Prügelknabe* for a group of post-revolutionary radicals. One of these was Richard Ashley, who claimed that although Waltz sought to purge the doctrinaire natural-science ideal from the study of International Relations, he nevertheless embraced a positivist philosophy of science. Waltz' *Theory* is only interested in power and in expanding social control, argued Ashley:

What emerges is a positivist structuralism that treats the given order as the natural order, limits, rather than expands political discourse, negates or trivializes the significance of variety across time and place, subordinates all practice to an interest in control, bows to the ideal of a social power beyond responsibility, and thereby deprives political interaction of those practical capacities which make social learning and creative change possible. What emerges is an ideology that anticipates, legitimizes, and orients a totalitarian project of global proportions (Ashley 1986, p. 258).

These were fighting words. Readers reacted strongly. Many thought it absurd to call Waltz' theory 'totalitarian'.

To appreciate Ashley's critique, it is helpful to make a brief detour to the

Dialectic of Enlightenment – a book which was written in exile (in Los Angeles) by two German refugees, Theodor Adorno and Max Horkheimer, in 1944 'when the end of the Nazi terror was within sight' (Adorno and Horkheimer 1979, p. ix). The authors begin by arguing that modern, positivist science is 'totalitarian', and that this totalitarian tendency originates with the Age of Enlightenment. But they hurry to add that the problem does not lie with the theoretical orientation of the Enlightenment project; rather, it lies with its practice. They recall that the vision of the Enlightenment was to emancipate humanity from superstition and alienation through the progressive operations of critical reason. In its eager desire to unmask superstition and reveal myths, the Enlightenment project created a vision of the natural world as abstract matter which was subject to human reason and control. Enlightenment science, with its methods of counting, weighing and calculating, would be the tool of human emancipation. 'From now on, matter would at last be mastered without any illusion of ruling or inherent powers, of hidden qualities. For the Enlightenment, whatever does not conform to the rule of computation and utility is suspect (p. 7). The big mistake, then, was to embrace 'the schema of calculability of the world'. Enlightenment scientists went astray when they adopted the view that 'that which does not reduce to numbers ... becomes an illusion; modern positivism writes it off as literature'.

Adorno and Horkheimer argue that modern science has reduced human reason to *mathesis* – i.e. to a specific form of reason. This specific form is presented as if it were reason as such; as if it were the only valid and legitimate form of rational thinking; as if it were science in its totality. When Ashley called Waltz' project 'totalitarian', this concept of *mathesis* informed his charge.

This portrayal of modern science as an oppressive straitjacket lies at the core of much post-structural theory. This is apparent in Jim George's *(Re)introduction to International Relations*. Its aim is to take issue with a discourse which, 'as "International Relations", reduces a complex and turbulent world to a patterned and rigidly ordered framework of understanding, derived from a particular representation of post-Renaissance European historical experience' (George 1994, p. ix). Rob Walker, similarly, intends to 'develop a sceptical stance about the possibility of understanding "world politics" through the categories of modern theories of "international relations"' (Walker 1993, p. ix).

Ashley, George, Walker and other post-structuralists are informed not only by Adorno's idea of a corrupting *mathesis*, but also by their status as refugees. Like Adorno, they claim to speak 'the language of exile' (Ashley and Walker 1990). Like him they adopted a metaphysical stance of restlessness and movement; of constantly being unsettled – and unsettling others (Said 1996, p. 53). Like him they adopted a mannered and convoluted style.

Notions of *mathesis* and exile, cores and margins inform a varied set of post-revolutionary International Relations theories which are often lumped together under the term 'post-structuralism'. It is a fashionable label. It is often uncritically applied and surrounded by conceptual unclarity. But it is helpful to recall that the post-structural impulse is Continental in origin – that its trunk grows from the turn-of-the-century Continental opponents of the liberal, Atlantic faith in progress (notably from Haeckel, Freud and Nietzsche).[8] Yet, in contemporary International Relations analysis, post-structural perspectives have been associated mainly with younger Anglo-American scholars who have distinguished themselves by an intense criticism of the prevailing (Anglo-American) methodology of Neo-Realism and neo-liberalism.

Some sceptics argue that post-structuralism is in essence a destructive project which cannot provide any constructive alternative to established social-science approaches. This is not accurate. In fact, post-structural approaches like 'archaeology', 'genealogy' and 'deconstruction' have contributed creatively to International Relations theory since the mid-1980s. 'Archaeology' is an analytic tool designed to 'excavate' a particular 'site' of knowledge and reach below the level of epistemology. Its purpose is to uncover more basic layers of meaning and identify the deeper 'internal rules' which guide scientific investigations. The archaeological approach has been famously used by Michel Foucault in several of his early historical studies of institutionalized (and thus marginalized) groups, such as the mad, the sick and the criminal. His *Order of Things* (1973 [1966]) has exerted a great influence on students of world affairs and teased many of them to write archaeologies of International-Relations knowledge – the present *History of International Relations Theory* being a case in point.

'Genealogy' (like 'archaeology') investigates the relationship between knowledge and power. But whereas archaeology focuses on knowledge (and language), genealogy emphasizes power (and discursive practices). Squarely put, 'genealogy' is historiography written in the light of current concerns. Genealogical investigations are undertaken to shine a critical light on unquestioned values and truth-claims by showing how all truths are, in fact, products of past practices. Foucault used this approach in several of his later works. But he was, like many other post-structural authors, inspired by Nietzsche (Foucault 1984b), who sought to trace moral rules back to concrete historical and social circumstances – ultimately to naked power struggles (Nietzsche 1994). Jens Bartelson, Bradley Klein and James Der Derian demonstrate the constructive contributions which such an approach may render the study of International Relations. Bartelson argues that the history of international relations is usually studied in the light of a modern concept of sovereignty. His *Genealogy of Sovereignty* (1995) relies on the late Foucault to criticize such accounts of international history and reveal 'the unthought foundations of our political knowledge' (p. 4). Klein, too, relies on Foucault. He argues in *Strategic Studies and World Order* (1994) that key concepts in strategic studies ('deterrence', 'balance of power', 'alliances' ...) acquire their meaning in concrete political circumstances, and that the meaning changes to sustain the shape of contemporary political life (p. 10). In *Writing Security* David Campbell (1992) draws on similar arguments to analyse US foreign and defence policies after the Cold War. In *On Diplomacy* (1987) Der Derian relies on Nietzsche, and argues that historians have tended to interpret diplomatic relations of the past in light of their own (modern) experiences. As a consequence they have mistakenly portrayed the history of diplomacy as a progressive evolution of rational negotiation; as a neat progression of reason and reasonable interaction. Der Derian boldly proposes to write an alternative history – one which conceptualizes 'diplomacy' not as the 'art of negotiation' (Nicolson 1954, p. 2), but through Nitzschean notions of power as 'mediation of estranged peoples organized in states which interact in a system' (Der Derian 1987, p. 42).⁹ The result is a very different diplomatic history – in fact, it is several different histories, which all seek to reveal the conceptual illusions which have so often deluded the more traditional historians of interstate relations (Der Derian 1995, pp. 380ff).

'Deconstruction' is a third post-structural approach. It, too, shines a critical light on unquestioned truth-claims. But deconstruction does not delve into the deeper layers of meaning; it 'plays off surfaces'. Rather than showing how truth-claims are shaped by history, it attempts to demonstrate their value-laden nature by exposing their internal contradictions. Deconstruction was developed by Jacques Derrida in the 1960s for purposes of literary criticism. In his view, Western thought has been in the habit of defining its key concepts in pairs of opposition – right/wrong, subject/object, value/fact, mind/body, form/content, theory/practice, particular/universal, self/other … While these pairs are usually presented as neutral descriptions, Derrida observes, it is in fact quietly understood that the terms are hierarchically arranged – that one of the terms is superior (or privileged) and the other inferior (or deferred). During the 1980s, deconstruction suddenly caught the attention of young International Relations scholars, who noted that key IR-concepts often come in pairs and thus were sitting ducks for deconstructionist techniques – war/peace, friend/foe, order/anarchy, Idealism/Realism, domestic/foreign, centre/periphery. Deconstruction seeks to reveal the criteria (and their ideological nature) which undergird this hierarchy of privilege. It seeks to expose power where it is claimed that only reason exists. In the essay 'Living on Border Lines' (1989) Richard Ashley relies on Derrida's techniques to deconstruct the dichotomy man/war which undergirds Kenneth Waltz' book *Man, State and War* (1959). In *Inside/outside* (1993) R. B. J. Walker draws on Nietzsche, Foucault and Derrida to 'destabilise seemingly opposed categories by showing how they are at once mutually constitutive and yet always in the process of dissolving into each other' (Walker 1993, p. 25). In *Simulating Sovereignty* Cynthia Weber (1995) relies on Baudrillard to explore the conceptual pair sovereignty/intervention, which, she argues, lies undiscussed at the heart of modern International Relations theory.

Post-structural authors tend to agree with Adorno and Horkheimer's view of modern science as an oppressive *mathesis*. The terms by which they characterize the mechanisms of oppression may vary from one author to the next – Foucault (1973, pp. 71ff) uses the word *mathesis*, but Lyotard uses the term 'meta-narratives', while Derrida refers to the iron cage of 'logocentrism'. But underneath the variations in labelling lies one constant, unifying notion: that the discourse of modern science forces upon its participants a narrowly-focused, exclusivist and intolerant scheme whose oppressive clutches it is imperative to escape. This notion is the irreducible core of post-structuralism. Stripped of all its linguistic jargon, post-structuralism hinges on the axiom that language is constitutive of social reality. The argument is that, since human beings grasp the world around them through language, language ought to be at the centre of their investigations about the world.

In this light it is easy to see that post-structural approaches to International Relations involve a change in focus: away from international actors, interactions and structures towards the concepts through which actors and interactions are understood. It redirects attention away from the world towards the discursive constructions by means of which the world is constituted – and towards the socio-linguistic processes through which these constructions are themselves constructed.

It is also easy to understand why so many critics repeatedly brush aside post-structural analysis as non-scientific or irrelevant: it puts no demand on its employers to touch empirical reality. Post-structural methods have driven some scholars to establish new arguments on solid, empirical bases (Foucault 1973; Der Derian 1987). But they have allowed others to lead aloof existences as parasites along the margins of established texts, lost in ever-multiplying interpretations and elaborate loops of constructivist self-reference.

The fate of the paradigms
The three core paradigms of International Relations research grew blurry and ambiguous during the 1990s. Like three plates of pudding moved from the safety of the freezer into hot, soapy water, the paradigms dissolved as they were immersed in post-Cold War realities. They dissolved and floated over into each other. Also, they mixed with other approaches.

Revolutionism has all but dissolved. Younger analysts have found its discourse of nineteenth-century evolutionism outmoded and its historic teleology simplistic. However, the radical attitudes which found a particular expression in the Revolutionist approach have been conserved in other, more properly post-modern approaches – among which ecologism and constructivism may be the most important.

Realism, too, is presenting itself in an altered suit. In the post-Cold War world it no longer allows itself to be unambiguously defined in terms of a state-centric analysis; it prefers to be associated with problems of level-of-analysis and anarchy. The focus on anarchy is an old, Realist notion (for 'among men as among states, anarchy, or the absence of government, is associated with the occurrence of violence' (Waltz 1979, p. 102). But efforts to explore the anarchic condition through economic models pushed Realist analysis in a liberal direction and, in some cases, well into the liberal camp. For anarchy, as Onuf (1989, pp. 18f) remarks, may simply be 'liberalism carried to its logical extreme'. The result is that the old, neat distinction between Realism and Rationalism has disappeared. The resulting confusion is exacerbated by Rationalists' importation of highly formal models from co-operation theory and institutional economics. For through this import Rationalism, too, began self-consciously to entertain the old Realist claim that anarchy is the distinctive condition in the international system. At century's end, representatives from the two old rival paradigms thus met in the economists' camp. Both explored the problem of anarchy, and they did this in common utilitarian and rationalistic ways.

New questions, new projects, new paradigms?

During the late 1980s and early 1990s, students of International Relations raised a great variety of new questions (Smith, Booth and Zalewski 1996) and sparked a good number of new projects. Have any of them occasioned the rise of new paradigms?

The question may be explored by addressing one of the most divisive issues in the study of post-Cold War International Relations: the origins of collective identities – nation, state, federation, *ethnie*, tribe, gender, class, culture, civilization …. It is a common claim in post-Cold War International Relations theory that collective identities are constructed through communicative acts. This claim is, in turn, attended by several scholarly reorientations. One of these is a movement in analytic focus away from objects and towards meanings. Thus, many students of International Relations are no longer preoccupied with states and state interaction; instead, they explore the meaning of 'state'. They ask how concepts like 'state' and 'statehood' are constructed and what marks the discourses through which 'state interaction' can be observed and described. These new debates do not discuss states and interstate structures (or patterns); they explore ways in which key concepts like 'states', 'structures' and 'patterns' are constructed. This change from objects to meanings is expressed in a renewed preoccupation with the basic concepts of the discipline – such as 'power', 'security', 'sovereignty', 'diplomacy' … It is also evident in a renewed interest in normative approaches to International Relations (C. Brown 1992) and in the interrelations of collective identities – either horizontal interrelationships (e.g. between different ethnic groups) or vertical ones (between identities on different levels – between region and nation, nation and territorial state, state and world society …).

One notable revival concerns the old idea that the construction of collective 'selves' is attended by constructions of collective 'others'. This argument has long been explored by anthropologists and by Continental political thinkers (Nietzsche 1994; Schmitt 1932; Todorov 1989). More recently it has been discussed by scholars of non-Western origins, who have explored Occidental attitudes towards the Orient (Said 1978; MacKenzie 1995) in order to identify 'an alternative perspective on modern oppression' (Nandy 1987, p. xv). Around the end of the Cold War, this idea also enjoyed a rapid revival among Western scholars, through whom it had a substantial impact on the study of International Relations. Nations and states were increasingly seen as constructed identities, whose interaction could be analysed as mutually constructed relations between 'Selves' and 'Others' (I. Neumann 1996).

This growth of a constructivist attitude has been attended by another reorientation as well: viz a growing acknowledgement of the limits of the traditional study 'International Relations'. A growing number of scholars have become aware of the fact that the study of world politics has largely been a parochial examination of European interstate interaction since the Peace of Westphalia. They have come to doubt the wisdom of this old focus, and wonder whether generalizations derived from the study of the Westphalian state system can be meaningful in our varied, multicultural world (Bozeman 1960). In an in-depth case study of contemporary Iran, Boroujerdi (1996) show how the Islamic intelligentsia discuss Nietzsche, Mannheim, Popper, Heidegger and others in order to fortify Islam against the West. In a vast macro-historical analysis, Ferguson and Mansbach (1996) extend the boundaries of International Relations in space and time. They include new regions (i.e. outside the West) and neglected epochs (before 1648), and add an important intercultural dimension to the field. By expanding their vision, they capture clearly the parochial nature of traditional International Relations analysis. They demonstrate how recent an actor the territorial state really is. They display its Western origins. They also show that central concepts like national unity and state sovereignty have been greatly exaggerated in the professional literature.

Reorientations such as these suggest that rather than producing novel paradigms, post-Cold War theory debates have largely bypassed the concept of paradigms altogether. The debate about the origins and nature of collective identities suggests quite strongly that the study of International Relations has in the 1990s turned away from such encompassing templates and instead approached basic issues of ontology and epistemology. It suggests that a constructivist turn affects the study of world affairs. Constructivism is not one theory. It is a family of theories. As such it has many members who share some characteristic family resemblances. The most central of these is a common concern about how world politics is socially constructed.

First, in order to position constructivism among other approaches to the study of international relations, it is helpful to begin with two questions. The first asks whether states or international structures are the most appropriate focus for the study; the second asks whether the international system is material or social in nature (Wendt and Friedheim 1996, p. 244). Constructivists tend to see international structures as the most appropriate focus for study, and to see the international system as largely social in nature. Thus, they distinguish themselves from (neo)liberals (who tend to focus on states and their social interaction), from (Neo)Realists (who tend to focus on states and their material capabilities), and from old-fashioned radicals (who tend to focus on international structures, but define them in material terms).[10]

Second, to illustrate the diversity within the constructivist family, it is useful to distinguish between two opposite ontological orientations: one of which may be labelled 'relativist' and the other 'empiricist'. The relativists dismiss the notion of an external reality which is accessible to the human mind. Their argument therefore falls back on human reason and reflection as the sole source of knowledge. Foucault illustrates the implications of this radical stand. For by rejecting the notion of a cognitively approachable world, he also dismissed any hope of ever observing and describing real-world events. Foucault would say to social scientists who look for patterns and order in world events that they are wasting their time (at best). He would tell them that the world is neither orderly nor disorderly; rather, it is what it appears to be. He would advise them to turn their attention away from the world and focus instead on human perceptions of the world. He would tell them to observe the observers and interpret the interpreters ... For, when push comes to shove, the only things a social scientist can really investigate are the various 'rhetorical renderings' which humans impose upon the world. A moderate and quite common interpretation of Foucault's position holds that a scholar cannot say everything; that for every claim made there are several other possible claims that are silenced (and many of these may be important). But there also exists a more radical inference – one that informs the approach of many post-men (Ashley, Klein, Walker and others) and that flirts with nihilism, because it is encumbered by a self-defeating implication that attends all relativistic positions: if the basic idea of an external reality is dismissed and if theory is reduced to social and linguistic constructions, then there is no reason to prefer any scholarly (including post-structuralist) arguments to those made by any accidental pedestrian. What is sauce for the goose is sauce for the gander. If relativism is consistently applied, it will destroy traditional scholarship; but it will also destroy its own foundations.

The empiricist members of the constructivist family avoid this paradox. They accept the notion that an external world exists and that it is cognitively approachable. At the same time they embrace the idea that human agents construct the social world which they inhabit. They see structures as the most appropriate focus for the study of society, but they are loath to consider it primary. They give primacy neither to subject (human agent) nor object ('society', social institutions or structures). They argue that each is constituted by the other through recurrent practices. Through deeds done, acts performed and words spoken, people construct the society around them. And they are, in turn, constituted by it. Underneath this idea lies a basic assumption about human nature: humans are active, social, creative beings. 'In the beginning was the deed', writes Onuf (1989, p. 36) with a nod to Wittgenstein. And he goes on to argue that subjects (agents) relate to objects in the world (including other agents) on the basis of the meanings that the objects have for them. Thus states relate to each other on the basis of meanings (and not by virtue of some distribution of power, as the Neo-Realists would have us believe). States separate enemies from friends simply because they see enemies as threatening and friends as co-operative (not because enemies are stronger and friends are weaker). So Wendt (1995, p. 73) can argue that '500 British nuclear weapons are less threatening to the United States than 5 North Korean weapons'. Wendt goes on to claim that actors acquire identities through involvement in recurrent practices – i.e. relatively stable, role-specific understandings of their 'self' (and expectations about their 'others'). Ruggie (1993a, pp 14ff) explains how recurrent practices give rise to collective understandings among participant actors: that they constitute patterned interrelationships which provide the bases for norms, rules and even laws, which then regulate interaction.

The constructivists make up a large family. There is a great distance between its relativist and its empiricist members. There is ample room for many different arguments between the extreme positions, and a great many of different claims have influenced the study of International Relations since the 1980s. For example, Ruggie's devastating critique of Waltz' *Theory* has an empirical–constructivist core. Ruggie (1986, 1993b) rejects the claim that international life has operated as an anarchic self-help system for centuries; he argues instead that the international system operates on codes of norms, rules and 'exchange considerations', and that these are constantly (re)constituted through recurrent practices. A similar logic lies at the heart of Kratochwil's works. He counters the realist image of the international system with a constructivist alternative: an ensemble of norms and rules that are constituted through recurrent practices. His constructivist vantage point, fortified with a keen knowledge of international law, provides Kratochwil (1989) with a powerful refutation of the notion that lies at the heart of Neo-Realist (and neo-liberal) analysis: the image of international politics as a normless anarchy.

The constructivists have a simple core claim in common: viz, that conceptualization is prior to observation; that the meaning of empirical facts depends on the conceptions that frame them. The great variety of members in the constructivist family allows for many variations on the constructivists' core theme. Towards the relativist corner one finds Nicholas Onuf (1989), who is informed by Wittgenstein and Foucault. Among the empirical members is Alexander Wendt, who draws on American pragmatists like Rorty and European sociologists like Giddens, Berger and Luckmann – and who easily converses with US regime theorists and neo-institutionalists (like Robert Keohane, who is a frequent gate-crasher of many such family gatherings). They all agree that the structures of international politics are outcomes of social interaction; that states are not static subjects, but dynamic agents; that state identities are not given, but (re)constituted through complex, historical, overlapping (often contradictory) practices – and therefore volatile, unstable, constantly changing; that the distinction between domestic politics and international relations is tenuous (Biersteker and Weber 1996).

Concluding remarks

Captain Lemuel Gulliver, it may be recalled, had a habit of commanding rickety vessels which were blown off course. On one occasion, he departed Europe and shipwrecked off the country of Lilliput, where the people were tiny and Gulliver a comparative giant. Here he advised the Emperor on issues of war and peace, and tended to observe Lilliputian affairs from a bird's-eye perspective of power and macro-strategy (Swift 1992, pp. 42ff). On a second occasion, Gulliver shipwrecked off the coast of North America and drifted ashore in Brobdingnag. He found the inhabitants so huge that he feared they might squash him under foot, and when he observed society he tended to focus on individuals who were predisposed towards reducing questions of politics 'to common sense and reason ...' (p. 143). A third occasion stranded Gulliver in a starkly divided country. On the one hand were the Yahoos, who were 'cunning, malicious, treacherous and revengeful'; on the other were the noble Houyhnhnms, who were 'endowed by nature with a general disposition to all virtues ...' (pp. 284, 285).

Students who first encounter post-Cold War International Relations theory may, at times, wonder if they have entered a land in which representatives from all the exotic civilizations visited by Gulliver were brought together to compose a multicultural community criss-crossed by conceptual divisions. Some scholars define their activities in relation to one of the three old competing paradigms. Others have jettisoned the paradigm approach altogether, arguing that it imposes a confining set of epistemological and ontological assumptions upon the study of world affairs (S. Smith 1992, p. 492).

But Gulliver also made a fourth voyage, during the course of which he travelled through Laputa, Balnibari, Luggnagg and Glubbdubdrib when his account of this trip is read in the light of post-Cold War debates, they emerge as the most interesting of his (mis)adventures. For these are journeys during which Gulliver converses eagerly on basic issues of science and philosophy. He reports on one scholar who has worked many years to extract sunshine from cucumbers. He notes that another has tried to convert human excrement back to its original food. That a third has contrived a method for building houses from the roof downwards. A fourth scholar, who was born blind, has long instructed several apprentices in the art of mixing colours for painters, which he taught them to distinguish by texture and smell. His technique has some flaws. Gulliver reports that the students were rather imperfect in their lessons, and that the professor himself happened to be generally mistaken – although he was 'much encouraged and esteemed by the whole fraternity' (Swift 1992, p. 192).

The new International Relations debate may appear confusing and fragmented at first sight. Some scholars claim that the international system is the most appropriate focus for International Relations; others focus on individual actors. Some emphasize material variables, while others stress the importance of social dynamics. However, one dividing line appears to blaze through the arguments and divide the late-twentieth century International Relations society into two camps: the 'scientists' on the one hand and the 'humanists' on the other. The scientists claim that human beings can be observed, counted and measured like rocks, trees, stars and other objects in nature. The humanists insist that the activities of humankind are not amenable to such traditional scientific treatment. The fronts of this struggle are old. French historian Hippolyte Taine formulated the scientific case in the mid–nineteenth century, when he claimed that cultural science is nothing other than a form of applied botany. The German historian Wilhelm Dilthey provided a famous retort when he argued that in the natural sciences objects of nature are classified and categorized by humanity: they do not categorize themselves. In the human sciences, by contrast, humanity always encounters a wealth of pre-existing categories and organizing principles. Thus, human life does not come to us as 'data', but as life already lived and sated with meanings and interpretations. The scientist–humanist struggle has been assessed by Droyson, Simmel, Weber and many others.[11] One recent assessment concludes thus:

One side has said that "explanation" (subsumption under predictive laws, roughly) presupposes, and cannot replace, "understanding". The other side has said that understanding simply is the ability to explain, that what their opponents call "understanding" is merely the primitive stage of groping around for exploratory hypotheses. Both sides are quite right (Rorty 1979, p. 347).

Why has the old struggle re-emerged in the 1990s? One common answer refers to the end of the Cold War. It holds that old Stalinist control structures unravelled – first in Eastern Europe, then in the Soviet Union itself; that these were momentous political events which unravelled the political structures of the East and shook established political paradigms in the West. For example, the fact that IR-scholars were just as surprised by the unravelling of the Eastern Bloc as everybody else raised the embarrassing question of whether long and specialized studies in International Relations do, in fact, yield any privileged insight into world affairs. This uncomfortable question was exploited by critics of the field's traditional method (Gaddis 1993). The failure to foresee the collapse of the USSR presented an opportunity for them to revel in the shortcomings of the positivist methodology and to present controversial alternatives. This mode of reasoning helps explain why new debates erupted in the late 1980s. But it does not explain why the anti-positivist critique was dressed in radical constructivist garments.

Another answer is linked to the communications revolution. New systems of telecommunications and new means of global transport and world travel have helped create a novel, intricate web of international transactions, organized and managed by transnational firms.[12] As these factors began to affect local markets under rules laid down by national governments, fundamental changes occurred in the economic base of states. And in interstate interaction as well. During the 1980s, the USSR and countries in Eastern Europe were lagging increasingly behind the technological development of the capitalist, Western world. As the communist world was not exempted from the communications revolution, the alterations helped pry open the traditionally closed, communist Eastern Bloc.

This is a seductive answer and a very popular one: the communications revolution acted as a corrosive on the Soviet system; it played its part in the unravelling of the Soviet empire and, thus, in the ending of the Cold War. But it is vague. Its gist cannot be denied – the developments in finance alone show that the communications revolution has altered human affairs in significant ways and on a global scale. But its appeal may lie just as much in the ideological message which informs the theories, for the argument itself is very often unsatisfactorily substantiated. Few authors include grounded accounts of the precise mechanisms of change. Bar the convincing instance of finance, most authors neglect to show how the new communications technologies actually alter world politics. They generally do not explain the ways in which new modes of electronic information do in fact erode the territorial state (and, by consequence, the entire Westphalian state system).[13] They do not demonstrate well how instant and personal access to the vast information resources of cyberspace will in fact liberate people all over the world.[14]

It is commonly accepted that the communications revolution has altered the world (although the jury is out on the diverse mechanisms of change and on the consequences of the alterations). It is less appreciated that it has also changed the ways in which human observers perceive the world. With a laptop computer connected to a mobile phone, an eager student of world affairs can sit anywhere on the earth – Tananarivo, Turkmenistan, Tupelow or Trondheim – and download detailed information on the political history or the economic conditions anywhere else. She can access the headlines of today's newspapers in London, New York, Paris or Tokyo. She can read hourly-updated world-news bulletins on the most interesting or fast-breaking stories. For more in-depth knowledge, she can access professional journals – and often even download articles or synopses. She can browse through entire 'virtual libraries' and visit 'virtual bookstores'.[15] On the threshold of the twenty-first century, time and space are suspended. Students of world affairs have direct, immediate access to the world they study – or rather: to virtual representations of it. This experience, aided by expansions in trade and interdependence, has demolished the traditional notions of national self-sufficiency and of sovereignty, and have undoubtedly affected the ways through which many post-modern authors have sought to reconceptualize world affairs.[16]

The communications revolution has changed the world and affected the ways in which we observe world politics. Furthermore, it has affected International Relations theorizing. The communications revolution has triggered a proliferation of speculation and theorizing about language and meaning. Political interactions have been increasingly discussed in terms of relations among meaning-producing subjects (including person–machine relations). International Relations have been discussed in the light of systems of symbols which provide the common medium through which meaningful messages are disseminated. The adoption of new terms and new conceptual schemes invariably leads to new perspectives, new models, new questions and new research projects.[17]

What will happen to the good old concepts and arguments of International Relations if continued communications revolutions make space irrelevant, interdependence acute, and national allegiance obsolete? What will happen to the nation state and, by extension, to the interstate system? One possible scenario lies in the sketches of Campanella, Crucé, Kant and other planners of a perpetual peace: that the erosion of state boundaries may result in a global federation of some kind. However, it remains as unclear now as it did then how such a federation should, in practice, be established. Will it be made by voluntary agreement (as recommended by for example Dante and Dubois)? In which case it involves an inordinate amount of faith in the benevolence of God or in the wisdom and kindness of Man. Or can it only be established through conquest (as argued by Rousseau)? In which case the continued presence of nuclear weapons forces one to wonder whether such an establishment might perhaps do more harm in the moment of conquest than it would guard against for ages.

Another possible scenario lies in the post-modern visions of a new medievalism. The erosion of states may give place to a secular incarnation of the heteronomous system (Ruggie 1986) of overlapping or segmented authority (P. Anderson 1979) that marked the medieval world (H. Bull 1977). R. Kaplan (1994) draws parallels between the disorder of the early Middle Ages and the breakdown of civil society in the contemporary West, and notes the similarities between the fenced and gated communities of postmodern suburbia and the walled and moated castles of medieval society. Alain Minc (1993) provides a detailed analysis of a new medievalism marked by the demise of organized social formations and the disappearance of central command; characterized by the emergence of fluid and ephemeral allegiances, of indetermination and flux, of a downgrading of reason as the principal guide of social behaviour and an upgrading of principles of pleasure. It is also marked by the re-emergence of old mythologies and superstitions which we thought were long dead and done with. The result is a world in which a multiplying variety of social formations are culturally interconnected through a universal, English-like language ('globish'). Politically it is divided by old civilizational and religious lines (like the old, reinvigorated division between Christianity and Islam). Economically, the world is an odd *bricolage* of late-twentieth century technology, nineteenth-century doctrines of free trade, and a neo-medieval kind of interstitial world-trade centres –

where an Italian nobleman might declare himself a vassal of a German prince (or a Canadian branch manager swear fealty to a Japanese CEO). All this is contained by a framework of international capitalism where multiple interwoven hierarchies constitute a-territorial networks of rival jurisdictions. 'City states like Hong Kong and Singapore revive extraterritorial "industrial zones" and multiply inside technically sovereign nation-states like Hanseatic Steelyards', comments Hobsbawm (1991, pp. 174f). And if he is right, a growing web of transnational business élites defy the distinction between internal and external affairs (Strayer 1970, p. 83; Ruggie 1993b, p. 154); territory will no longer alone determine identity and loyalty. And as a reaction to this, politicians of various countries are forced together to negotiate and devise institutions of 'international' governance. They seek to combat the fragmenting effects of global business and to preserve the relationship between geography and authority. In this light, efforts to integrate states into regional (con)federations could be read not in the spirit of Smith and Ricardo, but in the shadow of Clovis and Charlemagne. The European Union (EU) may not at all represent an economic effort to further the freedom of regional trade; it may be a political project to contain the disintegration of the European state and the Western state system.

If scenarios such are these are useful, it is not because they depict a new, post-Westphalian reality. Rather, they are useful because they are metaphors that help us make sense out of a period of postmodern turbulence. Territorial states are unlikely to wither away overnight. But their natures are bound to change. And their interactions will produce new institutions and structures. Past visions of 'empires' and 'federations' may help illuminate present efforts to build peaceful, post-Cold War relations in Europe – East as well as West of the Elbe. Medieval ideas of 'heteronomy' and 'usufructure' may help clarify the nature of the conflicts and quarrels which torment the post-Cold War West and the extra-Western world alike. Treated as metaphors, old visions and ideas may be turned and twisted until they produce new perspectives, unexpected visions, novel concepts, appropriate terms, innovative syntheses and other tools of theory-building which help us capture the rough outlines of post-modern international relations.

Notes

Notes to the Introduction

1   Dougherty and Pfaltzgraff's (1981) influential *Contending Theories of International Relations* is indicative of the literature. It devotes one page to Thucydides, Machiavelli, Crucé and other founding theorists of the discipline; it then devotes three pages to a reprisal of Edward H. Carr and 570 pages to twentieth-century theorists.

This disregard for the tradition of International Relations theory has been most famously noted by Wight (1968) and pursued by authors like Linklater (1982). The focus on current events has been most notable in the major US introductory texts to International Relations. Jones (1991), Kegley and Wittkopf (1995), Hughes (1991) and several others follow the encyclopedic example of Schuman (1933) and present exhaustive overviews of contemporary events and theories, but do not venture to explore the world prior to 1918. However, there is a tendency in more recent texts to follow the indispensable example of Holsti (1967) and include historical issues in the discussions: Ray (1987) sketches the aftermath of World War I (a major key to world politics in the 1990s); Pearson and Rochester (1988) have a summary of International Relations since the Treaty of Westphalia, Couloumbis and Wolfe (1990) have references to historical events and theorists interspersed throughout the text.

Two *caveats* must be added to this criticism of traditional literature. First, there have always existed notable exceptions to this a-historical mainstream trend. Among the most influential of these are Carr (1964), Hinsley (1963), Holsti (1987), Parkinson (1977) and Russell (1936). The authoritative texts of Aron (1966), Bull (1977), Cox (1987), Gilpin (1981 and 1987), Morgenthau (1978), Schwarzenberger (1951), Waltz (1959 and 1979) and many others are richly informed by history; however, they tend to advocate the realist paradigm, and are not strictly introductory overviews.

Second, the a-historical trend has been conspicuously bucked since the late 1980s by a renewed interest in historically informed theorizing – as indicated by a spate of journal articles and the books by Bartelson (1995), Buzan, Little and Jones (1993), Chanteur (1992), Der Derian (1987), Kauppi and Viotti (1992), Luard (1992), Olson and Groom (1991), Renouvin (1994), Thompson (1994), Walker (1993), Watson (1992), Williams (1992) and others.

Notes

Notes to Chapter 1

1 I capitalize 'International Relations' whenever it refers to the academic discipline. This is to distinguish it from the lower-case 'international relations, which I consider a more general term that denotes 'world politics' or 'world events'.

2 Terms like 'Europe', 'Italy', 'England', 'France' are anachronisms. Strictly speaking, it is not justified to use these modern labels when discussing the early Middle Ages, for there existed no cultural or political entities of such coherence or duration that they could fill the terms with any meaningful content. However, the alternative is worse: more appropriate designations would involve such elliptic descriptions that the few points covered in this hurried overview might easily be lost in ponderous prose.

3 Although this kingdom fell apart shortly after his death, Clovis made two important contributions which drove the Continent towards greater unity. First, many of the quarrelling Germanic kings were depicted as decendants of the same ancestor, Clovis' grandfather Meroveus – from whom the great variety of subsequent rulers derive their common label 'Merovingians'. Second, Clovis embraced the Catholic faith. He became the only Catholic ruler among the German kings, and got what no other Germanic ruler had: the support of the Church.

4 In England, Alfred the Great (871–99) organized a successful defence against the Viking invasions and won the allegiance of all Anglo-Saxons. In Germany, local counts and dukes repulsed the infringements of foreign attackers in the late 800s and managed to rebuild political stability from the local level. In the early 900s they elected themselves a king, Henry I (919–36). His son, Otto I, allied with the Church, repressed domestic rebellions, defeated the Magyars once and for all (955), and made good his claim to be king of Italy (962). Such ties were also evident in France, where political stability was similarly rebuilt in the early 900s from the local level by counts and dukes. In the late 900s the great lords of France chose Hugh Capet (987–96) as their king, and became his vassals. Hugh seized the old Carolingian crown, gave it to his own family, and thus founded the Capetian dynasty.

5 This staff was attached to the imperial post office (or the *drome*), one part of which was called the *scrinium barbarorum* (the Office of the Barbarians). The official in charge of this office was the *logothete* of the *drome*, who was responsible for the imperial post. As diplomatic relations evolved during the ninth and tenth centuries, the tasks of the *logothete* came to include the reception of foreign envoys, their formal introduction to the emperor and his court and the internal security of the empire. In practice it involved the constant gathering of intelligence pertaining to domestic security as well as to external relations with neighbouring societies, frequent (often daily) interviews with the emperor and the entertainment of visiting envoys – foreign visitors were treated lavishly, but also confined in special quarters and subject to constant surveillance.

The duties of the *logothete* also involved the collection of diplomatic information; not only from professional envoys, but also from merchants, missionaries, military men and foreign prisoners. In addition, information was collected from renegades – e.g. from Muslims like the eunuch Samonas, who entered the service of Byzantium around AD 900. Such intelligence was systematically stored in special archives. Here they could be retrieved upon request and inform the decisions of generals, ambassadors or emperors.

6 In AD 830 the Caliph al-Ma'mun founded the *Bayt al-Hikmah* ('the House of Wisdom') in Baghdad. It contained several astronomical observatories with scientific

288

equipment, a translation bureau and a vast library – which by the eleventh century claimed to have over a million volumes on its shelves. The translations of classical works represented a significant incentive to learning. Through the munificence of rulers and princes, large private and public libraries and schools were built. Caliph al-Hikim built the *Dar al-Hikmah* ('The Hall of Wisdom') in Cairo. The tenth-century library of Caliph al-Hakam in Córdova boasted more than 400,000 books. In 1065 a great university was founded in Baghdad. Soon after, universities were also built in Damascus, Jerusalem, Cairo, Córdova and other places.

7 The 'Mirror-of-Princes' genre include texts written in the form of advice to new rulers. The genre was introduced from Persian into Arabic as early as the eighth century, but it did not produce its most celebrated texts until the Caliphate found its final definition in the eleventh. The most famous Islamic example of the 'Mirror-of-Princes' genre in the Caliphate is probably the *Seyasat-nameh* ('Book of Government') written by Nizam al-Mulk (1018–92). Other famous examples include texts by Prince 'Onsor ol-Ma'ali Keyavns (10??–1098) and the mystic al-Ghazali (1058–1111). The genre emerged in Western Europe in the middle of the twelfth century (Berges 1938).

8 When Augustine observed that even the Roman Empire, that bastion of constancy and civility, was collapsing, he was forced to conclude that no earthly state can eternally ensure security from internal and external attack. Everything on earth is temporal. And although temporal rulers are ordained by God, they will always be victims of fear, envy, greed, vanity and ignorance. Because no earthly ruler can be permanently sheltered from such human frailties, there will always be wars, and there will always be an end to every earthly kingdom. Rome was no exception.

9 The formalization of civic representation in the king's council furnished the origins of the parliamant in England, the Cortes in Spain, the Reichstag in Germany, and the Estates-General in France. This development not only consolidated the territorial state, it also laid the foundations for the distinct form of the *Ständestaat* – a late-medieval regime type in which the monarch and his court emerged as the strong centre of political gravity, but where key decision-making bodies included representatives from the main estates of the country (Poggi 1978) – and, later, the absolute monarchy (P. Anderson 1979).

10 Aquinas explains that peace is the first aim of government and that God's laws must be obeyed above those of man. Furthermore, he acknowledges the importance of economic activities in human society. His proposition that basic material needs for food, shelter and clothing must be satisfied before man can be expected to engage in spiritual pursuits shows that he recognized the important role played by production. He also recognizes the realm of exchange, but he betrays a pronounced scepticism towards mercantile affairs. He associated these with profit-making and with 'artificial wealth' which he suspected because the lust for it knows no limits. Aquinas emphasizes that all exchange must be guided by a concern for justice, and is careful to specify that the just price of a commodity must be calculated by adding the costs of production to a reasonable payment to the producer in proportion to his social status (1947, pp. 1513–22). Financial activities, however, are reserved a harsh judgement in the *Summa*, where usury is abhorred in no uncertain terms. However, Acquinas does not expand upon issues of production, exchange or finance. He mostly repeated the strong scepticism towards mercantile affairs entertained by his contemporaries and by Aristotle.

11   Pierre Dubois is often hailed as the man who first proposed an international council or court of arbitration. But he did more. He also urged the council members to break associations with any state that initiated war and advocated concerted action against the aggressor state – thus foreshadowing Woodrow Wilson's doctrine of collective security by about 600 years.

It is hard to gauge the influence of *De recuperatione Terre Sancte* (which did not appear in print until 1611). But it seems to have been known to George Podiebrad and Marini, who, in the 1460s, proposed a scheme for an international body of arbitration which would settle disputes among kings (ter Meulen 1917). Dubois was clearly known to Erasmus and Suarez.

12   It should be added that, more surprisingly, the concept of the 'state' was not really within the range of the late-medieval vocabulary either. The ancients had used terms like *polis* or *imperium* to denote independent territorial associations. And when Dubois and Marsiglio display, towards the end of the Middle Ages, a gradual awareness that a new kind of political association was emerging in Europe, the idea of 'the state' came into being. The term emerged slowly and in many local variations (*status, stato, el estado, l'Etat, der Staat* ...). It was at first used with little clarity. And these unclarities reflected the complexity of the new experience and of the factors which gave rise to it. It was only by the fifteenth century that the term began to acquire a clearer political usage as a reference to a specific form of polity. Only after the Dutch proclamation of Independence (1581) was *status* frequently invested with a republican tone which contrasted a 'popular' or 'republican' association with a 'monarchic' one (Dyson 1980, pp. 25ff; Vincent 1987, pp. 16ff).

Notes to Chapter 2

1   Pico della Mirandola's *Oration on the Dignity of Man* (1965 [1486]) is one of the most famous Renaissance expressions of this new emphasis on man as a private person. This emphasis on the private and the individual is also strikingly apparent in the fresh development of a literary form which was rare in the Middle Ages, the biography – and most characteristically, in the autobiography, the most noteworthy instances of which were written by Cellini (1969) and Cardano (1930).

2   Francesco Poggio Braccioline (1380–1459) was one of many entrepreneurs in classical humanist culture. Dissatisfied with the low salaries he earned as a copyist for notaries and diplomats, he went into business for himself, tracking down and copying classical manuscripts. On his many expeditions all over Europe, Poggio found several important works which he copied. The originals were often neglected by their owners, and were lost or destroyed; Poggio's copies were preserved in Florence. In effect, copies like Poggio's are often the oldest testimonies extant about life in ancient Greece and Rome.

3   This claim goes against the established view, according to which 'it is the name of Machiavelli that has come to symbolise what the tradition of international relations theory is all about' (Walker 1993, p. 30).

Two comments help illuminate the interpretation set out here. First, it is quite common to assume that Machiavelli was a balance-of-power analyst and a key contributor to the tradition of International Relations theory. However, even a cursory glance at his writings suggests that Machiavelli's preoccupation was with domestic, not with international politics – he frequently discusses military affairs, but he rarely produces a sustained discussion of interstate relations. *The Prince* does not contain the modern phrase 'balance of power' – although it once (Chapter 20) refers to relations among Italy's (city)states as 'a sort of balance' ('uno certo modo bilanciata'); a description which some English-language editions have translated into 'a balance of power'. There is no doubt that Machiavelli is an important power-theorist; but it would be an exaggeration to call him a *balance*-of-power theorist.

Second, Machiavelli's most probing and direct discussion of international issues is found in neither *The Prince*, nor *The Discourses*, nor *The Art of War*; it is found in the dispatches he sent to Florence when he was on diplomatic missions on behalf of its ruling Council of Ten. It is possible that a systematic study of these dispatches will weaken the claim presented here and furnish the established view with a more convincing foundation.

4 *The Prince* consists of 26 short chapters, which can be grouped into four parts according to subject matter: Part One (Chs. 1–9) deals with principalities. It lists various types of principalities and explains the means by which they are acquired and maintained. Part Two (Chs. 10–14) discusses the claim that military power is the foundation of the State. Part Three (Chs. 15–23) deals with the prince and the qualities which will secure his rule. Part Four (Chs. 24–26) deals with the political situation in Italy in the 1520s.

Most commentaries emphasize the third part of the book – in most anthologies it is the third part's most wicked chapters, 17 and 18, which are most commonly reproduced. From the point of view of International Relations theory, the third part is not the most interesting. Rather, the book's short Part Two is far more revealing, for it is here that Machiavelli formulates his insights about the nature of the State and touches briefly upon relations among states in the form of war.

5 Pope Leo X (1513–21) appointed Guicciardini governor of Modena and Reggio and, later, commissioner of the papal armies. Pope Adrian VI (1522–23) demoted him. But Pope Clement VII (1523–34) made him president of the province of Romagna, the northernmost papal province (Quatela 1991).

6 While ambassador to Spain (1512), Guicciardini found the time to write *Relazione de Spagna* and *Discorso di Logrogno*. His book on Florentine politics, which is called *The Dialogue on the Government of Florence*, was begun in 1521 and completed three years later. In 1530 he wrote a long commentary entitled *Considerations on the 'Discourses' of Machiavelli*. Guicciardini's biographical works include *The Consolatoria* (which discusses the merits of religion and philosophy), *Oratio Accusatoria* and *Oratio Defensoria* (Guicciardini 1994, pp. vii–xxxi; Quatela 1991).

7 C–28 refers to 'maxim' No. 28 in the compilation that Guicciardini himself made of his *Ricordi*: the so-called 'C-collection'. Guicciardini wrote several versions of his *Ricordi*. The first two were written during his ambassadorship in Spain (1512) and were little more than a collection of brief jottings (and are usually denoted as quartos 1 and 2, respectively – or Q¹ and Q²). After his return to Florence, Guicciardini apparently wrote another collection, which has subsequently been lost, but which has been denoted the A-collection. In 1528, he rewrote his maxims, added some new ones, and produced a collection of 181 *Ricordi* (the B-collection). In 1530, he completed his final compilation of 221 *Ricordi* (the C-collection). See Rubinstein (1970, pp. 20ff).

Notes to Chapter 3

1 Campanella wrote in his *Philosophia sensibus demonstrata* ('Philosophy Demonstrated by the Senses') of 1591 that philosophy must be based on methodic doubt (as later systematized by Descartes) and on self-conscious, human experience (as was later elaborated by Bacon). This book was interpreted as a critique of Scholastic Aristotelianism; its author was seized by the Inquisition and imprisoned for heresy. Campanella spent over 25 years in prison. And although he was subjected to deprivation and torture, he manged to write prolifically. In addition to *Philosophia* ..., a list of his books must include: *De monarchia Christianorum* ('On Christian Monarchy) of 1593; *Dialogo politico contra Luterani, Calvinisti ed altri eretici* ('Political Dialogue against Luterans, Calvinists and Other Heretics') of 1595; *La città del sole* ('The City of the Sun') of 1602; *Apologia pro Galilaeo* ('Apology for Galileo) of 1616; and *Atheismus triumphatus* ('Atheism led in triumph') [16??].

2 Botero's 'principle of population' is unmistakable in his *Reason of State* (Book 8, Ch. 4). However, it is restated with greater clarity and force his *Treatise Concerning the Causes of the Magnificence and Greatness of Cities* (1956 [1606]). In an account which foreshadows Malthus' *Essay on Population* by nearly 200 years, Botero claims that populations strive to increase to the full extent made possible by human fecundity (or mankind's *virtus generativa*); however since any society only offers limited means of subsistence (*virtus nutritiva*) unlimited population growth is always checked by limited resources. This limit asserts itself through want and misery, squalor and disease. It may also assert itself in wars, Botero intimates.

3 Pierino Belli (1502–75) offered thorough discussions of strategy and international law in his *De re militari et de bello* (1936 [1563]). Paolo Paruta (1540–98) discussed the balance of power among the Italian city-states in his *Discorsi politici* of 1599. Traiano Boccalini (1556–1613) portrayed the cynicism of statesmen in his influential satire *Ragguagli di Parnaso* ('Reports from Parnassus') of 1612 and discussed the European balance of power in his disillusioned commentaries upon Tacitus, *Osservazioni Politiche sopra I Sei Libri degli Annali di Cornelio Tacito* of 1678.

4 Bodin's Method divides human knowledge into three main branches: divine history, natural history and human history. In modern parlance these three branches would roughly cover theology, natural sciences and history/social sciences respectively (Bodin 1945, p. 2). That that division provided a lasting vantage point for Bodin's scholarship is evident from his treatment of each of the three branches separately in his three major works: his *Dialogue of Seven Wise Men* of 1593 is an exposition of the world's religions; *The Theatre of Nature* of 1596 is a treatise on the physical properties of the world; *The Six Books on the Commonwealth* of 1576 discusses human history and universal law.

5 Their common, secular perspective is obvious from the titles of their books: Scipione Ammirato, *Discorsi sopra C. Tacito* of 1594; Ciro Spontone, *Dodici libri del governo di stato* of 1599; Antonio Palazzo, *Discorso del governo e della ragion vera di stato* of 1606; Pietro Andrea Canonhiero, *Discorso del governo e della ragion vera di stato* of 1614; Ludovico Zuccoli, *Dissertatio de ratione status* of 1621; Federico Bonaventura, *Della region di stato* of 1623; Gabriel Zinano, *Della ragione degli stati* of 1626; Lodovico Settala, *Della ragion di stato* of 1627; Scipione Chiaramonti, *Della ragione di stato* of 1635. These authors are discussed in Meinecke (1957, Ch. 5) and Ferrari (1860, Part II, Section III).

Notes to Chapter 4

1   There is an enormous literature which seeks to explain the emergence of Western Europe and its modern institutions. Downing (1992, pp. 4ff) makes a useful division of this literature into five macrohistorical schools: (1) the German sociological approach (inspired by Weber and Hinze); (2) the modernization theorists (represented by the US Committee on Comparative Politics of the Social Science Research Council); (3) the 'bourgeois revolution' school (inspired by Adam Smith and Karl Marx); (4) the culturalist or idealist perspective (exemplified by Bendix); and (5) the Barrington Moore thesis.

2   Filmer's *Patriarcha* must have been written after 1635 but before 1640. It was circulated in manuscript form before it was finally published posthumously in 1680. Long before it was printed, it had earned its author the reputation of an extreme supporter of royal prerogatives (Laslett 1960, p. 71). The main reason why Filmer has become such a famoush representative for monarchic absolutism is less the sophistication of his argument and more the fact that he served as *Prügelknabe* in John Locke's landmark *First Treatise of Government* of 1688 (Laslett 1960).

3   For Filmer this division of the world into states was greatly enhanced by the confusion of Babel, whence God scattered man 'over the whole face of the earth' (*Genesis* 11:8). 'It is a common opinion that at the confusion of tongues there were seventy-two distinct nations erected', writes Filmer (1991, p. 7). This continued fragmentation of the earth into several smaller political units not only occurred with God's blessing, but with His direct participation. It was God, after all, who had created the confusion of Babel in the first place (Filmer 1991, p. 7).

4   Cineas ('Cyneas') was a Thessalian diplomat employed by Pyrrhus of Epinis (celebrated for his 'pyrrhic victories') in his war with Rome, and chiefly known for his observations that the Roman senate was 'an assembly of Kings' and that war with Rome was like fighting a many-headed hydra: hence presumably a type of figure for one who is well able to recognize unwelcome politico-strategic realities.

5   Russell (1936), for example, traces the evolution of Crucé's vision of a 'general assembly' of states from *The New Cyneas* through the writings of the Duke of Sully, via William Penn and the internationalist ideas of the Society of Friends (the Quakers) to twentieth-century statesmen like Woodrow Wilson and Franklin D. Roosevelt.

6   *De jure praedae* was a report commissioned by the Dutch East India Company, which was involved in a hot legal contest with Portuguese companies about prizes. Grotius realized that to prove that a Portuguese ship had been legally captured, he had to invalidate the claim that the Indian Ocean was Portugal's private property. He did this by relying on Vitoria's argument that all nations have a natural right to trade. This axiom furnished the basis for Grotius' famous claim that the open seas are free for all. When Grotius had completed his sizeable report (at the age of 26), its important 12th chapter was published under the title *Mare liberum* in 1609. To appreciate fully John Selden's *Mare clausum* in 1635, it is important to note that he wrote this text as an effort to rebut Grotius' *Mare liberum* (Selden 1652, pp. 447ff). The full text of Grotius' report was not published until 1868 (Klee 1946).

7   There are two major explanations for why natural law is eternal – both of them discussed by Selden (1652, pp. 12f). The first is medieval in origin. It was clearly expressed by Augustine, who formulated the doctrine that participation in God's thought is the moral and obligatory end of all intellectual pursuit. In the light of this explanation, nat-

ural law is but the formulation of a divinely inspired moral order. Natural law, in other words, is created by God.

The second explanation was developed in the seventeenth century, and is well represented by Thomas Hobbes. It holds that the basic, permanent characteristic of Man is his ability to reason. And since all humans are essentially alike, they are likely to reason in the same manner. The implication of Hobbes' argument is that through reason humans can logically deduce universal and self-evident rules for human behaviour. Natural law, in other words, is created by humanity.

The tendency of the seventeenth century was towards rejecting the former explanation and accepting the latter. This conforms to the larger theme of the age: the mounting tendency on the part of scholars and statesmen to remove both political authority and responsibility from the realm of the divine and place it in the hands of rational individuals. Thomas Hobbes formulated a pessimistic variation on this theme of the age. Émeric Crucé formulated an optimistic one. Hugo Grotius took a middle position.

8 Thomas Hobbes exemplifies the rebellious spirit of the age. Hobbes admits freely he has 'neglected the Ornament of quoting ancient Poets, Orators and Philosophers contrary to the custom of late time'. Indeed, he disapproves of authors who, instead of explaining their thoughts as clearly as possible, 'stick their corrupt Doctrine with the Cloves of other men's Wit'. It is, he complains 'an argument of Indigestion, when Greek and Latine Sentences unchewed come up again, as they use to doe, unchanged' (Hobbes 1951, p. 727).

9 Leibniz saw the 'state' much in the same way that he saw his 'monads' (Ross 1984, pp. 89ff). And although he did not elaborate on how discrete, impenetrable, territorial states were organs in a larger interstate organism, his 'monadology' suggests a complex vision of the interstate system – a composite organism in which each member is a unique, self-conscious society which is, in turn, composed of many smaller, self-conscious societies and so on, down the several levels of the multi-layered system. On the face of it, Leibniz' speculations are dense and abstract to the point of absurdity. However, their basic imagery gains by close acquaintance, exuding a seductive intellectual force rivalled in its generality only by the system which Hegel formulated a century later – and which also relied on self-consciousness as the key attribute of the state.

Notes to Chapter 5

1 That label has more than the usual difficulties by which such sobriquets are always attended. In common parlance the label conjures up images of intellectual upheavals, economic turbulence and rapid, indeed, revolutionary, political changes. In fact, most of the eighteenth century was not particularly turbulent. The first half of the century was not so much an age of energetic creation as it was a period of gestation; it was an epoch in which the fruits of the intellectual revolution of the seventeenth century were pondered, systematized, codified, steamlined, perfected, digested and commonly accepted. The Age of Enlightenment was also the Age of the Old Regime.

2 Locke's argument echoes Hobbes' in its claim that humanity created government through a social contract. However, Locke differed from Hobbes in several respects. First, whereas Hobbes saw natural rights as people's unlimited privilege to do anything they pleased, Locke saw natural rights as a set of specific rights limited by duties towards others. For example, Locke argued that human beings have a right to life, and defined

this in terms of a property right. All individuals own their own bodies and no one could be born the property of someone else – no one, then, could be born a slave or a serf. From this axiom Locke deduced that human beings have the right to own the products of their own labour. When people work, they 'mix their labour' with objects of nature, which thereby became their property. To Locke, it was as if labour enclosed parts of the great common which was nature.

Second, whereas Hobbes envisioned the state of nature as a condition of war, Locke saw it as a state of peace. If free and largely happy individuals agreed to set up a government, this was only because a few deluded or evil individuals insisted on exceeding their natural rights and taking the lives and property of others. In order to have an efficient defence against such people, it was necessary for peace-loving property-owners to organize a government which could legislate in accordance with natural rights and enforce this legislation. Consequently, Locke's state emphasized the legislative and the judicial aspects of government over the executive functions. A good government, Locke implied, is that which restricts its functions as much as possible to refining and enforcing the law.

Third, in contrast to Hobbes', Locke's social contract is not unconditional; it imposes mutual obligations on individual citizens as well as on the government. The citizen must agree to act in accordance with reason (and the God–given natural law which represents reason); for, Locke adds with emphasis, only rational individuals can be free. The government, on its part, must respect the contract. If the government threatens its citizens' rights (which it is its sole purpose to protect), then the citizens might consider the contract null and void. They may even as a last resort rebel against it.

3 This acknowledgement is quite explicit in Chapter 12 of Locke's *Second Treatise*, where he discusses the three aspects of governmental power: legislative, executive and federative. He explains that whereas the legislative and the executive powers pertain to domestic affairs, the federative power pertains to foreign relations – it encompasses 'the Power of War and Peace, Leagues and Alliances, and all the Transactions, with all Persons and Communities without the Commonwealth' (Locke 1960, p. 411). This point is further pursued by Cox (1960).

4 It is only for reasons of space that several noteworthy American authors – primary among whom are Benjamin Franklin (1706–90), Thomas Paine (1737–1809), Thomas Jefferson (1743–1818) and Alexander Hamilton (1756–1804) – are excluded from this discussion of Enlightenment theories. Both Franklin and Jefferson had diplomatic experience. Franklin spent several years in both England and France and drew upon his varied experiences for several political and economic treatises that touched upon international affairs. Two of his treatises are notable: *The Interest of Great Britain Considered with Regard to Her Colonies* ... of 1760 and his *Journal of the Negotiations for Peace* of 1782. These two essays, together with Franklin's 'Plan of union' of 1754, his *Positions to be Examined Concerning National Wealth* of 1769 and parts of his correspondance from Europe (e.g. his odd exchange with Pierre Gargaz on a project of perpetual peace) add up to an interesting American variant of the trade-focused Enlightenment arguments presented by Montesquieu, St-Pierre, Vattel, Voltaire and others.

Jefferson was America's representative in Paris for five years where he witnessed the early stages of the French Revolution; he was America's first Secretary of State (1788–94) and the new nation's third president (1801–09), and involved in the diplomatic difficulties caused by the Napoleonic Wars. Hamilton, as an active Secretary of the Treasury

Notes

(1789–95), was much concerned with the issues of international trade and foreign investments. Neither Jefferson nor Hamilton wrote sustained treatises on international affairs; however, their many scattered writings on related subjects – notably during the intense political feuds between them in the early 1790s, which reflect the struggle of the day between the schools of free trade and mercantilism (Hamilton 1928) – provide glimpses into the International Relations theories of the American Enlightenment (Varg 1970, pp. 70–94).

5   After the American Revolution, Vattel's authority continued undiminished because his definitions of liberty and equality coincided with those of the American *Declaration of Independence* (1776). Vattel and Locke greatly affected the foreign policies of the United States. The Americans were attracted to Vattel's (and Locke's) proposition that human beings are born free and endowed with natural rights; that nations are 'composed of men naturally free and independent, and who before the establishment of civil societies lived together in the state of nature' (Vattel 1863, p. lv). The Americans embraced fondly Vattel's argument that in certain circumstances a part of a nation had a right to separate itself from the rest (pp. 96–8).

6   In all fairness, Hume did provide several expositions as to how the balance-of-power principle operates in domestic politics (Hume 1985, pp. 42–6, 47–53 and 64–73). Extracts from Hume are found in Luard (1992, pp. 46–9, 386–9), and from Hume, Defoe, Bolingbroke and others in Wright (1975, pp. 39–87).

7   Godwin's *Enquiry Concerning Political Justice* opens with a resounding assault on Locke and the entire tradition of contract philosophy and liberal political thought; it concludes with the vision of a communal order marked by virtuous co-operation and social solidarity. Godwin pushes the preoccupation with individual freedom to such extremes that many observers see in Godwin's argument 'a philosophy of anarchism carried through to its logical conclusions' (Joll 1964, p. 31). Godwin also presented some of the themes from his *Enquiry* in fictional form, most notably in his novel *Caleb Williams* of 1794, but also in plays.

8   To put it more modern terms, Godwin moves from the facile, nation-level claim that democracies do not start wars, to the more sophisticated, dyadic claim that democracies do not fight each other. See Gleditsch and Hegre (1996) for a formulation of the more sophisticated claim; see Gates *et al.* (1996) for a critique.

9   This notion, that more knowledge (and especially more information about other peoples) encourages tolerance and thus serves the cause of peace, is ancient. But few theorists have drawn such a clear connection between commerce and increased knowledge as Montesquieu. After him, this connection has been elaborated in several projects on perpetual peace. Most authors, especially liberal Englishmen – e.g. Bentham (1843) and his Manchester followers (Blainey 1973) – have agreed that 'good things have resulted from this'. But some authors, notably German radicals – e.g. Herder (1829) and Fichte (1979), have argued that commerce corrupts mores and encourages conflicts and war.

10   Connections explored by Montesquieu are evident in de Forbonnais' entries on '*colonie*' and '*commerce*' in d'Alembert's famous *Encyclopédie*; they are noticable in the Abbé Raynal's celebrated *Histoire de Deux Indes* (1804 [1770].) The writings of Diderot (1713–84) echo with Montesquieu's ideas – his contributions to Raynal's *Histoire* suggest a connection between monarchic rule and colonialism; and in *Observations sur le Nakaz* of 1767 Diderot (1992) claims that absolute monarchs foment conflict and war. De Jau-

296

court repeated this point in the article he wrote on 'war' for the *Encyclopédie*. When d'Holbach (1773:II, pp. 137f) writes that wealth which is not the fruit of labour is a source of corruption, his argument is satiated with doubts about the ways in which monarchs wage wars and acquire colonies. The same attitudes inform Condorcet's attacks on slavery and his claims that freedoms of industry and commerce will both favour the distribution of wealth and prevent the concentration of power in the hands of a few individuals (Condorcet 1788).

11   After this chapter was written, Rousseau's major writings on international relations were finally brought together in English translations by Hoffmann and Fidler (1991). Their volume contains a long and valuable introductory essay.

12   Rousseau published neither his *Judgement* on Saint-Pierre nor his thoughts on colonialism. As a foreigner in France, he feared that government agents would identify him as a dangerous subversive, handle him 'roughly' and expel him (Rousseau 1978, p. 394; Cranston 1991, pp. 26ff; Starobinski 1988, pp. 201ff). The French government had good cause for concern. For in France, as in Britain and America, the Enlightenment celebration of human reason, individual liberty and the social contract drove demands for human liberation – through revolution if necessary.

13   Rousseau's argument has regularly been misunderstood. Most commentators have failed to connect Rousseau's theories of alienation and History to his theory of International Relations. One reason for this failure is that most interpretations have focused on the *'Project for a perpetual peace'* and taken the text at face value. Most commentators have forgotten that this essay was originally intended as a presentation of St-Pierre's argument – which Rousseau found more 'superficial', 'impractical' and naïve the more he read of it. Consequently, the commentators have often confused Rousseau's rendition of St-Pierre's argument with Rousseau's own ideas. They have therefore tended to find the text unclear and contradictory, and to emerge confused from it. Thus James Madison (1953 [1792], p. 261) found the 'project of Rousseau ... preposterous and impotent'; whereas G. Lowes Dickinson (1927, p. xxii) found it to contain the blueprint for 'an institution which, rightly used, should at last bring jarring races and warring nations into the calm and prosperous haven of perpetual peace'. Even the ordinarily so acute Kenneth Waltz (1959, p. 185) seems to think that Rousseau, when push comes to shove, is a proponent of a world-wide federation. Our understanding of Rousseau's International Relations theories is likely to be greatly enhanced by placing the *Project* and his *Judgement* in the proper context of his other political writings – as is done here (and also by Hoffmann and Fidler, 1991). The publication of the diplomatic dispatches which Rousseau (1995 [1743/44]) wrote on behalf of the French ambassador to Venice (Cranston 1982, p. 173), may throw additional light on the development and nature of his argument.

Notes to Chapter 6

1   Factories and shops created solidarity among workers subjected to the wearisome pace set by the new machines. In the industrial cities huddled a new, proletarianized working class, as well as a city mob of unemployed and dispossessed. Since these two emerged together on the social scene, they raised the spectre of mass action and disorder for the established classes of society, whose members could not always distinguish between them.

2   Bentham, like Smith, recognized that politics is unavoidable because it provides nec-

essary services for society: legislation, maintenance of civil order and national defence. Yet politics should not interfere with the natural properties of the economic order. All forms of government intervention involve some degree of interruption of this order; whatever the legislator does, it is bound to be 'felt in the shape of hardship and coercion somewhere' (Stark 1952–4, p. 311).

3   Bentham wrote three major essays on international affairs: 'Objects of international law', 'War considered in respect of its causes and consequences' and 'A plan for a universal and perpetual peace'. These were all written in the late 1790s and are collected in a comparatively slim volume entitled *Principles of International Law* (which is included in Bentham's collected *Works* (1843), Vol. 2, pp. 531–61). A fourth essay, 'Emancipate your colonies' was issued separately (and is included in Bentham's *Works* (1843), Vol. 4, pp. 408–19).

4   Around 1800, Germany still consisted of some 300 states, principalities and free cities, loosely linked together as the Holy Roman Empire under the leadership of Francis I of Austria. Napoleon abolished this thousand-year-old empire when he vanquished the Austrians at Ulm and Austerlitz (1805) and the Prussians at Jena (1806). Clausewitz was not the only observer present at Jena who realized the importance of the concept of *Volk* in history and in international politics; Hegel was there too.

5   The degree to which the three ideologies of liberalism, radicalism and conservatism appear similar or different depends upon the vantage point of the observers. From the narrowly Eurocentric perspective adopted in this discussion, the differences far outweigh the similarities. However, it must be borne in mind that these ideologies all are products of a Western-Christian, largely Protestant political culture; thus, from a Buddhist or a Confucian perspective, the differences between them may appear rather minute.

6   Even after British thinkers provided more empirical and more easily accessible theories of evolution, Hegel continued to exert significant influence on the Anglo-American world through theorists like F. H. Bradley, J. E. McTaggert, T. H. Green, Josiah Royce and R. G. Collingwood.

7   Metternich grafted his world view on to a balance-of-power argument. Devoted to the cause of Austria's national interest, Metternich saw in liberal democracy a challenge to Austrian power in south-central Europe. Liberal Germans, for example, argued for greater unity among the 39 members of the German Confederation (*Bund*). If the members of the *Bund* could only remove the existing restrictions on transport, trade and travel and adopt democratic constitutions, then the forces of free exchange would stimulate the creation of wealth, binding the German states together in tight interdependence. Metternich saw that such an integration would seriously impede Austria's policies in Hungary, Italy and the Balkans. He therefore sought to persuade the local German rulers that the liberals were working to undermine the established order in central Europe.

   The landowning nobility east of the river Rhine also opposed the doctrines of Western-style reforms. Metternich skilfully exploited and accentuated the difference in socioeconomic structure and philosophical sentiment between the western and the central regions of Europe to his own benefit. By presenting Enlightenment ideals as an unwelcome intrusion on the part of Germany's expanding western neighbours, Metternich managed to foment a chauvinistic and xenophobic reaction which helped his cause and broadened the gap between the Atlantic and the Continental political traditions of Europe.

8 The sentiment surrounding these events are well represented by the texts of Alexis de Tocqueville (Clinton 1993).

9 This conflict within liberalism between 'optimistic non-interventionism' and 'messianic interventionism' – between a passive and an active state – has remained endemic, notably in US foreign policy (Waltz 1959).

10 List had studied Political Economy in the United States and carefully observed how American politicians had built up the new nation's industries behind a wall of selective tariffs. List especially admired Alexander Hamilton's efforts to escape the influence of Europe's imperial economies. He embraced Hamilton's claims: that a strong economy is an invaluable basis for a country's defence; that a government can intervene in the domestic economy and greatly encourage its rate of development; that in the modern age such development must be based on the superiority of manufacturing over agriculture (Hamilton 1928).

11 The upheavals of 1848 swept Metternich's reactionary regime away. Austria was a multinational empire embracing at least ten major nationalities, and the revolutionary sentiment which had ousted Metternich from power, had also fuelled demands for self-determination among various national groups and pushed the old Austrian empire close to fragmentation and political paralysis. In Germany, by contrast, the upheavals had stimulated the vision of a larger German *Volk*, and had strengthened the idea of a German Confederation (*Bund*).

In Bismarck's view, Prussia's old policy of a close alliance with Austria had become unviable. Prussia's interests could only be served by the establishment of a larger, Prussian-led German state. Such a policy would be resented by the smaller members of the German *Bund*, Bismarck realized: left to their own volition, the small states would seek to maximize their petty interests by striking a neutral position between the two major German actors, Austria and Prussia. If Prussia undertook to unify Germany, this would drive many minor states into Austria's embrace. Germany could only be unified through a war between Austria and Prussia. And if war was inevitable, Prussia should prepare for it sooner rather than later. His mind made up, Bismarck bided his time and waited for an opportunity to build up Prussia's military forces and for a constellation of forces in Europe which could allow Prussia to challenge Austria for the leadership of Germany.

Bismarck had his opportunity when King Wilhelm I appointed him Chancellor (1862). He immediately expanded Prussia's military forces, seeing this as the first, necessary step towards his goal of a unified Germany under Prussian leadership. His second step was to bring into the open the conflict of interest between Prussia and Austria: he allied with Austria in a war against Denmark over the duchies of Schleswig and Holstein [1864], and then he exploited the joint annexation of the duchies to trigger the conflict with Austria that he had so long sought. Through 1865, Bismarck allowed the animosities to deepen while he quietly discredited Austria in British, Russian and French eyes. When Austria was isolated diplomatically, he provoked Austria to declare war. Having prepared this war for four years, he crushed the Austrian army in seven weeks. He annexed both Schleswig and Holstein, together with the kingdom of Hanover, the duchies of Nassau and Hesse-Cassel and the free city of Frankfurt. These annexations dissolved the German Bund. In its place, Bismarck organized a North German Confederation (1867), which the newly enlarged Prussia joined with 21 other German states.

In 1870, Bismarck pursued his policy of violent unification by provoking war with

France, relying on traditional German fears of France to drive the remaining German states into the new Confederation. Again, he was wildly successful: Prussia defeated France in nine months, and the small states of Germany were unified under Prussian leadership.

Notes to Chapter 7

1 Religion plays an important role in this growth of princely power, for it allowed the princes to impose a distinct interpretation of Christianity upon their people. By translating the Bible from the universal Latin into a national language, a prince emphasized the distinctness of his nation (Eisenstein 1993, pp. 148ff; Anderson 1983, p. 41).

2 From the late 1830s on, Ranke wrote voluminous studies in which he sought to escape the seductive fashions of his times. He self-consciously strove to maximize the objectivity of his accounts by trying to write history 'as it really happened'. These studies included long discussions on the foreign relations of Europe's most powerful states. Ranke's historical method, his concept of 'Great Powers' and his study of their interaction add up to a much-underestimated contribution to the study of international relations and International Relations theory.

3 The first industrial revolution was driven by practical men, by artisans and engineers who improved traditional methods of production. The second was driven by scientists, by men who invented new types of commodities, and by capital. Innovations in smelting, working and rolling improved the quality of metals; new tools for cutting and welding improved large-scale commercial production of rails, plates, castings, tools and engines. The introduction of steel as the basic material for the construction of railroads, ships, buildings, machinery and weapons also introduced new products for the booming mass-consumer market. Goods which previous ages had never conceived of – the telegraph, the telephone, the radio, the gramophone, the electric lamp, the sewing machine, the machine gun, the bicycle, pneumatic tyres, the internal combustion engine, underground trains, the typewriter – appeared during the busy, optimistic 1860s (Barraclough 1976).

4 In the Americas, the United States industrialized at a rate which exceeded even that of Germany. In Asia, Japan took to electricity, petroleum engines, railways and steel-hulled ships at such a rapid pace that it had, by 1900, emerged as the primary power in the region. In 1850, Britain had possessed half the world's industrial production; by 1870, the figure had sunk to one-third; and by 1910 to one-sixth (Kennedy 1987, pp. 198ff).

5 This was particularly clear in the policies which the West adopted towards Africa. In 1875, less than one-tenth of Africa was claimed by European countries; by 1895, only one-tenth remained unappropriated. In the final quarter of the nineteenth century, Britain added over 4,250,000 square miles and 66,000,000 people to her empire. France added over 3,500,000 square miles and 6,500,000 people. The old empires of Portugal and the Netherlands increased only slightly; but Belgium, Italy and Germany each acquired new overseas empires. 'It was a historical novelty that most of the world should now belong to a handful of great European powers' (Thomson 1974, p. 498).

6 These tendencies began to emerge as features of consequence in intellectual life during the first decades of the twentieth century. They were then most immediately perceived in the abstract art of Klee (1879–1940), the atonal music of Schönberg (1875–1951)

and the poetry of Eliot (1888–1965). But the same sentiments are apparent in scientists' rejection of causality – they are most famously noticeable in Einstein's 'theory of relativity'.

Notes to Chapter 8

1   In 1924 the German economy collapsed – one US dollar was then worth four trillion marks. The collapse interrupted the West's financial ring-around-the-roses. American speculators stopped lending money to Germany. The Germans became unable to pay reparations to the Allies. The Allies, in turn, could no longer pay the instalments on their war debt to the United States. As American investors realized they stood to lose the billions of dollars they had loaned to Europe, they lost confidence in the economy.

In October 1929, the Wall Street stock market crashed. It thrust the world economy into a depression and dealt a severe blow to the capitalist ideals of a free-market economy and a liberal-democratic polity. These ideals were seriously challenged in the 1930s by two alternative visions of socio-economic organization. From the left emerged Marxist doctrines of a centrally planned economy; from the right emerged fascist doctrines of a corporate society. As the capitalist economies of the West staggered from one crisis to the next, fascist and Marxist strongmen appeared to conquer the recession through central planning and massive state intervention.

2   After World War I, the key liberal axioms of human rationality and historical progress were under continued attack from Darwinists, Marxists, Freudians and others. Biologists portrayed man not as God's creation but as a highly evolved animal whose faculties could be explained as adaptations to the environment. Psychologists argued that what was called reason was often only 'rationalization' – a finding of alleged 'reasons' to justify emotional needs. Historians claimed that historiography is conditioned by the author's own time and place. Sociologists and philosophers explained that groups, classes and entire nations construct elaborate collective myths – in Germany Scheler, Mannheim and others developed a 'sociology of knowledge' which investigated ways in which specific social conditions give rise to distinct 'ideologies'; in France Canguilhem, Bachelard and Koyré argued that specific epochs and cultures encourage distinct 'epistemologies'. Such investigations relativized human reason by portraying human thought and knowledge as reflections of a given socio-historical context. Even Physics, the hardest of all sciences, dissolved into relativism as Continental scientists like Mach, Einstein, Heisenberg, Schrödinger and others developed quantum mechanics, which removed causality from the physical universe and replaced it with cool calculi of probability.

3   Anti-war movements can be traced far back in history – as might be suggested by e.g. Euripides' *Trojan Women* (415 BC), such societies were established as far back as antiquity (cf. Beales 1931; M. Howard 1978; Mueller 1989). Important anti-war societies were formed in response to the Thirty Years War and the English Civil War. Among the first activists were the Quakers, whose anti-war sentiment was based on moral arguments against the taking of human life. After the Napoleonic Wars, secular anti-war societies emerged. Some of them justified their stand with aesthetic or humanistic arguments – such as Henry Thomas Buckle and Bertha von Suttner. Others expressed their opposition to war in pragmatic arguments – like Norman Angell, Ramsay Muir and Francis Delasi.

4 Angell (1909) is important, commonly misunderstood and deserving of a closer comment. To put it briefly, Angell addressed two widely accepted foreign-policy arguments in particular. The first was that superior force is the best defence. Angell saw this claim as a fruit of Social Darwinist attitudes (so widely accepted at the turn of the century), and refuted it as absurd. It implies, he wrote, that security for one state must be purchased at the cost of the insecurity of its neighbours, and a policy based on this claim could only result in arms races and war.

The second argument addressed was the claim that the territory and trade of one country can be conquered by another, and profitably added to the possessions of the victor. Angell saw this claim as dangerously obsolete. The economically-developed world of the twentieth century is far more complex than the more primitive economies of the past. In a seductive argument, which drew on liberal theorists like Smith, Bentham and Cobden, Angell described a modern world economy which involved international production, trade and credit. Disruptions in one country lead to disruptions in another, forcing producers and financiers in both countries to work together. In the new international environment, marked by complexity and interdependence, war would disrupt the entire world economy. It would hurt everyone, and had therefore become 'irrelevant to the end it has in view', argued Angell.

Angell's second point, which drew on liberal theories, has earned him a reputation as an idealist. His book has often been discussed as if it claimed that war could no longer be fought. But the argument is not as simplistic as that. In fact, on re-reading *The Great Illusion* at the threshold of the twenty-first century, one finds adumbrations of late-twentieth-century International Relations theory – Angell's discussion of the 'superior-force argument', for example, foreshadows the concept of the 'security dilemma' (Hertz 1950; Waltz 1979, pp. 186ff); and his refutation of the 'conquest-pays argument' more than hints at modern 'interdependence theory' (Muir 1933; Keohane and Nye 1977). Cf. Navari (1989) for a fine re-evaluation of Angell.

5 The tsar's initiative was disingenuous. But it was enthusiastically embraced by the peace movements whose eargerness created an international momentum which culminated in the Hague Peace Conferences of 1899 and 1907 – and took the tsar by surprise. The conferences modernized the codification of international law; in particular of the laws of war.

6 In a book which discussed various ways in which society controls its members, a former student of Woodrow Wilson's hinted at the international implications of this idea (Ross 1969). In 1917 the American Sociological Society devoted its annual meeting to the theme of 'social control', and applied the concept to interstate relations. One of its leading members, Charles H. Cooley, presented a paper on 'Social Control in International Relations', in which he looked beyond power politics to an 'organic international life' in which brute force would be replaced by benevolent social control – for example in the form of a league of nations (Cooley 1918).

7 Grant, Greenwood, Hughes, Kerr and Urquhart edited a propitious *Introduction to the Study of International Relations* in 1916. It is a thought-provoking little volume for two reasons. First, it is remarkably modern in terms of the topics it addresses – 'War and Peace since 1815' (Ch. 1), 'Causes of Modern Wars' (Ch. 2), 'International Economic Relations' (Ch. 3), 'International Law' (Ch. 4), 'Political Relations between Advanced and Backward Peoples' (Ch. 5) and 'International Relations and the Growth of Freedom'.

Some of these topics emerged as important foci in the study of International Relations during the final quarter of the twentieth century – e.g. in the form of International Political Economy, Dependency theories and Democracy–Peace Studies.

Second, this slim volume also distinguishes itself by what it does *not* include: most conspicuously, it includes a chapter on international law, but excludes speculations on wishful, legalistic peace plans. This represents a noticeable silence in an age in which International Relations texts were soon to be dominated by long-winded legal regulatory schemes. It is tempting to speculate whether exciting texts like Grant *et al.* (1916) – and Dupuis (1909), Angell (1909) and other authors who discussed interstate relations from a more interdisciplinary vantage point – suffocated in the new academic field of International Relations, whose members only breathed the rareified air of Wilsonian utopianism.

8 Written by Oppenheim (1937), Brierly (1928), Eagleton (1932), Lauterpacht (1933) and Zimmern (1936), respectively.

9 It is one of the persistent half-truths in contemporary International Relations that Carr's analysis represents the Realist approach. This opinion both rests on a superficial understanding of Carr's argument and overlooks its methodological aspect. A more interesting proposition maintains that Carr quietly draws on a radical (rather than a Realist) tradition of social thought, and gives a dialectical account of International Relations informed by Karl Mannheim's (1936) sociology of knowledge (rather than a simple comparison of utopian and realist points).

Notes to Chapter 9

1 Accordingly, Churchill opposed America's grand strategy to invade Europe through Normandy. If Anglo-American forces pushed the Nazi armies eastwards through France while Soviet forces drove the Germans westwards through Poland, then Anglo-American forces would ultimately encounter the Red Army in the heart of Europe. Churchill feared that whatever territories the Red Army occupied in this final offensive Stalin would try to keep after the war. As an alternative to the American plan, Churchill argued for an Anglo-American invasion of Europe from the south: through Italy and Greece. Anglo-American forces could then meet the Soviet Army in the eastern regions of Europe, block its movement westwards and prevent Stalin from occupying the central regions of the Continent.

Despite the invasions of Sicily and Italy in 1943, the primary Allied effort was launched in Normandy in 1944. As Churchill had feared, the Red Army did drive German forces westwards on a broad front through Poland, Czechoslovakia, Hungary and Romania and far into Austria and Germany. Detachments of Allied and Russian troops meet at Torgau on the Elbe River on 25 April 1945. When Germany surrendered, the Red Army occupied a vast area of eastern and central Europe. Stalin quickly began to instal pro-Soviet regimes in these occupied countries.

2 Cf. Fraenkel (1941), Neumann (1944), Arendt (1951) and Friedrich (1954). One of the most influential explorations of 'totalitarianism' is Friedrich and Brzezinski (1965).

3 One of the first 'think tanks' of the modern world may have been the naval academy which Portugal's Prince Henry the Navigator established in 1420 on the rocky promontory of Sagres. Prominent scholars from all over Europe were hired to come here to develop new ship models, to refine techniques of cartogarphy and instruments of navigation, and to study the doctrines of grand strategy and the most recent discoveries of the extra-European world.

4   The (largely American, common) notion that states are 'rational' actors flies in the face of the pessimistic anthropology which lies at the base of traditional Realism – at least if 'rational' refers to a condition in which a political actor has control over his actions, self-consciously collects information about his condition until it has become transparent, evaluates all options in a cool and calculated manner and acts in goal-optimizing ways. The pessimistic anthropology of arch-realism is clear in Niebuhr (1932) and fascinatingly captured in Kennan (1993).

Morgenthau insists that political scientists have a duty to approach political reality in a rational mode (1978, p. 5), but acknowledges that this is an unobtainable ideal for politicians (pp. 156ff), who are condemned to act on information which is uncertain and incomplete. This insight is also apparent in Machiavelli (e.g. 1961, pp. 39f), who notes that political actions have the greatest impact when taken early (when information is scarce and uncertain), and is often to no avail when taken late (when information is more abundant and certain). Some implications of this insight are drawn for example by Kissinger (1954, p. 329).

5   Increasingly ignored, Kennan resigned in 1950. He was replaced by hard-liner Paul Nitze, who immediately recommended further militarization of US foreign policies. Nitze's recommendations dominated the 1950 top-secret National Security Council Paper no. 68 (NSC-68), which set US foreign policy for a generation (LaFeber 1989, pp. 479ff).

6   Authors who discuss the fate of the earth in ecological terms also make use of the concept of systemic rationality. Rachel Carson (1962), Harold and Margaret Sprout (1965), Garret Hardin (1968) and others saw in industrial and demographic dynamics dangers which rivalled those of nuclear weapons. They described the earth as a vast system which operates according to distinct, complex and as yet partially unknown ecological rules. The fate of humankind, they argued, depended on the finite carrying capacity of the planet. Consequently, the ecological rules of the planet impose limits on human action.

7   The apparent strength and efficiency of communist organization made an immense impression on political leaders in Asia and Africa. In addition, there was the pragmatic attraction of Soviet aid: by adopting a Marxist-Leninist rhetoric, Third-World leaders might receive economic and military support from the USSR. It is also important to note that many Third-World leaders soon transcended Soviet orthodoxy. They accumulated experiences from their own anti-colonial struggles and drew theoretical lessons from them. Notably important were the early experiences with guerrilla wars. Mao Zedong had already in the 1930s formulated a new concept of national liberation: in the absence of an urban working class, he had organized a revolutionary movement on the basis of the peasant masses. Ho Chi Minh applied Mao's theories to Indo-China and lauched a peasant-based guerrilla war against the French and, later, the Americans from bases in the jungle. The Communist Party of Malaya engaged the British on the same premiss. The Dutch encountered similar opposition in Indonesia.

A strong, political euphoria swept the Third World in the wake of Mao's revolutionary victory in 1949 (Jian 1994). The British and the Dutch withdrew from Malaya and Indonesia during the 1950s. In 1954, France gave up its colonial struggle in Indo-China. When the United States refused to recognize Vietnam's independence, Ho Chi Minh's National Liberation Front (FLN) initated a second phase of its protracted guerrilla war: this time against American imperialism. In North Africa, French colonialism was challenged by the growing Algerian Movement for National Liberation (FNL). Frantz Fanon provided a seminal justification for wars of independence in his *Studies of a Dying Colonialism* (1964). With direct reference to Hegel's anti-liberal analysis, Fanon insisted that independence is never *given* to a nation; it must be *taken*. Fanon (1967) saw in the armed struggle against the white colonizers a violent therapy, a 'collective catharsis' which offered release from centuries of alienation and injustice.

In 1955, at a decisive conference of 29 Asian and African nations at Bandung, it was evident that the orthodox Soviet model for liberation and development was under attack from within the Marxist camp – for example, when the Conference condemned 'colonialism in all its manifestations', it was obvious that Soviet policies in Eastern Europe and Central Asia were included.

8   Throughout the post-war era, a variety of authors have proposed comparable three-fold divisions of International Relations theory (Waltz 1959; Wight 1991; McKinlay and Little 1986; Viotti and Kauppi 1987), but they have often used very different labels and contributed to the confusion of the discipline.

9   See note no. 5, above.

Notes to Chapter 10

1   The total value of the world's financial transactions has, traditionally, slightly exceeded the total value of traded goods and services – indicating that financial flows were tightly associated with trade. But this association was broken during the 1980s. By the mid-1980s, world trade in goods and services amounted to between $2.5 and $3 trillion a year, whereas the world's financial institutions turned over about $75 trillion a year – a volume at least 25 times that of world trade. In addition there were the foreign exchange transactions (in which the world's currencies were traded against each other), which ran at about $35 trillion a year – or 12 times the world-wide trade in goods and services. By the late 1980s, the value of the world's financial flows was nearly 100 times the world-wide value of trade in goods and services. It looks as if financial transactions emerged as a profitable, independent and rapidly growing part of the world economy during the 1980s. There is no one explanation for this development (Drucker 1986), but the computer revolution – the vast increase in the power of computers, computer software, satellites, fibre-optic cables, and high-speed electronic transfers – is certainly one major reason why financial flows have separated from trade in goods and services (Kennedy 1993, pp. 47ff).

2   When observed in the rear-view mirror, twentieth-century political history can be read as an epic struggle for pre-eminence between two rival ideologies, democracy and totalitarianism. Each ideology had its own state champions, and the struggle took place in two decisive rounds. World Wars I and II marked the first round, which assumed the form of an armed contest between liberal democracy on the one side and fascist and communist totalitarianism on the other, and concluded with the elimination of Hitlerite fascism. The Cold War was the second round. This was a long, stalemated, nuclear-age confrontation between the remaining two ideologies, and it concluded with the collapse of Stalinist communism.

3   Because they protest of the idea of modern science, these radical critics have often been lumped together under the catch-all labels of 'post-modernism or 'post-structuralism' – soubriquets which undoubtedly exaggerate the unity of the camp. Although 'post-

modernism' and 'post-structuralism' overlap considerably (and are sometimes used inter-changeably), the two terms are not identical. I see post-modernism as the broader term, denoting a general culture–critical attitude; whereas I reserve post-structuralism for a more narrowly focused stance on methodological and epistemological matters.

4   One of the deductions which offended many Realists was the proposition that system stability increases as the number of Great Powers diminishes. The logic of the argument is that as the number of Powers diminishes, the unilateral capabilities of each remaining Power increase – as does its interest in maintaining the system. The implication of the argument is that a bipolar system is the most stable of all Great-Power constellations, and that the Cold War has had a stabilizing effect in world events (Waltz 1979, pp. 163ff).

One of the deductions which offended the Rationalists was the claim that economic interaction and interdependence is of little consequence for world order. Economic col-laboration takes place, but it is always embedded in a competitive political framework and is 'always a marginal affair' (Waltz 1979, p. 206). And, adds Waltz, as the number of Great Powers diminishes, so does the extent of economic collaboration between them. The controversial implication is that international economic interdependence was lower during the Cold War (which was an age of bipolarity) than prior to World War I (which was an age of multipolarity).

5   Buzan uses examples like social revolution and technological innovation to demon-strate that Waltz is mistaken; that domestic change *cannot* be disregarded. Social revolu-tions occur within states, but have been known to affect interstate relations greatly – as was shown in 1789, when monarchies quaked before the prospect of triumphant repub-licanism, or in 1917, when capitalist states feared the spread of communism. The sudden rise of a strong revolutionary state, concludes Buzan (1991, p. 306) 'threatens not only the distribution of power, but also the domestic values and structures of all the states associated with the prevailing status quo'. The collapse of Soviet communism and the subsequent end of the Cold War is another illustration of Buzan's larger point: that changes within states affect the dynamics of interstate relations.

Technological innovation, too, occurs within states, but has been known to affect inter-action among states. On the one hand, new modes of production may increase a state's productivity, raise its wealth-creating capabilities, and enhance its position in the hierar-chy of states (as shown by the case of England during the Industrial Revolution). On the other, new modes of destruction may similarly trigger sudden changes in the system's relative distribution of capabilities (as in the case of the invention of the atomic bomb). Also, new modes of communication may alter the nature of interstate interaction – for example by improving the carrying capacity and the speed of transportation (of goods as well as troops), thereby enhancing the 'intensity' and the 'density' of global interaction' (p. 151).

6   It bears repeating that old-fashioned Realists tend to see the state as a historic cre-ation which has a temporal origin, a path of evolution and, most probably, an end. Niebuhr (1932), for example, did not think that the state was a particularly rational actor; nor did he think that Realism depended on the continued existence of the modern state. Morgenthau (1978, p. 10) seems to agree.

7   The Revolutionary paradigm in IR theory all but collapsed after the Cold War. The collapse did not come as a surprise. It had long been obvious that orthodox revolutionary arguments did not fit reality. First, they did not fit Third-World experience. In Africa

and Latin-America, 'dependency'-derived strategies of development had consistently met with disastrous failures – in spectacular contrast to the success of many newly-industrializing countries (NICs) in Asia, which followed development strategies derived from free-trade doctrines. Second, orthodox radical analysis most certainly did not fit the Second World. The collapse of the Eastern Bloc finally revealed the extent to which twentieth-century *Realsozialismus* was marked by economic backwardness, human oppression and political corruption – revelations which were embarrassing for Marxist radicals everywhere. Finally, revolutionary analysis did not fit the reality of the First World. By 1990, most capitalist countries of the West had moved out of old-fashioned industrialism and into 'post-industrial society'. The waning of industrialism meant the demise of the working class, of traditional working-class politics and of the Victorian, Marxist discourse in which it was framed.

8 To this can be added that the Continental, illiberal trunk bifurcates into a German and a French branch. The German branch may be best represented by the traditions of Sociology of Knowledge (Scheler and Mannheim), by left-wing Critical Theory (as represented most famously by the left-wing Frankfurt School, of which Adorno and Horkheimer were illustrious members), and by right-wing anti-modernists (notably Heidegger). The French branch is represented by French historians of science (Canguilhem, Bachelard and Koyré) and, later, the most illustrious participants in the French structuralist debates (Althusser, Lévi-Strauss, Barthes, Foucault, Derrida). The foliage of these two main branches is dense and intertwined. Miller (1993) has written an engaging and readable (but pithy and provocative Sado-Nietzschean) study of Foucault and the post-war generation of French intellectuals – to which Eribon (1994) has delivered a stinging counterattack.

9 On another occasion, Der Derian (1992, p. 1) plays off Will Rogers' definition of diplomacy as 'the art of saying "Nice doggie" until you can find a rock'. This is a far cry from the definitions used by traditional diplomatic historians like Nicolson (1954, p. 2) or Hamilton and Langhorne (1995, p. 1).

10 At the time this is written, there is no agreed-upon definition of 'constructivism'; the term is bandied recklessly about. Some authors see it as another label for 'post-structuralism'; others see in it a fruitful competitor to post-structuralism. That my definition is wider than any of these should be apparent from the text.

11 The struggle ought to have ended at the turn of the century with Max Weber. He argued that there are probably regularities in human behaviour, that they can be discovered by science, and that scientific methods can be called upon to help devise social theories and explain social and historical events. But it is insufficient to analyse society and history in terms of such theories, he continued. For scholars cannot readily deduce from general regularities to concrete events, because concrete events always have concrete causes. Weber then suggested that patterns in history tend to be the products of conceptualization rather than observation, and that social explanations necessarily involve subjective imagining on the part of the scientist.

Weber acknowledged that students of history and society work both by means of 'comprehensive historical intuition' and according to 'subjective experience'. He maintained that scientific and humanist approaches were different. He affirmed the legitimacy of both, limited each to particular spheres of usefulness, and explained their complementarity. This ought to have signalled an armistice among epistemological warriors. It did not. The tension remained. And it has occasioned vociferous epistemological debates every 30 years or so – in the 1920s and 1930s, in the 1960s, and, again, in the 1990s.

12   The advent of new means of global transportation irrevocably changed the old modes of world-wide transport and trade; it irreversibly altered traditional modes and relations of production. The rise of new systems of telecommunications, coupled with microelectronic processing units and user-friendly software programmes revolutionized world trade and finance. The smooth flows of monies and goods were additionally assisted by liberalization of the world economy, which, in turn, was intimately associated with the rapid globalization of firms and companies. By the early 1990s 'the growth of cross-national production networks of goods and services of some 35,000 transnational corporations and their more than 150,000 foreign affiliates [was] beginning to give rise to an international production system, organised and managed by transnational corporations' (UN 1993, p. 5).

13   Two things are worth noting here. First, that the unified sovereign territorial state still is an attractive ideal for many peoples and groups. In non-Western parts of the world, most particularly, the number of states has increased more than threefold since 1945; also, the territorial state has outcompeted several rival forms of political organization (Tilly 1994). Second, although new means of technology and new modes of communication have stimulated economic interdependence and helped erode the powers of states in many areas, technological developments have also increased state power in others. At the end of the twentieth century, many central governments have a greater capacity then ever for surveillance and regulation, and the regulatory powers of many states are stronger than they have ever been.

14   Statistics which describe the actual dissemination of personal computers (PCs) across the globe show that PCs are most densely clustered in the wealthy, liberal-democractic West, and far more thinly scattered across the Third World. If PCs liberate their users, then this extremely uneven distribution of PCs across the globe must necessarily occasion an equally uneven distribution of freedoms of information, knowledge and expression. Indeed, such statistics strongly suggest that the communications revolution is a Western phenomenon, and that it simply adds one more important power resource to those Western states which are already mighty and wealthy and enjoy a privileged position on the world scene.

15   Information about the history and conditions of countries can be accessed through http://www.yahoo.com/Regional/Country. An internet version of *The New York Times* can be accessed through http://nytimesfax.com/. Hourly updated world-news bulletins can be accessed e.g. through http://www.cnn.com/maps/cnn-header.map. An increasing number of professional journals are establishing home pages; the 'Monster List' (on http://www.enews.com/monster/international.html) provides more journal entries than most students can shake a stick at. An Internet Public Library is found at http://ipl.sils.umich.edu/; and a 'virtual bookstore' at http://www.comlab.ox.ac.uk/archive/publishers/bookstores.html. Much good information about the discipline of International Relations can be found through the home page of the International Studies Association (ISA): http://csf.colorado.edu/isa/index.html.

16   This could have dramatic consequences. The communications revolution represents a transition from the modern 'era of the book' to a post-modern 'age of the screen'. The old world image – traditionally represented by a world atlas containing about 200 coun-

tries coloured in different hues – has been replaced by an image of a borderless globe. Computer holograms have raised our awareness of the artificial nature of the boundaries of modern states and enhanced our awareness of the concepts through which we, until recently, observed and thought about world affairs. It has made it obvious that the old image offered by the world atlas was invented by European geographers during the infancy of the modern age. At that time it offered a way to classify the new territorial states which were emerging in Europe; the map-makers presented the world as a jigsaw puzzle of neat territorial pieces, and this presentation has ever since dominated the way we look at international relations (R. Kaplan 1994). However, recent events have done more than chip away at this old 'Westphalian notion' of a globe composed of independent and sovereign states. They have made us increasingly aware of the fact that this image is a clever, representational device. They have made us more aware of the context-dependent nature of our perceptions of the world. They have attuned us to the fact that concepts, images and perceptions are produced under distinct historical and civilizational conditions.

17 Psychologists have long relied, as a matter of course, on theories of communications to guide their investigations of the human mind as well as certain forms of therapy. Anthropologists, sociologists and social historians have long found in communications theory mechanisms by which mores, myths, identities and life-styles are passed from one generation to the next or from one segment of society to another – indeed, influential trend-setting sociologists define society itself as a self-producing system of communications (Habermas 1991; Luhmann 1995). Economists and political scientists also recognize that theories of communication and discourse help account for the regularities which sustain social order. Students of International Relations have since the 1960s tapped into theories of information processing, cybernetics, systems theory and other hi-tech related branches of communications theory to help understand world affairs (Pye 1963; Schelling 1966; Steinbruner 1974; Jervis 1976). But it was only during the 1980s that radical students discovered the critical potential inherent in theories of linguistics, semiology, symbolic interactionism and literary criticism. Given the centrality of communications theory in other fields of contemporary social sciences, the interesting question is not why radical students of International Relations discovered constructivist theories, but why it took them so long.

Bibliography

Adorno, T. and Horkheimer, M. (1979). *Dialectic of Enlightenment*. London: Verso [1944]

Airas, P. (1978). *Die geschichtlichen Wertungen Krieg und Friede von Friedrich dem Grossen bis Engels*. Rovaniemi: Pohjois-Suomen Historiallinen Yhdistys

Alker, H. (1992). 'The Humanist Moment in International Relations: Reflections on Machiavelli and Las Casas', *International Studies Quarterly*, 36:4, pp. 347–73

Allen, S H. (1920). *International Relations*. Princeton, NJ: Princeton University Press

Allison, G. (1971). *Essence of Decision*. Boston: Little, Brown

Anderson, B. (1983). *Imagined Communities*. London: NLB

Anderson, M. S. (1988). *War and Society in Europe of the Old Regime, 1618–1789*. London: Fontana Press

Anderson, P. (1979). *Lineages of the Absolutist State*. London: NLB

Angell, N. (1909). *The Great Illusion*. London: Heinemann

—— (1951). *After All*. London: Hamish Hamilton

Appleby, J. O. (1978). *Economic Thought and Ideology in Seventeenth Century England*. Princeton, NJ: Princeton University Press

Aquinas, T. (1947). *Summa Theologica*. New York: Benziger Brothers

Ardant, G. (1975), 'Financial Policy and Economic Infrastructure of Modern States and Nations', in Tilly (1975), pp. 164–242

Arendt, H. (1951). *The Origins of Totalitarianism*. New York: Harcourt, Brace

Aron, R. (1966). *Peace and War*. New York: Doubleday

—— (1986). *Clausewitz: Philosopher of War*. New York: Simon & Schuster

Artz, F. B. (1967). *The Mind of the Middle Ages*. Chicago: University of Chicago Press

Ashley, R. (1986). 'The Poverty of Neorealism', in Keohane (1986), pp. 255–300 [1984]

—— (1989). 'Living on Border Lines', in Der Derian and Shapiro (1989), eds., pp. 259–323

—— and Walker, R. B. J., eds. (1990). *International Studies Quarterly* (Special issue on post-structuralism), 34:3

Augustine of Hippo (1954). *The City of God*. New York: Fathers of the Church, Inc., Vol. VIII

Axelrod, R. (1984). *The Evolution of Cooperation*. New York: Basic Books

Bacon, F. (1852). 'Notes of a Speech Concerning a War with Spain', in *Works of Francis Bacon*, Vol. II, pp. 199–201. Philadelphia: Hart, Casey & Hart [1624]

Bagehot, W. (1889). 'Physics and Politics', *Works*, Vol. IV. Hartford, Conn: The Travelers Insurance Co. [1872]

Baran, P. and Sweezy, P. M. (1966). *Monopoly Capital*. New York: Monthly Review Press

Baron, H. (1952). 'Die Politische Entwicklung der Italienischen Renaissance', *Historische Zeitschrift*, 174, pp. 31–56

Barraclough, G. (1976). *An Introduction to Contemporary History*. Harmondsworth: Penguin

Barry, B. (1970). *Sociologists, Economists and Democracy*. London: Macmillan

Bartelson, N. (1995). *A Genealogy of Sovereignty*. Cambridge: Cambridge University Press

Batscha, Z. und Saage, R. eds. (1979). *Friedensutopien. Kant, Fichte, Schlegel, Görres*. Frankfuhrt-a.-M.: Suhrkamp

Baudrillard, J. (1995). *The Gulf War did not Take Place*. Bloomington, IN: Indiana University Press

Beales, A. C. F. (1931). *A History of Peace*. New York: Dial

Bebel, A. (1893). *Die Frau und der Sozialismus*. Stuttgart: Dietz

Becker, K. L. (1932). *The Heavenly City of the Eighteenth-Century Philosophers*. New Haven: Yale University Press

Belli, P. (1936). *A Treatise on Military Matters and Warfare*. Oxford: Clarendon Press [1563]

Bentham, J. (1843a). 'A Plan for an Universal and Perpetual Peace', in *Works*, Vol. II, pp. 546–61. Edinburgh: William Tait [*c*.1794]

—— (1843b). 'Emancipate you Colonies', in *Works*, Vol. 4, pp. 408–19. Edinburgh: William Tait

—— (1843c). 'Principles of International Law', in *Works*, Vol. 2, pp. 531–61. Edinburgh: William Tait

Berges, W. (1938). *Die Fürstenspiegel des hohen und späten Mittelalters*. Stuttgart: Hiersman Verlag

Berman, H. (1983). *Law and Revolution*. Cambridge: Harvard University Press

Bernhardi, F. von (1912). *Germany and the Next War*. New York: Longman, Green & Co

Bevin, E. (1945). 'On The Foreign Situation', memo by the Secretary of State for Foreign Affairs, 8. Nov. 1945, Foreign Office document (FO) 800.478 MIS/45/14; Public Records Office, London

Biersteker, T J. and Weber, C., eds (1996). *State Sovereignty as Social Construct*. Cambridge: Cambridge University Press

Bismarck, O. von (1898). *Bismarck, the Man and the Statesman*. London: Smith, Elder & Co

Blainey, G. (1973). *The Causes of War*. New York: The Free Press

Bloch, M. (1961). *Les Rois thaumaturges*. Paris: Colin

Bodin, J. (1945). *Method for the Easy Comprehension of History*. New York: Columbia University Press [1566]

—— (1967). *Six Books of the Commonwealth*. Oxford: Basil Blackwell [1576]

Bondanella, P. E. (1973). *Machiavelli and the Art of Renaissance Italy*. Detroit: Wayne

State University Press

Boroujerdi, M. (1996). *The Tormented Triumph of Nativism*. Syracuse, NY: Syracuse University Press

Bossuet, J.-B. (1824). *Politique*. Turin: Alliana [167?]

Botero, G. (1956). *The Reason of State and the Greatness of Cities*. New Haven: Yale University Press [1601?]

Bozeman, A. B. (1960). *Politics and Culture in International History*. Princeton, NJ: Princeton University Press

Bramhall, J. (1658). *Castigations of Mr. Hobbes his last animadversions in the case concerning liberty, and universal necessity. With an appendix concerning the Catching of Leviathan*. London: J. Crook

Braudel, F. (1972). *The Mediterranean*. New York: Harper & Row

Brennan, G. and Buchanan, J. (1985). *The Reasons of Rules*. Cambridge: Cambridge University Press

Brierly, J. L. (1928). *The Law of Nations*. New York: Oxford University Press

Brown, C. (1992). *International Relations Theory: New Normative Approaches*. New York: Harvester Wheatsheaf

Brown, P. M. (1923). *International Society*. New York: Macmillan

Buchanan, J. (1991). *The Economics and the Ethics of Constitutional Order*. Ann Arbor: University of Michigan Press

—— and Tullock, G. (1962). *The Calculus of Consent*. Ann Arbor: University of Michigan Press

Buckle, H. T. (1862). *History of Civilization in England*. New York: Appleton

Bukharin, N. (1973). *Imperialism and World Economy*. New York: Monthly Review Press [1915]

Bull, E. (1948). *Arbeiderklassen in norsk historie*. Oslo: Tiden Norsk Forlag

Bull, H. (1966). 'International Theory: The Case for a Classical Approach', *World Politics*, 18:3, pp. 361–77

—— (1977). *The Anarchical Society*. New York: Columbia University Press

Burke, E., ed. (1772). *The Annual Register* (Vol. XV). London: J. Dodsley

—— (1866). 'Letter to a Member of The National Assembly ...', in *Works*, Vol. IV, pp. 1–57. Boston: Little, Brown and Company [1791]

—— (1988). *Reflections on the Revolution in France*. Harmondsworth: Penguin [1790]

Burns, C. D. (1920). *International Politics*. London: Methuen

Burton, J. W. (1972). *World Society*. Cambridge: Cambridge University Press

Butterfield, H. and Wight, M. (1968). *Diplomatic Investigations*. Cambridge: Harvard University Press

Buzan, B. (1991). *People, States and Fear*. New York: Harvester Wheatsheaf

—— (1995a). 'The Present as a Historic Turning Point', Journal of Peace Research, 32:4, pp. 385–99

—— (1995b). 'The Level of Analysis Problem in International Relations Reconsidered', in Booth, K. and Smith, S., eds, *International Relations Theory Today*, pp. 198–217. Oxford: Polity Press

——, Little, R. and Jones, C. (1993). *The Logic of Anarchy*. New York: Columbia University Press

Callières, F. de (1983). *The Art of Diplomacy*. New York: Holmes & Meier [1716]

Campbell, D. (1992). *Writing Security*. Minneapolis, MN: Minnesota University Press

Cardano, G. (1930). *The Book of My Life*. New York: Dutton [1574]

Carr, E. H. (1964). *The Twenty-Year Crisis, 1919–1939*. New York: Harper and Row [1939]

Carson, R. (1962). *Silent Spring*. Boston: Houghton Mifflin

Castiglione, B. (1959). *Book of the Courtier*. New York: Doubleday [1528]

Cellini, B. (1969). *The Autobiography of Benvenuto Cellini*. New York: Macmillan [1728]

Chanteur, J. (1992). *From War to Peace*. Boulder, CO: Westview

Chartier, R., ed. (1987). *A History of Private Life*. Cambridge: Harvard University Press

Ch'en Po-ta (1953). *Stalin on the Chinese Revolution*. Peking: Foreign Languages Press

Chickering, R. (1975). *Imperial Germany and a World without War*. Princeton, NJ: Princeton University Press

Churchill, W. S. (1923). *The World Crisis*. London: Longman, Green

—— (1938). *Arms and the Covenant*. London: Harrap

Clausewitz, C. von (1922). 'Die Deutschen und die Franzosen', in Rothfels, H., ed., *Carl von Clausewitz: Politische Schriften und Briefe*, pp. 35–51. München: Drei Masken Verlag

—— (1962). 'I Believe and Profess,' in *War, Politics and Power*, pp. 301–4. Chicago: Henry Regnery

—— (1976). *On War*. Princeton, NJ: Princeton University Press [1832]

Clemenceau, G. (1930). *Grandeurs et misères d'une victoire*. Paris: Plon

Clinton, D. (1993), 'Tocqueville on democracy, obligation and the international system', *Review of International Studies*, 19:3, pp. 227–45

Cobden, R. (1973). *The Political Writings of Richard Cobden*, 2 vols. New York: Garland Publishing

Cole, G. D. H. ed. (1950). *The Social Contract and Discourses*. London: Dutton

Cole, P. R. (1939). *A History of Educational Thought*. Westport, Conn.: Greenwood Press

Condorcet, J.-A.-N. de Caritat, marquis de (1788). *Reflexions sur l'esclavage des nègres*. Neufchatel: Societé typographique [1781]

—— (1798). *Esquisse d'un tableau historique des progrès de l'esprit humain*. Paris: Agasse [1794]

Connolly, W. E. (1993). *Terms of Political Discourse*. Oxford: Blackwell [1974]

Cooley, C. H. (1918). *Social Process*. New York: Scribner's Sons

Cooper, R. (1968). *The Economics of Interdependence*. McGraw-Hill, New York

Couloumbis, T. A. and Wolfe, J. H. (1990). *Introduction to International Relations*. Englewood Cliffs, NJ: Prentice-Hall

Courtilz de Sandras, G. de (1686). *Nouveaux interêts des Princes de l'Europe, où l'on traite des Maximes qu'ils doivent observer pour se maintenir dans leurs Etats, et pour empêcher qu'ils ne se forme une Monarchie Universelle*. Cologne [the Hague]: Pierre Marteau

Cox, R. H. (1960). *Locke on War and Peace*. Oxford: Clarendon Press

Cox, R. W. (1987). *Production, Power and World Order*. New York: Columbia University Press

—— with Sinclair, T. J. (1996). *Approaches to World Order*. Cambridge: Cambridge University Press

Cranston, M. (1982). *Jean Jacques*. Chicago: University of Chicago Press

—— (1991). *The Noble Savage: Jean-Jacques Rousseau 1754–1762*. Chicago: University of Chicago Press

Crocker, L. G. (1974). *Jean-Jacques Rousseau*, 2 vols. New York: Macmillan
Cronin, V. (1967). *The Florentine Renaissance*. New York: E. P. Dutton & Co
Crook, P. (1994). *Darwinism, War and History*. Cambridge: Cambridge University Press
Crucé, É. (1972). *The New Cyneas*. New York: Garland Publishing [1623]
Cumberland, R. (1727). *A Treatise of the Law of Nature*. London: R. Philips [1672]
Darwin, C. (1958). *The Origin of Species*. New York: New American Library [1859]
—— (1962). *The Voyage of the Beagle*. New York: Doubleday [1839]
Davies, D. (1932). *Suicide or Sanity?* London: Williams & Norgate
Defoe, D. (1938). Editorial in *Review of the State of the English Nation*, Vol. 7, pp. 261–3 [1 June 1706]. New York: Columbia University Press
Derathé, R. (1979). *Jean-Jacques Rousseau et la science politique de son temps*. Paris: Libraire philosophique J. Vrin
Der Derian, J. (1987). *On Diplomacy*. Oxford: Blackwell
—— (1992). *Antidiplomacy*. Oxford: Blackwell
—— (1994). 'Simulation: The Highest Stage of Capitalism?', in Kellner, D., ed., *Baudrillard*, pp. 189–209. Oxford: Blackwell
——, ed. (1995). *International Theory: Critical Investigations*. London: Macmillan
—— and Shapiro, M., eds (1989). *International/Intertextual Relations*. Lexington, Mass: Lexington Books
Deutsch, K. W. (1953). *Nationalism and Social Communication*. New York: John Wiley
—— et al. (1957). *Political Community and the North Atlantic Area*. Princeton, NJ: Princeton University Press
Dickinson, G. L. (1927). 'Introduction', in Rousseau, J.-J., *A Project of Perpetual Peace*. London: R. Cobden-Sanderson
Dickson, P. (1972). *Think Tanks*. New York: Atheneum
Diderot, D. (1992). *Political Writings*. Cambridge: Cambridge University Press
Dougherty, J. E. and Pfaltzgraff, R. L. Jr, (1981). *Contending Theories of International Relations*. New York: Harper & Row
Downing, B. M. (1992). *The Military Revolution and Political Change*. Princeton, NJ: Princeton University Press
Doyle, M. (1983). 'Kant, Liberal Legacies and Foreign Affairs', *Philosophy and Public Affairs*, vol. 12, no. 3, pp. 441–73
Drucker, P. (1939). *The End of Economic Man*. New York: John Day Company
—— (1986). 'The Changed World Economy', *Foreign Affairs*, vol. 64, pp. 768–91
Duby, G. (1968). *Rural Economy and Country Life in the Medieval West*. London: Edward Arnold
Dunn, F. S. (1937). *Peaceful Change: A Study of International Procedures*. New York: Council on Foreign Relations
—— (1949). 'The Scope of International Relations', *World Politics*, 1:2, pp. 142–7
Dupuis, C. (1909). *Le Principe d'équilibre et le concert europeén*. Paris: Perrin & Compagnie
Dyson, K. (1980). *The State Tradition in Western Europe*. Oxford: Martin Robertson
Eagleton, C. (1932). *International Government*. New York: Ronald Press
—— (1937). *Analysis of the Problem of War*. New York: Ronald Press
—— and Wilcox, F. O., eds (1945). 'The United Nations: Peace and Security', *American Political Science Review*. 39:4, pp. 934–92

Eckstein, H. (1982). 'The Idea of Political Development', *World Politics*. 34:4, pp. 451–86

Eistenstein, E. L. (1993). *The Printing Revolution in Early Modern Europe*. Cambridge: Cambridge University Press

Elias, N. (1983), *The Court Society*, Pantheon, New York

Elton, G. R. (1981). *Reformation Europe*. Glasgow: Fontana/Collins

Engels, F. (1976). *Anti-Düring*. Peking: Foreign Languages Press [1878]

Eribon, D. (1994). *Michel Foucault et ses contemporains*. Paris: Fayard

Evans, P., ed. (1993). *Double-Edged Diplomacy*. Berkeley, CA: University of California Press

Fanon, F. (1963). *The Wretched of the Earth*. New York: Grove Press [1961]

—— (1967). *Black Skin, White Masks*. New York: Grove Press

—— (1968). *Studies in a Dying Colonialism*. New York: Monthly Review Press

Fébvre, L. (1942). *Le problème de l'incroyance au XVIe siècle*. Paris: Michel

—— and Martin, J.-H. (1976). *The Coming of the Book: The Impact of Printing*. London: NLB

Fénelon, F. de Salignac de la Mothe, (1815). 'On the necessity of forming alliances, both offensive and defensive, against a foreign power which manifestly aspires to universal monarchy', in anon., *A Collection of Scarce and Valuable Tracts on the most Interesting and Entertaining Subjects*, 2nd edn, Vol. XIII. London: Cadell, Davis, etc. [1700]

Ferguson, Y. H. (1996). *Politics: Authority, Identities and Ideology*. Columbia, SC: University of South Carolina Press

—— and Mansbach, R. W. (1988). *The Elusive Quest*. Columbia, SC: University of South Carolina Press

Ferrari, J. (1860). *Histoire de la raison d'État*. Paris: Michel Lévy Frères

Fichte, J. G. (1979a). 'Zum ewigen Frieden', in Batscha and Saage (1979), pp. 83–93 [1796]

—— (1979b). *Der geschlossende Handelsstaat*. Hamburg: Felix Meiner Verlag [1800]

Fichterman, H. (1964). *The Carolingian Empire*. New York: Harper & Row

Filmer, R. (1991). 'Patriarcha: a defence of the natural power of kings against the unnatural liberty of the people', in *Patriarcha and Other Writings*. Cambridge: Cambridge University Press [1680]

Finer, S. (1975). 'State- and nation-building in Europe', in Tilly (1975), pp. 84–164

Fischer, F. (1961). *Griff nach der Weltmacht*. Dusseldorf: Droste

Forsyth, M. G. *et al.* (1970). *The Theory of International Relations*. London: Allen & Unwin

Foucault, M. (1973). *The Order of Things*. New York: Random House [1966]

—— (1984a). 'What is Enlightenment', in Rabinow (1984), pp. 32–51

—— (1984b). 'Nietzsche, Genealogy, History', in Rabinow (1984), pp. 76–101

Fox, W. T. R. (1949). 'Interwar International Relations Research: The American Experience', *World Politics*. 1:1, pp. 67–80

——, ed. (1959). *Theoretical Aspects of International Relations*. Notre Dame: Notre Dame Press

Fraenkel, E. (1941). *The Dual State*. London: Oxford University Press

Frank, A. G. (1967). *Capitalism and Underdevelopment in Latin America*. New York: Monthly Review Press

Franke, W. (1968). 'The Italian City-State System as an International System', in Kaplan,

M., ed., *New Approaches to International Relations*, pp. 426–59. New York: St. Martin's Press

Frederick II (1981). *AntiMachiavel*. Athens, OH: Ohio University Press [1740]

Friedrich, C. J., ed. (1949). *The Philosophy of Kant*. New York: The Modern Library

—— (1954). *Totalitarianism*. Cambridge: Harvard University Press

—— and Brzezinski, Z. (1965). *Totalitarian Dictatorship and Autocracy*. Cambridge, MA: Harvard University Press

Fromkin, D. (1989). *A Peace to End all Peace*. New York: Avon Books

—— (1995). *In the Time of the Americans*. New York: Knopf

Frost, M. (1986). *Towards a Normative Theory of International Relations*. Cambridge: Cambridge University Press

Fukuyama, F. (1992). *The End of History and the Last Man*. New York: Free Press

Gaddis, J. L. (1993). 'International Relations Theory and the End of the Cold War', *International Security*, 17:3, pp. 5–58

Ganshof, F.-L. (1994), 'Le Moyen Age' in Renouvin (1995), pp. 15–243 [1953]

Gardner, L. C. (1984). *A Covenant with Power*. New York: Oxford University Press

Gasman, D. (1971). *The Scientific Origins of National Socialism*. London: Macdonald

Gates, S., Knutsen, T. L. and Moses, J. W. (1996). 'Democracy and Peace: A More Skeptical View', *Journal of Peace Research*, 33:1, pp. 1–11

Geiss, I. (1993). *Europa – Vielfalt und Einheit*. Mannheim: B.I.-Taschenbuchverlag

Gellner, E. (1983). *Nations and Nationalism*. Oxford: Blackwell

Gentili, A. (1964). *De Jure Belli Libri Tres*. New York: Oceana Publications [1612]

Gentz, F. (1806). *Fragments upon the Present State of the Political Balance of Europe*. London: M. Peltier

—— (1953), 'Über den ewigen Frieden', in Raumer, K. von (ed.), *Ewiger Friede*. München: Verlag Karl Alber Freiburg

George, J. (1994). *Discourses of Global Politics: A Critical (Re)Introduction to International Relations*. Boulder, CO: Lynne Rienner

Gilbert, F. (1965). *Machiavelli and Guicciardini*. Princeton, NJ: Princeton University Press

Gilpin, R. (1981). *War and Change in World Politics*. New York: Cambridge University Press

—— (1986). 'The Richness of the Tradition of Political Realism', in Keohane (1986), pp. 301–22. New York: Columbia University Press

—— (1987). *The Political Economy of International Relations*. Princeton, NJ: Princeton University Press

Gleditsch, N. P. and Hegre, H. (1996). 'Peace and Democracy: Three Levels of Analysis', *Journal of Conflict Resolution*, forthcoming

Godwin, W. (1985). *Enquiry Concerning Political Justice*. Harmondsworth: Penguin [1793]

Goertz, G. (1994). *Contexts of International Politics*. Cambridge: Cambridge University Press

Gordon, D. C. (1989). *Images of the West*. Totowa, NJ: Rowman & Littlefield

Görres, J. (1979), 'Der allgemeine Frieden – Ein Ideal', in Batscha and Saage (1979), pp. 126–77 [1798]

Gough, J. W. (1936). *The Social Contract*. Oxford: Clarendon Press

Grampp, W. D. (1965). *Economic Liberalism*. New York: Random House

Grant, A. J. *et al.* (1916). *An Introduction to the Study of International Relations*. London: Macmillan & Co

Grant, R. and Newland, K., eds. (1991). *Gender and International Relations*. Buckingham: Milton Keynes/Open University Press

Gregory of Tours (1974). *The History of the Franks*. Harmondsworth: Penguin [593?]

Grey, E. (1925). *Twenty-Five Years*, Vol. 2. New York: Frederick A. Stokes

Grotius, H. (1853). *De Jure Belli ac Pacis*. Cambridge: Cambridge University Press [1625]

Grunebaum, G. E. von (1946). *Medieval Islam*. Chicago University Press, Chicago

Guevara, E. (1961). *On Guerrilla Warfare*. New York: Praeger

Guicciardini, F. (1969). *The History of Italy*. London: Collier-Macmillan [1561]

—— (1970). *Maxims and Reflections of a Renaissance Statesman*. Gloucester, Mass.: Peter Smith [1857]

—— (1994). *Dialogue on the Government of Florence*. Cambridge: Cambridge University Press

Gumplowicz, L. (1909). *Der Rassenkampf*. Innsbruck: Wagner'sche Universitätsbuchhandlung [1885]

Gunn, J. A. W. (1969). *Politics and the Public Interest in the Seventeenth Century*. London: Routledge & Kegan Paul

Gunnell, J. G. (1978). 'The Myth of the Tradition', *American Political Science Review*, 72:1, pp. 122–35

Gwatkin, H. M. *et al.*, eds (1968). *Germany and the Western Empire*. Cambridge: Cambridge University Press

Haas, E. (1964). *Beyond the Nation State: Functionalism and International Organization*. Stanford, CA: Stanford University Press

Haas, P., ed. (1992). *International Organization* (Special Issue on Epistemic Communities), 46:1

Habermas, J. (1991). *Communication and the Evolution of Society*. Cambridge: Polity Press

Haeckel, E. (1896). *The Evolution of Man*. New York: Appleton

—— (1900). *The Riddle of the Universe*. New York: Harper & Brothers

Hale, J. R. (1981). 'International relations in the West', in Hay, D., ed., *The Renaissance 1493–1520*, 2nd edn, pp. 259–92. Cambridge: Cambridge University Press [1957]

Hall, J. A. (1986). *Powers and Liberties*. Harmondsworth: Penguin

Halliday, F. (1994). *Rethinking International Relations*. London: Macmillan

Hamilton, A. (1928). 'Report on the Subject of Manufactures', in Cole, Arthur H., ed., *Industrial and Commercial Correspondence of Alexander Hamilton*. Chicago: A. W. Shaw Co. [1791]

——, Jay, J. and Madison, J. (1937). *The Federalist*. New York: Modern Library [1788]

Hamilton, K. and Langhorne, R. (1995). *The Practice of Diplomacy*. London: Routledge

Hampson, N. (1968). *The Enlightenment*. Harmondsworth: Penguin

Hancock, W. K. (1937). *Survey of British Commonwealth Affairs*, Vol. I. London: Oxford University Press

Hanke, L. (1974). *All Mankind is One*. De Kalb, IL: Northern Illinois University Press

Harbutt, F. (1988). *The Iron Curtain*. Oxford: Oxford University Press

Hardin, G. (1968). 'The Tragedy of the Commons', *Science*, 13 December, pp. 1243–8

Haushofer, K. (1928). *Bausteine zur Geopolitik*. Berlin-Grünewald: Vowinkel

Hawtrey, R. G. (1952). *Economic Aspects of Sovereignty*. London: Longman Green

Hayek, F. A. (1944). *The Road to Serfdom*. Chicago: University of Chicago Press

Heatley, D. P. (1919). *Diplomacy and the Study of International Relations*. Oxford: Clarendon Press

Heckscher, E. (1935). *Mercantilism*. London: Allen & Unwin

Hegel, G. W. F. (1980). *Philosophy of Right*. London: Oxford University Press [1821]

Heilbroner, R. L. (1986). *he Nature and Logic of Capitalism*. New York: W.W. Norton

Herder, J. G. von (1829). *Briefe zur Beförderungen der Humanität*. Stuttgart: Cotta

Hertz, J. (1942). 'Power Politics and World Organization', *American Political Science Review*, 36:6, pp. 1039–52

—— (1950). 'Idealist Internationalism and the Security Dilemma', *World Politics*, 2:2, pp. 157–80

—— (1951). *Political Realism and Political Idealism*. Chicago: University of Chicago Press

—— (1957). 'The Rise and Demise of the Territorial State', *World Politics*, 9:4, pp. 473–93

Hilferding, R. (1955). *Das Finanzkapital*. Berlin: Dietz Verlag [1910]

Hinsley, F. H. (1963). *Power and the Pursuit of Peace*. Cambridge: Cambridge University Press

Hintz, S. I. (1962). *The Hunting of Leviathan*. Cambridge: Cambridge University Press.

Hirschman, A. O. (1981). *The Passions and the Interests*. Princeton, NJ: Princeton University Press [1977]

Hitler, A. (1943). *Mein Kampf*. Boston: Houghton Mifflin

Hobbes, T. (1951). *Leviathan*. Harmondsworth: Penguin [1651]

Hobsbawm, E. (1962). *The Age of Revolution: 1789–1848*. New York: New American Library

—— (1969). *Industry and Empire*. Harmondsworth: Penguin

—— (1991). *Nations and Nationalism since 1780*. Cambridge: Cambridge University Press

—— (1994). *The Age of Extremes*. London: Michael Joseph

Hobson, J. A. (1902). *Imperialism*. London: J. Pott

Hodges, C. (1931). *Background of International Relations*. New York: Wiley

Hoffmann, S. (1987), 'An American Social Science', in *Janus and Minerva*, pp. 3–24. Boulder, CO: Westview [1977]

Hoffmann, S. and Fidler, D. P., eds. (1991). *Rousseau on International Relations*. Oxford: Clarendon Press

Holbach, P. H. T., baron de (1773). *Système social*. London: Marc-Michel Rey

Holsti, K. (1967). *International Politics*. Englewood Cliffs, NJ: Prentice-Hall

—— (1987). *The Dividing Discipline*. London: Allen & Unwin

—— (1996). *The State, war, and the State of War*. Cambridge: Cambridge University Press

Holsti, O. (1972). *Crisis, Escalation, War*. Montreal: McGill-Queen's University Press

Homer-Dixon, T. (1994), 'Environmental Scarcities and Violent Conflict', *International Security*, 19:1, pp. 5–40

Howard, M. (1978). *War and the Liberal Conscience*. New Brunswick, NJ: Rutgers University Press

—— (1984). *War in European History*. London: Oxford University Press

Howard, R. (1995). 'Occidentalism, Human Rights and the Obligation of Western Scholars', *Canadian Journal of African Studies*, 29:1, pp. 110–11

Hughes, B. B. (1991). *Continuity and Change in World Politics*. Englewood Cliffs, NJ: Prentice-Hall

Hull, C. (1948). *Memoirs*, Vol. I. New York: Macmillan

Hume, D. (1985). *Essays. Moral, Political and Literary*. Indianapolis: Liberty Classics [1741]

Huntington, S. (1991). *The Third Wave*. Norman: University of Oklahoma Press

Hussey, J. M. (1966). *The Byzantine Empire*. Cambridge: Cambridge University Press

James, M. R. (1968a). 'Learning and Literature till the Death of Bede', in Gwatkin. *et al.* (1968), pp. 485–513

—— (1968b). 'Learning and Literature till Pope Sylvester II', in Gwatkin *et al.* (1968), pp. 514–38

Janet, P. (1887). *Histoire de la science politique. Ses rapports avec la morale*, Vol. I. Paris: Alcan

Janis, I. (1972). *Groupthink*. Boston: Houghton Mifflin

Jervis, R. (1976). *Perception and Misperception in International Politics*. Princeton, NJ: Princeton University Press

Jevons, W. (1888). *The Theory of Political Economy*. London: Macmillan [1871]

—— (1909). *The Coal Question*. London: Macmillan [1865]

Jian, C. (1994). *China's Road to the Korean War*. New York: Columbia University Press

Joll, J. (1964). *The Anarchists*. London: Eyre & Spottiswoode

Jones, W. S. (1991). *The Logic of International Relations*. New York: Harper Collins

Kant, I. (1949a). 'What is Enlightenment'? in Friedrich (1949), pp. 132–40 [1784]

—— (1949b). 'Idea for a Universal History with Cosmopolitan Intent', in Friedrich (1949), pp. 116–31 [1784]

—— (1970a). 'On the Commonplace', in Forsyth *et al.* (1970), pp. 192–200 [1793]

—— (1970b). 'Perpetual Peace', in Forsyth *et al.* (1970), pp. 200–45 [1795]

—— (1991). 'A Renewed Attempt to Answer the Question: "Is the Human Race Continually Improving?"' in Reiss (1991), pp. 177–91 [17..]

Kaplan, M. (1957). *System and Process in International Politics*. New York: John Wiley

Kaplan, R. (1994). 'The Coming Anarchy', *Atlantic Monthly*, 275:2 (February), pp. 44ff

Kauppi, M. V. and Viotti, P. R. (1992). *The Global Philosophers*. New York: Macmillan

Kautsky, Karl (1970). 'Ultra-imperialism', in *New Left Review*, 59, pp. 41–7 [1914]

Keen, M. H. (1963). *The Laws of War in the Late Middle Ages*. London: Routledge & Kegan Paul

Keens-Soper, H. M. A. and Schweizer, K. (1983). 'Introduction', in Callières, François de, ed., *The Art of Diplomacy*, pp. 1–53. New York: Leicester University Press, Holmes & Meier

Kegley, C. W., Jr and Wittkopf, E. R. (1995). *World Politics*. New York: St Martins

Kennan, G. F. (1946). 'The Chargé in the Soviet Union (Kennan) to the Secretary of State', in *Foreign Relations of the United States, 1946*, GPO, Washington D.C., 1969, VI, Telegram 861.00/2–2246 [Moscow, 22 February 1946], pp. 700–7

—— (1950). *American Diplomacy*. Chicago: University of Chicago Press

—— (1956). *Soviet–American Relations: 1917–1920*. Princeton, NJ: Princeton University Press

—— (1967). *Memoires 1925–1950*. New York: Little, Brown and Co

—— (1993). *Around the Cragged Hill*. New York: W.W. Norton

Kennedy, P. (1987). *The Rise and Fall of the Great Powers*. New York: Random House
—— (1993). *Preparing for the Twenty-First Century*. London: HarperCollins
Keohane, R. O. (1982). 'The Demand for International Regimes', *International Organization*, 36:3, pp. 325–55
—— (1984). *After Hegemony*. Princeton, NJ: Princeton University Press
—— ed. (1986). *Neo-Realism and its Critics*. New York: Columbia University Press
—— (1988). 'International Institutions: Two Approaches', *International Studies Quarterly*, 32:4, pp. 379–96
—— and Nye, J. S. (1977). *Power and Interdependence*. New York: Little Brown and Co
Keynes, J. M. (1920). *The Economic Consequences of the Peace*. London: Macmillan & Co
Kidd, B. (1894). *Social Evolution*. London: Macmillan & Co
Kirk, G. (1949). 'Materials for The Study of International Relations', *World Politics*, 1:4, pp. 426–31
Kissinger, H. A. (1954). *A World Restored*. Boston: Houghton Mifflin
—— (1968). 'The White Revolutionary: Reflections on Bismarck', *Daedalus*, 97:3, pp. 888–924
—— (1994). *Diplomacy*. New York: Simon & Schuster
Klee, H. (1946). *Hugo Grotius und Johannes Selden*. Berne: Verla Paul Haupt
Klein, B. S. (1994). *Strategic Studies and World Order*. Cambridge: Cambridge University Press
Kline, M. (1977). *Mathematics in Western Culture*. Harmondsworth: Penguin
Kluckhohn, C. (1949). 'Russian Research at Harvard', *World Politics*, 1:2, pp. 266–71
Knutsen, T. L. (1994). 'Re-Reading Rousseau in the Post-Cold War World', *Journal of Peace Research*, 31:3, pp. 247–63
Krasner, S. (1982). 'Structural Causes and Regime Consequences', *International Organization*, 36:1, pp. 185–205
Kratochwil, F. V. (1989). *Rules, Norms and Decisions*. Cambridge: Cambridge University Press
Kubalkova, V. and Cruikshank, A. A. (1980). *Marxism–Leninism and Theory of International Relations*. London: Routledge & Kegan Paul
Kuttner, R. (1991). *The End of Laissez-Faire*. New York: Knopf
LaFeber, W. (1989). *The American Age*. New York: W. W. Norton
Lange, C. (1919). *Histoire de l'internationalisme*. Kristiania: Publications de l'Institut Nobel norvégien, tome IV
Lansing, R. (1935). *War Memoires of Robert Lansing, Secretary of State*. Indianapolis: Bobbs-Merrill
Lapid, Y. (1989). 'The Third Debate', *International Relations Quarterly*, 33:3, pp. 235–55
Laslett, P. (1960). 'Introduction', in Locke (1960), pp. 15–136
Laue, T. von (1987). *The World Revolution of Westernization*. Oxford: Oxford University Press
Lauterpacht, H. (1933). *The Function of Law in International Community*. New York: Oxford University Press
Lawrence, T. J. (1919). *The Society of Nations*. New York: Oxford University Press
Lebow, N. R. and Strauss, B. S., eds (1991). *Hegemonic Rivalry*. Boulder, CO: Westview Press
Leibniz, G. von (1963). 'Entretien de Philarète et d'Eugène sur la question du temps', in

Politische Schriften, Vol. II, pp. 278–339. Berlin: Akademie-Verlag [1677]

Lenczowski, G. (1952). *The Middle East in World Affairs*. Ithaca, NY: Cornell University Press

Lenin, V. (1975a). 'Decree on Peace', in Tucker (1975), pp. 540–2. New York: W. W. Norton

—— (1975b). 'Imperialism, the Highest Stage of Capitalism', in Tucker (1975), pp. 204–75

Leonard, I. A. (1949). *Books of the Brave*. Massachusetts: Harvard University Press

Link, A. S., ed. (1967). *The Public Papers of Woodrow Wilson*, Vol. V. Princeton, NJ: Princeton University Press

—— (1971). *The Higher Realism of Woodrow Wilson*. Nashville: Vanderbilt University Press

Linklater, A. (1982). *Men and Citizens in the Theory of International Relations*. New York: St Martin's Press

—— (1990). *Beyond Realism and Marxism*. London: Macmillan

Lippmann, W. (1943). *U.S. Foreign Policy*. Boston: Little, Brown and Co

—— (1947). *The Cold War*. New York: Harper

List, F. (1927). 'Das Natürliche System der Politischen Ökonomie', in *Werke*, Vol. IV, pp. 154–550. Berlin: Reimar Hobbing [1837]

—— (1930). 'Das Nationale System der Politischen Ökonomie', in *Werke*, Vol. VI, pp. 1–433. Berlin: Reimar Hobbing [1841]

Locke, J. (1960). *Two Treatises of Government*. Cambridge: Cambridge University Press [1689]

Luard, E. (1992). *Basic Texts in International Relations*. New York: St Martin's

Luce, H. (1941). *The American Century*. New York: Farrar & Rinehart

Luhmann, N. (1995). *Social Systems*. Stanford, CA: Stanford University Press

Luxemburg, R. (1951). *Accumulation of Capital*. Yale University Press, New Haven [1913]

Lyotard, J.-F. (1983). 'Answering the Question: What is Postmodernism', in Hassan, I and Hassan S., eds, *Innovation/Renovation*, pp. 71–82. Madison, WI: University of Wisconsin Press

Machiavelli, N. (1961). *The Prince*. Harmondsworth: Penguin

MacKenzie, J. M. (1995). *Orientalism*. Manchester: Manchester University Press

Mackinder, H. (1904). 'The Geographical Pivot of History', *Geographical Journal*, 23 pp. 421–44

McKinlay, R. D. and Little, R. (1986). *Global Problems and World Order*. Madison, WI: University of Wisconsin Press

Macpherson, C. B. (1962). *The Political Theory of Possessive Individualism*. Oxford: Clarendon Press

Madison, J. (1953), 'Is Universal Peace Possible', in *The Complete Madison*. New York: Harper & Brothers, pp. 260–62 [1792]

Malthus, T. (1982). *An Essay on the Principle of Population*. Harmondsworth: Penguin [1798]

Mandeville, B. de (1924). *Fable of the Bees: or Private Vices, Publick Benefits*. Oxford: Clarendon Press [1714]

Mandrou, R. (1978). *From Humanism to Science, 1480–1700*. Harmondsworth: Penguin

Mannheim, K. (1936). *Ideology and Utopia*. New York: Harcourt, Brace

Mansbridge, J. J. (1990). *Beyond Self-Interest*. Chicago: University of Chicago Press

Mansfield, H. C. (1996). *Machiavelli's Virtue*. Chicago: University of Chicago Press

Mantoux, P. *et al.* (1938). *The World in Crisis*. New York: Longman, Green

Mao Zedong (1964). 'Problems of Strategy in China's Revolutionary War', in *Selected Works*, Vol. I, pp. 179–248. Peking: Foreign Languages Press [1936]

—— (1965a). 'The Role of the Chinese Communist Party in the National War', in *Selected Works*, Vol. II, pp. 195–212 Peking: Foreign Languages Press [1938]

—— (1965b). 'On Protracted War', in *Selected Works*, Vol. II, pp. 113–94. Peking: Foreign Languages Press [1937]

—— (1965c). 'Talks at The Yenan Forum on Literature And Art', in *Selected Works*, Vol. III, pp. 69–99. Peking: Foreign Languiages Press [1942]

Marriott, J. A. (1937). *Commonwealth or Anarchy?* London: P. Allan

Marsiglio of Padua (1993). *Writings on the Empire. Defensor minor and De translatione Imperii*. Cambridge: Cambridge University Press [1324]

Marx, K. (1964a). 'Marx and Engels in Manchester', in *Werke*, Vol. XXX, pp. 130–1. Berlin: Dietz Verlag

—— (1964b). 'Marx and Ferdinand Lassalle in Berlin', in *Werke*, Vol. XXX, pp. 577–79. Berlin: Dietz Verlag

—— (1972). 'The Future Results of the British Rule in India', in *On Colonialism*, pp. 81–8. New York: International Publishers [1853]

—— (1975a). 'Critique of Hegel's Dialectic And General Philosophy', in Hoare, Quentin, ed., *Karl Marx: Early Writings*, pp. 379–400. New York: Random House [1843–44]

—— (1975b). 'Preface to A Contribution to The Critique of Political Economy', in Hoare, Quentin, ed., *Karl Marx: Early Writings*, pp. 424–9. New York: Random House [1859]

—— (1977). *Capital*, Vol. I. New York: Vintage Books [1867]

—— and Engels, F. (1974). 'Manifesto of the Communist Party,' in Fernback, D., ed., *Karl Marx: Political Writings*, Vol. I, pp. 67–99. New York: Random House

Mazzini, G. (1945). *Selected Writings*. London: Lindsay Drommond

Meinecke, F. (1957). *Machiavellism*. New Haven: Yale University Press [1924]

Mészáros, I. (1970). *Marx' Theory of Alienation*. New York: Harper & Row

Mill, J. S. (1866). *Principles of Political Economy*, 2 vols. London: Longman, Green, Reader and Dyer

Miller, J. (1993). *The Passion of Michel Foucault*. London: HarperCollins

Miller, L. (1994). *Global Order*. Boulder, CO: Westview Press

Minc, A. (1993). *Le nouveau moyen age*. Paris: Gallimard

Minogue, K. (1985). *Alien Powers*. New York: St Martin's Press

Mitrany, D. (1933). *The Progress of International Government*. New Haven: Yale University Press

—— (1966). *A Working Peace System*. Chicago: Quadrangle [1943]

Molnar, M. (1975). *Marx, Engels et le politique international*. Paris: Gallimard

Momigliano, A., ed. (1963). *The Conflict between Paganism and Christianity in the 4th Century*. Oxford: Clarendon Press

Montaigne, M. de (1935). *The Essays of Michel de Montaigne*, vol. I. New York: Knopf

Montesquieu, C. L. de Secondat, baron de (1990). *The Spirit of the Laws*. Chicago: Encyclopædia Britannica [1748]

Moore, B., Jr (1966). *Social Origins of Dictatorship and Democracy*. Boston: Beacon Press
—— (1978). *Injustice: The Social Bases of Obedience and Revolt*. New York: Sharpe
Morgenthau, H. J. (1967). 'To Intervene Or Not to Intervene', *Foreign Affairs*, 45:3, pp. 424–36
—— (1978). *Politics Among Nations*. New York: Knopf [1948]
Morley, J. (1881). *The Life of Richard Cobden*. Boston: Robert Brothers
Mueller, J. (1989). *Retreat from Doomsday*. New York: Basic Books
Muir, R. (1918). *National Self-Government, Its Growth and Principles, The Culmination of Modern History*. London: Constable & Co
—— (1933). *The Interdependent World and Its Problems*. London: Constable & Co
Mussolini, B. (1933). *The Political and Social Doctrine of Fascism*. London: Hogarth Press
Nandy, A. (1987). *Traditions, Tyranny, and Utopias*. Delhi: Oxford University Press
Nardin, T. and Mapel, D. R. (1993). *Traditions of International Ethics*. Cambridge: Cambridge University Press
Navari, C. (1989). 'The Great Illusion Revisited', *Review of International Studies*, 15, pp. 341–58
Nedham, M. (1659). *Interest will not Lie, or a View of England's True Interest*. London: (no publisher identified)
Needham, J. (1969). *The Grand Titration*. London: Allen & Unwin
Neumann, F. L. (1944). *Behemoth*. New York: Octagon Books
Neumann, I. (1996). 'Self and Other in International Relations', *European Journal of International Relations*, 2:2, pp. 139–74
Ngugi wa Thiong'o (1986). *Decolonizing the Mind*. London: James Currey
Nicolson, H. G. (1954). *Evolution of the Diplomatic Method*. London: Constable
—— (1988). *Diplomacy*. Washington, DC: Georgetown University, School of Foreign Service [1939]
Niebuhr, R. (1932). *Moral Man and Immoral Society*. New York: Scribner's Sons
—— (1936). *Doom and Dawn*. New York: Eddy and Page
—— (1942). 'Plans for World Reorganization', *Christianity and Crisis*, 2, p. 4
—— (1949). *Faith and History*. New York: Scribner's Sons
—— (1950a). 'American Conservatism And The World Crisis', *Yale Review*, 40, pp. 385–97
—— (1950b). 'A Protest against A Dilemma's Two Horns', *World Politics*, 2:3, pp. 338–45
—— (1955). *The Self and the Dramas of History*. New York: Scribner's Sons
—— (1959). *The Structure of Nations and Empires*. New York: Scribner's Sons
Nietzsche, F. (1960). 'Aus dem Nachlass der Achtzigerjahre', *Werke*, Vol. III, p. 917. Munich: Carl Hansen Verlag [188?]
—— (1994). *On the Genealogy of Morality*. Cambridge: Cambridge University Press [1887]
North, D. (1981). *Structure and Change in Economic History*. New York: W. W. Norton
—— (1990). *Institutions, Institutional Change and Economic Performance*. Cambridge: Cambridge University Press
O'Donnell, J. J. (1979). *Cassiodorus*. Los Angeles: University of California Press
Olson, W. C. and Groom, A. J. R. (1991). *International Relations Then And Now*. London: Routledge
Onuf, N. (1989). *World of Our Making*. Columbia, SC: University of South Carolina Press

Oppenheim, L. F. L (1937). *International Law* London: Longman, Green

Oppenheimer, J. R. (1953). 'Atomic Weapons And American Policy', *Foreign Affairs*, 31, pp. 525–35

Organski, A. F. K. and Kugler, J. (1980). *The War Ledger*. Chicago: University of ChicagoPress

Orlans, H. (1972). *he Nonprofit Research Institute*. New York: McGraw-Hill

Oye, K. A., ed. (1986). *Cooperation under Anarchy*. Princeton, NJ: Princeton University Press

Palmer, R. R. (1951). *A History of the Modern World*. New York: Knopf

Pannekoek, A. (1912). *Marxism and Darwinism*. Chicago: Charles H. Kerr & Company Co-operative

Pannikar, K. K. (1953). *Asia and Western Dominance*. New York: John Day Co

Parker, G., ed. (1978). *The General Crisis of the Seventeenth Century*. London: Routledge & Kegan Paul

Parkinson, F. (1977). *The Philosophy of International Relations*. Los Angeles: Sage

Paul the Deacon (1974). *History of the Lombards*. Philadelphia: University of Pennsylvania Press [797?]

Pearson, F. S. and Rochester, J. M. (1988). *International Relations*. New York: Random House

Pecquet, A. (1757). *L'Esprit des maximes politiques*. Paris: Chez Prault père

Penn, W. (1986). *Essai d'un Projet pour rendre la Paix de l'Europe solide et durable*. York: William Sessions [1693?]

Perkins, H. L. (1959). *The Moral and Political Philosophy of the Abbé de Saint-Pierre*. Geneva: Librairie E. Droc

Peterson, V. S. (1993). *Global Gender Issues*. Boulder, CO: Westview Press

Pico della Mirandola, G. (1965). *On the Dignity of Man*. Indianapolis: Bobbs-Merrill [1486]

Pitkin, H. F. (1984). *Fortune is a Woman*. Berkeley: University of California Press

Poggi, G. (1978). *The Development of the Modern State*. Stanford: Stanford University Press

Popper, K. (1945). *The Open Society and Its Enemies*. London: Routledge and Sons

—— (1957). *The Poverty of Historicism*. Boston: Beacon Press

—— (1959). *The Logic of Scientific Discovery*. London: Hutchinson [1930]

Postan, M. M. *et al.*, eds (1965). *Cambridge Economic History of Europe*, Vol. III, pp. 42–118. Cambridge: Cambridge University Press

Potter, P. B. (1922). *An Introduction to the Study of International Organization*. New York: Appelton-Century

Pufendorf, S. (1991). *On the Duty of Man and Citizen*. Cambridge: Cambridge University Press [1673]

Pye, L. W., ed. (1963). *Communications and Political Development* Princeton, NJ: Princeton University Press

Quatela, A. (1991). *Invito alla lettura di Guicciardini*. Milan: Mursia

Raab, F. (1964). *The English Face of Machiavelli*. London: Routledge

Rabinow, P., ed. (1984). *The Foucault Reader*. New York: Pantheon

Ratzel, F. (1896). 'Die Gesetze des raumlichen Wachstums der Staaten', *Petermanns Mitteilungen*, 42, pp. 101ff

—— (1903). *olitische Geographie* Munich: R. Oldenbourg

Ray, J. L. (1987). *lobal Politics*. Boston: Houghton Mifflin

Raynal, G. T. (1804). *Philosofisk og Politisk Historie om Eurpæernes handel og Besiddelser i Ost- og Vest-Indien*. København: Sebastian Popp [1770]

Reich, R. (1991). *The Work of Nations*. New York: Knopf

Reiss, H., ed. (1991). *Kant: Political Writings*. Cambridge: Cambridge University Press

Renouvin, P., ed. (1994). *Histoire des relations internationales*, Vol. I. Paris: Hachette [1953]

Ricardo, D. (1984). *The Principles of Political Economy and Taxation*. London: Everyman's Library [1817]

Risse-Kappen, T. (1995). *Bringing Transnational Relations Back In* Cambridge: Cambridge University Press

Rohan, H., Duc de (1673). *Interêts et maximes des Princes et des Estates souverains*. Cologne: (no publisher identified) [1638]

Roosen, W. (1986). *Daniel Defoe and Diplomacy*. Selinsgrove: Susquehanna University-Press

Roover, R. de (1965). 'The Organization of Trade', in Postan *et al.* (1965), pp. 42–118

Rorty, R. (1979). *Philosophy and the Mirror of Nature*. Princeton, NJ: Princeton University Press

Rosecrance, R. (1963). *Action and Reaction in World Politics*. Boston: Little, Brown

Rosenau, J. N. (1995). 'Governance in the Twenty-first Century', *Global Governance*, 1:1, pp. 13–44

Rosenau, J. N. and Knorr, K., eds (1969). *Contending Approaches to International Politics*. Princeton, NJ: Princeton University Press

Ross, E. (1969). *Social Control: A Survey of the Foundations of Order*. Cleveland: Press of Case Western Reserve University [1901]

Ross, M. (1984). *Leibniz*. Oxford: Oxford University Press

Rousseau, J.-J. (1950a). 'Discourse on The Origin And Basis of Inequality among Men', in Cole, G. D. H. (1950), *The Social Contract and Discourses*, pp. 175–282. London: Dutton [1755]

—— (1950b). 'Social Contract', in Cole, G. D. H. (1950), pp. 1–142 [1762]

—— (1950c). 'Discourse on Political Economy', in Cole, G. D. H. (1950), pp. 283–330 [1755]

—— (1964a). 'Extrait du projet de paix perpétuelle', in *Oeuvres Complètes*, Vol. III, pp. 563–90. Paris: Bibliothèque de la Pleiade [1760]

—— (1964b). 'Jugement sur le projet de paix perpétuelle', in *Oeuvres Complètes*, Vol. III, pp. 591–600. Paris: Bibliothèque de la Pleiade [1782]

—— (1964c). 'Que l'État de guerre nait de l'état social', in *Oeuvres Complètes*, Vol. III, pp. 601–13. Paris: Bibliothèque de la Pleiade [1896]

—— (1964d). 'Considérations sur le gouvernement de Pologne', in *Oeuvres Complètes*, Vol. III, pp. 953–1044. Paris: Bibliothèque de la Pleiade [1782]

—— (1978). *The Confessions*. Harmondsworth: Penguin [1782]

—— (1995). *Oeuvres Complètes*, Vol. V. Paris: Gallimard

Rubinstein, N. (1970). 'Introduction', in Guicciardini (1969), pp. 7–33

Ruggie, J. G. (1986). 'Continuity and Transformation in the World Polity', in Keohane (1986), pp. 131–58 [1983]

——, ed. (1993a). *Multilateralism Matters*. New York: Columbia University Press

—— (1993b). 'Territoriality and Beyond', *International Organization* 47:1, pp. 139–75

Rummel, R. J. (1985). 'Libertarian Propositions on Violence within and between Nations', *Journal of Conflict Resolution*, 29:3, pp. 419–55

Runciman, S. (1992). *The First Crusade*. Cambridge: Cambridge University Press [1951]

Russell, F. M. (1936). *Theories of International Relations*. New York: D. Appleton-Century Co

Russett, B. (1993). *Grasping the Democratic Peace*. Princeton, NJ: Princeton University Press

Said, E. W. (1978). *Orientalism*. London: Routledge & Kegan Paul

—— (1996). *Representations of the Intellectual*. New York: Random House

Satow, E. (1917). *A Guide to Diplomatic Practice*. London: Longman, Green & Co

Schelling, T. (1966). *The Strategy of Conflict*. Cambridge: Harvard University Press

Schlegel, F. (1979), 'Versuch über den Begriff des Republikanismus', in Batscha and Saage, pp. 93–110 [1796]

Schmitt, C. (1932). *Das Begriff des politischen*. Berlin: Duncker & Humblott

Schuman, F. L. (1933). *International Politics: An Introduction to the Western State System*. New York: McGraw-Hill

Schumpeter, J. A. (1954). *A History of Economic Analysis*. New York: Oxford University Press

—— (1976). 'Die Krise der Steuerstaats', in Hickel, R., *Rudolf Goldscheid, Joseph Schumpeter: Die Okonomie der Staatsfinanzen*. Frankfurt a.M. Suhrkamp [1918]

Schwarzenberger, G. (1951). *Power Politics*. New York: Praeger

Scott, J. B., ed. (1920). *The Proceedings of the Hague Peace Conference*. New York: Oxford University Press

Scuton, R. (1986). *Spinoza*. New York: Oxford University Press.

Searle, J. (1993). 'Rationality and Realism, What is at Stake?' *Daedalus*, 122;4, pp. 55–83

Selden, J. (1652). *Of the Dominions or Ownership of the Sea*. London: William Du-Gard [163?]

Semmel, B., ed. (1981). *Marxism and the Science of War*. London: Oxford University-Press

Sheehan, M. (1996). *The Balance of Power*. London: Routledge

Shirer, W. L. (1983). *The Rise and Fall of the Third Reich*. New York: Fawcett Crest [1950]

Shotwell, J. T. (1936). *On the Rim of the Abyss*. New York: Macmillan

Simonds, F. and Emeny, F. (1935). *The Great Powers in World Politics*. New York: American Book Co

Singer, J. D. (1969). 'The Incompleat Theorist: Insight without Evidence', in Rosenau and Knorr (1969), eds, pp. 63–86

Skinner, Q. (1981). *Machiavelli*. Oxford: Oxford University Press

Smith, A. (1976). *The Wealth of Nations*. Oxford: Clarendon Press [1776]

Smith, A. D. (1991). *National Identity*. Harmondsworth: Penguin

Smith, D. M., ed. (1966). *American Intervention 1917*. Boston: Houghton Mifflin

Smith, H. (1990). 'The Womb of War', *Review of International Studies*, 16:1, pp. 39–58

Smith, S. (1992). 'The Forty Years' Detour', *Millennium*, 21:3, pp. 489–506

Smith, S., Booth, K. and Zalewski, M. (1996). *International Theory: Positivism and*

Beyond. Cambridge: Cambridge University Press

Souleyman, E. V. (1972). *The Vision of World Peace in Seventeenth and Eighteenth-Century France*. New York: Kennekat Press [1941]

Sonnino, P. (1981), 'Introduction', in Frederick II (1981), pp. 1–23

Southern, R. W. (1953). *The Making of the Middle Ages*. New Haven: Yale University Press

Spector, I. (1962). *The First Russian Revolution: Its Impact on Asia*. New Jersey: Englewood Cliffs

Spencer, H. (1846). *Principles of Biology*. London: Williams and Norgate

—— (1897). *Social Statics*. New York: D. Appleton and Co

Spero, J. E. (1990). *The Politics of International Economic Relations*. New York: St Martin's Press

Spinoza, B. de (1951a). 'Theologico-political treatise', in *Works*, Vol. I, pp. 1–265. New York: Dover Publications [1670]

—— (1951b). 'Ethics', in *Works*, Vol. II, pp. 43– 270. New York: Dover Publications [1677]

—— (1951c). 'A Political Treatise', in *Works*, Vol. I, pp. 279–385. New York: Dover Publications [1677]

Sprout, H. and Sprout, M. (1965). *The Ecological Perspectives on Human Affairs*. Princeton, NJ: Princeton University Press

Spykman, N. J. (1944). *America's Strategy in World Politics*. New York: Harcourt, Brace and Co

Stalin, J. V. (1946). *Speech Delivered by J. V. Stalin at a Meeting of Voters of the Stalin Electoral Area of Moscow, February 9, 1946*. Washington, DC: Embassy of the Soviet Union

—— (1953). 'The Twelfth Congress of the R.C.P.(B.)', in *Works*, Vol. V, pp. 191–200. Moscow: Foreign Languages Publishing House [1923]

Stark, W., ed. (1952–54). *Jeremy Bentham's Economic Writings* Vol. III. London: Allen & Unwin

Starobinski, J. (1988). *Jean-Jacques Rousseau*. Chicago University Press

Stavrianos, L. S. (1981). *Global Rift*. New York: William Morrow and Co

Steel, R. (1980). *Walter Lippmann and the American Century*. Boston: Little, Brown and Co

Stein, A. (1982). 'Coordination and Collaboration: Regimes in an Anarchic World', *International Organization*, 36:2, pp. 299–325

—— (1990). *Why Nations Cooperate*. Ithaca, NY: Cornell University Press

Steinbruner, J. D. (1974). *The Cybernetic Theory of Decision*. Princeton, NJ: Princeton University Press

Stephanson, A. (1989). *Kennan and the Art of Foreign Policy*. Cambridge: Harvard University Press

Stopford J. and Strange, S. (1992). *Rival States, Rival Firms*. Cambridge: Cambridge University Press

Strange, S. (1992). 'States, firms and diplomacy', in *International Affairs*, 68:1, pp. 1–15

—— (1994). 'Wake up, Krasner! The World *has* Changed', in *Review of International Political Economy*, 1:2, pp. 209–19

Strayer, J. R. (1955). *Western Europe in the Middle Ages*. New York: Appleton-Century-

Crofts
—— (1970). *On the Medieval Origins of the Modern State*. Princeton, NJ: Princeton University Press

Sumner, W. G. (1954). *What the Social Classes Owe Each Other*. Caldwell, ID: The Caxton Printers, Ltd. [1883]

—— (1965). 'War', in *The Conquest of the United States by Spain and other Essays*, pp. 200–35. Chicago: Henry Regenry Company [1903]

Suttner, B. von (1914). *Lay Down Your Arms!* New York: Longman, Green

Swift, J. (1992). *Gulliver's Travels*. Hertfordshire: Wordsworth [1726]

Sylvester, C. (1994). *Feminist Theory and International Relations in a Postmodern Era*. Cambridge: Cambridge University Press

Szücs, J. (1990). *Die drei historischen Regionen Europas*. Frankfurt a.M: Verlag Neue Kritik

Talmon, J. L. (1952). *The Origins of Totalitarian Democracy*. London: Secker & Warburg

—— (1960). *Political Messianism*. London: Secker and Warburg

Taylor, A. J. P. (1967). *Bismarck*. New York: Random House

—— (1980). *Revolutions and Revolutionaries*. New York: Atheneum

ter Meulen, J. (1917). *Internationalen Organisation in seiner Entwicklung*. The Hague: Martinus Nijhoff

Thompson, K. W. (1994). *Fathers of International Thought*. Baton Rouge, LA: Louisiana State University Press

Thomson, D. (1974). *Europe Since Napoleon*. Harmondsworth: Penguin

Thucydides (1972). *The Peloponnesian War*. Harmondsworth: Penguin [*c*.402 BC]

Tilly, C., ed. (1975). *The Formation of Nation States in Western Europe*. Princeton, NJ: Princeton University Press

—— (1984). *Big Structures, Large Processes, Huge Comparisons*. New York: Russell Sage

—— (1994). *Coercion, Capital, and European States, AD 990–1992*. Oxford: Blackwell

Todorov, T. (1989). *Nous et les autres*. Paris: Editions du Seuil

Treitschke, H. von (1916). *Politics*. London: Macmillan

Tucker, R. C., ed. (1975). *The Lenin Anthology*. New York: W. W. Norton

Tully, J. (1993). *An Approach to Political Philosophy: Locke in Contexts*. Cambridge: Cambridge University Press

Ulam, Adam (1971). *The Rivals*. New York: Viking Press

—— (1974). *Expansion and Coexistence*. New York: Holt Rinehart and Winston

UN (1993). *World Investments Report 1992*. New York: United Nations

Varg, P. A. (1970). *Foreign Policies of the Founding Fathers*. Baltimore, MD: Penguin Books

Vasquez, J. (1983). *The Power of Power Politics*. New Brunswick, NJ: Rutgers University Press

Vattel, E. de (1863). *The Law of Nations or the Principles of Natural Law Applied to the Conduct and to the Affairs of Nations and of Sovereigns*. Philadelphia: T. & J. W. Johnson [1758]

Veblen, T. (1939). *Imperial Germany and the Industrial Revolution* New York: Viking Press [1915]

Vincent, A. (1987). *heories of the State*. Oxford: Blackwell

Viotti, P. R. and Kauppi, M. V. (1987). *International Relations Theory*. New York: Macmillan

Viroli, M. (1995). *For Love of Country*. Oxford: Clarendon Press

Vitoria, F. de (1934a). 'On the Indians Recently Discovered', in Scott, J. B., *The Spanish Origin of International Law*, Appendix A. Oxford: Clarendon Press [1532]

—— (1934b). 'On the Law of War Made by the Spaniards on the Barbarians', in Scott, J. B., *The Spanish Origin of International Law*, Appendix B. Oxford: Clarendon Press [153?]

Vogler, J and Imber, M. F., eds (1996). *The Environment and International Relations*. London: Routledge

Voltaire (1967). 'Guerre', *Dictionnaire Philosophique*, pp. 228–33. Paris: Garnier Frères [1764]

—— (1980). *Letters on England*. Harmondsworth: Penguin

Walker, R. B. J. (1993). *Inside/Outside: International Relations as Political Theory*. Cambridge: Cambridge University Press

Wall, I. M. (1983). *French Communism in the Era of Stalin*. Westport, Conn.: Greenwood Press

Wallace-Hadrill, J. M. (1956). *The Barbarian West, 400–1000*. Hutcheson, London

Wallensteen P. and Sollenberg, M. (1995), 'After the Cold War: Emerging Patterns of Armed Conflict 1989–94', *Journal of Peace Research*, 32:3, pp. 345–60

Wallerstein, I. (1974; 1980; 1989 and forthcoming). *The Modern World-System*, Vols. I–IV. New York: Academic Press

Waltz, K. N. (1959). *Man, the State and War*. New York: Columbia University Press

—— (1979). *Theory of International Relations*. Reading, Mass.: Addison-Wesley

Walworth, A. C. (1969). *Woodrow Wilson*, Vol II. . Baltimore: Penguin

Watson, A. (1992). *The Evolution of International Society*. London: Routledge

Weber, C. (1995). *Simulating Sovereignty*. Cambridge: Cambridge University Press

Weber, M. (1994). *Political Writings*. Cambridge: Cambridge University Press

Weikart, R. (1993). 'The Origins of Social Darwinism in Germany, 1859–1995', *Journal of the History of Ideas*, 54:3, pp. 469–89

Wendt, A. (1995). 'Constructing International Politics', *International Security*, 20:1, pp. 71–81

—— and Friedheim, D. (1996). 'Hierarchy under Anarchy', in Biersteker and Weber (1996), pp. 240–78

White, L. (1972). 'The Expansion of Technology 500–1500', in Cipolla, C. M., ed., *The Fontana Economic History of Europe*, Vol. I, pp. 143–74. London: Collins/Fontana

Wight, M. (1968). 'Why is There No International Theory?' in Butterfield and Wight (1968), pp. 17–35

—— (1987). 'An Anatomy of International Thought,' *Review of International Studies*, 13, pp. 221–7

—— (1991). *International Theory: The Three Traditions*. Leicester: Leicester University Press

—— (1995). *Power Politics*. Leicester: Leicester University Press [1978]

Williams, H. (1992). *International Relations in Political Theory*. Milton Keynes, Herts.: Open University Press

Wiltse, C. M. (1960). *The Jeffersonian Tradition in American Democracy*. New York: Hill and Wang

Winch, D. (1996). *Riches and Poverty*. Cambridge: Cambridge University Press

Wolf, E. (1982). *Europe and The People without History*. Berkeley: University of California Press

Wolfers, A. (1951). 'The Pole of Power and the Pole of Indifference', *World Politics*, 4:1, pp. 39–63

—— (1959). 'The Actors in International Politics', in Fox (1959), pp. 83–107

Wright, M., ed. (1975). *Theory and Practice of the Balance of Power, 1486–1914*. London: J. M. Dent & Sons

Yergin, D. (1991). *The Prize*. New York: Simon & Schuster

York, E. (1919). *Leagues of Nations*. New York: Swarthmore University Press

Zimmern, A. E. (1936). *The League of Nations and the Rule of Law 1918–35*. London: Macmillan

Index

feudal society/feudalism 15, 26, 91, 180, 219, 252
  disintegrating order 90
  'happily extinct everywhere' 152
  industry 156
  organization 58
Fichte, Johann Gottlieb 144, 173, 176, 190
Ficino, Marsilio 41
Fielding, Henry 139
Filmer, Robert 92–3, 107, 119, 293
finance 78, 87, 185–6, 210, 260, 261
'First International' (1864) 158
Flanders 202, 212
Flashman, Harry P. 259
Florence 38, 39, 41, 42, 43
foreign policy 26–7, 105, 117, 158, 212, 234, 237
  Abbasid 20
  arch-realist discussions of decisions 242
  based on military might 243
  deliberations to the public 240
  education in 239
  fascist 221
  'handbook' 127
  imperialist 222
  important goal 94
  king's prerogative to make 118
  orientations of European states 187
  realist 232, 235, 240
fortuna 43, 44, 54
Foucault, Michel 38, 111, 141, 149, 275–7 *passim*, 280, 281
Frachetta, Girolamo 80
France 65, 113, 146, 168, 175, 206, 217, 226, 232
  belligerence 162
  chartered companies 90
  colonial war 243
  costly war to maintain overseas possessions 205
  Europe dominated by 89
  evolution of a strong state 84
  growth of parliamentary politics 29
  mandates 207
  mercantilism 94

military matters 87, 173, 182
  monarchs/monarchies 16, 31
  philosophes 183
  programme for new post-war order (1916) 203
  Prussia's quick victory over (1871) 148
  radical ideas 153
  recruitment of able-bodied men from India and Vietnam 228
  revolutions 125, 128, 145, 146, 153, 156–60 *passim*, 166, 171, 181, 257
  Russia allied with 202, 218
  Saracen attacks 14
  see also Charles VIII; Charles X; Francis I; Henry IV; Louis XIV; Louis-Philippe; Napoleon; Philippe IV
Francis I, king of France 47
Franco-Prussian War (1871) 218
Frank, André Gunder 251–2
Frankish kingdoms 14
Franklin, Benjamin 295
Franz Ferdinand, Archduke and Crown Prince of Austria 202
Franz Joseph I, emperor of Austria-Hungary 208
Frederick II (the Great), king of Prussia 112, 125, 126–7
free market 171, 173, 209, 210, 250, 251
  doctrine as 'pure ideology' 190
  world economy 234
free trade 151, 153, 170, 172, 174, 187
  nineteenth-century doctrines 285
  see also comparative advantage
free will 52, 53, 198, 223
freedom 131, 136, 163, 166, 168, 171, 199, 210
  absolute 104
  conflict between affluence and 132
  historical evolution of 188
  individual 79, 95, 122, 128, 151, 158, 170, 194
  natural right to 130, 154
  religious 80, 94, 235
  social stability and political order necessary for 160

destroyed 207
free movement of 147
slave 187
uncompensated 89
urbanization of 184
see also division of labour
Labour parties 185, 221, 232, 233
Lake Copaïs, battle of (1311) 29
landlords/landowners 89, 117, 147, 157, 205
language(s) 111, 131, 182, 201, 275
  Arabic 19
  common 180
  constitutive of social reality 277
  Germanic 20
  Greek 16
  Latin 13–14
  nation defined in terms of 183
  speculation and theorizing about 284
  universal 285
Lansing, Robert 205
Las Casas, Bartoloméo de 66–7
Latin 13–14, 30, 41, 180
Latin America 233, 251
Lauterpacht, Hersh 217
law(s) 32, 35, 69, 143
  canon 25, 33
  civil 76, 72, 73, 98, 106, 262, 267
  constitutional 74–5
  customary 25–6, 33
  diplomatic 145
  in international politics 164
  limits to the authority of 217
  market 200
  political institutions backed by 133
  religion and 25–7
  sovereignty associated with 105
  traditional, breakdown of 110
  voting 176
  see also international law; natural law; laws of nature
laws of nature 74, 76, 111, 119, 140
  deduced 225
  living a healthy life in accordance with 198
  self-equilibrating 153

violation of 209
'lay' scholars 40–1
League of Cognac 47
League of Nations 97, 206–8 *passim*, 213, 215–17 *passim*
Lebensraum 221
Lee, Joseph 109
left-wing (political) 153, 154, 155, 223, 233, 255
Leibniz, Gottfried Wilhelm 91, 100, 107, 112
Lenin, Vladimir Ilyich 205–6, 216, 225, 226, 229, 256, 272
  communism and 219–21
  denunciation of imperialism 228
  primary heir of the Enlightenment project 223
  theories of International Relations 232
  theory of colonial wars 251
Leo III, Byzantine emperor 18
Leo VI, Byzantine Emperor 18
Leo X, Pope 47
Lessing, Gotthold 141
le Tellier, Michel 87
letters of indulgence 61
levée en masse 146, 181
lexicographers 183
'liberal arts' 41
liberalism 145, 198, 214, 225, 226, 234, 255
  challenges presented by 161
  containing 170, 174–5
  Continental response/reaction to 174, 219
  free-market 176
  growth of 179
  moral pretensions of 201
  opposed 162, 197
  profoundly transformed 193
  rejected doctrines of 221
  self-congratulatory, radicalism developed as a critique of 165
  split between 'classic' and 'reformist' 171
  striking its newest roots 210
  tattered remains of 247